Euro-skepticism

Europe Today
Series Editor: Ronald Tiersky

Europe Today: National Politics, European Integration, and European Security
Edited by Ronald Tiersky

Uniting Europe: European Integration and the Post-Cold War World
By John Van Oudenaren

Euro-skepticism

A Reader

Edited by
Ronald Tiersky

ROWMAN & LITTLEFIELD PUBLISHERS, INC.
Lanham • Boulder • New York • Oxford

ROWMAN & LITTLEFIELD PUBLISHERS, INC.

Published in the United States of America
by Rowman & Littlefield Publishers, Inc.
4720 Boston Way, Lanham, Maryland 20706
www.rowmanlittlefield.com

12 Hid's Copse Road, Cumnor Hill, Oxford OX2 9JJ, England

British Library Cataloguing in Publication Information Available

Library of Congress Cataloging-in-Publication Data

Euro-skepticism : a reader / edited by Ronald Tiersky.
    p. cm. — (Europe today)
    Includes bibliographical references and index.
    ISBN 0-7425-1053-0 (alk. paper) — ISBN 0-7425-1054-9 (pbk. : alk. paper)
    1. European federation. 2. Nationalism—Europe. I. Tiersky, Ronald, 1944-
II. Europe today (Rowman and Littlefield, inc.)

JN15 .E7455 2001
341.242'2—dc21   2001019532

Printed in the United States of America

♾ ™ The paper used in this publication meets the minimum requirements of
American National Standard for Information Sciences—Permanence of Paper
for Printed Library Materials, ANSI/NISO Z39.48-1992.

For Vanessa and Alexandre
Who were, it seems, born skeptical

Contents

Acknowledgments

This book came rapidly together when, as noted in the introduction, it became clear to me as general editor that some kind of teaching reader in "Euro-skepticism" was lacking in the Europe Today series. I had in mind, had indeed already been assigning to my students at Amherst College, several of the texts included here. Susan McEachern, executive editor at Rowman & Littlefield, has my sincerest thanks for her quick, positive reaction, which got us from idea to book in seriously unscholarly time. More than that, I want to acknowledge her knowledgeable and generous care of the series. She has, from her days at Westview Press to her current trusteeship, become a force in her own right in the publishing of serious books on European politics.

For help with technical aspects of the manuscript, Heather Werner and Alexandre Tiersky have my gratitude.

EU member states
Candidate states negotiating accession
Candidate state, not negotiating

Possible Dates of Accession

2003–2007	Cyprus
	Czech Republic
	Estonia
	Hungary
	Latvia
	Lithuania
	Malta
	Poland
	Slovakia
	Slovenia
2008–2010	Bulgaria
	Romania
2010–?	Turkey

FINLAND

SWEDEN

Helsinki

Stockholm
Tallinn
BALTIC
SEA
ESTONIA

Moscow

RUSSIA

LATVIA
Riga

Copenhagen

LITHUANIA
Vilnius

BELARUS

Minsk

Berlin
Warsaw

POLAND

Kiev

UKRAINE

Prague
CZECH. REPUBLIC

SLOVAKIA
Bratislava

Moldova
Chisinau

Vienna

AUSTRIA

Budapest

HUNGARY
SLOVENIA
Ljubljana

ROMANIA

Zagreb CROATIA
Bucharest

BLACK SEA

BOSNIA Belgrade
Sarajevo SERBIA
BULGARIA

ADRIATIC MONTENEGRO
SEA
Sofia

Rome
Skopje

Tirana MACEDONIA

Ankara

ALBANIA

GREECE AEGEAN
SEA

TURKEY

Athens

SICILY

Nicosia

Valletta
MALTA

IONIAN SEA

CYPRUS

LEBANON
Beirut

CHAPTER 1

Introduction: Euro-skepticism and "Europe"

Ronald Tiersky

Europe and "Europe"—by the use of quotation marks Euro-skeptics indicate a difference of worldview concerning European integration between themselves and the enthusiasts of an increasingly federal European Union (EU). Different premises, different goals: "Europe," to the Euro-skeptic, is too much Europe, an ill-conceived and dangerous erosion of European nation-states. The difference between Europe and "Europe" is a great debate in which the Euro-skeptic side has not been sufficiently aired in American teaching about European integration.

For Euro-enthusiasts, says British Euro-skeptic Noel Malcolm (in chapter 8), "Europe is a project, a concept, a cause: the final goal that the European Community (EC) has been moving toward ever since its hesitant beginnings in the 1950s." This idealist vision of "Europe" is the desire for a historic new unification of the Old Continent, nothing less than the creation, out of Europe's supposedly outdated national states, of a new entity in international affairs. "Europe" means the goal of a unified federal Europe as a new economic and political structure in the world. The achievement of this new "Europe," in short, would mean a Europe once again a puissance, once again a great power, a Europe that is more than an economic and financial center, let alone, as Bismarck once said disdainfully, "a mere geographical expression."

Euro-skeptics, on the contrary, believe passionately that this vision of European integration is a mistake, indeed, that it is impossible. In Malcolm's words (chapter 8), "Those who are in favor of Europe [no quotes], that is, those who favor increasing the freedom and prosperity of all who live on the European continent—should view the creation of this hugely artificial political entity with a mixture of alarm and dismay." Much of the European Union, for Euro-skeptics, is a bureaucratic elitist roof erected over the heads of its nation-states and peoples. It is in this sense a fundamentally wrongheaded construction in permanent danger of deadlock or regression, and with a permanent taint of illegitimacy. The federalist and supranationalist aspects of the European Union dilute the sovereignty of its member states. And since it is still, and will long be, the nation-states of Europe that are its basic political units, and thus the framework of citizen identity and political democracy, the EU, or rather the "Europe" aspect of the European integration process, suppresses much of the political-democratic vitality of Europe's political parties and peoples without replacing it with something else. So warned the fount of Euro-skepticism Charles de Gaulle in the 1960s, so spoke Margaret Thatcher in the 1980s, and so speak Euro-skeptics of the year 2001.

Another issue is the relation of "Europe" and the United States. Euro-enthusiasts believe either that a cooperative relationship can be built within what used to be called the Atlantic community, or that a "European Europe," an independent Europe with its own foreign policy, diplomatic, and security identity, can and should exist on its own. Euro-skeptics, to the contrary, question whether a "Europe" independent of the United States, a "European Europe" pursuing its own new continentwide interests, is not a historic folly bound to collapse because of its own internal weaknesses and contradictions so tragically displayed to the world during the twentieth century. Would the goal of a "European Europe," as Professor Robert Conquest suggests in chapter 19, turn out to be, wished for or not, destructive of "the West, and indeed divisive of 'European' civilization itself; . . . implicitly, and often explicitly, anti-American"?

This reader is a supplementary text in Rowman & Littlefield's new Europe Today series, in which the first volume was my own edited, *Europe Today: National Politics, European Integration, and European Security* (1999). The second volume to appear was John Vanoudenauren's well-received *Uniting Europe: European Integration and the Post-Cold War World* (2000). Soon to follow will be Erik Jones's book on the politics of monetary union, Jochen Lorentzen's on the social effects (and defects) of integration, and several country books, starting with Patrick McCarthy on Britain. While all these books are being done by established scholars, meaning they are serious works of scholarship, they are all dedicated to the broader pedagogical task of the Europe Today series: to provide college and university students with compelling new writing on Europe at the beginning of a new century.

Yet history must not be left out of the equation, above all regarding the Old Continent. I thought this book to be indispensable for the Europe Today series because a presentation of Euro-skeptical points of view and political action has been lacking in American college texts about European integration. Professors have tended to be Euro-philes, and American writing, especially in teaching materials, has been weighted in favor of the "Europe" project, if only by virtue of following the rocky but overall progressive functionalist spread of European integration from the Coal and Steel Community to the Common Market to the Single Market to Maastricht and beyond. The Euroskeptic side needed to be heard more distinctly and in depth.

Moreover, prior to the EU's Nice summit of December 2000, negotiations about enlargement and institutional reform ("widening" and "deepening") elicited an unexpected public expression of government views on ultimate goals and structures of European integration, to begin with the possibility of writing a formal constitution for the European Union. The timing for this book seems all the more appropriate.

The first order of business is to disambiguate the meanings of Euro-skepticism. What is Euro-skepticism, and how should it be distinguished from cousin concepts such as Euro-pessimism, Euro-cynicism, and Euro-phobia?

It would be a mistake to try to be overprecise about our terms. Euro-skepticism and its cousin concepts are journalistic, informal labels rather than formal political theory or even political party labels. Such categories are not tightly contained and mutually exclusive, and a single political party, for example the British Conservative party, can be split down the middle between Euro-skeptics and Euro-philes.

"Skeptic" descends from the Greek "skeptikos," which meant to be thoughtful and inquiring in a general sense, as opposed to easy acceptance of others' arguments. A skeptic today, according to *Webster's Unabridged*, is "a person who habitually doubts, questions, or suspends judgment upon matters generally accepted." Skepticism, so goes the definition, is "a philosophical doctrine that the truth of all knowledge must always be in question and that inquiry must be a process of doubting." Therefore, Euro-skepticism can be defined as a permanent doubting of "Europe" as a great project, a vigilance about European integration conceived as building a new and powerful political actor in the international system, a "European Europe" that would constitute a new force in a multipolar world as opposed to the contemporary American-dominated unipolar system. Euro-skeptics are not against what they see as realistic advantageous cooperation among various groups of European states for greater peace and prosperity. But "mainstream" Euro-skeptics are hostile to the idea of trying to build a European-level power, a "European Europe" that would have its own continental interests and would tend—this is very important—to exclude the United States from Europe's political and security affairs, perhaps even provoking American hostility toward Europe as a natural response to the assertion of a common European identity. But far right, "national" and anti-"Europe" parties such as the French National Front (FN) and the Austrian Freedom party (FP) reject American influence in Europe as well as European federalism.

"Euro-pessimism," as contrasted with Euro-skepticism, comes in two forms. It can mean a period—for example the Euro-pessimistic 1970s—or it can mean a pessimism about the European integration enterprise as a whole. Stanley Hoffmann's well-known 1966 essay, "Obstinate or Obsolete?: France, European Integration, and the Fate of the Nation-State" (see chapter 3) is an example of both. Measuring integration from the federalist point of view of "Europe's" founders, this conceptual masterpiece was a Euro-pessimistic analysis both of the condition of European integration in the early 1960s and of the outlook for "Europe" in the long term. Hoffmann's pessimistic conclusion that a Europe "beyond the nation-state" had missed its moment—at a time when integration ran on the French clock of Charles de Gaulle—made sense considered from the point of view that "Europe" was, or should have been, the goal from the beginning. A functionalist might have concluded that the clock was, despite the general's "empty chair" boycott of European Economic Community (EEC) meetings, still ticking along, for example in accelerated progress in abolishing intra-EEC tariffs, achieved two years ahead of schedule in 1968.

"Euro-phobia" and "Euro-cynicism" are exotic extensions of Euro-skepticism. These terms group a diverse collection of anti-federalist politicians and observers who believe that the "Europe" project cannot help but be an anti-national, anti-democratic, conspiracy-without-a-center of bureaucratic social democrats, whose goal, perhaps unwitting, is to turn Europe into a superstate controlled by a technocratic managerial elite. For the Euro-cynic, "Europe" constitutes a new version of what French writer Jacques Ellul decades ago called the "technological illusion," a hidden, perhaps not even conscious agenda, whose goal or end point must be a drift toward a society "guided" by "experts."

The positive program of Euro-skepticism is, in any case, not national isolation but an intergovernmental and confederal European Union anchored in two ways: the minimum necessary integration for peace and prosperity coupled with the maximum preservation of national sovereignty. The precise mix of these goals is of course a matter of judgment and sometimes disagreement. Euro-skeptics are a diverse lot, although they would all share Frenchman Charles Pasqua's definition of preserving national sovereignty and independence as keeping "the power to say no." For Euro-skeptics the European goal should be a "family of nations," not a merging of peoples; integration not unification.

In American scholarly study of European integration there was from the beginning an enthusiasm for the project. Integration, even if only in the free half of the cold-war-divided continent, seemed a good thing in so many ways for the west Europeans. It promised reconstructed economies, good in themselves and vital in recreating politically resilient societies during the cold war. More than that, after decades of nationalist self-destruction, to get beyond the nation-state seemed a necessity in historical terms and a good cause in moral terms. Thus, for three or four decades, from the European Coal and Steel Community's initiation in the early 1950s to the great European revolution of 1989–1991, Americans studying European integration generally couldn't help favoring it.

In addition, west European socialists and social democrats, who in the 1950s opposed the integration of western European countries as a "capitalist" coup that would perpetuate a divided Europe, changed their outlook. True enough, the west European communist parties, especially the French (PCF) and Italian (PCI), continued to oppose the EEC. But as western Europe's socialists became parties of government, they argued that European integration could become infused with social democracy's ideals and moral values. Willy Brandt, the German Social Democratic party chancellor (1969–1974), brought the West German SPD decisively into the mainstream of European Community efforts. In the 1970s and 1980s, François Mitterrand, Felipe Gonzalez, and Mario Soares led a similar change of opinion in the French, Spanish, and Portuguese left-wing parties.

The west European socialists' embrace of European integration created a paradox, however, since it seemed to confirm the argument of British conservative prime minister and Euro-skeptic Margaret Thatcher (in office 1979–1990) that European integration was becoming evermore socialist, which to her mind also meant, as in the failed planned Soviet-style economies, bureaucratic and technocratic. Her own theme, stated emphatically in the famous speech at Bruges in September 1988 (included in this book as chapter 5), was that Britain wanted no part of "Brussels' bureaucratic socialism." Thatcher's rhetorical dagger was pointed first of all at Jacques Delors, president of the European Commission (1985–1995) and a French Socialist by affiliation.

This mainstreaming of Europe's left-wing parties plus the opportunities for social progress created by the European revolution of 1991 have in recent years brought a significant change of attitude among many Americans who analyze European integration, especially younger scholars with left-wing sympathies. With the cold war's security dangers no longer an issue overriding all others, European integration should now be held more accountable than before to basic contrasts between progressive and conservative values. The ideological free ride of European integration, ipso facto moral acceptance among scholars of "Europe" as a goal, is ending. Researchers judging the success of European integration are less impressed today by, for example, the supremacy of European law over national law or the achievement of a full single integrated market. They are more impressed by the continued thinness of "social" Europe, by continuing (and widening) regional disparities, and by the need for today's EU member states to deal effectively with the "poor cousin" problems that face the coming eastern enlargement. The mood among academics is shifting perceptibly to socially focused, class-based policy analyses, which often enough conclude that "Europe" may be no better for disadvantaged groups than the old national politics.

The selections in this reader follow along roughly with the history of European integration itself. But they do not give a chronological account of key moments so much as they provide vivid expressions of Euro-skeptic points of view, for which the occasion is almost always some event or debate or policy discussion. It obviously would have made no sense to try to update the texts presented here, which does of course presume some historical knowledge on the part of students and guidance from teachers.

The coming period in European integration—first of all the related problems of institutional reform and eastern enlargement—will be even more rough and ready than previous periods of great change and turmoil. Freedom is always a dilemma. The cold war constraints and alibis are gone, internal national interests are less inhibited, and those outside the European Union—candidate members, the United States, Russia, and other foreign partners and *demandeurs*—will each in its own way ask Europe (or "Europe") for more.

What will the European response be? Europeans are facing once again at the start of a new century what is for them now an old question: Decline or renewal? Much has changed—European economic power and international financial potential are unmistakable. But much is the same—the gnawing question of Europe's desire and political will to be once again master in its own house and a great power on the world stage, the question, in other words, of European self-respect. Is the Euro-skeptical sentiment, in this existential debate, a mere rearguard discourse of the privileged, or, to the contrary, is it, as Euro-skeptics believe, the contemporary expression of Europe's finest hours?

CHAPTER 2

Europe

Charles de Gaulle

Charles de Gaulle (1890-1970) was France's most illustrious military and political leader of the twentieth century. First a victorious general leading the Free French in World War II, he later became the founder and first president (1958-1969) of the Fifth Republic. De Gaulle was universally recognized as France's hero despite all partisan disagreements, including with the large French Communist party of the epoch.

He saved the nation twice, the first time following France's defeat by the Germans in 1940. De Gaulle rejected the truce negotiated by the new prime minister Marshal Philippe Pétain, instead fleeing to London, where he, with only a few like-minded fighters, began organizing the Free French forces. By the time of the liberation of Paris in August 1944, de Gaulle had become undisputed leader of the French Resistance. "Le Général," as he was usually called even as president, rescued the country again from disaster in May 1958 when he took power, recalled from retirement by the National Assembly, to deal with the "dirty war" in Algeria, the violent combination of Algerian national liberation insurgence and rebellion in the French military's own ranks in Algiers. Civil unrest, even some sort of civil war, loomed in France as well as in Algeria. Some French people wanted to agree to Algerian independence while ultracolonialist diehards demanded that Algeria remain "French Algeria."

At the same moment, de Gaulle had to decide what attitude he would adopt toward the Rome Treaty creating the EEC, which had been signed in 1957. He decided to accept it. One reason was its economic advantages for France, especially a guarantee by West Germany and other partners to subsidize French agriculture, but de Gaulle also was wagering that lower intra-EEC tariffs would stimulate and modernize a generally protectionist French industry rather than annihilate it through competition.

7

The deciding factor, however, was the Rome Treaty's intergovernmental structure of authority. The Common Market would be based on national sovereignty, putting ultimate authority in the council of ministers (thus national governments, thus the permanent threat of national interested veto powers), rather than in the supranational commission where "Europeans" held sway. In the middle 1960s Walter Hallstein, first president of the EEC commission, tried to enlarge the commission's powers at the expense of national governments and to get for the EEC its own budgetary resources, through a right to tax, and to strengthen federalist/supranationalist tendencies over intergovernmentalism, which de Gaulle called a "Europe des patries," a Europe of the National States. In response, for seven months (July 1965–January 1966), de Gaulle implemented a French boycott of council of ministers meetings called the "empty chair" policy. This French insistence on national sovereignty and resistance to institutional imperialism by the commission resulted in the so-called Luxembourg compromise of January 1966, a document that upheld the right of any state to resort to a veto "when very important [national] issues are at stake." The document, to assuage other EEC members, said that defining what "important" meant required full consultation of all states. In general, de Gaulle had stopped, at least temporarily, the supranationalist/federalist gains of what he called the "stateless, unaccountable" bureaucrats who supposedly ran the EEC.

In this, de Gaulle consolidated his historic position as the fount of Euro-skepticism, meaning rejection of all delegation of national sovereignty to the Community except that which was absolutely necessary and which intergovernmental cooperation could not achieve. Later Euro-skeptics have taken this to mean a rejection of the federalist euro and the European Central Bank. But such issues are matters of judgment, even if basic tendencies seem to be clear enough. In other words, one cannot say for certain what Charles de Gaulle might have decided about the euro or any other question today in changed circumstances. De Gaulle once told an aide that "a federal Europe is unthinkable now, but in fifty years who can say?" That was in 1960.

The following chapter from the General's Memoirs of Hope, *written in haste after his resignation from office in April 1969 at the age of seventy-nine, is his last statement on Europe. De Gaulle had planned a three-volume set of memoirs of his years as president, in parallel to his three-volume* War Memoirs. *Death permitted only the first volume and part of the second.*

War gives birth and brings death to nations. In the meantime, it never ceases to loom over their existence. For us French, the development of our national life, our political regimes and our world position from 1815 to 1870 was determined by the hostile coalition which united the nations of Europe against the Revolution, the dazzling victories and then the downfall of Napoleon, and finally the disastrous treaties which sanctioned so many battles. Thereafter, during the forty-four years of the "armed truce," it was our defeat, our secret desire to avenge it, but also the fear that a united Germany might inflict another on us, that dominated our actions at home and abroad. Although the gigantic effort put forth by our people in the First World War opened the way to renewal, we closed it upon ourselves by failing to consolidate our military victory, by forgoing the reparations which would have provided us with the means of industrializing our country and thus compensating for our enormous human and material losses, and, finally, by withdrawing into a passive strategic and foreign policy which left Europe a prey to Hitler's ambitions. Now, in the aftermath of the last conflict in which she had all but perished, on what premises was France to base her progress and her actions?

The first of these premises was that, in spite of everything, she was alive, sovereign and victorious. That was undoubtedly a marvel. Who would have thought that, after suffering an unparalleled disaster, after witnessing the subjection of her rulers to the authority of the enemy, after undergoing the ravages of the two greatest battles of the war and, in the meantime, prolonged plundering by the invader, after enduring the systematic abasement inflicted on her by a regime founded on surrender and humiliation, she would ever heal the wounds inflicted on her body and her soul? Who would not have sworn that her liberation, if it was to come, would be due to foreigners alone and that they would decide what was to become of her at home and abroad? Who, in the almost total extinction of her resistance, had not condemned as absurd the hope that one day the enemy would surrender to her at the same time as to her allies? Nevertheless, in the end she had emerged from the struggle with her frontiers and her unity intact, in control of her own affairs, and in the ranks of the victors. There was nothing, therefore, to prevent her now from being what she intended to be and doing what she wished to do.

This was all the more true because, for the first time in her history, she was unhampered by any threat from her immediate neighbors. Germany, dismembered, had ceased to be a formidable and domineering power. Italy regretted having turned her ambitions against us. The alliance with England, preserved by Free France, and the process of decolonization which had removed old grievances, ensured that the wind of mistrust no longer blew across the English Channel. Bonds of affection and common interest were bringing a serene France and a pacified Spain closer together across the Pyrenees. And what enmities could possibly spring up from the friendly lands of

Belgium, Luxembourg, Holland or neutral Switzerland? Thus we were relieved of the state of constant tension in which dangerous neighbors once held us and which gravely hampered our activities.

It is true that, while France had lost her special vocation of being constantly in danger, the whole world was now haunted by the permanent fear of global conflict. Two empires, the American and the Soviet, now become giants in comparison with the old powers, confronted each other with their forces, their hegemonies and their ideologies. Both were in possession of nuclear armaments which could at any moment shake the entire world, and which made each of them omnipotent protectors in their respective camps. This perilous balance was liable to tip over eventually into limitless war unless it evolved into a general *détente*. For France, reduced in wealth and power by the conflicts in which she had been engaged over the past two centuries, dangerously exposed by her geographical position at the edge of the Old World and facing the New, mortally vulnerable by reason of her size and population, peace was obviously of vital importance. And, as it happened, circumstances now ordained that she should appoint herself its champion. For she was in the singular position of having no claims on what others possessed while they had nothing to claim from her, and of harboring no grievances on her own behalf against either of the giants, for whose peoples she cherished a traditional friendship confirmed by recent events, while they felt an exceptional attachment to her. In short, if there was a voice that might be listened to and a policy that might be effective with a view to setting up a new order to replace the Cold War, that voice and that policy were pre-eminently those of France. But only on condition that they were really her own and that the hand she held out in friendship was free.

At the same time, France now enjoyed a vast fund of interest and trust among peoples whose future was in gestation but who refused to pay allegiance to either of the rival dominations. China, endowed with such reserves of manpower and resources, that limitless possibilities were open to her for the future; Japan, re-creating an independent world role on the basis of economic strength; India, at grips with problems of subsistence as vast as her size, but ultimately destined to turn towards the outside world; a great number of old and new States in Africa, Asia and Latin America which accepted aid from either or both of the two camps for the immediate needs of their development, but refused to align themselves—all these now looked by choice towards France. True, until she had completed the process of decolonization, they bitterly criticized her, but the criticisms soon ceased when she had liberated her former possessions. It remained for her to exploit the potential of respect, admiration and prestige which existed in her favor over a large part of the globe provided that, as the world expected of her, she served the universal cause of human dignity and progress.

Thus the same destiny which had enabled France to survive the terrible crisis of the war, offered to her afterwards, in spite of all she had lost over the past two centuries in terms of relative power and wealth, a leading international role which suited her genius, responded to her interests and matched her means. I was naturally determined that she should play this role, the more so since I believed that the internal transformation, the political stability and the social progress without which she would unquestionably be doomed to disorder and decline demanded that she should once again feel herself invested with world responsibility. Such was my philosophy. What was my policy to be as regards the practical problems that faced our country abroad?

Apart from that of Algeria, and our colonies, which was for us to settle on our own, these problems were of such scope and range that their solution would be a very lengthy undertaking, unless a new war should chance to come and cut the Gordian knots tied by the previous one. Hence a sustained and continuous policy was required to deal with them, and this was precisely what, in contrast to the unending shifts and changes of the past, our new institutions made possible.

But what exactly were these problems? First of all there was Germany, divided into three by the existence of a parliamentary republic in the West, a Communist dictatorship in the East, and a special status for Berlin, a prey to the internal strains imposed by this state of affairs and the principal pawn in the rivalry between the two camps. There was Europe, impelled by reason and sentiment towards unification after the terrible convulsions which had torn it apart but radically divided by the Iron Curtain, the Cold War and the enforced subjection of its eastern half to Soviet domination. There was the organization imposed on the Atlantic alliance, which amounted to the military and political subordination of Western Europe to the United States of America. There was the problem of aid for the development of the Third World, which was used by Washington and Moscow as a battleground for their rivalry. There were crises in the East, in Africa, in Asia and in Latin America, which the rival interventions of the two giants rendered chronic and incurable. And there were the international institutions in which the two opposing camps polarized judgments on all subjects and prohibited impartiality.

In each of these fields, I wanted France to play an active part. In this poor world which deserved to be handled gently and each of whose leaders was weighed down with grave difficulties, we had to advance step by step, acting as circumstances demanded and respecting the susceptibilities of all. I myself had struck many a blow in my time, but never at the pride of a people nor at the dignity of its leaders. Yet it was essential that what we did and said should be independent of others. From the moment of my return to power, that was our rule—such a complete change of attitude on the part of our country that the world political scene was suddenly and profoundly transformed.

It is true that the Eastern camp at first confined itself to watching to see what new attitude emerged in Paris. But our Western partners, among whom up till then official France had submissively taken its place under the hegemony known as Atlantic solidarity, could not help being put out. However, they would eventually resign themselves to the new situation. It must be said that the experience of dealing with de Gaulle which some of them had had during the war, and all of them after it, meant that they did not expect this Republic to be as easy to handle as the previous one. Still, there was a general feeling in their chancelleries, their parliaments and their newspapers that the ordeal would be a brief one, that de Gaulle would inevitably disappear after a while, and that everything would then be as it had been before. On the other hand, there was no lack of people in these countries, especially among the masses, who were not at all displeased by France's recovery and who felt a certain satisfaction, or envy perhaps, when they saw her shaking off a supremacy which weighed heavily on the whole of the Old World. Added to this were the feelings which foreign crowds were kind enough to entertain for me personally and which, each time I came in contact with them, they demonstrated with a fervor that impressed their governments. On the whole, in spite of the annoyance that was felt, the malicious remarks that were made, the unfavorable articles and aggressive caricatures that proliferated, the outside world would soon accommodate itself to a France who was once more behaving like a great power, and henceforth would follow her every action and her every word with an attention that had long been lacking.

I was to find rather less resignation in what was said and written in quarters which had hitherto been looked upon as the fountainhead of French political thought. For there it had long been more or less taken for granted that our country should take no action that was not dictated to it from outside. No doubt this attitude of mind dated from the time when the dangers which threatened France forced her continually to seek support from abroad, and when the instability of the political regime prevented the government from taking upon itself the risks of major decisions. Even before the First World War, in its alliance with Russia, the Third Republic had had to undertake to respect the Treaty of Frankfurt and let St. Petersburg lead the way rather than Paris. It is true that, during the long battle subsequently fought on our soil in alliance with the English, the Belgians and finally the Americans, the leading role and then the supreme command fell to the French, who in fact provided the principal effort. But was it not primarily the Anglo-Saxons' cry of "Halt!" that brought the sudden cessation of hostilities on November 11, 1918, at the very moment when we were about to pluck the fruits of victory? Were not the wishes and promises of the American President the dominant factor in the Treaty of Versailles, which admittedly restored Alsace and Lorraine to us but left the enemy's unity, territory and resources intact? And afterwards, was it not to gratify the wishes of Washington and London that the government in Paris surrendered the guarantees we had secured and renounced the reparations which Germany owed us in exchange for specious schemes offered to us by America? When the Hitlerian threat appeared and the Führer ventured to move his troops into the Rhineland, and preventive or repressive action on our part would have been enough to bring about his retreat and discomfiture at a time when he was still short of armaments, did not our ministers remain passive because England failed to take the initiative? At the time of the Austrian Anschluss, then the dismemberment and annexation of Czechoslovakia by the Reich, from whence did French acquiescence stem if not from the example of the English? In the surrender of Vichy to the invader's law and in the "collaboration" designed to make our country participate in a so-called European order which in fact was purely Germanic, was there not a trace of this long inurement to satellite status? At the same time, even as I strove to preserve France's sovereign rights in relation to our allies while fighting the common enemy, whence sprang the reprobation voiced by even those closest to me, if not from the idea that we should always give way?

After so many lessons, it might have been thought that once the war was over, those who claimed to lead public opinion would be less inclined towards subordination. Far from it: for the leading school of thought in each political party, national self-effacement had become an established and flaunted doctrine. While for the Communists it was an absolute rule that Moscow is always right, all the old party formations professed the doctrine of "supra-nationalism," in other words France's submission to a law that was not her own. Hence the support for "Europe" seen as an edifice in which technocrats forming an "executive" and parliamentarians assuming legislative powers—the great majority of both being foreigners—would have the authority to decide the fate of the French people. Hence, too, the passion for the Atlantic organization which would put the security and therefore the policy of our country at the disposal of another. Hence, again, the eagerness to submit the acts of our government to the approval of international organizations in which, under a semblance of collective deliberation, the authority of the protector reigned supreme in every field, whether political, military, economic, technical or monetary, and in which our representatives would never dare to say "we want" but simply confine themselves to "pleading France's cause." Hence, finally, the constant fury aroused among the party-political breed by my actions in the name of an independent nation.

Nevertheless, I was to find no lack of support. Emotionally, I would have the backing of the French people, who, without being in the least inclined to arrogance, were determined to preserve their own identity, all the more so because they had nearly lost it and because others everywhere were ardently affirming theirs, whether in terms of sovereignty, language, culture, production or even sport. Whenever I expressed myself in public on these matters I felt a quiver of response. Politically, the organization which had been formed to follow me above and beyond all the old parties, and which had had a numerous and compact group elected to parliament, was to accompany me through thick and thin. Practically, I would have a stable government at my side, whose Prime Minister was convinced of France's right and duty to act on a world scale, and whose Foreign Minister displayed in his field an ability which few have equalled in the course of our arduous history.

Maurice Couve de Murville had the required gifts. Amid a welter of interlocking problems and tangled arguments he was immediately able to distinguish the essential from the accessory, so that he was clear and precise in matters which others deliberately made as obscure and ambiguous as possible. He had the experience, having dealt with many of the issues of the day and known most of the men in command in the course of a distinguished career. He had the confidence, certain as he was that the post to which I had nominated him would be his for a long time. He had the manner, being skilful at making contact by listening, observing and taking note, and then excelling, at the critical moment, in the authoritative formulation of a position from which he would never be deflected. He had the necessary faith, convinced as he was that France could survive only in the first rank of nations, that de Gaulle could put her back there, and that nothing in life was more important than working towards this goal.

This was what we were aiming for in the vast arena of Europe. I myself had always felt, and now more than ever, how much the nations which peopled it had in common. Being all of the same white race, with the same Christian origins and the same way of life, linked to one another since time immemorial by countless ties of thought, art, science, politics and trade, it was natural that they should come to form a whole, with its own character and organization in relation to the rest of the world. It was in pursuance of this destiny that the Roman emperors reigned over it, that Charlemagne, Charles V and Napoleon attempted to unite it, that Hitler sought to impose upon it his crushing domination. But it is a fact of some significance that not one of these federators succeeded in inducing the subject countries to surrender their individuality. On the contrary, arbitrary centralization always provoked an upsurge of violent nationalism by way of reaction. It was my belief that a united Europe could not today, any more than in previous times, be a fusion of its peoples, but that it could and should result from a systematic *rapprochement*. Everything prompted them towards this in an age of proliferating trade, international enterprises, science and technology which know no frontiers, rapid communications and widespread travel. My policy therefore aimed at the setting up of a concert of European States which in developing all sorts of ties between them would increase their interdependence and solidarity. From this starting-point, there was every reason to believe that the process of evolution might lead to their confederation, especially if they were one day to be threatened from the same source.

In practice this led us to put the European Economic Community into effect; to encourage the Six to concert together regularly in political matters;

to prevent certain others, in particular Great Britain, from dragging the West into an Atlantic system which would be totally incompatible with a European Europe, and indeed to persuade these centrifugal elements to integrate themselves with the Continent by changing their outlook, their habits and their customers; and finally to set an example of *détente* followed by understanding and co-operation with the countries of the Eastern bloc, in the belief that beyond all the prejudices and preconceptions of ideology and propaganda, it was peace and progress that answered the needs and desires of the inhabitants of both halves of an accidentally divided Europe.

At the heart of the problem and at the center of the continent lay Germany. It was her destiny to be the keystone of any European edifice, and yet her misdeeds had contributed more than anything else to tearing the Old World apart. True, now that she was sliced into three segments, with the forces of her conquerors stationed in each, she was no longer a direct threat to anyone. But how could the memory of her ambition, her audacity, her power and her tyranny be effaced from peoples' memories—an ambition which only yesterday had unleashed a military machine capable of crushing with one blow the armies of France and her allies; an audacity which, thanks to Italy's complicity, had carried her armies as far as Africa and the Nile basin; a power which, driving across Poland and Russia with Italian, Hungarian, Bulgarian and Rumanian aid, had reached the gates of Moscow and the foothills of the Caucasus; a tyranny whose reign had brought oppression, plunder and crime wherever the fortune of war took the German flag? Henceforth, every precaution must be taken to prevent Germany's evil genius from breaking loose again. But how could a real and lasting peace be built on foundations that were unacceptable to this great people? How could a genuine union of the continent be established without Germany being a part of it? How could the age-old threat of ruin and death be finally dispelled on either side of the Rhine as long as the old enmity remained?

On the all-important question of Germany's future, my mind was made up. First of all, I believed that it would be unjust and dangerous to revise the *de facto* frontiers which the war had imposed on her. This meant that the Oder-Neisse line which separates her from Poland should remain her definitive boundary, that nothing should remain of her former claims in respect of Czechoslovakia, and that a new Anschluss in whatever form must be precluded. Furthermore, the right to possess or to manufacture atomic weapons—which in any case she had declared her intention to renounce—must in no circumstances be granted to her. This being so, I considered it essential that she should form an integral part of the organized system of co-operation between States which I envisaged for the whole of our continent. In this way the security of all nations between the Atlantic and the Urals would be guaranteed, and a change brought about in circumstances, attitudes and relationships which would doubtless ultimately permit the reunion of the three segments of the German people. In the meantime, the Federal Republic would have an essential role to play within the Economic Community and, should it ever materialize, in the political concert of the Six. Finally, I intended that France should weave a network of preferential ties with Germany, which would gradually lead the two peoples towards the mutual understanding and appreciation to which their natural instinct prompts them when they are no longer using up their energies in fighting each other.

By a stroke of good fortune, at the moment when I took up the reins once more in Paris, it happened that Konrad Adenauer, of all Germans the most capable and most willing to commit his country alongside France, was still at the head of the Bonn Government and would remain there for some time longer. This Rhinelander was imbued with a sense of the complementary nature of the Gauls and the Teutons which once fertilized the presence of the Roman Empire on the Rhine, brought success to the Franks and glory to Charlemagne, provided the rationale for Austrasia, justified the relations between the King of France and the Electors, set Germany afire with the flame of the Revolution, inspired Goethe, Heine, Madame de Staël and Victor Hugo, and in spite of the fierce struggles in which the two peoples were locked, continued to seek a path gropingly through the darkness. This patriot was aware of the barriers of hatred and distrust which the frenzied ambitions of Hitler, passionately obeyed by the German masses and their elite, had raised between his country and all its neighbors and which France alone, he knew, by offering the hand of friendship to the hereditary enemy, could succeed in breaking down. This politician, whose tenacious skill had up to now succeeded in maintaining the stability and progress of the Federal Republic, had to steer a careful course to ensure that neither the threat from the East nor the protection of the West endangered the fragile edifice of a State built from the ruins, and perceived the potential value at home and abroad of the resolute backing of the new French Republic.

As soon as he realized that my return was something more than an interlude, the Chancellor asked to see me. I received him at Colombey-les-deux-Eglises on September 14 and 15, 1958. It seemed to me appropriate to mark the occasion in some special way, and I felt that the atmosphere of a family house would be more striking than the splendor of a palace as a setting for the historic encounter between this old Frenchman and this very old German in the name of their two peoples. And so my wife and I offered the Chancellor the modest hospitality of La Boisserie.

When we were face to face, Konrad Adenauer came straight to the point. "I have come to you," he said, "because I consider that you are in a position to influence the course of events. Your personality, what you have already accomplished in the service of your country, the circumstances in which you returned to power—all this gives you the means to do so. Our two peoples are now for the first time in a position to put their relations on an entirely new basis of cordial co-operation. True, we are already on the right road in this respect. But what has been achieved so far has been due to circumstances which, though pressing enough in all conscience, are transitory by the time-scale of history: Germany's defeat and France's exhaustion. The question now is whether something more durable can be achieved. According to what you personally want and decide to do, France and Germany can either reach a genuine long-term understanding, to the immense benefit of themselves and of Europe, or else remain mutually estranged and thus doomed to oppose each other again to their joint detriment. If it is your aim to bring about a genuine *rapprochement* between our two countries, let me say that I am determined to work with you to this end, and that I myself have certain assets in this regard. I have held the office of Chancellor for eleven years, and in spite of my great age I hope to be able to do so for some time to come. The prestige I enjoy and my past record—the reprobation and contempt I showed for Hitler and his people and the maltreatment I and my family suffered at their hands—enable me to lead German policy in the desired direction. But you? What direction do you intend to give French policy?"

I told the Chancellor in reply that if we were together in my house it was because I felt that the moment had come for my country to adopt a new policy towards his. After the terrible ordeals inflicted on her as a result of Teutonic ambitions in 1870, 1914 and 1939, France now faced a Germany which had been defeated, dismantled and reduced to a pitiful international position, which entirely altered the circumstances of their relationship. Of course the French people would not readily forget what they had suffered in the past at the hands of their neighbor across the Rhine, or neglect the precautions which must be taken to safeguard their future. I had, indeed, before the end of hostilities, intended that such precautions should be physical and territorial. But in view of the momentous events which had occurred since then and the resulting situation for Germany, in view of the change of policy and outlook brought about in the Federal Republic by Konrad Adenauer's government, and in view of the overriding importance of the union of Europe, a union which above all demanded the co-operation of Paris and Bonn, I felt that we should try to reverse the course of history by reconciling our two peoples and uniting their efforts and abilities.

This said, Adenauer and I proceeded to consider how to put our aims into practice. We had no difficulty in agreeing on the fundamental principle that, instead of merging the respective policies of the two countries, as the theorists of the European Coal and Steel Community, Euratom and the European Defence Community sought to do, we should recognize that our positions were very different, and build on this fact. According to the Chancellor, there were three things which humiliated and handicapped Germany ventured to ask of France: first, to help her to recover the respect and trust of other nations which would restore her international position; secondly, to contribute towards her security *vis-à-vis* the Soviet camp, especially with regard to the threat that overshadowed Berlin; and thirdly, to recognize her right to reunification. I pointed out to the Chancellor that, in response to so many requests, France for her part had nothing to ask of Germany with respect to unity, security or rank, whereas she could certainly help to rehabilitate her erstwhile aggressor. She would do so—with what magnanimity!—in the name of the entente to be established between the two peoples, and of the balance of power, the unity and the peace of Europe. But to justify her support, she would insist that certain conditions be fulfilled on the German side. These were: acceptance of existing frontiers, an attitude of goodwill in relations with the East, complete renunciation of atomic armaments, and unremitting patience as regards reunification.

I must say that on these points the Chancellor's pragmatism reconciled him to my position. Devoted as he was to his country, he did not intend to make frontier revision the present and principal aim of his policy, knowing full well that to raise the matter would produce nothing but redoubled alarm and fury from Russia and Poland and reproachful anxiety in the West. Despite his unwavering hostility to the Communist regime and his fears of Muscovite imperialism, he by no means ruled out the possibility of a *modus vivendi.* "As early as 1955," he told me, "I paid an official visit to the Kremlin. I was the first Western Head of State or Government to have been there since the end of the war." He categorically denied that Germany had any intention of possessing atomic weapons, and was aware of the immediate threat to peace if it were otherwise. Although he longed with all his heart to see a united German State and an end to the totalitarian oppression imposed by the Communists, on behalf of the Soviets, in what he called "the Zone," I sensed in this Catholic Rhinelander, leader of a party of traditional democrats, a feeling that, in the event, the present Federal Republic might experience some uneasiness in incorporating outright the Prussian, Protestant and socialist complex of the eastern territories. In any case he agreed that, although this was a goal which Germany would never relinquish, no time limit should be set for its achievement.

We discussed Europe at length. Adenauer agreed with me that there could be no question of submerging the identity of our two nations in some stateless construction. He did, however, admit that Germany had drawn distinct advantages from the mystique of integration, and he was grateful to its French protagonists such as Jean Monnet and Robert Schuman for their gifts. But being Chancellor of a defeated, divided and threatened Germany, he naturally inclined towards a West European system which would ensure his country not only equal rights but also commanding influence, would provide powerful support against the East, and by its very existence would encourage the United States to remain in Europe and thus maintain its guarantee to Federal Germany. Adenauer set great store by this guarantee because, he said, "by providing for the security of the German people and putting them in good company, it diverts them from their obsession with isolation and the worship of power which, to their cost, drove them into Hitler's arms."

I told Adenauer that from a strictly national point of view France, unlike Germany, had no real need of an organization of Western Europe, since the war had damaged neither her reputation nor her territorial integrity. Nevertheless, she was in favor of a practical and, if possible, political *rapprochement* of all European States because her aim was general peace and progress. Meanwhile, on condition that her national identity remained unaffected, she was prepared to implement the Treaty of Rome and, further, to propose that the Six should meet regularly to discuss joint action on all the political problems facing the world. Difficulties would arise for the European Economic Community from the problem of agriculture, a solution to which was essential for France, and Britain's application for membership, which France felt must be turned down as long as Britain remained economically and politically what she was. On these two points, the French government was counting on the agreement of the German government, failing which a genuine union of the Six would be unattainable. "Personally," the Chancellor said, "I understand your reasons very well. But Germany on the whole is unfavorable to the agricultural Common Market and anxious to give satisfaction to Britain. However, since in my opinion nothing is more important than that the union of the Six should succeed, I promise to act in such a way that the two problems you have mentioned do not prevent its realization. As for the idea of regular political discussions with our partners, I am entirely in favor of it."

I assured the Chancellor that we in France considered it perfectly natural that Federal Germany should adhere unreservedly to the Atlantic Pact. How could she do otherwise? In this age of atomic weapons, as long as she was threatened by the Soviets, it was obvious that Germany needed the protection of the United States. But in this respect as in others, France was not in the same position. Hence, while continuing to belong to the alliance formed by the Treaty of Washington for mutual assistance in case of aggression, she planned to leave NATO sooner or later, the more so as she intended to equip herself with nuclear weapons which there could be no question of integrating into the system. More than anything else, political independence commensurate with my country's position and aims was essential to its survival in the future. The German Chancellor listened while I explained the reasons for this. "The French people," I told him, "had for centuries grown accustomed to think of their country as the mastodon of Europe. It was this sense of their greatness and the responsibilities it entailed that preserved their unity, although by nature, ever since the time of the Gauls, they have been inclined to divisions and airy illusions. Now once again circumstances—by which I mean France's salvation at the end of the war, her strong institutions, and the profound upheaval which the world is undergoing—offer them the chance of fulfilling an international mission, without which they would lose interest in themselves and fall into disruption. It is my view that every country in the world, including Germany, has a great deal to lose and nothing to gain from the eclipse of France. Anything that leads my country to give up the struggle represents a grave danger to us and a serious threat to others." "I agree with you," replied Adenauer, "and I am heartily glad to see France resume her rightful place in the world. Allow me to say, however, that the German people, although their genius is different from that of the French, have a similar need for dignity. Having seen you and listened to you, I feel confident that you are willing to help Germany recover that dignity." At the conclusion of our discussions, we agreed to establish direct and special links between our two countries in every field, and not to limit them to membership of organizations which extinguished their individual personalities. From then onwards we were to remain in close personal contact.

Two months later, on November 26, I paid a return visit to Adenauer at Bad-Kreuznach, accompanied by Michel Debré and Maurice Couve de Murville. The Chancellor was seconded by the dynamic Ludwig Erhard who, making the most of the enterprise and initiative of management, the constructive co-operation of the unions and the credits provided under the Marshall Plan, had restored his country's means of production and was now presiding over a remarkable economic achievement. Heinrich von Brentano, the Foreign Minister, was also there, as convinced as his chief that an understanding with France must henceforth be a basic principle of German policy. In the course of this meeting, the two governments set out the terms of their co-operation in accordance with what had been adumbrated at Colombey-les-deux-Eglises. In particular, they agreed to put an end to the negotiations conducted by Reginald Maudling which were calculated to submerge the Community of the Six at the outset in a vast free trade area together with England and eventually the whole of the West. At the same time, it was an opportunity for us French to assure the Germans, who were then in a state of acute anxiety, that we would oppose the change in the status of Berlin which Nikita Khrushchev was at that very moment threatening to impose.

From then until mid-1962, Konrad Adenauer and I were to write to each other on some forty occasions. We saw each other fifteen times, either in Paris, Marly or Rambouillet, or in Baden-Baden or Bonn. We spent more than a hundred hours in conversation, either in private, or with our ministers in attendance, or in the company of our families. Then, since it was my intention that the new relationship between the two nations, so long at enmity, should be solemnly consecrated, I invited the Chancellor to pay an official visit to France. Heinrich Lübke, President of the Federal Republic, had already made a discreet State visit in June 1961. Now, in July 1962, the Head of the German government made a public appearance in the squares and avenues of our capital. The welcome he received, particularly from the people in the street, testified to the esteem in which he was personally held, as well as to the fund of goodwill towards the policy of reconciliation and co-operation to which he had dedicated himself. After his Parisian reception, an impressive military ceremony took place at the camp of Mourmelon. There, General de Gaulle received Chancellor Konrad Adenauer before the colors. Standing side by side in a command car, they inspected a French and a German armored division which outvied one another in smartness and bearing. Then, with their ministers and many dignitaries around them, they watched these heavy units parade before them, while aerial formations from both countries flew overhead. The journey ended at Rheims, the symbol of our age-old traditions, but also the scene of many an encounter between the hereditary enemies, from the ancient Germanic invasions to the battles of the Marne. In the cathedral, whose wounds were still not fully healed, the first Frenchman and the first German came together to pray that on either side of the Rhine the deeds of friendship might for ever supplant the miseries of war.

Subsequently, and until the death of my illustrious friend, our relations were to progress at the same tempo and with the same cordiality. By and large, everything that was spoken, written and evinced between us was to do no more than develop and adapt to events the friendly agreement concluded in 1958. It is true that circumstances would produce some divergences of view. But these were always surmounted. Through us, the relations between France and Germany were established on foundations and in an atmosphere hitherto unknown in their history.

This co-operation between the two former enemies was a necessary but by no means a sufficient precondition for organized European co-operation. It is true that, judging merely by the spate of speeches and articles on the subject, the unification of our Continent might well appear to be a matter as simple as it was foreordained. But when the realities of needs, interests and preconceptions came into play, things took on an altogether different aspect. While fruitless bargaining with the British showed the fledgeling Community that good intentions are not enough to reconcile the irreconcilable, the Six found that even in the economic sphere alone the adjustment of their respective positions bristled with difficulties which could not be resolved solely in terms of the treaties concluded to that end. It had to be acknowledged that the so-called executives installed at the head of common institutions by virtue of the delusions of integration which had prevailed before my return, were helpless when it came to making and enforcing decisions, that only governments were in a position to do this, and then only as a result of negotiations carried out in due form between ministers or ambassadors.

In the case of the European Coal and Steel Community, for example, once it had used up the birthday presents bestowed upon it by its member States, none of them, be it said, for our benefit—French relinquishment of coke from the Ruhr, deliveries of coal and iron to Italy, financial subventions to the Benelux mines—the High Authority, although vested with very extensive theoretical powers and considerable resources, was soon overwhelmed by the problems presented by competing national requirements. Whether it was a matter of fixing the price of steel, or regulating fuel purchases from outside, or converting the collieries of the Borinage, the areopagus enthroned in Luxembourg was powerless to legislate. The result was a chronic decline in that organization, whose prime mover, Jean Monnet, had moreover resigned the presidency.

At the same time, in the case of Euratom, there seemed an irremediable disparity between the situation of France, equipped for some fifteen years past with an active Atomic Energy Commissariat, provided with numerous installations and already engaged in precise and far-reaching programs of research and development, and that of the other countries which, having done nothing on their own account, now wanted to use the funds of the common budget to obtain what they lacked by placing orders with American suppliers.

Lastly, in the case of the Economic Community, the adoption of the agricultural regulations in conjunction with the lowering of industrial tariffs raised obstacles which the Brussels Commission was unable to overcome on its own. It must be said that in this respect the spirit and terms of the Treaty of Rome did not meet our country's requirements. The industrial provisions were as precise and explicit as those concerning agriculture were vague. This was evidently due to the fact that our negotiators in 1957, caught up in the dream of a supra-national Europe and anxious at any price to settle for something approaching it, had not felt it their duty to insist that a French interest, no matter how crucial, should receive satisfaction at the outset. It would, therefore, be necessary either to obtain it *en route,* or to liquidate the Common Market. Meanwhile, determined though it was to have its way in the end, the French government was able to allow the machinery of the Treaty of Rome to be set in motion thanks to the recovery of our balance of payments and the stabilization of the franc. In December 1958 it announced that it would implement the inaugural measures which were scheduled for New Year's Day, in particular a ten per cent tariff cut and a twenty per cent quota increase.

Once initiated, the implementation of the Common Market was to give rise to a vast outgrowth of not only technical but also diplomatic activity. For, irrespective of its very wide economic scope, the operation proved to be hedged about with specifically political intentions calculated to prevent our country from being its own master. Hence, while the Community was taking shape, I was obliged on several occasions to intervene in order to repel the threats which overshadowed our cause.

The first arose from the original ambivalence of the institution. Was its objective—in itself momentous enough—the harmonization of the practical interests of the six States, their economic solidarity in face of the outside world and, if possible, their co-operation in foreign policy? Or did it aim to achieve the total fusion of their respective economies and policies in a single entity with its own government, parliament and laws, ruling in every respect its French, German, Italian, Dutch, Belgian and Luxembourg subjects, who would become fellow-citizens of an artificial motherland, the brainchild of the technocrats? Needless to say, having no taste for make-believe, I adopted the former conception. But the latter carried all the hopes and illusions of the supra-national school.

For these champions of integration, the European executive was already alive and kicking: it was the Commission of the Economic Community, made up, admittedly, of representatives nominated by the six States but, thereafter, in no way dependent on them. Judging by the chorus of those who wanted Europe to be a federation, albeit without a federator, all the authority, initiative and control of the exchequer which are the prerogatives of government in the economic sphere must in future belong to this brigade of experts, not only within the Community but also—and this could be indefinitely extensible—from the point of view of relations with other countries. As for the national ministers, who could not as yet be dispensed with in their executive capacity, they had only to be summoned periodically to Brussels, where they would receive the Commission's instructions in their specialized fields. At the same time, the mythmongers wanted to exhibit the Assembly in Strasbourg, consisting of deputies and senators delegated by the legislatures of the member countries, as a "European parliament" which, while having no effective power, provided the Brussels "executive" with a semblance of democratic responsibility.

Walter Hallstein was the Chairman of the Commission. He was ardently wedded to the thesis of the super-State, and bent all his skilful efforts towards giving the Community the character and appearance of one. He had made Brussels, where he resided, into a sort of capital. There he sat, surrounded with all the trappings of sovereignty, directing his colleagues, allocating jobs among them, controlling several thousand officials who were appointed, promoted and remunerated at his discretion, receiving the credentials of foreign ambassadors, laying claim to high honors on the occasion of his official visits, concerned above all to further the amalgamation of the Six, believing that the pressure of events would bring about what he envisaged. But after meeting him more than once and observing his activities, I felt that although Walter Hallstein was in his way a sincere European, he was first and foremost a German who was ambitious for his own country. For in the Europe that he sought lay the framework in which his country could first of all regain, free of charge, the respectability and equality of rights which the frenzy and defeat of Hitler had cost it, then acquire the preponderant influence which its economic strength would no doubt earn it, and finally ensure that the cause of its frontiers and its unity was backed by a powerful coalition in accordance with the doctrine to which, as Foreign Minister of the Federal Republic, he had formerly given his name. These factors did not alter my esteem and regard for Walter Hallstein, but the goals I was pursuing on behalf of France were incompatible with such projects.

The fundamental divergence between the way the Brussels Commission conceived its role and my own government's insistence, while looking to the Commission for expert advice, that important measures should be subordinated to the decisions of the individual States, nurtured an atmosphere of latent discord. But since the Treaty specified that during the inaugural period no decision was valid unless unanimous, it was enough to enforce its application to ensure that there was no infringement of French sovereignty. So during this period the institution took wing in what was and must remain the economic sphere without being subjected to any mortal political crisis, in spite of frequent clashes. Moreover, in November 1959, at the initiative of Paris, it was decided that the six Foreign Ministers should meet at three-monthly intervals to examine the overall situation and its various implications and to report back to their own governments, which would have the last word if the need arose. It may be imagined that ours did not allow itself to be led.

But it was not only from the political angle that the new-fledged Community had to undergo the truth test. Even in the economic sphere two formidable obstacles, secreting all kinds of contradictory interests and calculations, threatened to bar its way. These were, of course, the external tariff and agriculture, which were closely bound up with one another. True, on signing the Treaty, our partners had seemed to accept that common taxes should be imposed upon foreign goods as customs duties were reduced within the Community. But although they all recognized in principle that this procedure was essential to their solidarity, some of them were nonetheless irked by it because it deprived them of trade facilities which had hitherto been intrinsic to their existence. They therefore wanted the common external tariff to be as low as possible and in any case so elastic that their habits would not be disturbed. The same countries, for the same reasons, were in no hurry to see the Six take upon themselves the consumption and, therefore, the cost of continental farm products, nearly half of which happened to be French. For instance Germany, nearly two-thirds of whose food was imported cheaply from outside the Community in exchange for manufactured goods, would have liked to see a Common Market for industrial goods only, in which case the Federal Republic would inevitably have had an overwhelming advantage. This was unacceptable to France. We therefore had to put up a fight in Brussels.

The battle was long and hard. Our partners, who bitterly regretted our having changed Republics, had been counting on us once again to sacrifice our own cause to "European integration," as had happened successively with the Coal and Steel Community, in which all the advantages went to others at our expense; with Euratom, for which our country put up practically the entire stake without a *quid pro quo,* and, moreover submitted her atomic assets to foreign supervision; and with the Treaty of Rome, which did not settle the agricultural question which was of paramount importance to ourselves. But now France was determined to get what she needed, and in any case her demands were consistent with the logic of the Community system. So her requirements were eventually met.

In May 1960, at our urgent insistence, the Six agreed to establish the external tariff and to adopt a timetable for the decisions to be taken on agricultural policy. In December of the same year, while urging an acceleration of the process of lowering customs barriers between them, they agreed that all imports of foodstuffs from elsewhere should be liable to an enormous financial levy at the expense of the purchasing State. And in January 1962 they adopted the decisive resolutions.

For at this date, now that the first phase of application was completed, it had to be decided whether or not, in pursuance of the terms of the Treaty, to proceed to the second phase, a kind of point of no return, involving a fifty per cent reduction in customs duties. We French were determined to seize the opportunity to tear aside the veil and induce our partners to make formal commitments on what we regarded as essential. When they proved reluctant to give way, and indeed showed signs of some disquieting reservations, I judged that now or never was the moment to take the bull by the horns. Our ministers in Brussels, Couve de Murville, Baumgartner and Pisani, made it quite clear that we were prepared to withdraw from the Community if our requirements were not met. I myself wrote in similar terms to Chancellor Adenauer, whose government was our principal antagonist in this matter, and repeated it by formal telegram on the evening of the final debate. Feeling ran high in the capitals of the Six. In France, the parties and most of the newspapers, echoing foreign opinion, were disturbed and scandalized by the attitude of General de Gaulle, whose intransigence was threatening "the hopes of Europe." But France and common sense prevailed. During the night of January 13-14, 1962, after some dramatic exchanges, the Council of Ministers of the six States formally decided to admit agriculture into the Common Market, laid down there and then a broad basis for its implementation, and made the necessary arrangements to establish the agricultural regulations on the same footing and at the same time as the rest. Whereupon the implementation of the Treaty was able to enter its second phase.

But how far could it go, in view of the difficulties which the British were doing their utmost to raise, and the tendency of our five partners to submit to their influence? It was not surprising that Great Britain should be radically opposed to the whole venture, since by virtue of her geography and therefore her policy, she has never been willing to see the Continent united or to merge with it herself. In a sense it might almost be said that therein lay the whole history of Europe for the past eight hundred years. As for the present, our neighbors across the Channel, adapted to free trade by the maritime nature of their economic life, could not sincerely agree to shut themselves up behind a continental tariff wall, still less to buy their food dear from us rather than import it cheap from everywhere else, for example the Commonwealth. But without the common tariff and agricultural preference, there could be no valid European Community. Hence at the time of the preliminary studies and discussions that led up to the Treaty of Rome, the London government, which was represented at the outset, had soon withdrawn. Then, with the intention of undermining the project of the Six, it had proposed that they should join a vast European free trade area with itself and various others. Things had reached this stage when I returned to power.

As early as June 29, 1958, Prime Minister Harold Macmillan had come to see me in Paris. In the midst of our friendly discussions which touched upon a great many topics, he suddenly declared with great feeling: "The Common Market is the Continental System all over again. Britain cannot accept it. I beg you to give it up. Otherwise, we shall be embarking on a war which will doubtless be economic at first but which runs the risk of gradually spreading into other fields." Ignoring the overstatement, I tried to pacify the English Premier, at the same time asking him why the United Kingdom should object to seeing the Six establish a system of preference such as existed inside the Commonwealth. Meanwhile, his minister Reginald Maudling was actively engaged inside the so-called Organization for European Economic Co-operation, to which Britain belonged, in negotiations which were keeping the Six in suspense, and delaying the launching of the Community by proposing that the latter should be absorbed and, consequently, dissolved in a free trade area. Harold Macmillan wrote me a number of very pressing letters in an effort to obtain my compliance. But my government broke the spell, and made it clear that it would not agree to anything which did not include the common external tariff and an agricultural arrangement. London then appeared to abandon its policy of obstruction and, suddenly changing course, set up its own European Free Trade Association, with the Scandinavians, Portugal, Switzerland and Austria. At once, our Brussels partners dropped all their hesitations and set about launching the Common Market.

But the match had merely been postponed. In the middle of 1961 the British returned to the offensive. Having failed from without to prevent the birth of the Community, they now planned to paralyze it from within. Instead of calling for an end to it, they now declared that they themselves were eager to join, and proposed examining the conditions on which they might do so, "provided that their special relationships with the Commonwealth and their associates in the Free Trade area were taken into consideration, as well as their special interests in respect of agriculture." To submit to this would obviously have meant abandoning the Common Market as originally conceived. Our partners could not bring themselves to do so. But, on the other hand, it was beyond their power to say "No" to England. So, affecting to believe that the squaring of the circle was a practical proposition, they proceeded to discuss a series of projects and counter-projects in Brussels with the British minister Edward Heath, which threw nothing but doubt on the future of the Community. I could see the day approaching when I should either have to remove the obstruction and put an end to the tergiversation, or else extricate France from an enterprise which had gone astray almost as soon as it had begun. At all events, as could have been foreseen, it was now clear to all that in order to achieve the unification of Europe, individual states are the only valid elements, that when their national interest is at stake nothing and nobody must be allowed to force their hands, and that co-operation between them is the only road that will lead anywhere.

In this respect what is true of economics is even truer of politics. And this is no more than natural. What depths of illusion or prejudice would have to be plumbed in order to believe that European nations forged through long centuries by endless exertion and suffering, each with its own geography, history, language, traditions and institutions, could cease to be themselves and form a single entity? What a perfunctory view is reflected in the parallel often naïvely drawn between what Europe ought to do and what the United States have done, when the latter was created from nothing in a completely new territory by successive waves of uprooted colonists? For the Six in particular, how was it conceivable that their external aims should suddenly become identical when their origins, situations and ambitions were so very different? In the matter of decolonization, which France was about to bring to a conclusion, what part could her neighbors play? If, from time immemorial, it had been in her nature to accomplish "God's work,"[1] to disseminate freedom of thought, to be a champion of humanity, why should it *ipso facto* become the concern of her partners? Germany, baulked by defeat of her hopes of supremacy, divided at present and suspected by many of seeking her revenge, was now a wounded giant. By what token should her wounds automatically be shared by others? Given the fact that Italy, having ceased to be an annex of the Germanic or the French empires, and thwarted of her Balkan ambitions, remained a peninsular power confined to the Mediterranean and naturally located within the orbit of the maritime nations, why should she throw in her lot with the Continentals? By what miracle would the Netherlands, which had always owed its livelihood to shipping and its independence to overseas resources, allow itself to be swallowed up by the land powers? How could Belgium, hard put to it to maintain the juxtaposition of Flemings and Walloons in a single entity ever since a compromise between rival powers had turned her into a State, genuinely devote herself to anything else? Lying at the center of the territorial arrangements which had succeeded the rivalries of the two great countries bordering on the Moselle, what major concern could the people of Luxembourg have other than the survival of Luxembourg?

On the other hand, while recognizing that each of these countries had its own national personality which it must preserve, there was no reason why they should not organize concerted action in every sphere, arrange for their ministers to meet regularly and their Heads of State or Government periodically, set up permanent organs to discuss politics, economics, culture and defense, have these subjects debated in the normal way by an assembly of delegates from their respective parliaments, acquire the taste and habit of examining together problems of common interest, and as far as possible adopt a united attitude towards them. Linked with what was already being practiced in the economic sphere in Brussels and Luxembourg, might not this general co-operation lead to a European policy as regards progress, security, influence, external relations, aid to the developing countries, and finally and above all as regards peace? Might not the grouping thus formed by the Six gradually attract the other States of the Continent into joining in on the same terms? And perhaps in this way, by opposing war, which is the history of men, that united Europe which is the dream of the wise might ultimately be achieved.

Before discussing this with the German Chancellor, I had put the idea to the Italian Prime Minister. Amintore Fanfani came to visit me on August 7, 1958. I was to receive him again in December and in January. Each of these meetings made me appreciate his wide-ranging intellect, his prudent judgment and his urbanity. Through him, I saw an Italy anxious to keep in touch with everything that was afoot, willing to join in on condition that she was treated with the consideration due to a nation with a very great past and a very important future, ready to subscribe to declarations of principle which expressed good intentions, but careful not to commit herself too deeply. This was the case as regards European unity. The head of the Italian government was certainly in favor of it. He even shared the supra-national leanings bequeathed to him by de Gasperi. Yet, comfortably ignoring an obvious contradiction, he did not want anything done without England, although he was well aware that England was opposed to integration. While paying lip-service to the solidarity of the peoples of the Old World, he did not feel that this should lead them to alter their ties—however dependent—with the United States. In particular, the organization of the Atlantic alliance must on no account be modified. However, he did not spurn my plan for organized political co-operation among the Six, though he reserved judgment on the terms and conditions until these came up for discussion.

Soon afterwards, as it happened, I was to make direct contact with the Italian government and people. Our neighbors were celebrating the centenary of the Franco-Piedmontese victories of 1859. When I was invited to take part by the President of the Republic, Giovanni Gronchi, I accepted with alacrity. Couve de Murville and Guillaumat came too. Milan welcomed me on June 23 amid a storm of cheers. I met with the same enthusiasm the following day during a military parade in which French troops took part alongside the Italian Army. At Magenta too, and then at Solferino, where an enormous crowd had gathered and where I made a speech on the battlefield, fervent demonstrations left no doubt as to public feeling towards our country and General de Gaulle. In the course of the religious service the Archbishop of Milan, Monsignor Montini, the future Pope Paul VI, gave a sermon imbued with a deep affection for France. The same warmth was evident during the reception given to me at the Capitol shortly afterwards by the municipality of Rome. There could be no better proof of the aberration represented by the aggression committed against us nineteen years before on the orders of Mussolini. But nothing could be more encouraging for the future relations between the two kindred nations. President Gronchi, Prime Minister Antonio Segni and Foreign Minister Giuseppe Pella agreed on this point with myself and the ministers who accompanied me.

Nevertheless our discussions, first on the train which took us to Rome, then at the Quirinal Palace, where my wife and I were the guests of the Head of State and Signora Gronchi and where the two Presidents forgathered with members of their governments, revealed attitudes on either side which were far from identical. We French wanted to proceed towards a European Europe. The Italians set the utmost store by the maintenance of existing relations with the Anglo-Saxons. Basically, the Rome government favored integration because under cover of that mythical apparatus it could maneuver to its heart's content, because there was nothing in such a structure that could interfere with the protective hegemony of Washington, and because in any case it saw it as a temporary arrangement until the arrival of the English. Soon I was to discover that the Benelux countries took the same view. Just as French economic and social vested interests and political parties clamored for the transformation of France, but resisted any reform that altered the established order, so the unification of the Continent whose necessity was proclaimed by the ruling circles of our European partners and by our own coteries, came up against a wall of reservations, exegeses and counterbids whenever I attempted to clear the way for it. But I reflected that if Rome was not built in a day, it was in the nature of things that the construction of Europe should require protracted efforts.

In the matter of perseverance, I received the best possible reminder in the Vatican. I was received there by Pope John XXIII. The pomp and pageantry displayed for the occasion demonstrated his exceptional concern for France. He was gratified to hear what I had to say about our efforts towards national renewal, since he knew our country well and had witnessed its former political confusion at close range as Nuncio in Paris. Then, with an anxiety tempered by his natural serenity, the sovereign pontiff spoke of the spiritual perturbation inflicted on Christendom by the gigantic upheavals of the century. Among all the peoples of Europe and Asia which had been subjected to Communism, the Catholic community was oppressed and cut off from Rome. But everywhere else, under free regimes, a sort of diffuse rebelliousness was undermining, if not religion then at least its practices, its rules, its hierarchy and its rites. Nevertheless, however much anxiety this situation might cause him, the Pope saw it as no more than another in the long series of crises which the Church had faced and surmounted ever since the time of Christ. He believed that by putting into practice its own values of inspiration and self-examination it would not fail once more to regain its equilibrium. It was to this that he proposed to dedicate his pontificate. After my wife had been introduced, John XXIII gave us his blessing. We never saw him again.

Europe, for its part, had no certainty of eternal life. However, by regrouping in order to come to grips with its own problems, perhaps it too might take on a new lease of life. But with all the talk and counter-talk about unity, no plan for such a confrontation had ever been submitted to the Six. I took it upon myself to do so once it had become clear that our country was extricating herself from the Algerian problem and about to regain her freedom of action. My intention was to invite the Heads of State or Government to Paris, so that France could present her proposals in a setting commensurate with the subject. Chancellor Adenauer was the first to be informed. In July 1960 at Rambouillet, where I had invited him to stay, I announced to him my plan for a summit conference and explained to him how, in my view, the political co-operation of the Six should be run by periodic meetings of their leaders and, in the interim, by the work of permanent bodies which would prepare the ground for the meetings and follow up the decisions. He and I were agreed on the essentials. In August, I confided my plan to Jan de Quay, Prime Minister of the Netherlands, and Joseph Luns, the Foreign Minister, when they came to Paris. As expected, I found them orientated far less towards the Continent than towards America and England, and above all anxious to see the latter join the Six on no matter what terms. Much the same was true of the Belgians, Gaston Eyskens, the Prime Minister, and Paul-Henri Spaak, once again in charge of Foreign Affairs, when I received them too at the Elysée. There also the cautious Luxembourg ministers Pierre Werner and Eugène Schauss were welcomed in their turn. In the meantime, I had conferred at leisure with Amintore Fanfani, once again Prime Minister of Italy, and Antonio Segni when they came to stay at Rambouillet, and had had a further discussion with Konrad Adenauer in Bonn.

In addition, as was my wont, I saw fit to apprise the public of my plans. In the course of a press conference on September 5, I gave details of what was being undertaken. After saying that "to build Europe, which means to unite Europe, is an essential aim of our policy," I declared that to this end it was necessary "to proceed, not on the basis of dreams, but in accordance with realities. Now, what are the realities of Europe? What are the pillars on which it can be built? The truth is that those pillars are the States of Europe . . . States each of which, indeed, has its own genius, history and language, its own sorrows, glories and ambitions; but States that are the only entities with the right to give orders and the power to be obeyed." Then, while recognizing "the technical value of certain more or less extra-national or supra-national organisms," I pointed out that they were not and could not be politically effective, as was proved by what was happening at that very moment in the European Coal and Steel Community, Euratom and the Brussels Community. I insisted that, "although it is perfectly natural for the States of Europe to have specialist bodies available to prepare and whenever necessary to follow up their decisions, those decisions must be their own." Then I outlined my plan: "To arrange for the regular co-operation of the States of Western Europe in the political, economic and cultural spheres, as well as that of defense, is an aim that France deems desirable, possible and practical. . . . It will entail organized, regular consultations between the governments concerned and the work of specialist bodies in each of the common domains, subordinated to those governments. It will entail periodic deliberations by an assembly made up of delegates of the national parliaments. It must also, in my view, entail as soon as possible a solemn European referendum, in order to give this new departure for Europe the popular backing which is essential to it." I concluded: "If we set out on this road . . . links will be forged, habits will be developed, and, as time does its work, it is possible that we will come to take further steps towards European unity."

On February 10 and 11, in the Salon de l'Horloge in the Quai d'Orsay, I presided over a meeting of Prime Ministers, Foreign Ministers, higher civil servants and ambassadors of Germany, Italy, the Netherlands, Belgium, Luxembourg and France. The discussion was lively, because the doubts and misgivings were considerable. Needless to say, they all had to do with America and England. In response to my formal proposal to establish political co-operation among the Six forthwith, Adenauer gave his entire approval. Werner followed suit. Fanfani concurred, with certain reservations. Eyskens and Wigny raised no objections at first. But Luns, with some asperity, expressed all kinds of hesitations; whereupon Eyskens adopted the same attitude. It was clear that Holland and Belgium, small powers bordering on the North Sea, always on their guard against the "great ones" of the Continent and traditionally protected by the British Navy, now superseded by the Americans, did not take kindly to a system from which the Anglo-Saxons were excluded. But it was no less obvious that if the western half of the Old World remained subordinated to the New, Europe would never be European, nor would she ever be able to bring her two halves together. However, the prevailing impression at the conclusion of this encounter was that Europe had taken its first steps towards unity, that all the participants had been highly interested and gratified to meet and deliberate together, and, in short, that we should attempt to go further. To this end, it was agreed that there should be a second meeting in Bonn in three months' time, and that with a view to this next summit conference a political commission made up of representatives of the Six should draw up proposals in Paris for the organization of their co-operation in every sphere.

In view of the magnitude of the obstacles, however, there was little likelihood of immediate success. Indeed, an active campaign to impede it was launched at once behind the scenes. The supporters of unconditional British entry into the economic and—should it materialize—the political Community concerted their negative efforts with those of the champions of supranationalism, without the evident contradiction between the two theses in the least deflecting them from working together to combat the French solution. When I went to Bonn on May 20, I became aware of the commotion aroused there by the positive attitude which the Chancellor had adopted in my favor. Upon receiving the King and Queen of the Belgians, who were given a whole-hearted welcome by the Parisians at the end of the same month, I naturally took the opportunity to express to the young sovereigns and to their country the warm feelings of France, but I also listened to Spaak, who accompanied them, while he repeated to me his unfavorable views on the question of political co-operation among the Six. At the same time, there were nothing but echoes of dubiety from Italy and of criticism from Holland.

In spite of everything, after some delay the second meeting of Heads of State and Government took place in Bonn on July 18 and 19. Each of the delegations took up a similar position as in Paris. But since Chancellor Adenauer and General de Gaulle once again expressed their firm agreement, the opposition moderated its virulence. And when the Germans took everybody off after the session for an excursion and a luncheon on the Rhine, scarcely a cloud overshadowed the European effusions. The decision taken by the conference was to proceed on the lines advocated by the French government. To this end, the Political Commission already set up under the chairmanship of Christian Fouchet was instructed to draw up the text of a formal treaty which could be ratified by a summit meeting to be held subsequently in Rome.

Caution and the proprieties had thus prevented the higher authorities from parading their differences. But they were inevitably to come to light during the proceedings of the Fouchet Commission. A single project was submitted to it—that of France. Germany continued to support it. But the determined opposition of Holland and Belgium and the calculated indecision of Italy were to ensure that it came to nothing. At one moment it had looked as though the Rome Government was coming round to the Paris–Bonn viewpoint, and this would certainly have decided the issue. On April 4, 1962, I had gone to Turin to see Amintore Fanfani again. Our discussion led me to believe that we were in agreement on the somewhat amended text of the Fouchet Plan. No doubt this was true, that day, of my interlocutor himself. For the Italian statesman had sufficient taste for great issues and sense of the higher necessities of our day to want his country to be a pillar of European unity together with France and Germany. But so simple and categorical a resolve would have been out of keeping with the political complexities characteristic of our transalpine cousins. It was for this reason that when the Foreign Ministers of the Six met in Paris on April 17 to make their governments' final positions known, Antonio Segni turned down the French plan. This was Spaak's cue to speak out for all the dissentients. Warmly supported by Luns, he declared that Belgium would not sign the treaty, "even if it suited her as it was," as long as England was not a member of the Community. Some days later he wrote to me to say that Belgium was ready to conclude an agreement among the Six on condition that the Political Commission destined in our plan to be an instrument of the Council of States was set up as a power independent of the governments. Thus, without the slightest embarrassment, Spaak simultaneously embraced the two mutually exclusive theses of the supporters of Anglo-Saxon hegemony and the champions of supra-nationalism.

From then on, things were to remain in abeyance before it became known whether the French offer to initiate the co-operation of the sundered Old World was to be, for history, "some armada foundered in eternal error," or, for the future, a fair hope riding the waves.

NOTE

1. "Les gestes de Dieu": a reference to the Frankish motto, *Gesta dei per francos.*

CHAPTER 3

Obstinate or Obsolete?: France, European Integration, and the Fate of the Nation-State

Stanley Hoffmann

Stanley Hoffmann has long been recognized as one of the premier commentators on French politics and society, on European integration, and on ethics and international affairs. He was born in Vienna, spent his formative and university years in France, 1929–1955. He has taught at Harvard since 1955, and was founding chairman of the Center for European Studies, 1969–1995. His wide-ranging teaching interests include French intellectual and political history, American foreign policy, ethics and international relations, the sociology of war, and contemporary European history. Among his best-known books are Gulliver's Troubles *(1968);* Decline or Renewal? France since the 1930s *(1974);* Primacy or World Order? American Foreign Policy since the Cold War *(1978);* Duties beyond Borders *(1981); and* The European Sisyphus: Essays on Europe, 1964–1994 (1995), *from which this chapter is taken. It originally was published in a longer version as "Obstinate or Obsolete: The Fate of the Nation-State and the Case of Western Europe," in* Daedalus, *Summer 1966, and has been republished several times since. This surely should be read as partly a product of its time, just following the "empty chair" crisis provoked by French president de Gaulle. Professor Hoffmann's Euro-pessimism, given in relation to federalist hopes of the 1960s, contrasts with different analytical judgments at other times.*

I

The critical issue for every student of world order is the fate of the nation-state. In the nuclear age, the fragmentation of the world into countless units, each of which has a claim to independence, is obviously dangerous for peace and illogical for welfare. The dynamism that animates these units—when they are not merely city-states of limited expanse or dynastic states manipulated by the Prince's calculations, but nation-states that pour into their foreign policy the collective pride, ambitions, fears, prejudices, and images of large masses of people—is particularly formidable.[1] An abstract theorist could argue that any system of autonomous units follows the same basic rules, whatever the nature of the units. But in practice, i.e., in history, their substance matters as much as their form; the story of world affairs since the French Revolution is not simply one more sequence in the ballet of sovereign states; it is a story of fires and upheavals propagated by nationalism. A claim to sovereignty based on historical tradition and dynastic legitimacy alone has never had the fervor, the self-righteous assertiveness which a similar claim based on the idea and feelings of nationhood presents: in world politics, the dynamic function of nationalism is to constitute nation-states by amalgamation or by splintering, and its emotional function is to supply a good conscience to leaders who see their task as the achievement of nationhood, the defense of the nation, or the expansion of a national mission.[2]

This is where the drama lies. The nation-state is at the same time a form of social organization and—in practice if not in every theory—a factor of international nonintegration. But those who argue in favor of a world under more centralized power or integrated in networks of regional or functional agencies, tend to forget Comte's old maxim that *on ne détruit que ce qu'on remplace.* Any new "formula" would have to provide world order, of course, but also the kind of social organization in which leaders, elites, and citizens feel at home. There is currently no agreement on what such a formula is;[3] as a result, nation-states—often inchoate, economically absurd, administratively ramshackle, and impotent yet dangerous in international politics—remain the basic units despite the remonstrations and exhortations. They go on *faute de mieux* despite their alleged obsolescence. Indeed, they profit from man's incapacity to bring about a better world order, and their very existence stands as an obstacle to their replacement.

If there was one part of the world in which men of good will thought that nation-states could be superseded, it was Western Europe. Pierre Hassner, one of France's most subtle commentators on international politics, has reminded us of E. H. Carr's bold prediction of 1945: "We shall not see again a Europe of twenty, and a world of more than sixty independent states."[4]

Reprinted by permission of the author from *Decline or Renewal: France since the 1930s* (New York: Viking, 1974), 71-106.

Statesmen have invented original schemes for moving Western Europe "beyond the nation-state,"[5] and political scientists have studied their efforts with a care from which emotional involvement was not absent. The conditions seemed ideal. After World War II, nationalism seemed at a low ebb, and an adequate formula and method for building a substitute had apparently been devised. Thirty years after the end of the war—a period longer than the interwar era—observers have had to revise their judgments. The most optimistic put their hope in the chances which the future may still harbor, rather than in the propelling power of the present. Less optimistic ones, like myself, try simply to understand what went wrong.

My own conclusion is sad and simple. The nations in Western Europe have not been able to stop time and fragment space. The political unification of Europe might have succeeded if, on one hand, its nations had not been caught in the whirlpool of different concerns, arising from profoundly different internal circumstances and outside legacies, and if, on the other hand, they had been able or obliged to concentrate on "community-building" to the exclusion of other external and domestic problems. The involvement of policymakers in issues among which community-building is merely one has meant that the divergences among foreign policies have increased, not decreased.

Every international system owes its inner logic and its unfolding to a diversity of domestic determinants, geohistorical situations, and outside aims among its units. Every international system based on fragmentation tends to reproduce diversity through the dynamics of unevenness (so well understood by Lenin, albeit applied only in the economic realm by him). But there is no inherent reason why a fragmented international system need rule out certain developments in which critics of the nation-state have put their bets or their hopes. Why must the system be built of a diversity of *nations?* Could it not be a diversity of regions, of "federating" blocs superseding the nation-state, just as the dynastic state replaced the feudal puzzle? Or else, could not the logic of conflagration-fed-by-hostility lead to unification, the kind of catastrophic unification among exhausted yet interdependent nations which Kant sketched? Let us remember that the unity movement in Europe was an attempt to create a regional entity, and that its origins and dynamics resembled, on the reduced scale of a half-continent, the process Kant dreamed up in his *Idea of Universal History.*[6]

The answers are not entirely provided either by the legitimacy of national self-determination, the only principle which transcends all blocs and ideologies, since everyone pays lip service to it, or by the newness of many nation-states, which wrested their independence from another power in a nationalist upsurge and are unlikely to give up what they obtained so recently. But conversely, the legitimacy of the nation-state does not by itself guarantee the nation-state's survival in the international state of nature, and the appeal of nationalism as an emancipating passion does not assure that the nation-state must everywhere remain the basic form of social organization in a world where many nations are old and settled and where the shortcomings of the nation-state are obvious.

No, the real answers are provided by two unique features in the present international system. First of all, it is the first truly *global* international system. Regional subsystems have only a reduced autonomy; the "relationships of major tension" blanket the whole planet; interdependencies in the world economy affect all the non-Communist nations and begin to affect the Soviet group of nations. Domestic polities are dominated not so much by a region's problems as by purely local or purely global ones; these join to divert a region's members from the affairs of their area, and indeed make isolated treatment of those affairs impossible. As a result, each nation, new or old, is placed in an orbit of its own from which it is quite difficult to move away: the attraction of regional forces is offset by the pull of all the other forces. Or, to change the metaphor, the nations that coexist in the same apparently separate "home" of a geographical region cannot escape the smells and noises that come from outside through all the windows and doors, or the view of outlying houses from which the interference issues. With diverse pasts, moved by diverse tempers, living in different parts of the house, inescapably yet differently subjected and attracted to the outside world, the residents react unevenly to their exposure and calculate conflictingly how they could either reduce the disturbance or affect in turn the people in the other houses. Adjusting their own relations within the house is subordinated to their divergences about the outside world; the "regional subsystem" becomes a stake in the rivalry of its members about the system as a whole.

The common home could still prevail if the residents were forced to come to terms, either by one of them, or by the fear of a threatening neighbor. This is where the second unique feature of the present situation intervenes. What tends to perpetuate the nation-states decisively in the present system is the new set of conditions that govern and restrict the rule of force: Damocles' sword has become a boomerang, and the ideological legitimacy of the nation-state is protected by the tameness of the world jungle. Force in the nuclear age is still the "midwife of societies," insofar as revolutionary war begets new nations or new regimes in existing nations; but the use of force along traditional lines for conquest and expansion—a use that made "permeable" feudal units obsolete and replaced them with modern states built on "blood and iron"—has become too dangerous. The legitimacy of the feudal unit could be undermined by the rule of force—the big fish swallowing small fish by national might; or subtly and legitimately, so to speak, through dynastic weddings or acquisitions that consolidated larger units. But a system based on national self-determination rules out the latter, and a system in which force is a blunted weapon rules out the former. The new restrictions on violence even tend to pay to national borders the tribute of vice to virtue: violence that dons the cloak of revolution, or that persists in the form of interstate wars only when these accompany revolutions and conflicts in divided countries, perversely respects borders—it infiltrates them rather than crossing them overtly. Thus, all that is left for unification is what one might call "national self-abdication" or self-abnegation, the eventual willingness of nations to try something else. But global involvement hinders rather than helps here, and the atrophy of war removes the most pressing incentive. What a nation-state cannot provide alone—in economics or defense—it can still provide through means far less drastic than hara-kiri. For while it is true that economic interdependence in all its forms—trade, investments, travel, the management of monetary institutions—has weakened the autonomy of the nation-state, eroded its monetary, business, or tax policies, submitted its government to a host of transnational pressures,[7] it is not clear that a merger of nations would plug the sieve's holes rather than make the sieve bigger.

These two features bestow solidity to the principle of national self-determination, and resilience to the U.N. They also give shape to the "relationship of major tension": the conflict between the United States and the Soviet Union. As the superpowers find that what makes their power overwhelming also makes it less usable (or usable only to deter one another and to deny each other gains), lesser states discover that under the umbrella of the nuclear stalemate they are not condemned to death, and that they indeed have an impressive nuisance power. Thus, as the superpowers compete in a muted form all over the globe, the nation-state becomes the universal point of salience, to use the language of strategy—the lowest common denominator in the competition.

Other international systems merely conserved diversity; the present system profoundly conserves the diversity of nation-states despite all its revolutionary features. Rousseau's dream, concerned both with the prevalence of the general will (i.e., the nation-state) and with peace, was to create communities insulated from one another. In history, where "the essence and drama of nationalism is not to be alone in the world,"[8] the clash of noninsulated states has tended to create more nation-states and more wars. Today, Rousseau's ideals come closer to reality, but in a most un-Rousseauian way. The nation-states prevail in peace, they are not superseded because a fragile peace keeps the Kantian doctor away, they are not replaced because their very involvement in the world preserves their separateness. The "new Europe" dreamed of by the Europeans could not be established by force. Left to the wills and calculations of its members, the new formula did not jell because Europeans could not agree on their role in the world. The failure of an experiment made under apparently ideal conditions tells us a great deal, for it shows that a unification movement can fail not only when a surge of nationalism occurs in one important part but also when differences in how the national interest is assessed rule out agreement on the shape and purpose of the new, supranational whole.

The word nationalism is notoriously slippery. What I suggest is the following threefold distinction, which may be helpful in analyzing the interaction between the nation-state and the international system:

1. There is *national consciousness* (What the French call *sentiment national*)—a sense of "cohesion and distinctiveness,"[9] which sets one group off from other groups. My point is that this sense, which has important effects on international relations when it is shared by people who have not achieved statehood, is rather "neutral" once the nation and the state coincide. That is, the existence of national consciousness does not dictate foreign policy, does not indicate whether a people's "image" of foreigners is friendly or unfriendly, and does not indicate whether or not the nation's leaders will be willing to accept sacrifices of sovereignty. One cannot even posit that a strong national consciousness will be an obstacle to supranational unification, for it is perfectly conceivable that a nation might convince itself that its "cohesion and distinctiveness" will be best preserved in a larger entity.

2. For lack of a better phrase, I shall call it the *national situation.* Any nation-state—indeed, any state—is, to borrow Sartre's language, thrown into the world. Its situation is made up of internal features (these, in an individual, would be called heredity and character) and its position in the world. The state of national consciousness in the nation is only one element in the situation. It is a composite of objective data (social structure and political system, geography, formal commitments to other nations) and subjective factors (values, prejudices, opinions, reflexes, traditions toward and assessments of others, and others' attitudes and approaches). Some of its components are intractable, others flexible and changeable. Any statesman, whether a fervent patriot or not, must define the nation's foreign policy by taking this situation into account; even if he is convinced of the obsolescence of the nation-state (or of *his* nation-state), the steps he can and will take to overcome it will be affected by the fact that he speaks—to borrow de Gaulle's language this time—for the nation as it is in the world as it is. He cannot act as if his nation-state did not exist, or as if the world were other than it is. The national situation may facilitate unification moves, even when national consciousness is strong. It may be an obstacle, even when national consciousness is weak. The point is that even when the policy-maker tries to move "beyond the nation-state" he can do so only by taking the nation along, with its baggage of memories and problems—with its situation. I do not want to suggest that the situation is a "given" that dictates policy; but it sets up complicated limits that affect freedom of choice.[10]

3. I will reserve the term *"nationalism"* for a specific meaning: it is one of the numerous ways in which political leaders and elites may interpret the dictates, or suggestions, of the national situation. It is one of the ways of using the margin the national situation leaves. Whereas national consciousness is a feeling, and the national situation a condition, nationalism is a doctrine or an ideology—the doctrine or ideology that gives

absolute value and top priority to the nation in world affairs. The consequences of this may vary immensely. Nationalism may imply expansion (i.e., the attempt to establish the supremacy of one's nation over others) or merely defense; it may entail the notion of a universal mission or, on the contrary, insulation. It may be peaceful or pugnacious.[11] It is less a determinant than a criterion of choice, an attitude that shapes the choices made. But whatever its manifestations or content, it always follows the rule common to all manifestations of nationalism: it always pours the content into one mold, the preservation of the nation as the highest good. Nationalism thus affects, *at least* negatively, the way in which the freedom of choice left by the national situation will be used; indeed, it may collide with, and try to disregard or overcome, the limits which the situation sets.

The relation between these three factors is complicated. Nationalism (in the sense of the will to establish a nation-state) can be triggered by, and in turn activate, national consciousness in oppressed nationalities; but in colonial areas as well as in mature nation-states, nationalism can also be a substitute for a weak or fading national consciousness. In nation-states that are going concerns, national consciousness encourages nationalism only in certain kinds of national situations. A nationalist leader may assess the national situation in exactly the same way a nonnationalist one does, but the former may promote policies the latter would have rejected and oppose moves the latter would have undertaken. That bane of international relations theory, the national interest, could be defined as follows: N.I. = National situation × outlook of the foreign-policy-makers.

It is obvious that a similar national situation can result in differing foreign policies, depending in particular on whether or not there is a nationalist policy-maker. It is obvious also that the national interests in different nations cannot be defined in easily compatible terms if the respective outlooks are nationalist, even when the situations are not so different. But the same incompatibility may obtain, even if the outlooks are not nationalistic, when the situations are indeed very different.

II

Let us now look at the fate of the six nation-states in continental Western Europe, first by examining the basic features of their national situations, then by commenting upon the process of European unification, later by discussing its results, and finally by drawing some lessons.

Western Europe in the postwar years has been characterized by features that have affected all of its nations. But each of these features has affected each of the six nations in a different way.

The first feature—the most hopeful one from the viewpoint of the uni-fiers—was a temporary demise of nationalism. In the defeated countries—Germany and Italy—nationalism was associated with the regimes that had led the nations into war, defeat, and destruction. The collapse of two national ide-ologies that had been bellicose, aggressive, and imperialistic brought about an almost total discredit for nationalism in every guise. Among the nations of Western Europe on the Allied side, the most remarkable thing was that the terrible years of occupation and Resistance did not result in a resurgence of chauvinism. Amusingly enough, it was the French Communist Party that dis-played the most nationalistic tone; on the whole, the Resistance movements showed an acute awareness of the dangers of nationalist celebrations and national fragmentation in Western Europe. The Resistance itself had a kind of supranational dimension; none of the national Resistance movements could have survived without outside support, and the nations whose honor they saved were liberated rather than victorious. All this militated against any upsurge of the kind of cramped chauvinism that had followed the victory of World War I, just as in Germany the completeness of the disaster and the impossibility of blaming traitors crushed any potential revival of the smol-dering nationalism-of-resentment that had undermined the Weimar Republic. There was, in other words, above and beyond the differences in national sit-uations between indubitable losers and dubious winners, the general feeling of a common defeat and the hope of a common future: Resistance platforms often emphasized the need for a union, or federation, of Western Europe.

The demise of nationalism affected the various nations of the half-continent differently. There were significant differences in national consciousness, for one thing. In liberated France, nationalism was low, but patriotic sentiment was extremely high. The circumstances in which the hated Nazis were expelled and the domestic collaborators purged amounted to a rediscovery by the French of their own political community: the nation seemed to have redeemed its "cohe-sion and distinctiveness." On the contrary, in Germany especially, the destruc-tion of nationalism seemed to have been accompanied by a lowered national consciousness as well: what was distinctive was guilt and shame, and the all too cohesive nation-state was torn apart by partition, occupation zones, regional parochialisms blessed by the victors. Italy was in slightly better shape than Ger-many, in part because of its Resistance movements.

The defeated nations—Germany in particular—were in the position of patients on whom drastic surgery has been performed and who lie prostrate, dependent for their every movement on surgeons and nurses. Even if one had wanted to restore the nation to the pinnacle of values and objectives, one could not have done so except with the help and consent of one's guardians—and they were unlikely to support such a drive. In other words, the situation set strict limits on the possibility of any kind of nationalism, expansive or insulating. The lost territories were beyond recuperation; a healing period of *repli,* comparable to that which had marked the early foreign policy of the Third Republic, was not conceivable either.

On the other hand, France and, to a lesser extent, Belgium and Holland, were not so well protected. For, although the prevalence of the nation meant little in the immediate European context, it meant a great deal in the imperial one: if the circumstances of the Liberation kept national consciousness from veering into nationalism in one realm, the same circumstances tended to encourage such a turn with respect to the colonies. Cut down to size in Europe, these nations were bound to act as if they could call upon their overseas possessions to redress the balance; accustomed, through their association of nationalism with Nazi and Fascist imperialism, to equate chauvinism only with expansion, they would not be so easily discouraged from a nationalism of defense, aimed at preserving the "national mission" overseas. The Dutch lost most of their empire early, and found themselves in not so different a situation from the German and Italian amputees. The Belgians remained serene long enough not to have nationalistic fevers about the huge colony that seemed to give them no trouble until the day when it broke off—brutally, painfully, but irremediably. The French, however, suffered almost at once from dis-imperial dyspepsia, and the long, losing battle they fought gave continual rise to nationalist tantrums. The French inclination to nationalism was higher anyway, because there was one political force that was clearly nationalist. It had presided over the Liberation, given what unity it had to the Resistance, and achieved a highly original convergence of Jacobin universalism and "traditionalist," right-wing, defensive nationalism. This was the force of General de Gaulle. His resignation in 1946 meant, as Alfred Grosser suggests,[12] the defeat of a doctrine that put priority not only on foreign affairs but also on *Notre Dame la France.* The incident that led to his departure—a conflict over the military budget—was symbolic enough of the demise of nationalism. But his durability, first as a political leader, later as a "capital that belongs to all and to none," reflected a lasting French nostalgia for nationalism; and it was equally symbolic that the crisis which returned him to power was a crisis over Algeria.

The second feature common to all the West European national situations, yet affecting them differently, was the "political collapse of Europe." Europe did not merely lose power and wealth: such losses can be repaired, as the aftermath of World War I had shown. Europe, previously the heart of the international system, the locus of the world organization, the fount of international law, fell under what de Gaulle has called "the two hegemonies." The phrase is, obviously, inaccurate and insulting. One of those hegemonies took a highly imperial form, and thus discouraged and prevented the creation in Eastern Europe of any regional entity capable of overcoming the prewar national rivalries. But the American hegemony in Western Europe, different as it is, has been a basic fact of life, even though it was more "situational" than deliberate. Its effects were better than usual, insofar as the hegemony was restricted to areas where the European nations had become either impotent or incapable of recovery on their own. The dominated had considerable freedom of maneuver, and indeed the American presence prodded them into recovery, power recuperation, and regional unity; it favored both individual and collective emancipation. But the effects were in a way worse, because the laxity meant that each party could react to this feature of all the national situations—i.e., American hegemony—according to the distinctive *other* features of the national situation. American domination was only one part of the picture. Hence the following paradox: American prodding and the individual and collective impotence of West European nations ought logically to have pushed the latter toward unity-for-emancipation. But the autonomy that each West European nation retained gave it an array of choices: between accepting and rejecting dependence on the United States, between unity as a weapon for emancipation and unity as a way to make dependence more comfortable. It would have been a miracle if all the nations had made the same choice. To define one's position toward the United States was the common imperative, but each one has defined it in his own way.

At first, this diversity did not appear to be an obstacle to the unification movement. As Ernst Haas has shown,[13] the movement grew on ambiguity. Those who accepted American hegemony as a lasting fact of European life as well as those who did not could submerge their disagreement while building a regional entity: for the former, it was the most effective way to continue to receive American protection and contribute to America's mission and, for the latter, it was the most effective way to challenge American predominance. But there are limits to the credit of ambiguity. The split could not be concealed once the new Europe was asked to tackle matters of "high politics"— i.e., go beyond the purely internal economic problems of little impact or dependence on relations with America.[14] It is therefore no surprise that this split should have disrupted unification in 1953–54, when the problem of German rearmament was raised, and in 1962–68, when de Gaulle challenged the United States across the globe.[15]

This is how the diversity of national situations operated. First, it produced (and produces) a basic division between nations I would call resigned, and nations I would call resisters. The resigned ones included the smaller countries, aware of their weakness, realizing that the Soviet threat could not be met by Europeans alone, accustomed to dependence on external protectors, grateful to America for the unique features of its protection, and looking forward to an important role for Europe but not in the realm of high politics. In the past, Italy had tried to act as a great power without protectors, but those days were over, and acceptance of American hegemony gave the creaky Italian political system a kind of double cushion—against the threat of communism, and also against the need to spend too much energy and money on re-

armament. For the smaller states as well as for Italy, acceptance of U.S. hegemony was like an insurance policy which protected them against having to
give priority to foreign affairs. Germany, on the other hand, accepted dependence on the United States not merely as a comfort, but as a necessity as vital
as breathing. West Germany's geographical position put it on the front line,
its partition contributed to making security a supreme goal, the stanch anti-
communism of its leadership ruled out any search for security along the lines
of neutrality. There followed not only acceptance of American leadership but
also a wish to do everything possible to tie the United States to Western
Europe. Gaining equality with other nations was another vital goal for Germany, and it could be reached only through cooperation with the most powerful of the occupying forces. Defeat, division, and danger conspired to make
West Germany switch from its imperialistic nationalism of the Nazi era to a
dependence which was apparently submissive, yet also productive (of security and status gains) under Adenauer.

As for the resisters, they, like the West Germans, gave priority to foreign
affairs—but not in the same perspective. The French reading of geography
and history was different.[16] To be sure, the French saw the need for security
against the Soviet Union, but the "tyranny of the cold war" operated differently in France. French feelings of hostility toward Russia were much more
moderate than in Germany, and, although it may be too strong to speak of a
nostalgia for the wartime Grand Alliance, it is not false to say that hope of an
ultimate détente allowing for European reunification, a return of the Russians
to moderation, and an emancipation of the continent from its "two hegemonies" never died. The French time perspective has consistently differed
from, say, the German: the urgency of the Soviet threat never overshadowed
the desire for, and belief in, a less tense international system. Whereas West
Germany's continuity with its past was wrecked and repudiated, France (like
Britain) looked back to the days when Europe held the center of the stage and
forward to a time when Europe might again be an actor, not a stake: the anom-
aly was the present, not the past. Also, on colonial matters, France (more than
Britain) often found little to distinguish America's reprobation from Soviet
hostility. And France worried not only about possible Soviet thrusts but also
about Germany's potential threats: the fearful anticipation of a reborn German national consciousness and nationalism has marked all French leaders.
An additional reason for dreading the perpetuation of American hegemony
and the freezing of the cold war was the fear that such a course would make
Germany the main beneficiary of America's favors. Germany looked East with
some terror, but there was only one foe there; when the French looked East,
they saw two nations to fear; each could be used as an ally against the other—
but for the time being the Soviet danger was the greater, and if Germany was
built up too much against Russia, the security gained in one respect would be
compromised in another.[17]

The diversity of national situations also operated in another way. As I have suggested, situations limit and affect but do not command choices. A general desire for overcoming the cold war and American hegemony did not make for a general agreement on how to do so. What I have called the resisters were divided, and this division became decisive. If all the resisters had calculated that the best way to reach France's objectives was the construction of a powerful West European entity which could rival U.S. might, turn the bipolar contest into a triangle, and wrest advantages from both Russia and America, the "ambiguity" of the movement (between resigned *and* resisting forces) might not have damaged the enterprise until much later. But those who reasoned along the lines just described—like Jean Monnet—were sharply divided from those who feared that a sacrifice of national sovereignty to supranational institutions might entail loss of control over the direction of the European undertaking. Two kinds of people took this second line: the nationalists who were still eager to preserve all the resources of French diplomacy and strategy, in order, in the present, to concentrate on overseas fronts and, later, to promote whatever policies would be required, rather than let a foreign body decide; and, on the other hand, men like Mendès-France, who were not nationalists in the sense I use the term in this chapter, but who thought that the continental European construction was not France's best way of coping with her situation, who thought priority should be given to the search for a détente, the liberalization of the empire, the reform of the economy.[18]

The success of the European movement required, first, that those suspicious of European integration remain a minority—not only throughout the six nations but in their leadership, not only in the parliaments but above all in the executive branches. This requirement was met in 1950-53 and in 1955-58, but not in the crucial months for EDC in 1953-54, and no longer after 1958. The movement proceeded after 1958 in a dialectic of ambiguity. However, there was a second requirement for success: that the "minute of truth"—when the European elites would have to ask about the ultimate political direction of their community—be postponed as long as possible; i.e., that the cold war remain sufficiently intense to impose even on the "resisters" priority for the kind of security that presupposed U.S. protection—priority for the *urgent* over the *long-term important.* But this requirement was shaken during the brief period of nervous demobilization that followed Stalin's death in 1953-54, and then was gradually undermined by a third basic feature in Europe's postwar situation. Before we turn to it, one remark must be made: in French foreign policy, "resistance by European integration" prevailed over "resistance by self-reliance" only so long as France was bogged down in colonial wars; it was this important and purely French element in France's national situation whose ups and downs affected quite decisively the method of "resistance."[19]

The divisions and contradictions described above were sharpened by a third common feature which emerged in the mid-1950s and whose effects developed progressively: the nuclear stalemate between the United States and the Soviet Union. The effect of the "balance of terror" on the Western Alliance has been analyzed so often and well[20] that nothing needs to be added here; still, we might usefully inquire how Europe's gradual discovery of the uncertainties of America's nuclear protection affected the other factors we have discussed above.

The first thing we can say is that the nuclear balance of terror worsened the split between French "resistance" and West German "resignation." The dominant political elites in West Germany thought it merely added urgency to their previous calculation of interest. From the West German position, the nuclear stalemate was thought to increase the danger for the West: the United States was relatively weaker, the Soviet Union stronger and more of a threat. Indeed, the Social Democrats switched from their increasingly furtive thoughts of neutrality to outright endorsement of the Christian Democratic support of NATO. If America's nuclear monopoly was broken, if America's guarantee was weakened, West Germany needed a policy that was respectful enough of the United States' main concerns, so that the United States would feel obligated to keep its mantle of protection over West Germany and not be tempted into negotiating a détente at its expense. West German docility would be the condition for, and counterpart of, American entanglement in Europe. The West German reaction to a development that (if General Gallois' logic were followed) might lead to the prevalence of "polycentrism" over bipolarity was to search for ways of exorcising the former and preserving the latter. On the whole, the smaller nations and Italy, while not at all fearful about the consequences of polycentrism (quite the contrary), were nevertheless not shaken out of their "resignation." The mere appearance of parity of nuclear peril was not enough to make them eager or able to give priority to an activist foreign policy.

In France, the balance of terror reinforced the attitude of resistance. The goal of emancipation now became a real possibility. A superpower stalemate meant increased security for the lesser powers: however much they might complain about the decrease of American protection, there was a heightened feeling of protection against war in general. What the West Germans saw as a liability, the French considered an opportunity. West Germany's situation, and its low national consciousness, induced most German leaders to choose what might be called a "minimizing" interpretation of the new situation. France's situation—its high national consciousness and, after 1958, Gaullist doctrine—induced French political elites to choose a "maximizing" interpretation. They believed that the increasing costs of the use of nuclear force made actual use less likely, U.S. protection less certain but also less essential, Europe's recovery of not merely wealth but power more desirable and possible. This recovery of power would help bring about the much desired prevalence of polycentrism over bipolarity.[21]

As this feud shows, the balance of terror heightened the division over method among the "resisters." On one hand, it provided new arguments for those who thought that emancipation could be achieved only by uniting Western Europe; that individual national efforts would be too ridiculously weak to amount to anything but a waste in resources; but that a collective effort could exploit the new situation and make Western Europe a true partner of the United States. On the other hand, those who feared that the "united way" could become a frustrating deviation reasoned that the theory of graduated deterrence justified the acquisition of nuclear weapons by a middle-size power with limited resources and that this acquisition would considerably increase the political influence and prestige of the nation. The increased costs of force ruled out, in any case, what in the past had been the most disastrous effect of the mushrooming of sovereign states—a warlike, expansionist nationalism—but they simultaneously made the value of small- or middle-size nations good again. According to this argument, the "united way" would be a dead end, since some, and not exactly the least significant, of the associates had no desire for collective European power at the possible expense of American protection.

Until the nuclear stalemate became a fact of European life, opposition to a supranational West European entity had come only from a fraction of the "resisters." In the early 1950s the United States had strongly—too strongly—urged the establishment of a European defense system, for it had not been considered likely to challenge America's own military predominance. In the 1960s the United States no longer urged the West Europeans to build such a system. American leadership developed a deep concern for maintaining centralized control over NATO forces, i.e., for preserving bipolarity, and a growing realization that Europe's appetite would not stop short of nuclear weapons. As a result, some of the "resigned ones," instead of endorsing European integration unreservedly, for the first time now showed themselves of two minds: they were willing to pursue integration in economic and social fields, but less so in matters of defense, lest NATO be weakened. It is significant that the Dutch resisted de Gaulle's efforts in 1960–62 to include defense in a confederal scheme, and that West German leaders put some hopes in the MLF—a scheme that would have tied European nations one by one to the United States—rather than in a revised and revived EDC. Inevitably, such mental reservations of those who had been among the champions of supranationality could only confirm the suspicions of "resisters" who had distrusted the "Monnet method" from the beginning. Thus, the national situation of West Germany in particular—a situation in which the U.S. policy of reliance on West Germany as an anchor for U.S. influence on the continent played an important part—damaged the European movement: West German leaders were largely successful in their drive to entangle the United States but found that the price they had to pay was a decreasing ability to push for European integration. European integration and dependence on the United States were no longer automatically compatible.

This long discussion of the different responses to common situations has been necessary as an antidote to the usual way of discussing European integration, which has focused on process. The self-propelling power of the unifying process is severely constrained by the associates' views on ends and means. In order to go "beyond the nation-state," one must do more than set up procedures in adequate "background" and "process conditions." A procedure is not a purpose, a process is not a policy.

III

Still, since the process of European integration is its most original feature, we must examine it, too.[22] We have been witnessing a kind of race between the logic of integration set up by Monnet (analyzed by Haas) and the logic of diversity (analyzed above). According to the former, the double pressure of necessity (the interdependence of the European social fabric, which will oblige statesmen to integrate even sectors originally left uncoordinated) and of men (the action of the supranational agents) will gradually restrict the national governments' freedom of movement. In such a milieu, nationalism will become a futile and anachronistic exercise, and the national consciousness itself will, so to speak, be impregnated with an awareness of the higher interest in union. The logic of diversity, by contrast, sets limits on the degree to which the "spill-over" process can curtail the governments' freedom of action; it restricts to the area of welfare the domain in which the logic of functional integration can operate; indeed, insofar as discrepancies in other areas prevail, even issues belonging in the area of welfare may become infected by the disharmony, because of the links that exist among all areas. The logic of integration is that of a blender which crunches up the most diverse products, replacing their different tastes and perfumes with one, presumably delicious juice. One expects a finer synthesis: ambiguity helps because each "ingredient" can hope that its taste will predominate at the end. The logic of diversity is the opposite: it suggests that, in areas of key importance to the national interest, nations prefer the self-controlled uncertainty of national self-reliance, to the uncontrolled uncertainty of the blending process; ambiguity carries one only part of the way. The logic of integration assumes that it is possible to fool each one of the associates some of the time because his overall gain will still exceed his occasional losses, even if his calculations turn out wrong here or there. The logic of diversity implies that losses on one vital issue are not compensated for by gains on other issues (especially not on other less vital issues): nobody wants to be fooled. The logic of integration regards the uncertainties of the supranational function process as creative;

the logic of diversity sees them as destructive past a certain threshold. Ambiguity lures and lulls the national consciousness into integration as long as the benefits are high, the costs low, the expectations considerable. Ambiguity may arouse and stiffen national consciousness into nationalism if the benefits are low, the losses high, the hopes dashed or deferred. Functional integration's gamble could be won only if the method had sufficient potency to promise a permanent excess of gains over losses, and of hopes over frustrations. Theoretically, this may be true of economic integration. It is not true of political integration (in the sense of "high politics").

The success of the approach symbolized by Monnet depended, and depends still, on his winning a triple gamble: on goals, on methods, on results. As for goals, it is a gamble on the possibility of substituting motion as an end in itself, for agreement on ends. It is a fact that Europe's transnational integrationist elites did not agree on whether the object of the community-building enterprise ought to be a new superstate—i.e., a federal potential nation, à la U.S.A.—or whether the object was to demonstrate that power politics could be overcome in cooperation and compromise, that one could build a radically new kind of unit, change the nature and not merely the scale of the game. Monnet himself was ambiguous on this score; Walter Hallstein leaned in the first direction, many of Monnet's public relations men in the second.[23] Nor did the integrationists agree on whether the main goal was to create a regional "security-community,"[24] i.e., to pacify a former hotbed of wars, or to create an entity whose position and strength could decisively affect the cold war in particular and international relations in general. Now, it is perfectly possible for a movement to use its continental nationalists as well as its antipower idealists, its inward-looking and outward-looking politicians—but only as long as there is no need to make a choice. Decisions on tariffs do not require such choices. Decisions on agriculture begin to raise basic problems of orientation. Decisions on foreign policy and membership and defense cannot be reached unless the goals are clarified, nor can decisions on monetary union (past the first stage of narrowing fluctuations between currencies). One cannot be all things to all people all of the time.

As for methods, there was a gamble that supranational functionalism would irresistibly rise. Monnet assumed, first, that national sovereignty, already devalued by events, could be chewed up leaf by leaf like an artichoke. He assumed, second, that the dilemma of the West European governments—having to choose between an integration that tied their hands and stopping a movement that benefited their people—could be exploited in favor of integration by men representing the common good, endowed with superior expertise, initiative, deadlines, and package deals. Finally, he assumed that this approach would take into account the interests of the greater powers and prevent the crushing of the smaller ones. The troubles with this gamble have been numerous. Even an artichoke has a heart, and it remains intact after the leaves have been eaten. It is of course true that successful economic and social integration in Western Europe would considerably limit the freedom governments continued to enjoy (in theory) in diplomacy and strategy, but why should one assume that they would not be aware of it? As the artichoke is slowly eaten, the governments become ever more vigilant. To be sure, their dilemma suggests that they might not do anything about it: they would be powerless to save the heart. But this would be true only if governments never put what they consider essential interests of the nation above the particular interest of certain categories of nationals, if superior expertise were always either a supranational monopoly or the solution of an issue at hand, if package deals were effective in every argument, and, above all, if the governments' representatives were always determined to behave in an EEC way, rather than as agents of states that are unwilling to accept a supranational community whatever the conditions. Functional integration may indeed give lasting satisfaction to the smaller powers precisely because it is for them that the ratio of "welfare politics" to high politics is highest, and that the chance of gaining benefits through intergovernmental methods that reflect rather than correct the power differential between the big and the small is poorest. But this is also why the method is not likely à la longue to satisfy the bigger powers as much: facing them, the supranational civil servants, for all their skill and legal powers, are a bit like Jonahs trying to turn whales into jellyfish. Of course, the idea is ultimately to move from an administrative procedure, in which supranational civil servants enter a dialogue with national ministers, to a truly federal procedure in which a federal cabinet is responsible to a federal parliament; but what is thus presented as linear progress may turn out to be a vicious circle, since the ministers hold the key to the transformation, and may refuse it unless the goals are defined and the results already achieved are satisfactory.

There was a gamble about results as well. The experience of European integration would mean net benefits for all and bring about progress toward community formation. Progress could be measured by the following yardsticks: in the realm of interstate relations, an increasing transfer of power to new common agencies, and the prevalence of solutions "upgrading the common interest" over other kinds of compromises; in the realm of transnational society, an increasing flow of communications; in the area of national consciousness (which is important both for interstate relations, since it may limit the statesmen's discretion, and for transnational society, because it affects the scope and meaning of the communications), an increasing compatibility of views about external issues. The results achieved in Western Europe so far are mixed: dubious on the last count, positive (but not unlimited) on the second, and marked on the first by unexpected features. There was some strengthening of the authority of the EEC Commission until 1965, and in various areas there was some "upgrading of common interests." On the other hand, the Commission's unfortunate attempt to consolidate those gains at de Gaulle's expense in the spring of 1965 brought about a startling setback for the whole enterprise; in their negotiations, the members have conspicuously failed to find a common interest in some vital areas (energy, transport, industrial and investment policies), and sometimes reached apparently "integrating" decisions only after the most ungainly, traditional kind of bargaining, in which such uncommunity-like methods as threats, ultimatums, and retaliatory moves were used. In other words, either the ideal was not reached, or it was reached in a way that was its opposite and its destroyer. If we look at the institutions of the Common Market as an incipient political system for Europe, we find that their authority is limited, their structure weak, their popular base restricted and distant.[25]

It is therefore not surprising if the uncertainty about results already achieved contributes to uncertainty about future prospects. The divisions among partisans of integration make it hard to predict where the "Monnet method" will lead if the process were to continue along the lines so fondly planned by the French "*inspirateur.*" Will the enterprise become an effective federation, or will it become a mere façade behind which all the divergences and rivalries continue to be played out? It was nonetheless remarkable that Gaullist and American fears should converge in one respect: de Gaulle consistently warned that applying the supranational method to the area of high politics would dilute national responsibility in a way that would benefit only the United States; incapable of defining a coherent policy, the "technocrats" would leave vital decisions to the United States, at least by default. On the contrary, many Americans have come to believe on the basis of some of the EEC's actions in agriculture and trade that a united Europe would be able to challenge U.S. leadership much more effectively than the separate European states ever could. The truth of the matter is that nobody knows: a method is not a policy, a process is not a direction; the results achieved so far are too specialized and the way in which they have been reached is too bumpy to allow one to extrapolate and project safely. The face of a united Europe has not begun to emerge; there are just a few lines, but one does not know whether the supranational technique would finally give Western Europe the features of a going concern or those of a Fourth Republic writ large—the ambitions of a world power or the complacency of parochialism. The range of possibilities is so broad, the alternatives are so extreme, that the more the Six, and now the Nine, move into the stormy waters of high politics, the less they, and outside powers such as the United States that may be affected by their acts, are willing to extend the credit of hope and to make new wagers: neither Gaullist France nor America has been willing to risk a major loss of control. Contrary to the French proverb, in the process of functional integration, only the first steps do not cost much.

Two important general lessons can be drawn from a study of the process of integration. The first concerns the limits of the functional method: its relative success in the relatively painless area where it works relatively well lifts the participants of EEC to a new level of issues where the method does not work well any more—like swimmers whose skill at moving quickly away from the shore brings them to a point where the waters are stormy and deep, at a time when fatigue is setting in, and none of the questions about ultimate goal, direction, or endurance has been answered. The functional process was used in order to "make Europe"; once Europe began being made, the question had to be asked: "Making Europe, what for?" The process is like a grinder, a machine that works only when someone keeps giving it something to grind. When the members of EEC start quarreling and stop providing, the machine stops. For a while, the machine worked because the European governments poured into it a common determination to integrate their economies in order to maximize wealth. But with their wealth increasing, the question of what to do with it was bound to arise: a capability of supplying means does not *ipso facto* provide the ends, and it is about the ends that quarrels broke out. Each member state is willing to live with the others, but not on terms too different from his own; and the Nine are not in the position of the three miserable prisoners of *No Exit*. Transforming a dependent "subsystem" proved to be one thing; defining its relations to all other subsystems and to the international system in general has turned out to be quite another.

The model of functional integration—a substitute for the kind of instant federation that governments had not been prepared to accept—shows its origins in important respects. It is essentially an administrative model, which relies on bureaucratic expertise to promote a policy that political decisionmakers are technically incapable of shaping (something like French planning under the Fourth Republic). The hope was that in the interstices of political bickering the administrators could build up a consensus, but it was a mistake to believe that a formula that works well within certain limits is a panacea— and that even within the limits of "welfare politics" administrative skill can always overcome the disastrous effects of political paralysis or mismanagement. Moreover, the model assumes that the basic political decisions, to be prepared and pursued by EEC civil servants but formally made by the governments, would be reached through a process of short-term bargaining, by politicians whose mode of operation is empirical muddling through of the kind that puts immediate advantages above long-term pursuits. This model corresponds well to the reality of parliamentary politics with a weak executive branch—for example, the politics of the Fourth Republic—but it was a mistake to believe that all political regimes would conform to this rather sorry image, and to ignore the disastrous results that the original example produced whenever conflicts over values and fundamental choices made mere empirical groping useless or worse than useless.[26]

The second lesson we should draw from the origin of the integration model is even more discouraging for advocates of functionalism. To revert to the analogy of the grinder, what happened in 1965 was that the machine, piqued by the slowing down of supply, suddenly suggested to its users that in the future the supplying of material to be ground be left to the machine. Bureaucratic institutions tend to become actors with a stake in their own survival and expansion. The same thing happens often enough within a state whose political system is ineffective. But here we are dealing not with one but with several political systems, and the reason for the relative ineffectiveness of the EEC's Council of Ministers may be the excessive toughness, not weakness, of the national political systems involved. In other words, by trying to be a force, the bureaucracy here, inevitably, turns into a factor that the nations try to control or at least affect. A new complication is thus added to all the substantive issues that divide the participants. Thus, the agricultural problem could have been solved "technically," since the governments had previously reached basic compromises, and had more or less agreed on the relations between Common Market and outside agriculture. But the way these accords were reached left scars, and the nature of the agreement meant a victory for one state (France) over another (West Germany). The whole issue was reopened, due not to the states' but to the Commission's initiative. In the crisis of 1965, the Commission's overly bold proposal for a common agricultural policy (along pro-French lines) *cum* supranationality (against French determination) did allow some of the Six, hostile in fact to the substantive proposals, to endorse the Commission's plan and stand up as champions of supranationality, while knowing that the French would block the scheme; the French, eager to get their partners committed to a protected agricultural market, preferred to postpone the realization of this goal rather than let the Commission's autonomy grow, and used the Commission's rashness as a pretext for trying to kill supranationality altogether; and the West German government, not too kindly disposed toward the Commission whose initiatives and economic inspiration were hardly in line with Erhard's views, found itself defending it (its head, now under French attack, was a German). To be sure, the Commission's dilemma had become acute: either its members resigned themselves to being merely patient brokers to their quarreling clients, and letting them set the pace; or else they tried to behave according to the ideal type of the Monnet method *and* as if a genuine community had already been established. But if prudence meant sluggishness, anticipation meant delay. Since 1965, all the important issues—including Britain's entry—have been hammered out between governments. The Commission has been discreet. This has not ended the arguments about the need for "stronger" institutions. Haggling about the kind of machinery one wants is a polite method for appearing to want to keep working together, while disagreeing completely on what one wants the machinery for.

IV

We must come now to the balance sheet of the "European experiment." The most visible result is the survival of Europe's nations. To be sure, they survive transformed: swept by the "age of mass consumption," caught in an apparently inexorable process of industrialization, urbanization, and democratization, they become more alike in social structure, in economic and social policies, even in physical appearance; there is a spectacular break between the past, which so many monuments bring to constant memory, and a rationalized future that puts them closer to American industrial society than to the issues of their own history. These similarities are promoted by the Common Market itself. It is of no mean consequence that the prospect of a collapse of the EEC should bring anguish to various interest groups, some of which fought its establishment: the transnational linkages of businessmen and farmers are part of the transformation. And no West European nation is a world power any longer in the traditional sense—i.e., in the sense either of having physical establishments backed by military might in various parts of the globe, or of possessing in Europe armed forces superior to those of any non-European power.

And yet they survive as nations. In foreign affairs and defense, not only has power not been transferred to European organs but France has actually taken power away from NATO. Differences in the calculations of national interest broadened with the advent of the balance of terror, as I have already argued. Even when, after 1968, these calculations came closer, they converged on avoiding rather than promoting foreign and defense policies: Brandt's Bonn has wanted to avoid upsetting Washington or Moscow; Pompidou had decided to lift the European car out of the bog by no longer raising the issues that had, with de Gaulle at the wheel, stuck it there. Paradoxically, the post-Czechoslovakia rapprochement in the *Ostpolitiken* of Paris, London, and Bonn has not brought about much of a "spill-over" into European political cooperation. Policies toward the United States have remained different, and even the *Ostpolitiken* are not identical. A common inability to affect the superpowers' détente or their rivalry in the Middle East has not been translated into a common stand either on force reductions (or build-up) or on oil-sharing. As for intra-European communications, the indubitably solid economic network of the EEC has not been complemented by a network of social and cultural communications; the links between some European societies and the United States are stronger than the links among them. Even in the realm of economic relations, the Common Market for goods has not been complemented by a system of pan-West European enterprises: firms that are unable to compete with rivals in the EEC often associate with American firms rather than merge with their European rivals; or else the mergers are between national firms and help to build up national monopolies. Finally, European statesmen express views about external issues that often appear to reflect and support their divergent definitions of the national interest; or, while superficially favorable to "Europe," they fail to show any active enthusiasm or great passion.[27] There is no common European outlook. Nor is there a common *projet*, a common conception of Europe's role in world affairs or Europe's possible contribution to the solution of problems characteristic of all industrial societies.

To some extent, the obstacles lie in the present condition of national consciousness. In two respects, similarities have emerged in recent years. There has been a rebirth of German national consciousness, largely because the bold attempt at fastening Germany's shattered consciousness directly to a new European one did not succeed: the existence of a West German national situation gradually reawakened a German national awareness, and reduced the gap between West Germany and France in this area. Moreover, the national consciences in Western Europe are alike in one sense: they are not like Rousseau's general will, a combination of mores and moves that define the purposes of the national community with intellectual clarity and emotional involvement. Today's national consciousness in Europe is negative rather than positive. There is still, in each nation, a *"vouloir-vivre collectif."* But it is not a "daily plebiscite" *for* something. It is, in some parts, a daily routine, a community based on habit rather than on common tasks, an identity that is received rather than shaped. Thus West Germany's sense of "cohesion and distinctiveness" is the result of the survival and recovery of a West German state in a world of nations rather than a specific willed set of imperatives. In other parts, national consciousness is a daily refusal rather than a daily creation, a desire to preserve a certain heritage (however waning, and less because it is meaningful today than because it is one's own) rather than a determination to define a common destiny, an identity that is hollow rather than full, and marked more by bad humor toward foreign influences than by any positive contribution.

To be sure, negative or hollow national consciousness need not be a liability for the champions of integration: general wills à la Rousseau could function as obstacles to any fusion of sovereignty. But a patriotic consciousness that survives in a kind of nonpurposive complacency can be a drag on any policy: it does not carry statesmen forward in the way an intense and positive "general will" prods leaders who act on behalf of national goals, or in the way in which European federalists have sometimes hoped that enlightened national patriotisms would encourage Europe's leaders to build a new European community. The French may not have a sense of national purpose, but, precisely because their patriotism has been tested so often and so long, because pressures from the outside world have continued throughout the postwar era to batter their concerns and their conceits, and because modernization, now accepted and even desired, also undermines their cherished traditional values and their still enforced traditional authority patterns, French national consciousness resists any suggestion of abdication, resignation, *repli.* (So much so that the "Europeans" themselves have presented European integration as an opportunity for getting French views shared by others instead of stressing the "community" side of the enterprise.[28]) West Germany's national consciousness, on the other hand, is marked by a genuine distaste for or timidity toward what might be called the power activities of a national community on the world stage; hence the West Germans tend to shy away from the problems of "high politics" which a united Europe would have to face and avoidance of which only delays unity; a tendency, at first, to refuse to make policy choices and, later, to pretend (to oneself and to others) that no such choices are required, that there is no incompatibility between a "European Europe" and an Atlantic partnership and a reconciliation with the East. In one case, a defensive excess of self-confidence makes unity on terms other than one's own difficult; in the other case, an equally defensive lack of self-confidence projects into the foreign undertakings of the nation and weakens the foundations of the common European enterprise.

And yet, if the "national consciousness" of each European nation could be isolated from all other elements of the national situation, one would, I think, conclude that the main reasons for the endurance of the nation-state lie elsewhere.

They lie, first of all, in the differences in national situations, exacerbated by the interaction between each of the West European member states and the present international system. Earlier, we looked at specific instances of such differences; let us return to them in a more analytic way. One part of each national situation is the purely *domestic* component. In a modern nation-state, the importance of the political system—in the triple sense of functional scope, authority, and popular basis—is a formidable obstacle to integration. It is easier to overcome the parochialism of a political system with only a slender administrative structure, than it is to dismantle a political system which rests on "socially mobilized" and mobilizing parties and pressure groups, and which handles an enormous variety of social and economic services with a huge bureaucracy. To be sure, it was Monnet's hope and tactic to dismantle the fortress by redirecting the allegiance of parties and pressure groups toward the new central institutions of Europe, by endowing the latter with the ability to compete with the national governments in setting up social services. In other words, the authority of the new European political system would deepen as its scope broadened and its popular basis expanded. The success of this attempt to dry up the national ponds by diverting their waters into a new, supranational pool depended on three prerequisites which have not been met: with respect to popular basis, the prevalence of parties and pressure groups over executive branches; with respect to scope, the self-sustaining and expanding capacity of the new central bureaucracy; with respect to both scope and popular basis, the development of transnational political issues of interest to all political forces and peoples across boundary lines.

The executive establishment of the modern political state has one remarkable feature: it owes much of its legitimacy and power to the support of popularly based parties and pressure groups, but it also enjoys a degree of autonomy that allows it to resist pressures, manipulate opposition, manufacture support. Even the weak Fourth Republic evaded pressure toward "transnationalism" and diluted the dose of "bargaining politics" along supranational lines. Even the EEC civil servants' careers are made and unmade in national capitals. Above all, each nation's political life continues to be dominated by "parochial" issues: each political system is like a thermos bottle that keeps the liquid inside warm, or lukewarm. It is as if, for the mythical common man, the nation-state were still the most satisfying—indeed, the most rewarding— form of social organization in existence.[29] If we look at the states' behavior, we find that each reacted to the transnational forces that vitiated its autonomy by trying to tighten control on what was left. Multinational enterprises erase borders, but research, development, and technology, far from being "Europeanized," have been nationalized. The growing similarity and interdependence of West European industrial societies have not led to political integration. Indeed, insofar as all of them have become the scene of constant, often unruly group bargaining—what Raymond Aron has termed the politics of querulous satisfaction—their ability to divert attention to integration has been small. And, within the EEC's institutions, empirical muddling through— the political mode of operation of such societies—has been powerless to overcome paralysis whenever the members were divided (industrial and energy policy, social and regional policy, space, control of foreign investments) or to allow for the drastic revision of policies which incremental adjustments cannot save (agriculture).

The European political process has never come close to resembling that of any West European democracy because it has been starved of common and distinctive European issues. If we look at the issues that have dominated European politics, we find two distinct categories. One is that of problems peculiar to each nation—Italy's battle of Reds vs. Blacks, or its concern for the Mezzogiorno; Belgium's linguistic clashes; West Germany's "social economy" and liquidation of the past; France's postwar constitutional troubles and party splintering, later the nature and future of Gaullist presidentialism and the fallout from May 1968. Here, whatever the transnational party and interest-group alignments in the EEC, the dominant motifs have been purely national. The other category of issues are international ones (including European unity). But here, the *external* components of each national situation have thwarted the emergence of a common European political system comparable to that of each nation. Here, the weight of geography and history—a history of nations—has kept the nation-states in their watertight compartments.

It is no accident if France, the initiator of the European-unity process, has also been its chief troublemaker; for by reason of history and geography France's position differed from everyone else's in the Community (and was actually closer to Britain's). For West Germany, integration meant a leap from opprobrium and impotence to respectability and equal rights; for the smaller powers, it meant exchanging a very modest dose of autonomy for participation in a potentially strong and rich grouping. France could not help being much more ambivalent, for integration meant on one hand an avenue for leadership and the shaping of a powerful bloc, but, on the other, the acceptance of permanent restrictions on French autonomy. A once-great power inherits from its past a whole set of habits and reflexes that make it conduct policy as if it were still or could become again a great power (unless those habits and reflexes have been smashed, as Germany's were). In other words, integration meant an almost certain improvement in the national situation of the other five nations; but for France it could be a deterioration or an adventure.[30] There is no better example here than the issue of nuclear weapons. Integration in nuclear matters meant, for France, giving up the possibility of having a nuclear force of her own, perhaps never being certain that a united Europe would create a common nuclear deterrent, at best contributing to a European nuclear force that would put West Germany in the same position as France. But the French decision to pursue the logic of diversity, while giving her her own nuclear force, also made a European nuclear solution more difficult and increased France's distance from West Germany. Moreover, a geographical difference corroborated the historical one: France had lasting colonial involvements. Not only did they intensify national consciousness; they also contributed to France's ambivalence toward European integration. The worse France's overseas plight became, the more European integration was preached as a kind of compensatory mechanism. But this meant that European integration had to be given a "national" rather than a "supranational" color; it meant that the French tried to tie their European partners to France's overseas concerns, much against these partners' better judgment; above all, it meant that there was a competition for public attention and for official energies between the European and overseas components of French foreign affairs. The great-power reflex and the colonial legacy combined in a policy of cooperation with France's former imperial possessions despite the cost; overseas cooperation is presented as a policy that has transfigured the colonial legacy and that manifests the great-power reflex.[31]

Thus, national situations multiplied the effects of differences among the various national consciences. But the endurance of the nation-state in France is due also to a revival of nationalism. Even without de Gaulle, the differences analyzed above would have slowed down European integration; but his personal contribution to the crisis of integration was enormous. Not only did he raise questions that were inescapable in the long run but he tried to impose his own answers. De Gaulle changed French policy from ambivalence toward supranational integration to outright hostility; from a reluctance to force the European states to dispel the ambiguities of "united Europe" to an almost gleeful determination to bring out differences into the open. De Gaulle also changed the national situations of the others, which sharpened antagonisms and led to a kind of cumulative retreat from integration.

It is true that the General was an empiricist, and that his analysis of the European situation was to a large extent irrefutable. What could be more sensible than starting from what exists (the nation-states), refusing to act as if what does not yet exist (a united Europe) were already established? But pragmatism is always at the service of ends, explicit or not. (The definition of a bad foreign policy could be: a foreign policy that uses rigid means at the service of explicit ends, or whose flexible means do not serve clearly-thought-out ends.) De Gaulle's empiricism was a superb display of skill, but on behalf of a thoroughly nonempirical doctrine. It is obvious that his distrust of supranational integration, perfectly comprehensible as a starting point, nevertheless resulted in a kind of freezing of integration and perpetuation of the nation-state. If his chief foreign-policy objective had been the creation of a European entity acting as a world power, his "empirical" *starting point* would have been a most unrealistic *method*. But it was not his supreme objective, and Europe not his supreme value.

De Gaulle's doctrine was a "universalist nationalism." That is, he saw France's mission as world-wide, not local and defensive; but this meant that Europe was just one corner of the tapestry, a means, not an end. "Things being what they are," it is better to have separate nation-states than it is to have a larger entity; while the latter could undoubtedly act better as a forceful competitor in the world's contests, it would have to be coherent to do so, and it was more likely to be incoherent, given the divisions of its members and the leverage interested outsiders possess over some of the insiders. The size of the unit was less important than its "cohesion and distinctiveness," for effectiveness is not merely a function of material resources: if the unit has no capacity to turn resources to action, the only beneficiaries are its rivals. In a contest with giants, a confident David is better than a disturbed Goliath. This is a choice that reflects a doctrine; de Gaulle's refusal to gamble on European unity went along with a willingness to gamble on the continuing potency of the French nation-state. Joseph Schumpeter defined imperialism as an object-less quest; de Gaulle's nationalism was a kind of permanent quest with varying content but never any other cause than itself.

Every great leader has his built-in flaw, since this is a world where roses have thorns. De Gaulle's was the self-fulfilling prophecy. Distrustful of any Europe but his own, his acts made Europe anything but his. Here we must turn to the effect of his policy on France's partners. First of all, there was a matter of style. Wanting European cooperation, not integration, de Gaulle refused to treat the Community organs as Community organs; but, wanting to force his views about cooperation on nations still attached to the goal of integration, he paradoxically had to try to achieve cooperation for a common policy in a way that smacked of conflict, not cooperation, of unilateralism, not compromise. Thus we witnessed not just a retreat from the Monnet method to, say, the kind of intergovernmental cooperation that marks the Organization for Economic Cooperation and Development (OECD), but to a kind of grand strategy of nonmilitary conflict, a kind of political cold war of maneuver and "chicken." With compromises wrested by ultimatums, concessions obtained not through package deals but under the threat of boycotts, it is not surprising if even the Commission ended by playing the General's game instead of turning whatever cheek was left. Its spring 1965 agricultural plan was as outright a challenge to de Gaulle as his veto of January 1963 had been an affront to the Community spirit. Just as de Gaulle had tried to force West Germany to sacrifice her farmers to the idea of a European entity, the Commission tried to call his bluff by forcing him to choose between French farmers' interests and the French national interest in a "European Europe" for agriculture, on one hand, and his own hostility to supranationality and the French national interest in the free use of French resources, on the other. Playing his game, the Commission also played into his hands, allowing him to apply the Schelling tactic of "if you do not do what I ask, I will blow my brains out on your new suit," and in the end buying his return at the price of a sacrifice of integration.[32] In other words, he forced each member state to treat the EEC no longer as an end in itself; and he drove even its constituted bodies to bringing grist to his mill.

But de Gaulle's effect on his partners was a matter of policy as well. Here we must examine Franco-German relations. Had West Germany been willing to follow France, he would have given priority to the construction of a "half-Europe" that would thereafter have been a magnet (as well as a guarantee of German harmlessness) to the East. West Germany's refusal led him to put a "Europe from the Atlantic to the Urals" on the same plane as a "European Europe" in the West; for the containment of West Germany, no longer assured in a disunited Western Europe of the Six, could still be gotten in a larger framework. The implications were important. First, there was a considerable change in West Germany's national situation. Whereas for more than fifteen years the United States and France tacitly carried out Robert Schuman's recommendation—"never leave Germany to herself"—the Franco-American competition for German support, the Gaullist refusal to tie West Germany to France in a federal Europe (so to speak, for the knot's sake), and America's disastrous emulation of the sorcerer's apprentice in titillating German interest in nuclear strategy or weapons-sharing, had all been factors that loosened the bonds between Germany and the West. Consequently, the domestic component of West Germany's national situation was also affected.

Still concerned with security as well as with German reunification, but less and less able to believe that loyalty to their allies would deliver all the goods, the West German leaders and elites felt less dependent and constrained. Of course, objectively, the external constraints remain compelling. But de Gaulle's effect on Germany was, if not a rebirth of German nationalism, at least a change in the situation that gives national German action some chances. The temptation to use economic power to reach one's goals and the example of one's allies competing for accommodation with one's foe could not be resisted forever, especially when the past was full of precedents. To be sure, a nationalist Germany may well find itself as unable to shake the walls or to escape through the bars as Gaullist France was unable to forge the "European Europe." But the paradox of a revisionist France, trying to change the international system to her advantage despite her complete lack of "traditional" grievances (lost territories, military discrimination, and so forth), and a Germany with many grievances behaving in fact like a *status quo* power, could not last forever. The result, after 1969, was a West German *Ostpolitik* that followed France's example and solemnly acknowledged the inviolability of the *status quo,* yet in so doing asserted Bonn's right to an independent foreign policy. Of course, a less aggressively ambitious France might not have prevented West Germany from trying to follow its own path one day: the possibility of someone else's imitative *hubris* is no reason for *effacement;* but because the "essence and drama" of nationalism lie in the meeting with others, the risk of contagion—a risk that was part of de Gaulle's larger gamble—could not be disregarded.

Thus the nation-state survives, preserved by the resilience of national political systems, by the interaction between separate nations and a single international system, and by leaders who believe in the primacy of "high politics" over managerial politics and in the primacy of the nation.

V

This long balance sheet leaves us with many questions. What are the prospects in Western Europe? What generalizations can we draw from the whole experience? Is there no chance for the European Community? Is it condemned to be, at best, a success in economics and a fiasco in "high politics?"[33]

While nothing (not even the Common Market) is irreversible, no important event leaves the world unmarked, and after the event one can never pick up the pieces as if nothing had happened. This is true of the Common Market, and it is true also of General de Gaulle. It is not easy to sweep under the rug the curls of dust he willfully placed in the sunlight; it is not easy to ignore the questions he asked, even if his answers were rejected, since they are the questions any European enterprise would face sooner or later. Even the passing of his kind of nationalism has not transformed the national situations of the European states so deeply that all the cleavages discussed here have suddenly disappeared. To be sure, the failure of Britain's policy of maintaining close ties with the United States led to an "agonizing reappraisal" in London that in turn led to Britain's third, and successful, application to the EEC. In this respect, as well as in the rest of the Common Market, de Gaulle's disappearance eased the strains. France stopped trying to promote cooperation through cold war and lifted the veto on Britain. Yet Pompidou has combined a more conciliatory style with the Gaullist habit of raising questions about ends, at least in the economic part of the enterprise to which he has decided to devote his efforts. Even in this more moderate realm, the results have been mixed and do not disprove the previous analysis.

The diversity of national situations has been manifest again. The only part of Pompidou's grand design that his EEC partners have endorsed, a monetary union, has been badly battered. The common float of West European currencies, decided in March 1973, is limited (excluding the pound sterling and the lira) and fragile. West Germany's preference for economically liberal solutions, and the priority she gives to the fight against inflation, have made her suspicious of too strictly monetary a scheme, for she fears that would allow other nations to pursue both more statist and more lax economic policies while counting on help from the strong German mark to save them from trouble. But France's priorities—on full employment and peace and quiet on the labor front, even at the price of inflation, on modernizing without provoking widespread discontent, and on preserving the common agricultural policy (essential to protect her peasants from currency fluctuations)—and the French civil service's fondness for controls have led her to put monetary union ahead of economic harmonization. Moreover, the French have another target beyond EEC—the position of the dollar as a world currency—and they want to use monetary union as a lever to limit the influx of short-term capital from outside Europe. The West Germans (and, in all likelihood, the British) are opposed to controls on capital, out of a deeper attachment to and need for free trade, and out of a continuing desire not to antagonize the United States. But the economic union many Germans would prefer is considered by the French as something in which European distinctiveness would be diluted to America's advantage, and as a potential Deutschmark zone.[34] In order to prevent a new slowdown following the Community's enlargement, Pompidou tried to go beyond the economic realm by proposing a political secretariat, à la Fouchet, and to give his European policy the momentum of popular support, through a referendum. But the former proposal only underlined the old battle about institutions—which conceals, as before, a contest between French designs for Europe (hence her refusal to have that secretariat located in Brussels, along with NATO) and the others' desire to postpone the question of ends by escaping into supranationality. And the fiasco of the

French referendum (which confirmed the relative indifference of French public opinion and proved that Pompidou's temporary return to the politics of ambiguity had not paid off[35]) forced him to dig in his heels in more orthodox Gaullist fashion. The road is rocky, and the car sputters, even after the smooth but modest European summit conference of October 1972. America's demands for EEC "concessions" on agriculture and external trade policy, and America's overt linkage of economics and security have once again divided the EEC between those who, for domestic or foreign-policy reasons, are eager to accommodate Washington, and France's desire to build a "European Europe"—at least in the economic realm, where Western Europe's collective power is greatest, and whose importance in world politics has grown apace with détente and the nuclear stalemate.

These setbacks do not mean that the European enterprise is doomed. One can conceive of a set of circumstances in which a speedy forward march could succeed: Western Europe could become West Germany's least frustrating framework at a moment when MBFR or U.S. unilateral cuts might oblige Bonn's leaders to envisage a spill-over of EEC into defense and diplomacy, Western Europe could be seen as Britain's best avenue of leadership in such circumstances, Western Europe could serve as the best compensation for a French political system that would again be beset by domestic troubles and in which "Europe" would be once more an alibi. Western Europe could become a full-fledged economic, military, and diplomatic entity through a major external shock inflicted by either superpower or by both, or through a deliberate, gradual transformation planned in concert with Washington and acceptable to Moscow. But such progress depends on the timely convergence of too many variables to be counted on—and now, in the external component of each West European state's national situation, not only American but Soviet moves and positions have a decisive (if divisive) effect. Within the Community's institutions, daily reality brings a permanent confrontation of national interests that may erode the nation-state's edges but perpetuates their will to exist.[36]

The European experience is of general significance. It tells us about the conditions which the national situations of the units engaged in an attempt to integrate must meet, lest the attempt be unsuccessful. Those situations ought to be similar, of course; but what matters is the nature of the similarity. Insofar as domestic circumstances are concerned, two conditions are essential. The units must be political communities, not in a substantive sense (common values, à la Rousseau) but in a formal one (many links of communications, and common habits and rules, across regional differences and across the borders of ethnic groups, tribes, or classes).[37] In other words, transnational integration presupposes integration within each unit.[38] These units need not be nation-states, in the sense of communities endowed with external sovereignty under international law; but if a newly independent state is a mere shell with no true community yet, the divisions within the population will badly hinder any trans-state integration: domestic integration is a prerequisite for it and will be a primary goal of any leader who tries to be more than the representative of a sect, class, tribe, or ethnic group. This explains why Latin American integration remains a chimera, and also why it has been so difficult in Africa and Asia to move beyond the nation-state. In many cases, the state is there, but not yet the nation.

Students of supranational integration have rightly stressed the importance of pluralistic social structures and elite groups in the units that try to integrate. But success here also requires that in each unit there be executive leaders who represent those sections of the elites which advocate union and whose power depends on the support of the integrationist elites and groups. Since many of the new states are single-party states with so-called charismatic (or should one say authoritarian?) leaders, this internal condition for unification is often missing.

As far as external conditions are concerned, what matters is not that the units be in "objectively" similar situations but that there be "subjective" similarity—a conviction on the part of the policy-makers that the similarity exists. The implication—and this is crucial—is that one must examine more than the relation of each unit to the international system at the moment. The similarity that matters is a similarity in the way different statesmen interpret historical and geographical experience and outline the future in the light of this experience. Integration means a common choice of a common future, but that requires certain attitudes about the past and the present.

As for the past, supranational integration is likely to be more successful when the voyager's baggage is light. If the state's past international experiences have been long or complex, if the state has enjoyed an autonomous existence on the world scene for a long time, integration will not be easy. Is it an accident that the only successful example of voluntary unification in the modern world is that of the United States (a fusion of units that had been colonies, not states, where neither the machinery of the state nor foreign-policy traditions had had time to develop)? In one sense, ridding a nation of overseas commitments (such as France and Britain have done) should make their luggage lighter. But, as we have seen in the case of France, old burdens tend to be replaced by new ties, the old *imperium* leaves lasting concerns, and the old responsibilities leave a continuing sense of responsibility.

The kind of similarity required in the present concerns the relation of the units to the international system. When a similarity in national situations is one of distance or insulation from the system, as was the case of the American states and to a large extent the case of Switzerland after the Reformation, concentration on the difficult job of unification becomes possible. A capital obstacle to integration anywhere in the world today is the loss of such distance, the impossibility of such insulation in the echo chamber of the present international system. But this obstacle can sometimes be removed.

For there is a second question: the degree of compulsion in the international system. When the national situations are similar because of an overwhelming external threat (as was originally the case with the Swiss cantons and the American ex-colonies), unification for survival or security may be imperative. A compelling threat can make up for different pasts and impose a common destination. One can argue that this was Western Europe's condition in the first ten years after the end of World War II, but a countervailing force could be seen in the different pulls of different pasts, with different kinds of involvements in the international system. The nations of Western Europe assessed differently the degree to which the threat from the East superseded other aspects of international politics. It was not an accident that the nation which considered the menace entirely compelling was Germany, divided and literally confronted with the threat, to the exclusion of almost everything else. It was not an accident that France and Britain never let the threat from the East dominate their entire foreign policy. In any case, Western Europe today is no longer dominated by the Soviet threat. Today's international system inflates each national situation, while it removes some of sovereignty's sting. In a way, the relative impotence of force, the postponement of the minute of truth, should reduce the significance of all differences in national situations. But since this is still a competitive system of fragmented states, Rousseau's iron logic applies: each state tries to exploit whatever margin of difference it has; and, since it ultimately matters much less than before, the incentive to unification in order to "pull more weight" is slim. The breakdown of the Soviet and American camps and the kind of weightlessness that nations have in the new international system because of the restrictions on force encourage different visions of the future, or a tendency to take the hazards and chances of a diverse present as they come, rather than planning too much for an inscrutable future. A rational observer, outside the contest, can argue that—precisely because the stakes in the international contest are more symbolic than real—nation-states ought to be willing to unite, for the outcome would be a new actor whose power could really be great enough to make a difference. But the logic of competition operates the other way. It conforms to the French proverb: one thing possessed is worth more than two things promised. In the immediate postwar system, it seemed that European nations were obliged to choose between insecurity apart or an Atlantic shelter together. The "halfway house" of Western Europe got started but did not progress far before the advent of an era in which separateness became attractive again.

The dialectic of fragmentation and unity gives the drama of Europe much of its pathos. In a "finished world," dominated by two giant powers, in a crowded world that resists the sweep of any one power's universal mission, there is something absurd and pathetic in the tenacious persistence of separate European national wills. Yet precisely because so many of the differences among them are expressed in the realm of foreign affairs, integration becomes difficult.

It has become possible for scholars to argue that integration is proceeding *and* that the nation-state is more than ever the basic unit without being contradictory, for recent definitions of integration "beyond the nation-state" point not toward a new kind of political community, but merely toward an "obscur[ing of] the boundaries between the system of international organizations and the environment provided by member states."[39]

There are important implications here. One is, not so paradoxically, that the nation-state is vindicated as the basic unit. So far, anything that is "beyond" is "less": cooperative arrangements with a varying degree of autonomy, power, and legitimacy exist, but there has been no transfer of allegiance to their institutions, and their authority is limited, conditional, dependent, and reversible. There is more than a kernel of truth in the federalist critique of functional integration. So far, the "transferring [of] exclusive expectations of benefits from the nation-state to some larger entity"[40] leaves the nation-state as the main focus of expectations, and as the initiator, pace-setter, supervisor, and often destroyer of the larger entity. In the international arena the state is still the highest possessor of power, and while not every state is a political community, there is as yet no political community more inclusive than the state. To be sure, the military function of the nation-state is in crisis, but since the whole world is "permeable" to nuclear weapons, any new type of unit would face the same horror, and since the prospect of that horror makes conquest less likely, the decline of the state's capacity to defend its citizens is not total, nor even so great as to force the nation-state itself into decline.

The endurance of the nation-state is demonstrated not only by the frustrations of functionalism but also by both the promise and the failure of federalism. On one hand, federalism offers a way of going "beyond the nation-state," but it consists in building a new and larger nation-state. The scale is new, not the story, the gauge, not the game. The federalist model applies the Rousseauistic scheme for the creation of a nation to the "making of Europe"; it aims at establishing a unit marked by central power and based on the general will of a European people. The federalists are right in insisting that Western Europe's best chance of being an effective entity would be not to go "beyond the nation-state," but to become a larger nation-state in the process of formation and in the business of world politics: i.e., to become a sovereign political community in at least the formal sense. The success of federalism would be a tribute to the durability of the nation-state; its failure so far is due to the irrelevance of the model. Not only is there no general will of a European people because there is as of now no European people, but the institutions that could gradually (and theoretically) shape the separate nations into one people are not the ones that are most likely to do so. The internal problems of Europe involve matters that can be resolved by technical decisions by civil servants and ministers, rather than general wills and assemblies. (A general will to prosperity is not very operational.) The external problems of Europe are matters for executives and diplomats. And when the common organs set up by the national governments try to act as a European executive and parliament, they have to do so in a fog maintained around them by the governments, and are slapped down if they try to dispel the fog and reach the people themselves. In other words, Europe cannot be what some nations have been, a people that creates its state. Nor can it be what some of the oldest states are and many of the new ones aspire to be: a people created by the state. It has to wait until the separate states decide that their peoples are close enough to justify setting up a European state that will weld the many into the one; and we have just examined why such a joint decision has been missing. The factors that make the federalist model irrelevant to diverse and divided nations also make all forms of union short of federalism precarious. Functionalism is too unstable for complete political unification. It may integrate economies, but then either the nations will proceed to a full political merger (which economic integration does not guarantee), in which case the federal model will be vindicated, or else the national situations will continue to diverge, and functionalism will be merely a way of tying together the pre-existing nations in areas deemed of common interest. Between the cooperation of existing nations and the breaking in of a new one there is no stable middle ground. A federation that succeeds becomes a nation; one that fails leads to secession; halfway attempts like supranational functionalism must either snowball or roll back.

But the nation-state survives transformed. Among the men who see "national sovereignty" as the nemesis of mankind, those who put their hopes in regional superstates are illogical, those who put their hopes in a world state are utopian, those who put their hopes in functional political communities more inclusive than the nation-state are too optimistic. What has to be understood and studied now is, rather than the creation of rival communities, the transformation of "national sovereignty." The model of the nation-state derives from the international law and relations of the past, when there were only a few players on the stage and violence was less risky; it applies only fitfully to the situation today. The basic unit has become more heterogeneous as it has proliferated; the stage is occupied by players whose very numbers force each one to strut, but its combustibility nevertheless keeps them from pushing their luck. The nation-state today may be a new wine in old bottles, or in bottles that are sometimes only a mediocre imitation of the old; it is not the same old wine.[41] What must be examined is not just the legal capacity of the sovereign state but the *de facto* capacity at its disposal. Granted the scope of its authority, how much of it can be used and with what results? There are many ways of going "beyond the nation-state," and some modify the substance without altering the form or creating new forms. To be sure, as long as the old form is there, as long as the nation-state is the supreme authority, there is a danger for peace and for welfare. Gullivers tied by Lilliputians rather than crushed by Titans can wake up and break their ties. Men who slug it out with fists and knives, prisoners in a chain gang, are all men, yet their freedom of action is not the same. An examination of the international implications of "nation-statehood" today and yesterday is at least as important as the ritual attack on the nation-state.

Prospects of genuine European unification would improve if the international system created conditions and incentives for moving "beyond the nation-state." In a world where many more units succeeded in becoming genuine nations with pluralistic structures, and where, on the other hand, multipolarity led to greater autonomy for the subsystems and to new interstate wars, the conditions of unification would be met at least in some parts of the world: a less universal and intense involvement in global affairs, a more compelling threat of violence, greater internal harmony might allow the nation-state to supersede itself. But even so, the result might simply be an agglomeration of smaller nation-states into fewer, bigger ones. There are more things in the heaven and earth of the future than in any philosophy of international relations.

NOTES

1. See Pierre Renouvin and Jean-Baptiste Duroselle, *Introduction to the History of International Relations* (New York, 1966).

2. In a way, the weaker the foundations on which the nation rests, the shriller the assertions become.

3. On this point, see Rupert Emerson, *From Empire to Nation* (Cambridge, Mass., 1962), Chapter 9; and Raymond Aron, *Peace and War Among Nations* (New York, 1964), Chapter 11.

4. E. H. Carr, *Nationalism and After* (London, 1965), p. 51, quoted in Pierre Hassner, "Nationalisme et relations internationales," *Revue française de science politique*, XV, No. 3 (June 1965), 499–528.

5. See Ernst B. Haas, *Beyond the Nation-State* (Stanford, Cal., 1964).

6. On this point, see my essay "Rousseau on War and Peace," in *The State of War* (New York, 1965).

7. See for instance Richard Cooper, "Economic Interdependence and Foreign Policy in the 70's," *World Politics,* January 1972; and Robert O. Keohane and Joseph S. Nye, Jr., eds., *Transnational Relations and World Politics* (Cambridge, Mass., 1972).

8. Hassner, *op. cit.,* p. 523.

9. Karl W. Deutsch, *Nationalism and Social Communication* (Cambridge, Mass., 1953), p. 147.

10. A more systematic and exhaustive analysis would have to discriminate rigorously among the various components of the national situation. If the purpose of the analysis is to help one understand the relations between the nation-state and the in-

ternational system, it would be especially necessary to assess: 1) the degree to which each of these components is an unchangeable given (or a given unchangeable over a long period of time) or, on the contrary, an element that can be transformed by will and action; 2) the hierarchy of importance and the order of urgency that political elites and decision-makers establish among the components.

11. See Raoul Girardet, "Autour de l'idéologie nationaliste," *Revue française de science politique*, XV, No. 3 (June, 1965), 423–45; and Hassner, *op. cit.*, pp. 516–19.

12. Alfred Grosser, *French Foreign Policy under de Gaulle* (Boston, 1965).

13. Haas, *The Uniting of Europe* (Stanford, Cal., 1958).

14. See my discussion in "The European Process of Atlantic Cross-Purposes," *Journal of Common Market Studies*, February 1965, pp. 85–101. The success of internal economic integration raised these external issues far earlier than many expected.

15. The latter case is self-evident; the first, less so, since the crisis over EDC was primarily an "intra-European" split between the French and the Germans. But there was more to it than this. EDC was accepted mostly by nations who thought that Europe could not and should not refuse to do what the United States had demanded—i.e., rearm in order to share the defense of the half-continent with the United States and incite the United States to remain its primary defender; EDC was rejected by nations who feared that it would freeze existing power relationships.

16. Although there was a minority of "resigned ones" in France, like Paul Reynaud.

17. An impressive continuity marks French efforts to preserve the difference between France's position and West Germany's: from the *préalables* and protocols to EDC, to Mendès-France's Brussels proposals, to de Gaulle's opposition to any nuclear role for Germany.

18. France's "integrationist resisters," like Monnet himself, often choose not to stress the "resistance" aspect of their long-term vision, but nevertheless aimed ultimately at establishing in Western Europe not a junior partner of the United States but a "second force" in the West. Mendès-France's political vision never put the nation at the top of the hierarchy of values, but in 1954 (especially in his ill-fated demands for a revision of EDC at the Brussels meeting in August) and in 1957 (when he voted against the Common Market), his actual policies did put priority on national reform over external entanglements.

19. It is no coincidence that EDC was rejected six weeks after the end of the war in Indochina, that the Common Market treaty was signed by France while war raged in Algeria, that de Gaulle's sharpest attack on the "Monnet method" followed the Évian agreements that ended the Algerian war. The weight of the French national situation affected and inflected the course of even so nationalist a leader as de Gaulle. Even he went along with the "Monnet method" (however grudgingly) until the end of the Algerian war. It is not a coincidence either that the French leaders most suspicious of the imprisoning effects of the EEC were those who labored hardest at improving the national situation by removing colonial burdens (Mendès-France, de Gaulle), and that the French rulers who followed Monnet and tried to orient the pride of France toward leadership of a united Europe were those who failed to improve the national situation overseas (the MRP, Mollet). The one French politician who sought both European integration *and* imperial "disengagement" was Antoine Pinay.

20. Especially by Henry Kissinger in *The Troubled Partnership* (New York, 1965) and Raymond Aron in *The Great Debate* (New York, 1964).

21. One should not forget that the original decisions that led to the French nuclear *force de frappe* were made before de Gaulle, and opposition to the national deterrent came from men who did not at all object to de Gaulle's argument that Europe as a whole should stop being a client of the United States.

22. See my previous discussion in "Discord in Community," in F. Wilcox and H. F. Haviland, Jr., eds., *The Atlantic Community* (New York, 1963), pp. 3–31; and "Europe's Identity Crisis," *Daedalus,* Fall 1964, pp. 1244–97.

23. See, for instance, Max Kohnstamm, "The European Tide," in Stephen R. Graubard, ed., *A New Europe?* (Boston, 1964), pp. 140–73.

24. See Karl W. Deutsch, *et al., Political Community and the North Atlantic Area* (Princeton, N.J., 1957).

25. Under authority, I include three distinct notions: autonomy (the capacity to act independently of the governments, particularly financially), power (control over acts of others), and legitimacy (being accepted as the "rightful" center of action).

26. Compare decolonization. Along similar lines, see Francis Rosenstiel, *Le principe de "Supranationalité"* (Paris, 1962).

27. See the analysis of a recent French public-opinion poll by Raoul Girardet, "Du fait national aux necessités européennes," *Contrepoint,* Spring 1971.

28. On this point, see Raymond Aron and Daniel Lerner, eds., *France Defeats EDC* (New York, 1957).

29. See Emerson, *loc. cit.*

30. Britain's refusal to join EEC, before 1961, could not fail to increase French hesitations, for integration without Britain meant equality with Germany, and a clear-cut difference between France's position and Britain's, i.e., a reversal of French aspirations and traditions. Britain has on the whole rejected the "resignation-resistance" dilemma—and as a result, both the aspects of its foreign policy that appeared like resignation to U.S. predominance and the aspects that implied resistance to decline have contributed to the crisis of European integration: for France's vetoes in January 1963 and November 1967 meant a French refusal to let into Europe a power that had just confirmed its military ties to the United States, but Britain's previous desire to play a world role and aversion to "fading into Europe" encouraged France's own misgivings about integration.

31. See Grosser, *op. cit.,* Chapter 4.

32. See Thomas Schelling, *Strategy of Conflict* (Cambridge, Mass., 1960).

33. The best balance sheet (despite its jargon) is in Leon N. Lindberg and Stuart A. Scheingold, *Europe's Would-Be Polity* (Englewood Cliffs, N.J., 1970). For a more detailed assessment of current developments, see my contribution to Wolfram Hanrieder, ed., *The United States and Western Europe in the 70s* (Cambridge, Mass.: Winthrop Publishers, 1974).

34. For a good discussion of the 1971 crisis, see Guy Berger, Edward L. Morse, and Michel Albert's articles in *Revue française de science politique,* April 1972.

35. The question asked of the voters—whether to approve Britain's entry into EEC, given "the new perspectives open to Europe" (undefined)—was too clever by half. Pompidou's speeches veered from "Europeanism" to "Gaullism," and a sizable part of the Gaullist electorate abstained or deserted.

36. See Maurice Couve de Murville, *Une Politique étrangère* (Paris, 1971), p. 382.

37. Haas's definition of a political community in his *The Uniting of Europe,* p. 5 ("a

condition in which specific groups and individuals show more loyalty to their central political institutions than to any other political authority") is not very helpful in the case of states marked by severe domestic cleavages. There might be more loyalty to the center than to any other political authority merely because there is no other *political* authority, and yet one would still not be in the presence of anything like an integrated society.

38. The distinctions I suggest are like marks on a continuum.

1. At one end, there are *cooperative arrangements* whose institutions have no autonomy from the various governments (OECD, the U.N. in most respects). These arrangements range from truly cooperative to hegemonial, i.e., from representing all the members to asserting the domination and extending the will of one of them.

2. Then there are *entities* with *central institutions* that have some authority, in the sense of legal autonomy from the components and legal power all over the territory. But these are *not* political communities in the formal sense, because there may be discontinuities in communications or transactions among the components, or because the cleavages within the entity deprive the central institutions of autonomy or effective power. (States such as the Congo or certain Latin American republics fall in this category, supranational entities like the EEC, and, within the limits of effective military integration, NATO.) These entities may be very resilient if they are states, endowed with international personality and institutions that have a formal monopoly or at least superiority of force over internal challenges; but if they are supranational (and especially if they are not simply an arrangement disguising the hegemony of one of the members), they are likely to be unstable, since the "central" institutions will be challenged by the central institutions of the component states. In other words, supranational entities will tend either to retrogress toward stage 1 or to progress toward stage 3.

3. Next come entities that are *political communities* in the *formal* but not the substantive sense. That is, their central institutions have autonomy and power, there are common habits, and the community's rules are enforced across internal barriers, but the central institutions do not have legitimacy all over the territory, and the habits and rules are not based on common values concerning the polity. This is the case with many nation-states which have "national consciousness" but are not political communities in the last sense.

4. Here I refer to nation-states whose central institutions are wholly autonomous, effectively powerful and legitimate, and whose society has shared values concerning the polity. These are political communities in the *substantive* sense. Needless to say, there are not many of them. The difference between stage 3 and 4 is largely a difference in the level and scope of consensus. I would reserve the term national to states in those two stages.

39. Haas, *Beyond the Nation-State,* p. 29.

40. Haas and Philippe C. Schmitter, "Economics and Differential Patterns of Political Integration," *International Organization,* XVIII, No. 4 (Autumn 1964), 705–710.

41. Some assert that it is not even the old bottle, so great are the effects of transnational forces on the nation-states. See Keohane and Nye, *op. cit.*

CHAPTER 4

The Babel Express: Relations with the European Community, 1987-1990

Margaret Thatcher

Margaret Thatcher, born in 1925, was the British "Iron Lady" conservative prime minister, 1979-1990. She styled herself a "conviction politician" rather than the sort of compromise-oriented or "wet" politician who had dominated the Conservative party since the 1950s. Prior to becoming prime minister, she had very limited high-level experience, having been education minister (1970-1974) in the Edward Heath government, brought down in a losing confrontation with the labor unions. Surprisingly, in 1975 she was named leader, presumptively a transition figure while the "boys" sorted things out, of a Tory party in much disarray. With her as prime ministerial candidate, however, the Conservatives won three successive general elections. Thatcher became as authoritarian a party and government leader as she was successful. Finally in 1990 she was obliged to resign as prime minister by an internal revolt of her Tory colleagues. They would no longer accept her rigidity, her lack of toleration for disagreement, and her strict and often arrogant "politics of conviction."

Thatcher's time in office contained several remarkable successes however. She began with an economic policy much like Ronald Reagan's, focusing on tax cuts, budget cuts, and—a British but not American issue—privatization of state-owned enterprises. The British economy, like Reagan's American economy, dipped sharply before an upsurge of growth saved both leaders. In 1982 Thatcher responded in "Iron Lady" fashion with a successful military expedition to retake the Falkland Islands (the Malvinas in Spanish) from the Argentine government's invasion. In 1984-1985 she took on and outlasted the heretofore unstoppable British labor union movement that had humbled the Heath government a decade earlier. The Trades Union Congress has never regained its strength from that confrontation. Majority stakes in many public utilities were sold off to the private sector. Local government independence was restricted and "rate-capping," or fixed limits on property tax calculations, further narrowed municipal council influence.

All through her time in office in the 1980s, foreign policy issues were crucial. A staunch, unapologetic anticommunist, she stood with President Ronald Reagan and American policy toward the Soviet Union. She naturally welcomed the collapse of communist regimes in central and eastern Europe, as well as the Soviet Union's demise.

With regard to European integration, Thatcher was a successor to Charles de Gaulle, and wanted a European Community based on national states and national sovereignty, not supranationalism and federalism. The British Conservative party had long been split between a Euro-skeptic majority, of which she was the leader in the 1980s, and a minority favorable to closer, federalist-type links to the Continent, of which Michael Heseltine was a leading figure. However, during the European revolution of 1989–1991 the added concern arose of reunified Germany. Thatcher worried that a reunified Germany would be too strong economically, demographically, and thus geopolitically, for a federal-type Europe. Euro-skepticism in general, in other words, was overlaid and intensified by concern about the new Germany's potentiality for, as it was said, "winning in peace what it wasn't able to win in war," i.e. European dominance. Thatcher tried to little avail to convince French president François Mitterrand to take a stand of some kind against German reunification. The most she could do was to advocate rapid enlargement of the European Community so that supranationalism and federalism, as expressed in qualified majority decision making, would become more difficult. German strength might thus be diluted. Thatcher's view was, so to speak, a 1960s Gaullism brought up to date to face the problems of the 1990s. However, she left office with Germany reunified, with the Maastricht treaty planning for a single European currency by 1999, and with her own party still divided between Euro-skeptics and those who saw Britain's future ineluctably tied up with the Continent's plans, above all with Franco-German projects. John Major, Thatcher's successor as leader, could not resolve the dispute in the Conservative party over policy toward European integration. Today, under the new leader, William Hague, the Tories still remain seriously divided, although the majority Euro-skeptic position continues against British membership of the euro-zone.

I have already described how during my second term of office as Prime Minister certain harmful features and tendencies in the European Community started to become evident. Against the notable gains constituted by the securing of Britain's budget rebate and progress towards a real Common—or 'Single'—Market had to be set a more powerful Commission ambitious for power, an inclination towards bureaucratic rather than market solutions to economic problems and the re-emergence of a Franco-German axis with its own covert federalist and protectionist agenda. As yet, however, the full implications of all this were unclear—even to me, distrustful as I always was of that un-British combination of high-flown rhetoric and pork-barrel politics which passed for European statesmanship.

Indeed, the first three European Councils of my second term were very much of the traditional mould, dominated by finance and agriculture: and their outcome was equally traditional—a British victory on points. But from then on the Community environment in which I had to operate became increasingly alien and frequently poisonous. The disputes were no longer about tactical or temporary issues but about the whole future direction of the Community and its relations with the wider world changing so fast outside it. The Franco-German axis became more evident; and with the unification of Germany that relationship became still more lop-sided, with German dominance increasingly pronounced.

The Franco-German federalist project was wholeheartedly supported by a variety of different elements within the Community—by poorer southern countries who expected a substantial pay-off in exchange for its accomplishment; by northern businesses which hoped to foist their own high costs on to their competitors; by socialists because of the scope it offered for state intervention; by Christian Democrats whose political tradition was firmly corporatist; and, of course, by the Commission which saw itself as the nucleus of a supranational government. In the face of these powerful forces I sought for allies within the Community and sometimes found them; and so my strategic retreat in the face of majorities I could not block was also punctuated by tactical victories.

Ultimately, however, there was no option but to stake out a radically different position from the direction in which most of the Community seemed intent on going, to raise the flag of national sovereignty, free trade and free enterprise—and fight. Isolated I might be in the European Community—but taking the wider perspective, the federalists were the real isolationists, clinging grimly to a half-Europe when Europe as a whole was being liberated; toying with protectionism when truly global markets were emerging; obsessed with schemes of centralization when the greatest attempt at centralization— the Soviet Union—was on the point of collapse. If there was ever an idea whose time had come and gone it was surely that of the artificial mega-state. I was, therefore, convinced not just that I was right about the way forward for Europe, but confident that if the Government and Party I led kept their nerve we would be vindicated by intellectual developments and international events.

FINANCE AND FARMING

After the 1987 general election I was in just the mood to force the Community to live up to its previous protestations of virtue. For all the talk of financial rectitude at and since the Fontainebleau Council of 1984, there had still been no effective budget discipline and no binding limits on spending under the CAP. The rebate I had won had limited our net contribution from rising to a totally unacceptable level; but several of our Community partners now wanted to cut or eliminate it. There was a large Community budget deficit which was starting to concentrate minds. But from the Commission it had provoked the traditional answer to any financial problem—an increase in the Community's 'own resources.' They wanted to increase that sum not just to the 1.6 per cent of VAT which we had agreed at Fontainebleau might happen in 1988, but to 1.4 per cent of Community countries' GNP (equivalent to 2.2 per cent of VAT receipts). There was also on the table a pretty blatantly protectionist proposal, strongly supported by the French, for an Oils and Fats tax. This was, it is true, to be matched by measures to control spending on agriculture where huge sums were going on storing and disposing of surpluses, and to improve budget discipline. But these were not tough enough. Moreover, the Commission was still trying to whittle away at what I had secured at Fontainebleau by proposing to change our rebate mechanism. And M. Delors also wanted to double the structural funds (that is, spending on Community regional and social policy). This last proposal was, naturally, more than welcome to the southern member states and Ireland which expected to gain most from it.

Who were my allies? However unreliable the French and Germans would be when it came to cutting agricultural spending on which their politically influential farmers depended, I knew that at least I could look to them for support in trying to resist the huge increase in structural funds. I also had in M. Chirac, the Gaullist French Prime Minister, an ally in resisting the large increase proposed in 'own resources.' But my main allies—though inclined to be critical of our rebate—were the Dutch. Such then was the technically and politically complicated scene which I knew confronted me when I went to Brussels for the European Council meeting on Tuesday 29 and Wednesday 30 June 1987.

It was an intensely hot, humid day when I arrived. On the way from the airport, my car was pelted with water balloons by the less dangerous Euro-fanatics outside the Council. Inside, the possibilities of bad-tempered disagreement were maximized by the weak chairmanship of M. Martens, the Belgian Prime Minister and Council President. He allowed no less than four hours of discussion of the proposed Oils and Fats tax, which the Germans, the Dutch and I had not the slightest intention of accepting.

Generally, I was among the best briefed heads of government on these occasions—partly because I always did my homework and partly because I had a truly superb official team to help me. Perhaps the mainstay of this was David Williamson, who came from the Ministry of Agriculture to the key European policy role in the Cabinet Office and finally—and deservedly—became Secretary-General of the Commission. The intricacies of European Community policy, particularly finance, really test one's intellectual ability and capacity for clear thinking. With the exception of those of the presidency, the different delegations' officials were not present during the proceedings themselves; so the Foreign Secretary of the day wrote manuscript notes which were passed out to our people, against which the conclusions recorded by the presidency would be checked.

On this occasion (and at Copenhagen later) the complexity of some of the matters under discussion was absurd. They should have been dealt with by Agriculture or Finance or Foreign ministers: but there never seemed the will to take real decisions at this level and so heads of government would be left discussing matters which would boggle the mind of the City's top accountants.

The general view was that this first Brussels Council was a 'failure' and that I was responsible for it. There was only a little truth in either proposition. It was in any case unreasonable to think that with such a large number of contentious and complicated matters on the agenda agreement would be reached on the first serious attempt. Moreover, a good deal of progress was made on the key questions of finance and agriculture. It was accepted that budget discipline should be 'binding and effective,' that it should apply to 'commitments' (that is basically what the Agriculture ministers agreed to spend) as well as actual payments, and that additional regulations (that is Community 'laws') would be adopted to keep the level of spending within the budget. The worst aspect—unacceptable to me—was that they wanted to build into the 'agricultural guideline'—that is the total permitted spending on agriculture—the present level of overspending. The package as a whole was not sufficiently tight for me to agree to an increase in 'own resources.' So the other heads of government left Brussels aware that I had lost none of my willingness to say no.

I met two of the key players in Berlin in September, where I was attending the IDU Conference. I had a working breakfast with M. Chirac at the British Ambassador's residence. Not for nothing was he known by his compatriots as 'le bulldozer': and on more than one occasion I had to make it clear that the lady was not for bulldozing. He was a marked contrast to President Mitterrand. M. Chirac was blunt, direct, forceful, argumentative, had a sure grasp of detail and a profound interest in economics. The President was quieter, more urbane, a self-conscious French intellectual, fascinated by foreign policy, bored by detail, possibly contemptuous of economics. Oddly enough I liked both of them.

M. Chirac had apparently chastised me as a 'housewife' in Brussels in June 1987 and was to make an unprintable remark about me in a heated exchange at Brussels in February 1988. But I generally found him somewhat easier to deal with than President Mitterrand, because he said what he thought and because his public actions bore a greater similarity to his privately expressed views. I was, as M. Chirac knew, none too happy about the arrangements which led to the release of French hostages from Lebanon and which were widely considered to have overstepped the mark as regards the principle of refusal to deal with terrorists. (M. Chirac furiously reproached me at a reception at the Copenhagen Council for allegedly leaking criticism of what the French had done: in fact I could lay my hand on my heart and assure him that we had done no such thing.) To be fair, the French had been of great assistance to us in the matter of intercepting the arms shipment from the *Eksund*. And of course M. Chirac and I were very much on the same wave-length politically. He had done much to make the Gaullists (the RPR—*Rassemblement pour la République*) into a modern right-of-centre party, committed to free enterprise. This was of great significance not just to France but in the long term to Europe and the western alliance. I was disappointed, though not very surprised, at the way in which the wily President Mitterrand managed to turn the process of 'cohabitation' against the Right. At this time, though, it was the imminence of the French elections rather than their likely outcome which was the problem. For it was clear to me that neither M. Chirac nor President Mitterrand would be anxious to be seen taking tough action on agriculture when French farmers' votes would soon be needed.

Nor for that matter would Chancellor Kohl whom I saw for tea that afternoon in the German government guesthouse. He confessed to me that he too had had his domestic political difficulties. His farming supporters had stayed away from the polls in two recent Land elections which had led to bad results for the CDU. The small farmer was, he said, a great element of stability in Germany. He said he was prepared to make some sacrifices but it would take four or five years to 'get over the hill.' I retorted that we did not have four or five years. We must act on agricultural overspending now. But I did not come away from the meeting any more optimistic about the likely outcome of the next Council.

It was too much to expect, when I landed at an icy Copenhagen on Thursday 4 December, that the papers would not be full of allusions to the famous battle of Copenhagen, when Nelson, ignoring signalled orders by the device of holding a telescope to his blind eye, attacked and blew the opposing fleet out of the water. In fact, as at Brussels earlier, it was a magnifying glass—or perhaps a pocket calculator—which were most in order on this occasion, such was the complexity of the matters under discussion. At least we had the amiable Poul Schluter, the Conservative Danish Prime Minister, in the chair. The Danes were anxious to continue receiving as much as possible from the CAP. But of all the other Community countries they were the most anti-federalist. So there was a basic sympathy between us, even if not always a meeting of minds.

Discussions of the ideas put forward at Brussels had been continuing in the Agriculture Council and between officials and the Commission. But since then the pressure had increased to cut back our rebate. The Danes had unhelpfully brought it back into the limelight in their 'bidding letter' inviting heads of government to the Council. There was also continuing discussion about what should constitute the Community's 'own resources.' But for me everything really hinged—everything that is apart from the maintenance of our rebate on which I would not compromise—on the measures to control agriculture spending. The position here was far from satisfactory. I was still unhappy about the 'agricultural guideline' being proposed. But even more important was the way in which the Commission's idea of applying 'stabilizers' was to be put into effect. There were basically two possible ways of cutting agricultural subsidies. One was to tax overproduction by means of what—in another piece of Community jargon—was described as a 'coresponsibility levy.' This might have a place, but it was not the best method. The other way was to apply automatic and cumulative price cuts once a certain level of production was breached. This was the 'stabilizer' mechanism. It then fell to be discussed what the 'minimum quantity' of any particular commodity would be before the mechanism began to operate—for different agricultural products would require different formulae according to the market in which they were being produced—and what the price cuts should be.

It is also worth adding, however, one other possibility which I never actually advanced as an alternative to either of these routes but which from time to time I considered. This was to revert to a national system of subsidy for agriculture, thus bypassing the whole cumbersome Community apparatus altogether. It would, of course, have required a complete rethink of the regime imposed by the Community and could only have been possible if other countries had wanted to pursue the same approach. The disadvantage would have been that individual countries would have been competing in subsidy and probably our farmers would have lost out in that race to the French and Germans. It would only have been desirable if agriculture had been brought effectively under the GATT—and the difficulty of doing that was to become increasingly evident. But I was definitely attracted to a scheme by which each nation took financial responsibility for writing off surplus agricultural stocks and proposed this, without much success. I also raised with Helmut Kohl, when I saw him just before the Copenhagen Council, whether it might not be better if Germany used nationally financed aids to assist her small farmers—though these must not be used to finance increased production. (I recalled, of course, how he had essentially adopted this approach at an earlier Council [at Fontainebleau].) But though he took the point nothing came of it. I realized that the only immediate way to rein in Community spending on agriculture was within a Community framework.

My pre-Council meeting with Chancellor Kohl also revealed him to be even more preoccupied than before with his farming vote. He wanted a Community-financed 'set-aside' scheme, by which farmers would essentially be paid not to farm efficiently—something which ultimately demonstrated the Mad Hatter economics of the CAP. I was prepared to agree to this, as I told him, as long as we got effective stabilizers as well. I was also very tough with him about the prospect of increases in the Community's 'own resources,' on which I knew Chancellor Kohl was willing to see a large increase (ultimately at the expense of the German taxpayer) in order to keep his farmers happy. So by the time the Council opened we knew where we stood.

Once it was clear that the French—principally for electoral reasons—were prepared to back the Germans on a formula for stabilizers which could not conceivably contain agriculture spending, it was evident that no satisfactory conclusion could be reached. Neither I nor Mr. Lubbers of the Netherlands would agree to anything on these lines. The Commission added another split by pressing hard for a doubling of the structural funds, which pitted the northern against the southern Europeans. But it was not an acrimonious occasion. It was agreed that a special European Council would be held in Brussels the following February.

There were a number of long faces at the end of the Copenhagen Council. But mine was not among them. I knew that little by little I was winning the argument inside and outside the Council for the kind of solution I wanted. I told the other heads of government to cheer up and reminded them—with a little irony, for I suspected that some of them needed no reminding—of how difficult things had been at Brussels on the eve of the Fontainebleau summit and then how at the next moment what was insoluble suddenly seemed easy. Why should it not happen again in Brussels? President Mitterrand observed wryly that he was really not quite sure whether it was easier to deal with Madame Thatcher when she was difficult or when she was cheerful. Evidently he did remember.

But it was by no means certain that we would reach agreement at the forthcoming special European Council. I was prepared to make some compromises; after all, the question of precisely when and how agricultural stabilizers would bite was the sort of matter even people intent on checking agricultural spending could legitimately disagree about. But far more difficult to gauge was whether Messrs. Mitterrand and Chirac and Herr Kohl would think it worth their while achieving a settlement on terms which some of their farmers would find unpalatable.

By now the French election campaigns were in full swing and the rivalry between President and Prime Minister was intense, with 'cohabitation' nothing more than a fiction. Accordingly, when they arrived in London for an Anglo-French summit on Friday 29 January 1988, the important discussions I had with President Mitterrand and Prime Minister Chirac had to be at separate meetings. The contrast between their respective styles was once again evident. President Mitterrand was not in good form and had a heavy cold, which I hoped he would not pass on to me: I seem to have an unfailing ability to attract any passing cold germ. Nor was he properly briefed about the difficult European Community matters on which I wanted to concentrate and he had to break off half way through to receive explanations from Jacques Attali, his adviser. He was obviously relieved when the conversation turned to defence and foreign affairs. I was not sure that I had got very far by the end of the discussion, though as always it had been agreeable enough.

The same could not, however, be said of my meeting with M. Chirac, who was in robust form. He began very frankly, saying that with the presidential elections just three months away he had a real political problem with the forthcoming Council. His own interest, he said, lay in a failure at Brussels. But for wider international reasons he was prepared to work for success. Lest I conclude that this meant he was going to be a push-over, he spelt out for me precisely what his strategy was. He said that we could either settle at Brussels or wait until the financial pressure built up on the Community because of its lack of money. But in that case we would be under the Greek presidency, which he was certainly right in describing as offering an 'uncertain prospect.' If the British continued to block the settlement on agriculture at Brussels which the rest of the Community—by which he meant the French and the Germans—wanted we would be isolated and attention would focus on our rebate. I replied that this was evidently no time for diplomatic language. If he thought that ganging up with the Germans to 'isolate Mrs. T' was going to work, he was sadly mistaken. I had no fear at all of being isolated because I was demanding that agricultural surpluses be brought under control. M. Chirac again insisted that if there was to be a row it would turn out not to be about surpluses but about Britain's rebate. I advised him not to threaten me and promised that if there was no satisfactory solution on agricultural spending and our rebate, there would be no increase in 'own resources.' But he continued to insist then and over lunch that the present German presidency's proposals were the furthest France was prepared to go.

How much of this was Gallic bluff I could not know. But it certainly made it all the more important to gauge precisely what the German position was. The fact that the Germans had the presidency meant, as always, that they had less scope for openly advocating their own interests, but this was more than made up for by the extra influence it would give them behind the scenes. . . .

Overnight the Commission came up with a compromise package. But this was rejected by the Germans and the Council broke up for bilateral meetings without any paper as a basis for discussion. Chancellor Kohl was now the key, both as President of the Council and because if the Germans were prepared to do a deal on agricultural spending the French were unlikely to stand out against it. So late that afternoon Ruud Lubbers, Hans van den Broek, Jacques Delors, Geoffrey Howe and I went in to see Chancellor Kohl who was accompanied by Herr Genscher and several other officials. Chancellor Kohl's style of diplomacy is even more direct than mine. He was never above banging the table and on this occasion he spoke in a parade-ground bellow throughout. He said that Germany was making sacrifices, particularly the German farmers. I replied that British farmers were facing sacrifices too and that I was being asked to accept too large an increase in structural funds and too high a ceiling—1.3 per cent of GNP—for Community 'own resources.' The argument went back and forth. M. Delors now proposed a 1.2 per cent ceiling. This prompted alarmed protests from Chancellor Kohl who thought that it might jeopardize his farmers' set-aside scheme. But I said that I would think further about what had been proposed. I was aware that the Dutch were becoming restive and would probably not be prepared to stand out against what was now on offer. In any case, it was necessary to discuss with my officials precisely what the package would mean and I could only do this in private. What I did insist upon, however, was that it should all be set out clearly on paper. As it turned out this was one of my better decisions.

I had a long discussion with Geoffrey Howe and my officials. We argued through each element. It seemed to me that the discipline was going to prove tighter and more effective than I had earlier thought—and perhaps than others had really understood. So when the full Council reconvened I was able to join in giving broad support to the proposals in the paper which was now circulated.

Anyone who imagined that it would now all be plain sailing underrated the French. The agreement we had reached covered the main agricultural products at issue. But it assumed that the other products for which stabilizers had been agreed at Copenhagen would also be covered. To everyone's surprise President Mitterrand and M. Chirac would not agree to this. A heated argument erupted which lasted more than four hours about their proposal to have the stabilizers for 'other products' referred to the Agriculture Council. In the end a Danish suggestion that it should go to a Foreign ministers' meeting in ten days' time was agreed. Ruud Lubbers and I insisted that our agreement to the overall package was conditional on the Foreign ministers not reopening the Copenhagen agreement on 'other products.' In fact, the French had to concede the issue when the Foreign ministers met.

I was right to settle when I did. I had secured my basic aims: effective and legally binding controls on expenditure, measures to reduce agricultural surpluses in which automatic price cuts were the principal weapon, no Oils and

Fats tax, and Britain's rebate which had saved us some £3 billion in the past three years secure. I had had to concede a little on the threshold at which stabilizers began to work. I had had to compromise over the structural funds. I had reluctantly agreed a new 1.2 per cent of GNP ceiling for Community 'own resources.' But it was much better than a draw. Agricultural surpluses started to fall quite sharply and the new measures to enforce budget discipline were successful. None of that, of course, changed the fundamental direction or defects of the Community. The CAP was still wasteful and costly. Britain was still making a financial contribution which I considered too high. The bureaucratic and centralizing tendencies remained. But within its limits the February 1988 Brussels Agreement was not at all bad.

FREE TRADE V. PROTECTION

It is fair to say that from about this point onwards—early 1988—the agenda in Europe began to take an increasingly unwelcome shape. It also began to deviate sharply from that being pursued in the wider international community. That does not mean, however, that my own relations with other European heads of government worsened at a personal level; far from it. I was sorry—though not surprised—to see the Right beaten in the French presidential elections. But I sent a message of congratulations to President Mitterrand and went to see him in Paris that June to talk about the international scene in general and the forthcoming Toronto G7 summit and Hanover European Council in particular.

I found him in understandably good humour now that he had been freed from the domestic torment of 'cohabitation' with the Right. He was pressing a scheme—not dissimilar to one advanced by Nigel Lawson—to tackle the crippling level of Third World debt. I would have had more sympathy with his ideas if France had not been so determinedly protectionist, an approach which did far more harm to poorer countries than any amount of overseas aid did good. The French line was expressed—or rather concealed—in a splendid piece of Euro-jargon: the concept of 'globality.' That is to say progress must be made on all the issues before the GATT at roughly the same pace, a transparent device for avoiding concentration on the thorniest issue—that of agricultural subsidies and protection. He was also keen to have a committee of 'wise men' set up to report on how to achieve economic and monetary union; he specifically hankered after a European Central Bank. I roundly rejected this. I said that the proposal for such a bank was motivated by political not technical considerations and that this was not an area for playing games. The President smiled and said that it was nice to be reminded that I knew how to say no. But I had no illusion that he was going to desist because of that. . . .

As the dispute over measuring agricultural subsidies exemplified, free trade is something which almost everyone subscribes to in principle and finds politically painful in practice. Britain always had everything to gain from a global open trading system. The United States too traditionally believed in free trade. But Britain's own trade policy was now in the hands of the Community, which contained a majority of countries with a tradition of cartels and corporatism and a politically influential agricultural sector. We were in a minority in Europe when it came to deciding trade policy. As for the United States, its huge trade deficit had given a protectionist turn to policy which President Reagan, a convinced free trader, found difficulty resisting. For its part, Japan not only subsidized and protected its agriculture more than anyone else; it also continued to place obstacles in the way of foreign imports of nonagricultural goods and services. Consequently, I increasingly had to look to the 'Cairns Group' of fourteen countries (which includes Canada, Australia, and Argentina) and to Third World countries, anxious to export their agriculture and textiles, to bring pressure on this wealthy western protection racket. I always regarded free trade as far more important than all the other ambitious and often counter-productive strategies of global economic policy—for example the policies of 'co-ordinated growth' which led principally to inflation. Free trade provided a means not only for poorer countries to earn foreign currency and increase their peoples' standards of living. It was also a force for peace, freedom and political decentralization: peace, because economic links between nations reinforce mutual understanding with mutual interest; freedom, because trade between individuals bypasses the apparatus of the state and disperses power to customers not planners; political decentralization, because the size of the political unit is not dictated by the size of the market and vice versa.

After some two and a half hours of discussion on this subject at Toronto we achieved a broadly satisfactory communiqué. It reaffirmed the Uruguay round commitments and underlined the importance of its 'Medium Term Meeting,' while avoiding inclusion of what seemed to me the unrealistic United States objective of no agricultural subsidies by the year 2000. What remained to be seen was how the GATT negotiations now actually evolved. Had I been an optimist I might have drawn comfort from the fact that Toronto was the first time that M. Delors praised one of my speeches. But I kept my optimism in check.

DISCUSSION OF EMU

At Toronto I had an hour's meeting with Chancellor Kohl. Much of it focused on the forthcoming Hanover summit. Chancellor Kohl, supported by the German Finance Ministry and the Bundesbank, seemed ready now to plump for a committee of central bankers rather than academic experts—as the French and Hans-Dietrich Genscher wanted—to report on EMU. This I welcomed. But I restated my unbending hostility to setting up a European Central Bank. By now I was having to recognize that the chance of stopping the committee being set up at all was ebbing away; but I was determined to try to minimize the harm it would do. I also had to recognize that we were saddled with M. Delors as President of the Commission for another two years, since my own favoured candidate, Ruud Lubbers, was not going to stand and the French and Germans supported M. Delors. (In the end I bit the bullet and seconded M. Delors's reappointment myself.)

The Hanover Council turned out to be a fairly good-humoured if disputatious affair. The most important discussion took place on the first evening over dinner. Jacques Delors introduced the discussion of EMU. Chancellor Kohl suggested that a committee of Central Bank governors with a few outsiders be set up under M. Delors's chairmanship. In the ensuing discussion most of the heads of government wanted the report to centre on a European Central Bank. Poul Schluter opposed this and I supported him strongly, quoting from an excellent article by Karl Otto Pöhl, the President of the Bundesbank, to illustrate all the difficulties in the way of such an institution. We succeeded in getting mention of the Central Bank removed. But otherwise there was nothing I could do to stop the committee being set up. The Delors Group was to report back to the June 1989 European Council—that is in a year's time. I hoped that the Governor of the Bank of England and the sceptical Herr Pöhl would manage to put a spoke in the wheel of this particular vehicle of European integration; unfortunately, as I have already explained, that was not to be.

My problem throughout these discussions of EMU was twofold. First, of course, was the fact that I had so few allies; only Denmark, a small country with plenty of spirit but less weight, was with me. But I was fighting with one hand tied behind my back for another reason. As a 'future member' of the EEC, the UK had agreed a communiqué in Paris following a conference of heads of government in October 1972. This reaffirmed 'the resolve of the member states of the enlarged Community to move irrevocably [towards] Economic and Monetary Union, by confirming all the details of the acts passed by the Council and by the member states' representatives on 22 March 1971 and 21 March 1972.' Such language may have reflected Ted Heath's wishes. It certainly did not reflect mine. But there was no point in picking a quarrel which we would have lost. So I preferred to let sleeping dogs lie.

Then, of course, they woke up and started barking in the course of the negotiation of the Single European Act of 1985–6. I had not wanted any reference to EMU in at all. The Germans failed to support me and so the reference to EMU was inserted. But I had Article 20 of the Single European Act give my interpretation of what EMU meant; its title read: 'Co-operation in Economic and Monetary Policy (Economic and Monetary Union).' This enabled me to claim at subsequent forums that EMU now meant economic and monetary co-operation, not moving towards a single currency. There was a studied ambiguity about all this. Councils at Hanover in June 1988 and then at Madrid in 1989 referred back to the Single European Act's 'objective of progressive realization of economic and monetary union.' I was more or less happy with this, because it meant no more than co-operation. The rest of the European heads of government were equally happy, because they interpreted it as progress towards a European Central Bank and a single currency. But at some point, of course, these two interpretations would clash. And when they did I was bound to be fighting on ground not of my choosing.

For the fact was that the more I saw of how the Community operated the less I was attracted by any further steps on the road towards monetary integration. We advanced our proposals for a 'hard ecu.' We issued Treasury bills denominated in ecu terms. And (though this was done because it was in our own interests, not in order to please our European partners) we had swept away exchange controls before anyone else. All this was very *communautaire* in its way, as I never ceased to point out when criticized for resisting entry into the ERM. But my own preference was always for open markets, floating exchange rates and strong political and economic transatlantic links. In arguing for that alternative approach I was bound to be handicapped by the formal commitment to European 'economic and monetary union'—or indeed that of 'ever closer union' contained in the preamble to the original Treaty of Rome. These phrases predetermined many decisions which we thought we had reserved for future consideration. This gave a psychological advantage to my opponents, who never let an opportunity go by of making use of it.

THE BRUGES SPEECH

Not the least of those opponents was Jacques Delors. By the summer of 1988 he had altogether slipped his leash as a *fonctionnaire* and become a fully fledged political spokesman for federalism. The blurring of the roles of civil servants and elected representatives was more in the continental tradition than in ours. It proceeded from the widespread distrust which their voters had for politicians in countries like France and Italy. That same distrust also fuelled the federalist express. If you have no real confidence in the political system or political leaders of your own country you are bound to be more tolerant of foreigners of manifest intelligence, ability and integrity like M. Delors telling you how to run your affairs. Or to put it more bluntly, if I were an Italian I might prefer rule from Brussels too. But the mood in Britain was different. I sensed it. More than that, I shared it and I decided that the time had come to strike out against what I saw as the erosion of democracy by centralization and bureaucracy, and to set out an alternative view of Europe's future.

It was high time. It was clear that the momentum towards full blooded EMU, which I always recognized must mean political union too, was building. In July M. Delors told the European Parliament that 'we are not going to manage to take all the decisions needed between now and 1995 unless we see the beginnings of European government in one form or another,' and predicted that within ten years the Community would be the source of '80 per cent of our economic legislation and perhaps even our fiscal and social legislation as well.' In September he addressed the TUC in Bournemouth calling for measures to be taken on collective bargaining at the European level.

But there were also more subtle, less easily detectable, but perhaps even more important signs of the way things were going. That summer I commissioned a paper from officials which spelt out in precise detail how the Commission was pushing forward the frontiers of its 'competence' into new areas—culture, education, health and social security. It used a whole range of techniques. It set up 'advisory committees' whose membership was neither appointed by, nor answerable to, member states and which tended therefore to reach *communautaire* decisions. It carefully built up a library of declaratory language, largely drawn from the sort of vacuous nonsense which found its way into Council conclusions, in order to justify subsequent proposals. It used a special budgetary procedure, known as *'actions ponctuelles'* which enabled it to finance new projects without a legal base for doing so. But, most seriously of all, it consistently misemployed treaty articles requiring only a qualified majority to issue directives which it could not pass under articles which required unanimity.

Often, as over the environment, or later on health and hours of work, it was difficult to explain to the general public precisely why we opposed the specific measure the Commission wanted. When commissioners issued directives outside their competence they were careful to choose popular causes which had support among pressure groups in member countries, thus presenting themselves as the true friends of the British worker, pensioner and environmentalist. This made it politically difficult to resist the creeping expansion of the Commission's authority. In theory, it would have been possible to fight all this in the courts; for time after time the Commission were twisting the words and intentions of the European Council to its own ends. We did indeed fight, and won a number of cases on these grounds before the European Court of Justice (ECJ). But the advice from the lawyers was that in relation to questions of Community and Commission competence the ECJ would favour 'dynamic and expansive' interpretations of the treaty over restrictive ones. The dice were loaded against us.

The more I considered all this, the greater my frustration and the deeper my anger became. Were British democracy, parliamentary sovereignty, the common law, our traditional sense of fairness, our ability to run our own affairs in our own way to be subordinated to the demands of a remote European bureaucracy, resting on very different traditions? I had by now heard about as much of the European 'ideal' as I could take; I suspected that many others had too. In the name of this ideal, waste, corruption and abuse of power were reaching levels which no one who supported, as I had done, entry to the European Economic Community could have foreseen. Because Britain was the most stable and developed democracy in Europe we had perhaps most to lose from these developments. But Frenchmen who wanted to see France free to decide her own destiny would be losers too. So would Germans, who wished to retain their own currency, the deutschmark, which they had made the most credible in the world.

I was no less conscious of those millions of eastern Europeans living under communism. How could a tightly centralized, highly regulated, supranational European Community meet their aspirations and needs? Arguably, it was the Czechs, Poles and Hungarians who were the real—indeed the last—European 'idealists'; for to them Europe represented a precommunist past, an idea which symbolized the liberal values and national cultures that Marxism had sought unsuccessfully to snuff out.

This wider Europe, stretching perhaps to the Urals and certainly to include that New Europe across the Atlantic, was an entity which made at least historical and cultural sense. And in economic terms, only a truly global approach would do. This then was my thinking as I turned my mind to what would be the 'Bruges Speech.'

The hall in which I made my speech was oddly arranged. The platform from which I spoke was placed in the middle of the long side so that the audience stretched far to my left and right, with only a few rows in front of me. But the message got across well enough. And it was not only my hosts at the College of Europe in Bruges who got more than they bargained for. The Foreign Office had been pressing me for several years to accept an invitation to speak there to set out our European credentials.

I began by doing what the Foreign Office wished. I pointed out just how much Britain had contributed to Europe over the centuries and how much we still contributed, with 70,000 British servicemen stationed there. But what was Europe? I went on to remind my audience that, contrary to the pretensions of the European Community, it was not the only manifestation of European identity. 'We shall always look on Warsaw, Prague and Budapest as great European cities.' Indeed I went on to argue that western Europe had something to learn from the admittedly dreadful experience of its eastern neighbours and their strong and principled reaction to it:

> It is ironic that just when those countries, such as the Soviet Union, which have
> tried to run everything from the centre, are learning that success depends on dis-

persing power and decisions away from the centre, some in the Community seem to want to move in the opposite direction. We have not successfully rolled back the frontiers of the state in Britain only to see them reimposed at a European level, with a European super-state exercising a new dominance from Brussels.

There were, moreover, powerful non-economic reasons for the retention of sovereignty and, as far as possible, of power, by nation-states. Not only were such nations functioning democracies, but they also represented intractable political realities which it would be folly to seek to override or suppress in favour of a wider but as yet theoretical European nationhood. I pointed out:

Willing and active co-operation between independent sovereign states is the best way to build a successful European Community . . . Europe will be stronger precisely because it has France as France, Spain as Spain, Britain as Britain, each with its own customs, traditions and identity. It would be folly to try to fit them into some sort of identikit European personality.

I set out other guidelines for the future. Problems must be tackled practically: and there was plenty in the CAP which still needed tackling. We must have a European Single Market with the minimum of regulations—a Europe of enterprise. Europe must not be protectionist: and that must be reflected in our approach to the GATT. Finally, I stressed the great importance of NATO and warned against any development (as a result of Franco-German initiatives) of the Western European Union as an alternative to it.[1]

I ended on a high note, which was far from 'anti-European':

Let Europe be a family of nations, understanding each other better, appreciating each other more, doing more together, but relishing our national identity no less than our common European endeavour. Let us have a Europe which plays its full part in the wider world, which looks outward not inward, and which preserves that Atlantic Community—that Europe on both sides of the Atlantic—which is our noblest inheritance and our greatest strength.

Not even I would have predicted the furore the Bruges speech unleashed. In Britain, to the horror of the Euro-enthusiasts who believed that principled opposition to federalism had been ridiculed or browbeaten into silence, there was a great wave of popular support for what I had said. It was to become noisily apparent when I addressed the Conservative Party Conference the following month in much the same vein.

But the reaction in polite European circles—or at least the official reaction—was one of stunned outrage. The evening of my speech I had a vigorous argument over dinner in Brussels with M. Martens, his Deputy Prime Minister and Foreign minister. But perhaps that was only to be expected from a small country which thought it could wield more power inside a federal Europe than outside it.

From Brussels I flew to Spain on an official visit—the first by a British Prime Minister—with the press in hot pursuit, as the story rumbled on. My host, Felipe González, was as always the model of courtesy and charm. He prudently, if ambiguously, told me that 'careful study' of my Bruges speech 'could lead to some useful conclusions.' But most of our conversations concentrated on defence and on Gibraltar. Though relations had much improved since the Brussels Agreement of 1984 which reopened the Spanish-Gibraltar border, there was tension over the use of the airport. Spain was, I knew, doing so well out of the Community that I would never get a Socialist Spanish Prime Minister to challenge the arrangements that his country found so lucrative. Equally, I had no doubt that in the long term a proud, ancient nation like Spain would baulk at continued loss of national self-determination in exchange for German-financed subsidies. But that time had not yet arrived.

VISIT TO [CHANCELLOR KOHL AT] DEIDESHEIM

. . . And indeed the atmosphere at Deidesheim was otherwise amicable. It was jolly, quaint, sentimental and slightly overdone—*gemütlich* is, I think, the German word. Lunch consisted of potato soup, pig's stomach (which the German Chancellor clearly enjoyed), sausage, liver dumplings and sauerkraut.

Then we drove to the great cathedral of Speyer nearby, in whose crypt are to be found the tombs of at least four Holy Roman Emperors. As we entered the cathedral the organ struck up a Bach fugue. Chancellor Kohl, knowing how much I love church music, had thoughtfully arranged this gesture. Outside, a large crowd had gathered which I understood was telling the Chancellor how right he was to get British and American tanks off German soil and stop the low-level flying.

Only afterwards did I learn that Helmut Kohl had taken Charles Powell aside behind a tomb in the cathedral crypt to say that now I had seen him on his home ground, on the borders of France, surely I would understand that he—Helmut Kohl—was as much European as German. I understood what Helmut meant and I rather liked him for it. But I had to doubt his reasoning.

This desire among modern German politicians to merge their national identity in a wider European one is understandable enough, but it presents great difficulties to self-conscious nation-states in Europe. In effect, the Germans, because they are nervous of governing themselves, want to establish a European system in which no nation will govern itself. Such a system could only be unstable in the long term and, because of Germany's size and preponderance, is bound to be lop-sided. Obsession with a European Germany risks producing a German Europe. In fact this approach to the German problem is a delusion: it is also a distraction from the real task of German statesmanship, which must be to strengthen and deepen the post-1945 traditions of West German democracy under the new and admittedly challenging conditions of unification. That would both benefit Germany and reassure her neighbours. . . .

THE MADRID EUROPEAN COUNCIL

. . . I have already described how Geoffrey Howe and Nigel Lawson tried to hustle me into setting a date for sterling's entry into the ERM and how I avoided this at the Madrid Council in June 1989. In fact, as I had expected, the ERM was something of an irrelevance at Madrid. The two real issues were the handling of the Delors Report on EMU and the question of whether the Community should have its own Social Charter.

I was, of course, opposed root and branch to the whole approach of the Delors Report. But I was not in a position to prevent some kind of action being taken upon it. Consequently, I decided to stress three points. First, the Delors Report must not be the only basis for further work on EMU. It must be possible to introduce other ideas, such as our own of a hard ecu and a European Monetary Fund. Second, there must be nothing automatic about the process of moving towards EMU either as regards timing or content. In particular, we would not be bound now to what might be in Stage 2 or when it would be implemented. Third, there should be no decision now to go ahead with an Inter-Governmental Conference on the Report. A fall-back position would be that any such IGC must receive proper—and as lengthy as possible—preparation.

As regards the Social Charter, the issue was simpler. I considered it quite inappropriate for rules and regulations about working practices or welfare benefits to be set at Community level. The Social Charter was quite simply a socialist charter—devised by socialists in the Commission and favoured predominantly by socialist member states. I had been prepared to go along (with some misgivings) with the assertion in Council communiqués of the importance of the 'social dimension' of the Single Market. But I always considered that this meant the advantages in terms of jobs and living standards which would flow from freer trade.

The Foreign Office would probably have liked me to soften my stance. They liked to remind me of how Keith Joseph in Opposition had written a pamphlet on 'Why Britain Needs a Social Market Economy.' But the sort of 'social market' Keith and I advocated had precious little similarity with the way the term *'Sozialmarktwirtschaft'* had come to be used in Germany. There it had become a kind of corporatist, highly collectivized, 'consensus'-based economic system, which pushed up costs, suffered increasingly from market rigidities and relied on qualities of teutonic self-discipline to work at all. The extension of such a system throughout the Community would, of course, serve Germany well, in the short term at least, because it would impose German wage costs and overheads on poorer European countries which would otherwise have competed all too successfully with German goods and services. The fact that the cost of extending this system to the poorer countries would also be financed by huge transnational subsidies paid by the German taxpayer seemed to be overlooked by German politicians. But that is what happens when producer cartels rather than customer demands become dominant in any system, whether it is formally described as socialist or not.

When I went to Madrid I took with me a document setting out all the benefits enjoyed by British citizens—the Health Service, health and safety at work, pensions and benefits for the disabled, training provisions and so on. I also advanced the argument that the voluntary Council of Europe Social Charter was quite sufficient and that we did not need a Community document which would, I knew, be the basis of directives aimed at introducing the Delors brand of socialism by the back door.

Most of the first day's discussions in Madrid were taken up with EMU. Late in the afternoon we turned to the Single Market and the 'social dimension.' I have already described how I used my first speech to spell out my conditions for entering the ERM. But I also backed Poul Schluter who challenged paragraph 39 of the Delors Report, which essentially spelt out the 'in for a penny, in for a pound approach' which the federalists favoured. The other extreme was represented by France. President Mitterrand insisted on setting deadlines for an IGC and for completion of Stages 2 and 3, which at one point he suggested should be 31 December 1992.

The argument then turned to the Social Charter. I was sitting next to Sr. Cavaco Silva, the rather sound Portugese Prime Minister who would doubtless have been sounder still if his country was not so poor and the Germans quite so rich.

'Don't you see,' I said, 'that the Social Charter is intended to stop Portugal attracting investment from Germany because of your lower wage costs? This is German protectionism. There will be directives based on it and your jobs will be lost.' But he seemed unconvinced that the charter would be anything other than a general declaration. And perhaps he thought that if the Germans were prepared to pay enough in 'cohesion' money the deal would not be too bad. So I was alone in opposing the charter.

Ironically, when—on the second day of the Council—it came to the drafting of the section of the communiqué which dealt with EMU it was France who was the odd man out. Insofar as there could be an acceptable text which advanced us towards an unacceptable objective I felt that I had got it. All my requirements were satisfied by it. We could not stop an IGC because all it needed was a simple majority vote, but its outcome had been left open and its timing was unclear. President Mitterrand's attempt to have a deadline for Stages 2 and 3 inserted in the text was unsuccessful. To the irritation of Sr.

González, who had hoped to avoid more discussion, I made what I described as a 'unilateral declaration.' It ran:

> The United Kingdom notes that there is no automaticity about the move to nor the timing or content of Stage 2. The UK will take its decisions on these matters in the light of the progress which has by then been made in Stage 1, in particular over the completion of all measures agreed as being necessary to complete.

The phrasing was unpoetic but the meaning clear. This prompted President Mitterrand to make his own declaration to the effect that the IGC should meet as soon as possible after 1 July 1990. And so the Madrid Council came to an end not with a bang but two whimpers.

THE FRENCH REVOLUTION BICENTENNIAL

My disagreements with the French never led to ill-feeling. This was lucky for I was shortly to attend the G7 in Paris which had largely been overtaken by the hugely expensive—and for Parisians wildly inconvenient—celebrations of the Bicentennial of the French Revolution. The French Revolution is one of the few real watersheds in the history of political ideas. For most—though not all—Frenchmen it is nowadays accepted as the basis of the French state, so that even the most conservative Frenchman seems to sing 'the Marseillaise' with enthusiasm. For most other Europeans it is regarded with mixed feelings because it led to French armies devastating Europe, but it also stimulated movements which led eventually to national independence.

For me as a British Conservative, with Edmund Burke the father of Conservatism and first great perceptive critic of the Revolution as my ideological mentor, the events of 1789 represent a perennial illusion in politics. The French Revolution was a Utopian attempt to overthrow a traditional order— one with many imperfections, certainly—in the name of abstract ideas, formulated by vain intellectuals, which lapsed, not by chance but through weakness and wickedness, into purges, mass murder and war. In so many ways it anticipated the still more terrible Bolshevik Revolution of 1917. The English tradition of liberty, however, grew over the centuries: its most marked features are continuity, respect for law and a sense of balance, as demonstrated by the Glorious Revolution of 1688. When I was questioned about what the French Revolution had done for human rights by journalists from *Le Monde* on the eve of my visit I felt I ought to point out some of this. I said:

> Human rights did not begin with the French Revolution . . . [they] really stem from a mixture of Judaism and Christianity . . . [we English] had 1688, our quiet revolution, where Parliament exerted its will over the King . . . it was not the sort of Revolution that France's was . . . 'Liberty, equality, fraternity'—they forgot

obligations and duties I think. And then of course the fraternity went missing for a long time.

The headline over my remarks in *Le Monde* ran '"Les droits de l'homme n'ont pas commencé en France," nous déclare Mme Thatcher.'

It was on this note that I arrived in Paris for the Bicentennial. I brought with me for President Mitterrand a first edition of Charles Dickens's *A Tale of Two Cities,* which he, a connoisseur of such things, loved, but which also made somewhat more elegantly the same point as my interview. The celebrations themselves were on the scale which only a Hollywood studio—or France— could manage: an almost endless procession, a military parade, an opera with pride of place in the set being given to a huge guillotine.

The G7 summit itself definitely took second place to this pageantry. Indeed, this posed a potential problem. A large number of Third World heads of government had been invited to Paris to the celebrations and there seemed some prospect of President Mitterrand suddenly seeking to relaunch another 'North-South' dialogue of the sort we had thankfully left behind at Cancún. I alerted President Bush—arriving for his first G7—to this when I had a bilateral meeting with him at the US Embassy before the summit. He said that he thought there was a problem in blocking such a move without appearing a 'parsimonious bunch of don't cares.' I said that this did not seem to me to be much of a problem. Nor did it prove to be. The French in the end thought better of introducing this controversial idea, preferring to rest on the level of generalities.

George Bush and I made the familiar pleas for free trade under the GATT. President Mitterrand—with some help from me—got the text of his Declaration on Human Rights (with its obvious revolutionary symbolism) accepted almost word for word. There were discussions of the environment and drugs. In fact, everyone left happy and little of note was achieved. It was the sort of occasion which in earlier years had given international summitry a bad name. But President Mitterrand's final dinner for heads of government held in the new pyramid in the forecourt of the Louvre was one of the best I have ever eaten. Some traditions are too important for even the French to overthrow. . . .

THE FRANCO-GERMAN AXIS—AND 'POLITICAL UNION'

. . . The winter of 1989 saw those revolutionary changes which led to the collapse of communism in eastern Europe. In the longer term the emergence of free, independent and anti-socialist governments in the region would provide me with potential allies in my crusade for a wider, looser Europe. But the immediate effect, through the prospect and then the reality of German reunification, was to strengthen the hand of Chancellor Kohl and fuel the desire of President Mitterrand and M. Delors for a federal Europe which would 'bind in' the new Germany to a structure within which its preponderance would be checked. Although these matters are best dealt with later in the context of East-West relations, they formed the background to the ever more intense battles on monetary and political union in which I henceforth found myself engaged.

After Spain the European Community presidency passed to France. Partly in order to ensure that eastern Europe did not dominate the European Council scheduled for December at Strasbourg, President Mitterrand called a special Council in November in Paris specifically to discuss the consequences of events in the East and the fall of the Berlin Wall. He was also pressing hard for the creation of a European Bank of Reconstruction and Development (EBRD) in order to channel investment and assistance to the emerging democracies. I was sceptical about whether such an institution was really necessary. The case had not been made that aid of this dimension had to go through a European institution, as opposed to national or wider international ones. I conceded the point in Strasbourg; but my wishes were eventually met because the EBRD now sensibly involves the Americans and Japanese, not just the Europeans. President Mitterrand and I finally put together a deal in 1990: I agreed that his protégé Jacques Attali would be EBRD President and he agreed that the bank would be situated in London.

To some extent the French strategy of holding an 'unofficial' Paris Council on East-West relations worked because the Strasbourg Council concentrated—at least in its official sessions—heavily on the more narrowly European matters of EMU and the Social Charter. I was as strongly opposed to the holding of an IGC on economic and monetary union as ever. Equally, I had little hope of blocking it altogether. The French aim was to set a date for the IGC and this I still hoped to stave off. Until a few days before the start of the Council we were optimistic that the Germans would support us in calling for 'further preparation' before the IGC met. But in a classic demonstration of the way in which the Franco-German axis always seemed to re-form in time to dominate the proceedings, Chancellor Kohl went along with President Mitterrand's wishes. By the time I arrived in Strasbourg I knew that I would be more or less on my own. I decided to be sweetly reasonable throughout, since there was no point in causing gratuitous offence when I could not secure what I really wanted. It was agreed that the IGC would meet under the Italian presidency before the end of 1990, but after the German elections. As for the Social Charter at which I had directed my fire at Madrid, I reaffirmed that I was not prepared to endorse the text, my determination having been if anything strengthened by the fact that the Commission was now proposing to bring forward no fewer than forty-three separate proposals, including seventeen legally binding directives, in the areas which the charter covered. That effectively ended the discussion of the charter from our point of view. On EMU I would return to the fray in Rome.

In the first half of 1990, however, there was the Irish presidency to contend with. The unwelcome habit of calling extra 'informal' Councils proved catching. Charles Haughey decided that another one was needed in order to consider events in eastern Europe and the implications for the Community of German unification. Perhaps that is what Mr. Haughey really envisaged, but for others this was just an opportunity to keep up the federalist momentum.

'Political union' was now envisaged alongside 'monetary union.' In a sense, of course, this was only logical. A single currency and a single economic policy ultimately imply a single government. But behind the concept of 'political union' there lay a special Franco-German agenda. The French wanted to curb German power. To this end, they envisaged a stronger European Council with more majority voting: but they did not want to see the powers of the Commission or the European Parliament increased. The French were federalists on grounds of tactics rather than conviction. The Germans wanted 'political union' for different reasons and by different means. For them it was partly the price of achieving quick reunification with East Germany on their own terms and with all the benefits which would come from Community membership, partly a demonstration that the new Germany would not behave like the old Germany from Bismarck to Hitler. In this cause, the Germans were prepared to see more powers for the Commission and they gave special importance to increasing the power and authority of the European Parliament. So the Germans were federalists by conviction. The French pushed harder for political union: but it was the agenda of the Germans, who were increasingly the senior partner of the Franco-German axis, which was dominant.

For my part I was opposed to political union of either kind. But the only way that I could hope to stop it was by getting away from the standard Community approach whereby a combination of high-flown statements of principle and various procedural devices prevented substantive discussion of what was at stake until it was too late. Within the Community I must aim to open up the divisions between the French and the Germans. At home I must point out in striking language just what 'political union' would and would not mean if it was taken at all seriously. Far too much of the Community's history had consisted of including nebulous phrases in treaties and communiqués, then later clothing them with federal meaning which we had been assured they never possessed. Consequently, I decided that I would go to Dublin with a speech which would set out what political union was not and should never be. This seemed the best way of having all concerned define—and disagree about—what it was.

There was no doubt about how determined the French and Germans were in their federalist intentions. Shortly before the Council met in Dublin at the end of April President Mitterrand and Chancellor Kohl issued a joint public statement calling for the Dublin Council to 'initiate preparations for an Inter-

Governmental Conference on political union.' They also called on the Community to 'define and implement a common foreign and security policy.' President Mitterrand and Chancellor Kohl chose at about the same time to send a joint letter to the President of Lithuania urging temporary suspension of that country's declaration of independence in order to ease the way for talks with Moscow. As I took some pleasure in pointing out in my subsequent speech at the Council, this was done without any consultation with the rest of the Community, let alone NATO—it demonstrated that the likelihood of a common 'foreign and security policy' was somewhat remote.

I made my speech early on in the proceedings over a working lunch. I said that the way to dispel fears was to make clear what we did not mean when we were talking about political union. We did not mean that there would be a loss of national identity. Nor did we mean giving up separate heads of state, either the monarchies to which six of us were devoted or the presidencies which the other six member states favoured. We did not intend to suppress national parliaments; the European Parliament must have no role at the expense of national parliaments. We did not intend to change countries' electoral systems. We would not be altering the role of the Council of Ministers. Political union must not mean any greater centralization of powers in Europe at the expense of national governments and parliaments. There must be no weakening of the role of NATO and no attempt to turn foreign policy co-operation into a restriction on the rights of states to conduct their own foreign policy.

To deliver a ten-minute speech with one's tongue in one's cheek is as much a physical as a rhetorical achievement. For of course this was precisely the route which political union, if taken seriously, would go. Perhaps only my remarks about heads of state—which were widely reported—added a new element to the barely hidden agenda of the European Commission and those who thought like it. My speech did also have some immediate effect, for it rapidly became clear in the discussion that heads of government were either unable—or perhaps at this stage unwilling—to spell out precisely what political union meant for them. Top marks for calculated ambiguity, however, must surely have gone to Sig. Andreotti, who suggested that although we must set up an IGC on political union, it would be dangerous to try to reach a clear-cut definition of what political union was. Mr. Haughey wound up the discussion by announcing blandly that almost all the points I had mentioned in my remarks would be excluded from political union. And perhaps that was said with tongue in cheek as well.

At the end of June we were back in Dublin again. The Community Foreign ministers had been told to go away and produce a paper on political union for the European Council's consideration. I hoped that I had at least put down a marker against the sort of proposals which were likely to come before us at some future stage. But I was in no position to stop an IGC being called. I spent more time elaborating on our latest thinking on the hard ecu proposal. Anything that I could do to influence the discussions in the IGC on EMU which would run in parallel with that on political union was of value. I took most satisfaction, however, at this Council from stopping the Franco-German juggernaut in its tracks on the question of financial credits to the Soviet Union. I was not generally convinced that allowing former communist countries in eastern Europe—let alone the communist USSR—to build up more debt would do them any favours. Above all, any assistance must be properly targeted and must be intended to reward and promote practical reform rather than—as I was to put it in discussion at the G7 in Houston the following month—'providing an oxygen tent for the survival of much of the old system.'

President Mitterrand and Chancellor Kohl, however, were more interested in power politics and grand gestures. Shortly before the Dublin Council opened they had agreed to propose a multi-billion dollar loan to the Soviets and over dinner on the second day they tried to bounce the rest of us into endorsing this. I said that this was quite unacceptable. No board of directors of a company would ever behave in such an unbusiness-like way. We should not do so either. There must be a proper study done before any such decision was made. After much argument, which continued the following morning, my approach prevailed.

EMU AND THE GATT

Of the two, it was EMU rather than political union which posed the more immediate threat. What was so frustrating was that others who shared my views had a variety of reasons for not expressing them and preferring to let me receive the criticism for doing so. The weaker economies would have been devastated by a single currency, but they hoped to receive sufficient subsidies to make their acquiescence worthwhile. The classic case was that of Greece. I became all too used to a Greek chorus of support for whatever ambitious proposals Germany made.

Nor were the Germans at one on the move towards European economic and monetary union. From time to time Karl Otto Pöhl had been outspokenly critical of the concept. As I understood it, the pressure for EMU was coming from France which found it unacceptable to have monetary policy dominated by the deutschmark and the Bundesbank. The Bundesbank would not have had any problem sticking with the ERM rather than going further, but the political pressure for EMU was now very strong. I always had the highest respect for the Bundesbank and its record of keeping down inflation in Germany and I found it significant that those who contributed most to this achievement often had least time for a single European currency which would, of course, have meant the end of the deutschmark.

To get away from the often parochial atmosphere of the overfrequent European Councils to a meeting of the G7 was always a relief. That at Houston in July was the first chaired by President Bush, who was by now imposing very much his own style on the US Administration. These economic summits were by no means just 'economic' any longer: nor could they be when the economic and political world order was changing so radically and rapidly. In the forefront of all our minds was what needed to happen to ensure order, stability and tolerable prosperity in the lands of the crumbling USSR. But no less important was that at the G7 I could argue much more effectively for free trade and recruit allies for my cause than I could within the narrower framework of the Community.

It was scorching hot in Houston—so hot indeed that as heads of government stood watching the opening ceremonies the ever thoughtful and technology conscious Americans arranged for us to have special air conditioning around our feet, blowing up from the ground. . . .

THE ROME EUROPEAN COUNCIL

I flew into Rome at midday on Saturday 27 October knowing full well that this would be a difficult occasion. But I still did not realize how difficult. This time the excuse for holding an 'informal' Council before the formal Council in December was even more transparent than in Paris or Dublin. The idea was allegedly to take stock of preparations for the forthcoming CSCE summit and to discuss relations with the Soviet Union. In fact, the Italians wanted to pre-empt the outcome of the two IGCs on EMU and political union. Nobody bothered to explain why a special Council was necessary before the IGCs reported.

As always with the Italians, it was difficult throughout to distinguish confusion from guile: but plenty of both was evident. In his 'bidding letter' to the Council Sig. Andreotti made no mention of the need to discuss the GATT Uruguay round. I wrote back insisting that if the Community Trade and Agriculture ministers had not reached agreement on the Community offer on agriculture beforehand we must discuss the matter at Rome because time was running out.

More of a clue to the Italians' intentions was perhaps given by the Italian Foreign minister's letter which went so far as to suggest a provision for future transfer of powers from member states to the Community without treaty amendment. The Italians gave out—and it was well reported in the press— that they would be taking a moderate line, not pressing for a specific date for the start of Stage 2 of EMU and noting that Britain's hard ecu proposal must be taken seriously. A long and often contradictory list of proposals on political union had been drawn up by the presidency, including plans for a common foreign policy, extended Community competence, more majority voting, greater powers for the European Parliament and other matters. The precise purpose of this paper remained unclear. What I did not know was that behind the scenes the Italians had agreed with a proposal emanating from Germany and endorsed by Christian Democrat leaders from several European countries at an earlier caucus meeting that the GATT should not be discussed at the Council. Had there been such a discussion, of course, they would have found it more difficult to portray me as the odd one out and themselves as sea-green internationalists.

Chancellor Kohl had spoken publicly of the need to set deadlines for the work of the IGCs and for Stage 2 of EMU. But on the eve of the Rome Council he took a surprisingly soft line with Douglas Hurd, now Foreign Secretary, about his intentions. Herr Kohl suggested that perhaps the conclusions of the special Council could say something about a 'consensus building around the idea' of a specified starting date for Stage 2. But Douglas recorded his impression that the German Chancellor was not set on seeking even this much, and that he might be open to persuasion to drop references to any date. Moreover, Chancellor Kohl said that he did not oppose discussion of GATT in Rome. What he would not get into was negotiation of the Community position. He said that he recognized the importance of the Community's offer on agriculture in the GATT and accepted that December was a real deadline for the Uruguay round. He also recognized that Germany would have to compromise. He would be prepared to say tough things to the German farmers in due course—but not yet. Apparently he implied to Douglas that there could be a trade-off. If I was prepared to help him during the discussion of the GATT, he might be able to help me during the discussion on the EMU IGC. This, of course, turned out to be far from his real position.

I myself lunched with President Mitterrand at our embassy residence in Rome on the Saturday. He could not have been more friendly or amenable. I said that I was very disturbed at the Community's failure to agree a negotiating position on agriculture for the GATT negotiations. I understood that agreement had very nearly been reached after some sixteen hours of negotiations at the meeting of Agriculture and Trade ministers the previous day but had been blocked by the French. President Mitterrand said that this was all very difficult, that agriculture must not be looked at in isolation and that Europe—or more exactly France—should not be expected to make all the concessions at the GATT talks. He asked me when I proposed to raise the issue at the Council. I said that I would bring it up right at the beginning. I would demand that the Council make clear that the Community would table proposals within the next few days. Failure to do so would be a signal to the world that Europe was protectionist. President Mitterrand interjected that of course the Community was protectionist: that was the point of it. Clearly, there was not much to be gained by continuing this particular argument.

The French President did, however, agree with me—or so he claimed—

about the political union proposals. Indeed, he was highly critical of some of M. Delors's remarks and had no time at all for the European Parliament. Somewhat more surprisingly, President Mitterrand claimed that France, like Britain, wanted a common currency, not a single currency. This was not true. But let me be charitable—there may have been some confusion in translation. In any case, I detected no hostility or wish to force me into a corner.

I was too well versed in the ways of the Community to take all this *bonhomie* at face value. But even I was unprepared for the way things went once the Council formally opened. Sig. Andreotti made clear right at the beginning that there was no intention of discussing the GATT. I spoke briefly and took them to task for ignoring this crucial issue at such a time. I had hoped that someone other than me would intervene. But only Ruud Lubbers did and he raised a mild protest. Although something found its way into the communiqué, no one else was prepared to speak up for these imminent and crucial negotiations.

Then M. Delors reported on his recent meeting with Mr. Gorbachev. To my surprise, he proposed that the Council should issue a statement saying that the outer border of the Soviet Union must remain intact. Again I waited. But no one spoke. I just could not leave matters like this. I said that this was not for us in the Community to decide but for the peoples and Government of the Soviet Union. I pointed out that the Baltic States had in any case been illegally seized and incorporated in the USSR. In effect, we were denying them their claim to independence. M. Delors said that he had received an assurance from Mr. Gorbachev that the Baltic States would be freed, so we should not become alarmed on that point. I came back at him, saying that we had heard this sort of reassurance before from the Soviets; and, in any case, what about the other nations of the Soviet Union who might wish to leave it as well? At this point first Sr. González, then President Mitterrand and finally Chancellor Kohl intervened on my side and this ill-judged initiative foundered.

But the atmosphere went from bad for worse. The others were determined to insert in the communiqué provisions on political union, none of which I was prepared to accept. I said that I would not pre-empt the debate in the IGC and had a unilateral observation to this effect incorporated in the text. They also insisted on following the German proposal that Stage 2 of monetary union should begin on 1 January 1994. I would not accept this either. I had inserted in the communiqué the sentence:

> The United Kingdom, while ready to move beyond Stage 1 through the creation of a new monetary institution and a common Community currency, believes that decisions on the substance of that move should precede decisions on its timing.

They were not interested in compromise. My objections were heard in stony silence. I now had no support. I just had to say no.

In three years the European Community had gone from practical discussions about restoring order to the Community's finances to grandiose schemes of monetary and political union with firm timetables but no agreed substance—all without open, principled public debate on these questions either nationally or in European fora. Now at Rome the ultimate battle for the future of the Community had been joined. But I would have to return to London to win another battle on which the outcome in Europe would depend—that for the soul of the Parliamentary Conservative Party.

NOTE

1. The WEU was formed in 1948, principally for the purpose of military cooperation between Britain, France and the Benelux countries. Germany and Italy joined it in the 1950s. The WEU predated NATO, which has entirely overshadowed it.

CHAPTER 5

Speech at the College of Europe, Bruges, 20 September 1988

Margaret Thatcher

[Note by Robin Harris:] Measured by almost every criterion, the Bruges speech of September 1988 was the most important Mrs. Thatcher delivered during her time as Prime Minister. It was a direct response to the increasing interventionism and incipient federalism of the European Commission and its President, Jacques Delors. The pressure for European Economic and Monetary Union (EMU) was increasing. M. Delors had predicted that within ten years the Community would be the source of "80 per cent of our economic legislation, and perhaps even our fiscal and social legislation as well." In September he had addressed the British Trades Union Congress, advocating measures on collective bargaining to be taken at a European level.

But the Bruges speech was not limited to a rejection of this agenda. It also set out a new, alternative model for Europe—one of voluntary co-operation between independent nation states, free markets and open trade. Within the Conservative Party it exposed a gap, which in truth already existed, between a minority who were eager to see the merger of Britain with a new European superstate, and the majority who regarded such a prospect as unthinkable. In doing so, the Bruges speech can be said to have contributed towards the overthrow of Mrs. Thatcher as Prime Minister in 1990. But it also fundamentally reshaped political patterns and shifted public opinion on Europe, with consequences which, at the time of writing, are still unclear.

First, may I thank you for giving me the opportunity to return to Bruges—and in very different circumstances from my last visit shortly after the Zeebrugge ferry disaster, when Belgian courage and the devotion of your doctors and nurses saved so many British lives. Second, may I say what a pleasure it is to speak at the College of Europe under the distinguished leadership of its Rector, Professor Lukaszewski. The College plays a vital and increasingly important part in the life of the European Community. Third, may I also thank you for inviting me to deliver my address in this magnificent hall. What better place to speak of Europe's future than in a building which so gloriously recalls the greatness that Europe had already achieved over six hundred years ago?

Your city of Bruges has many other historical associations for us in Britain. Geoffrey Chaucer was a frequent visitor here. And the first book to be printed in the English language was produced here in Bruges by William Caxton.

BRITAIN AND EUROPE

Mr. Chairman, you have invited me to speak on the subject of Britain and Europe. Perhaps I should congratulate you on your courage. If you believe some of the things said and written about my views on Europe, it must seem rather like inviting Genghis Khan to speak on the virtues of peaceful co-existence!

I want to start by disposing of some myths about my country, Britain, and its relationship with Europe. And to do that I must say something about the identity of Europe itself.

Europe is not the creation of the Treaty of Rome. Nor is the European idea the property of any group or institution.

We British are as much heirs to the legacy of European culture as any other nation. Our links to the rest of Europe, the Continent of Europe, have been the *dominant* factor in our history. For three hundred years we were part of the Roman Empire, and our maps still trace the straight lines of the roads the Romans built. Our ancestors—Celts, Saxons and Danes—came from the Continent. Our nation was—in that favourite Community word—'restructured' under Norman and Angevin rule in the eleventh and twelfth centuries.

This year we celebrate the three hundredth anniversary of the Glorious Revolution, in which the British Crown passed to Prince William of Orange and Queen Mary.

Visit the great churches and cathedrals of Britain, read our literature and listen to our language: all bear witness to the cultural riches which we have drawn from Europe—and other Europeans from us.

We in Britain are rightly proud of the way in which, since Magna Carta in 1215, we have pioneered and developed representative institutions to stand as bastions of freedom. And proud too of the way in which for centuries Britain was a home for people from the rest of Europe who sought sanctuary from tyranny.

But we know that without the European legacy of political ideas we could not have achieved as much as we did. From classical and medieval thought we have borrowed that concept of the rule of law which marks out a civilized society from barbarism. And on that idea of Christendom—for long synonymous with Europe—with its recognition of the unique and spiritual nature of the individual, we still base our belief in personal liberty and other human rights.

Too often the history of Europe is described as a series of interminable wars and quarrels. Yet from our perspective today surely what strikes us most is our common experience. For instance, the story of how Europeans explored and colonized and—yes, without apology—civilized much of the world is an extraordinary tale of talent, skill and courage.

We British have in a special way contributed to Europe. Over the centuries we have fought to prevent Europe from falling under the dominance of a single power. We have fought and we have died for her freedom. Only miles from here in Belgium lie the bodies of 120,000 British soldiers who died in the First World War. Had it not been for that willingness to fight and to die, Europe would have been united long before now—but not in liberty, not in justice.

It was British support to resistance movements throughout the last war that helped to keep alive the flame of liberty in so many countries until the day of liberation.

Tomorrow, King Baudouin will attend a service in Brussels to commemorate the many brave Belgians who gave their lives in service with the Royal Air Force—a sacrifice which we shall never forget. It was from our island fortress that the liberation of Europe itself was mounted.

And still today we stand together. Nearly seventy thousand British servicemen are stationed on the mainland of Europe. All these things alone are proof of our commitment to Europe's future.

The European Community is *one* manifestation of that European identity. But it is not the only one. We must never forget that east of the Iron Curtain peoples who once enjoyed a full share of European culture, freedom and identity have been cut off from their roots. We shall always look on Warsaw, Prague and Budapest as great European cities. Nor should we forget that European values have helped to make the United States of America into the valiant defender of freedom which she has become.

EUROPE'S FUTURE

This is no arid chronicle of obscure facts from the dust-filled libraries of history. It is the record of nearly two thousand years of British involvement in Europe, co-operation with Europe and contribution to Europe, a contribution which today is as valid and as strong as ever.

Yes, we have looked also to wider horizons—as have others—and thank goodness for that, because Europe never would have prospered, and never will prosper, as a narrow-minded, inward-looking club.

The European Community belongs to *all* its members. It must reflect the traditions and aspirations of *all* its members.

And let me be quite clear: Britain does not dream of some cosy, isolated existence on the fringes of the European Community. Our destiny is in Europe, as part of the Community.

That is not to say that our future lies only in Europe. But nor does that of France or Spain or indeed any other member.

The Community is not an end in itself. Nor is it an institutional device to be constantly modified according to the dictates of some abstract intellectual concept. Nor must it be ossified by endless regulation. The European Community is the practical means by which Europe can ensure the future prosperity and security of its people in a world in which there are many other powerful nations and groups of nations.

We Europeans cannot afford to waste our energies on internal disputes or arcane institutional debates. They are no substitute for effective action. Europe has to be ready both to contribute in full measure to its own security and to compete commercially and industrially in a world in which success goes to the countries which encourage individual initiative and enterprise, rather than to those which attempt to diminish them.

This evening I want to set out some guiding principles for the future, which I believe will ensure that Europe does succeed, not just in economic and defence terms but also in the quality of life and the influence of its peoples.

WILLING CO-OPERATION BETWEEN SOVEREIGN STATES

My first guiding principle is this: willing and active co-operation between independent sovereign states is the best way to build a successful European Community. To try to suppress nationhood and concentrate power at the centre of a European conglomerate would be highly damaging and would jeopardize the objectives we seek to achieve. Europe will be stronger precisely because it has France as France, Spain as Spain, Britain as Britain, each with its own customs, traditions and identity. It would be folly to try to fit them into some sort of identikit European personality.

Some of the founding fathers of the Community thought that the United States of America might be its model. But the whole history of America is quite different from Europe. People went there to get away from the intolerance and constraints of life in Europe. They sought liberty and opportunity; and their strong sense of purpose has, over two centuries, helped create a new unity and pride in being American—just as our pride lies in being British, or Belgian, or Dutch, or German.

I am the first to say that on many great issues the countries of Europe should try to speak with a single voice. I want to see us work more closely on the things we can do better together than alone. Europe is stronger when we do so—whether it be in trade, in defence, or in our relations with the rest of the world.

But working more closely together does *not* require power to be centralized in Brussels or decisions to be taken by an appointed bureaucracy. Indeed, it is ironic that just when those countries such as the Soviet Union, which have tried to run everything from the centre, are learning that success depends on dispersing power and decisions away from the centre, some in the Community seem to want to move in the opposite direction. We have not successfully rolled back the frontiers of the state in Britain only to see them re-imposed at a European level, with a European super-state exercising a new dominance from Brussels.

Certainly we want to see Europe more united and with a greater sense of common purpose. But it must be in a way which preserves the different traditions, Parliamentary powers and sense of national pride in one's own country; for these have been the source of Europe's vitality through the centuries.

ENCOURAGING CHANGE

My second guiding principle is this: Community policies must tackle present problems in a *practical* way, however difficult that may be. If we cannot reform those Community policies which are patently wrong or ineffective and which are rightly causing public disquiet, then we shall not get the public's support for the Community's future development.

That is why the achievements of the European Council in Brussels last February are so important. It wasn't right that half the total Community budget was being spent on storing and disposing of surplus food. Now those stocks are being sharply reduced. It was absolutely right to decide that agriculture's share of the budget should be cut in order to free resources for other policies, such as helping the less well-off regions and training for jobs. It was right too to introduce tighter budgetary discipline to enforce these decisions and to bring total EC spending under better control.

Those who complained that the Community was spending so much time on financial detail missed the point. You cannot build on unsound foundations, financial or otherwise; and it was the fundamental reforms agreed last winter which paved the way for the remarkable progress which we have since made on the Single Market. But we cannot rest on what we have achieved to date. For example, the task of reforming the Common Agricultural Policy is far from complete. Certainly, Europe needs a stable and efficient farming industry. But the CAP has become unwieldy, inefficient and grossly expensive. Production of unwanted surpluses safeguards neither the income nor the future of farmers themselves. We must *continue* to pursue policies which relate supply more closely to market requirements, and which will reduce overproduction and limit costs. Of course, we must protect the villages and rural areas which are such an important part of our national life— but not by the instrument of agricultural prices.

Tackling these problems requires political courage. The Community will only damage itself in the eyes of its own people and the outside world if that courage is lacking.

EUROPE OPEN TO ENTERPRISE

My third guiding principle is the need for Community policies which encourage enterprise. If Europe is to flourish and create the jobs of the future, enterprise is the key. The basic framework is there: the Treaty of Rome itself was intended as a charter for economic liberty. But that is not how it has always been read, still less applied.

The lesson of the economic history of Europe in the seventies and eighties is that central planning and detailed control *don't* work, and that personal endeavour and initiative *do;* that a state-controlled economy is a recipe for low growth, and that free enterprise within a framework of law brings better results.

The aim of a Europe open to enterprise is the moving force behind the creation of the Single European Market by 1992. By getting rid of barriers, by making it possible for companies to operate on a Europe-wide scale, we can best compete with the United States, Japan and the other new economic powers emerging in Asia and elsewhere.

And that means action to *free* markets, action to *widen* choice, action to *reduce* government intervention. Our aim should *not* be more and more detailed regulation from the centre: it should be to deregulate and to remove the constraints on trade.

Britain has been in the lead in opening its markets to others. The City of London has long welcomed financial institutions from all over the world, which is why it is the biggest and most successful financial centre in Europe. We have opened our market for telecommunications equipment, introduced competition into the market for services and even into the network itself— steps which others in Europe are only now beginning to face. In air transport, we have taken the lead in liberalization and seen the benefits in cheaper fares and wider choice. Our coastal shipping trade is open to the merchant navies of Europe. I wish I could say the same of many other Community members.

Regarding *monetary matters,* let me say this: the key issue is *not* whether there should be a European Central Bank. The immediate and practical requirements are: to implement the Community's commitment to free movement of capital—in Britain we have it; and to the abolition throughout the Community of the exchange controls—in Britain we abolished them in 1979; to establish a genuinely free market in financial services, in banking, insurance, investment; to make greater use of the ecu. Britain is this autumn issuing ecu-denominated Treasury bills, and hopes to see other Community Governments increasingly do the same. These are the *real* requirements because they are what Community business and industry need, if they are to compete effectively in the wider world. And they are what the European consumer wants, for they will widen his choice and lower his costs.

It is to such basic practical steps that the Community's attention should be devoted. When those have been achieved, and sustained over a period of time, we shall be in a better position to judge the next moves.

It is the same with the *frontiers* between our countries. Of course we must make it easier for goods to pass through frontiers. Of course we must make it easier for our people to travel throughout the Community. But it is a matter of plain commonsense that we cannot totally abolish frontier controls if we are also to protect our citizens from crime and stop the movement of drugs, of terrorists, and of illegal immigrants. That was underlined graphically only three weeks ago, when one brave German customs officer, doing his duty on the frontier between Holland and Germany, struck a major blow against the terrorists of the IRA.

And before I leave the subject of the Single Market, may I say that we certainly do not need new regulations which raise the cost of employment and make Europe's labour market less flexible and less competitive with overseas suppliers. If we are to have a European Company Statute, it should contain the minimum regulations. And certainly we in Britain would fight attempts to introduce collectivism and corporatism at the European level—although what people wish to do in their own countries is a matter for them.

EUROPE OPEN TO THE WORLD

My fourth guiding principle is that Europe should not be protectionist. The expansion of the world economy requires us to continue the process of removing barriers to trade, and to do so in the multilateral negotiations in the GATT. It would be a betrayal if, while breaking down constraints on trade within Europe, the Community were to erect greater external protection. We must ensure that our approach to world trade is consistent with the liberalization we preach at home. We have a responsibility to give a lead on this, a responsibility which is particularly directed towards the less developed countries. They need not only aid; more than anything they need improved trading opportunities, if they are to gain the dignity of growing economic strength and independence.

EUROPE AND DEFENCE

My last guiding principle concerns the most fundamental issue: the European countries' role in defence. Europe must continue to maintain a sure defence through NATO. There can be no question of relaxing our efforts, even though it means taking difficult decisions and meeting heavy costs.

It is to NATO that we owe the peace that has been maintained over forty years. The fact is, things *are* going our way: the democratic model of a free enterprise society *has* proved itself superior; freedom *is* on the offensive, a peaceful offensive, the world over for the first time in my lifetime.

We must strive to maintain the United States's commitment to Europe's defence. That means recognizing the burden on their resources of the world role they undertake, and their point that their allies should play a full part in the defence of freedom, particularly as Europe grows wealthier. Increasingly they will look to Europe to play a part in out-of-area defence, as we have recently done in the Gulf. NATO and the WEU have long recognized where the problems with Europe's defences lie, and have pointed out the solutions. The time has come when we must give substance to our declarations about a strong defence effort with better value for money.

It's not an institutional problem. It's not a problem of drafting. It's something at once simpler and more profound: it is a question of political will and political courage, of convincing people in all our countries that we cannot rely for ever on others for our defence, but that each member of the Alliance must shoulder a fair share of the burden.

We must keep up public support for nuclear deterrence, remembering that obsolete weapons do not deter, hence the need for modernization. We must meet the requirements for effective conventional defence in Europe against Soviet forces, which are constantly being modernized. We should develop the WEU, not as an alternative to NATO, but as a means of strengthening Europe's contribution to the common defence of the West. Above all, at a time of change and uncertainty in the Soviet Union and Eastern Europe, we must preserve Europe's unity and resolve, so that whatever may happen our defence is sure.

At the same time, we must negotiate on arms control and keep the door wide open to co-operation on all the other issues covered by the Helsinki Accords.

But let us never forget that our way of life, our vision, and all that we hope to achieve is secured not by the rightness of our cause but by the strength of our defence. On this we must never falter, never fail.

THE BRITISH APPROACH

I believe it is not enough just to talk in general terms about a European vision or ideal. If we believe in it, we must chart the way ahead and identify the next steps. That's what I have tried to do this evening.

This approach does not require new documents. They are all there: the North Atlantic Treaty, the revised Brussels Treaty, and the Treaty of Rome, texts written by far-sighted men, a remarkable Belgian—Paul Henri Spaak—among them. However far we may want to go, the truth is that we can only get there one step at a time. What we need now is to take decisions on the next steps forward rather than let ourselves be distracted by Utopian goals. Utopia never comes, because we know we should not like it if it did.

Let Europe be a family of nations, understanding each other better, appreciating each other more, doing more together but relishing our national identity no less than our common European endeavour. Let us have a Europe which plays its full part in the wider world, which looks outward not inward, and which preserves that Atlantic Community—that Europe on both sides of the Atlantic—which is our noblest inheritance and our greatest strength.

May I thank you for the privilege of delivering this lecture in this great hall to this great College.

CHAPTER 6

Why the Norwegians Said No

Kate Hansen Bundt

Norway is, as Norwegian scholar Kate Hansen Bundt writes, the nation that has twice said no to "Europe." In 1972 the Norwegians held a consultative referendum, which advised their government against joining the European Community (EC). In 1994 a second referendum again produced a negative response, this time regarding a possible application for membership, the European Union (EU) created by the Maastricht treaty. Norway is the only country to have refused "Europe" in this way. But Hansen Bundt shows in this perceptive analysis how there is both more and less to Norway's "no" than meets the eye. On the one hand, Norwegian Euro-skepticism is deeply rooted in a society characterized by unusual geographical, socioeconomic, and cultural divisions. On the other hand, the prospects for a third referendum and EU membership are not as small as Norway's international reputation would indicate.

Kate Hansen Bundt is Director of Research at Europa-programmet, an Oslo-based think tank focusing on ongoing changes in European politics, economy, and security structures. She is particularly concerned with developments in Germany and central Europe, as well as European Union integration and enlargement. Her last book is Norway Said No *(2000), in Norwegian and also a Polish translation. She recently edited* Central Europe: Past, Present, and Future *(1996) and contributed to* Quo vadis, Germany? *(1998), both in Norwegian.*

In Finland foreign policy is decided by four people, in Sweden four hundred, in Denmark four hundred thousand, and in Norway four million.

Gro Harlem Brundtland, former prime minister of Norway

With editorial assistance by Ronald Tiersky.

"WHAT THE PEOPLE HAVE DECIDED,
ONLY THE PEOPLE CAN DISSOLVE"

Norway is a country roughly the size of unified Germany but with a population of only 4.4 million. Its pro-European governments have applied four times for membership in the European Community (EC) and European Union (EU), in 1962, 1967, 1970, and 1992. None of these applications went to fruition, however, and the Norwegian people themselves said no to joining the European integration process twice in referenda, in 1972 and 1994. If Norway is said to be a Euro-skeptical country, it is certainly a peculiar case.

The first three applications were made along with Great Britain's. French president Charles de Gaulle's veto of the British also became the main hindrance to Norway's entry in the 1960s. On the other hand, Norwegian governments reached membership application agreements with the EC in 1972, and once again with the Maastricht-created EU in 1994. But both times the Norwegians themselves backed away. Thin majorities rejected membership in ensuing referenda: 53.5 percent in 1972, and 52.2 percent in 1994.

Given the twenty-two-year time span, the nearly identical results are remarkable. On both occasions the Norwegian electorate was divided nearly evenly, with a minor victory for the No voters. But in 1994 almost one million voters were new since 1972. On the other hand, the main arguments and sociopolitical forces supporting the two Noes were almost identical. In 1994 as in 1972, the issue of joining the EC/EU uncovered a division in the electorate along a *center-periphery* axis, a center/periphery difference defined both geographically (a north/south cleavage) and sociologically (low versus high socioeconomic status). Thus, in 1994 it might have seemed as if nothing had changed in Norway during these years when Europe as a whole underwent a dramatic geopolitical revolution and remaking of institutions. Not only had the fall of the Berlin Wall (1989) ended the Cold War with the dissolution of the Soviet Union (1991); the collapse of Soviet domination and of the eastern and central European communist regimes had paved the way for a united Germany (1990), leaving the newly independent nations of the former Warsaw Pact with high hopes to join the EU and NATO.

To many people the negative outcome of the 1994 Norwegian referendum thus seemed paradoxical. Norway had been a committed NATO ally all through the Cold War period. Why should the country recoil from joining the EU, a political and economic organization that included almost all her allies, and that former neutrals such as Austria, Sweden, and Finland could accept?

It can be said that disappointment was indeed great for many Norwegians as well. Two interpretations were given domestically after the failed 1994 referendum. Among the No voters their victory was seen above all as a continuation of democratic Norwegian traditions. Not only was the second No a reaffirmation of the first people's decision in 1972, but both were seen as rooted in Norwegian traditions going back to the astonishingly democratic constitution of 1814, to the early introduction of parliamentarism in 1884, the peaceful dissolution of the Swedish-Norwegian Union in 1905, and the egalitarian ideals of the Norwegian welfare state throughout the twentieth century.

Among the defeated Yes voters, the country's national-democratic traditions and achievements were by no means denied, but the outcome was still interpreted as a chauvinistic and somewhat nationalistic or self-assertive decision. Some even suggested that Norwegian prestige and success at the Lillehammer XVII Winter Olympic Games deepened the No tendency heading into the referendum the following year. Among the most dedicated protagonists of membership a certain "elitist" disappointment among Yes voters also appeared, explaining the No as a victory of traditional values and provincialism in the countryside, which felt threatened by a sophisticated urban cosmopolitan culture and education.

But domestic explanations alone don't suffice. In 1994 resistance to EU membership was less than at any time before a solely "Norwegian affair."

The two Noes make Norway the only European nation ever to reject EC/EU membership.[1] But Norwegians are far from being the only people with doubts about different aspects of the European integration process. The 1992 Maastricht treaty, for example, triggered an uphill, complicated ratification process in several EU countries, and during the 1990s there were several national "opt-outs" regarding the Social Charter, the Single Currency, and other matters. There was some effect on the Norwegian process from these internal EU debates. The more federalist-inclined Maastricht treaty seems to have pushed Norway back from joining the EU in the 1990s, whereas Norwegians, at that point, might have voted to join the less binding EC framework that they rejected in 1972.

So the Norwegian case has both a domestic and a European level of explanation. Norway is unique in its relation to European integration, as is the Euroskepticism of its two referenda in 1972 and 1994. Moreover, psychology, as former Norwegian prime minister Kare Willoch once remarked, "is a heavily underestimated factor in political analysis." Perhaps a certain psychology is most important of all in explaining the "Norway-EU story" that follows. No other political issue has provoked such controversy in Norway in modern times than the relation of the country to European integration. It is a story of family quarrels, of divorces, and of close friends splitting up; of a political elite incapable of convincing its people of a policy it truly believed to be in the national interest; and it is also a story of vested political, geographical, ideological, and economic interests, cutting through traditional cleavages in Norwegian society. Behind all the rational interest factors, the decisive element was emotional, requiring psychological explanation.

1972 AND 1974: EXPLAINING THE REFERENDA RESULTS

External causes both times brought to a vote the issue of Norwegian membership in European integration. Great changes in European international politics as well as evolution of the EC/EU itself were at issue, in the 1960s and in the 1990s. Both times Norwegian leaders were worried about being marginalized, meaning that Norway would lose influence in European and Atlantic affairs. And both in 1972 and 1994 some of Norway's traditional strategic and economic partners in the European Free Trade Area (EFTA), which Norway had joined in 1960, changed their policy toward the EC/EU. In the 1960s it was Britain that turned on, and then off the Norwegian campaign, by her applications (1961, 1967, 1970) and subsequent EC refusals (1963, 1967). Britain finally joined the EC along with Denmark in 1973, but in the 1990s the Swedes played the earlier British role. The Swedish application in 1991, and to a lesser extent the Finnish application that followed in 1992, took the Norwegians by surprise, more or less obliging the Norwegian government to put the issue on the agenda again.

In addition, the 1994 referendum campaign resembled that of 1972, not only in the result but also in arguments put forth, campaign strategy, and the social bases of the opposed electorates. The situation after 1994, however, is different from in the years after 1972. Norwegian cooperation with the EC was a relatively minor issue then, with a free trade agreement reached in 1973 but little more. Today, Norway's relation to European integration has become a pervasive part of Norwegian politics and society, even if the referendum formally took the issue off the table. Even during a recent period when Norway was governed by a coalition of three No parties, no changes were made to existing Norwegian adjustments to the EU *acquis communautaire*, the totality of its policies, especially as concerned the European Economic Area (EEA) agreement of 1994.[2]

True enough, the first referendum in 1972 took place during the period when Norway entered her oil age. Increasing petroleum industry income throughout the 1970s and 1980s permitted an independent and to some extent different economic development in Norway than in the EC, whose economies were at that time in recession. By contrast, the EU area has now become economically reinvigorated. Norway cannot ignore this.

DECIDING HOW TO DECIDE

In any case, the Norwegian choice for or against the EC/EU in 1972 and 1994 was a national issue; thus, the question of what decision-making procedure would be used—parliamentary or referendum—became quite crucial, with the capacity to affect the outcome.

Choice of the referendum was a novelty in postwar Norway. Since 1814 a total of four had been held, the last (lifting a 1919 prohibition on alcohol) in 1926. According to the 1814 constitution, it was the Parliament, or *Storting,* that must decide, by three-quarters majority, on issues involving Norway's sovereignty. True, in 1949 Norway had joined NATO without asking the people, notwithstanding that this was a highly controversial decision both among politicians and in public opinion at that time. But already by 1962 the Parliament decided that a referendum would, at the appropriate time, decide Norway's relation to European integration. The 1949 decision to join NATO was much more vital and, given Norway's geopolitical situation, could not be left open to popular moods—even, or especially, since many Norwegians were worried that joining NATO would provoke the nearby Soviet Union. The decision to go to a referendum on European integration was mainly due to the fact of the internal split on the European issue in most of the major political parties.

The two referenda in 1972 and 1994 were, it must be emphasized, *advisory* rather than constitutionally binding votes. Yet it is now unthinkable to let the Storting settle the question, even with a three-quarters majority. The principle has become, "What the people have decided, only the people can dissolve." Without a positive referendum vote, Norway probably will never become an EU member.

THE DOMESTIC SITUATION: ELECTORATE
AND POLITICANS OUT OF STEP

Since the beginning of the 1960s an establishment political and economic elite strongly in favor of membership has stood against a Euro-skeptic grass-roots mass opinion. But the European issue also cross-cuts the traditional cleavages in Norwegian politics and society, such that strange sociopolitical and socioeconomic alliances are formed.

In both the 1972 and 1994 campaigns against EC/EU membership, rich farmers were allied with communists, nationalists with internationalists, and urban cultural radicals with religious fundamentalists from the countryside. In favor of membership, the main bulk of the establishment-governing Labor party was allied with its traditional political opponent, the large Conservative party. The main cleavage was, however, territorial, with a stronghold of No voters in the countryside opposing the Yes voters in the main cities and centers around the capital of Oslo.

Both times the Yes side had very good cards to play. The Labor party, Norway's largest and most influential party, was in office both in 1972 and 1994. It was supported by the bulk of the Norwegian business community. And in 1994, contrary to 1972, the Norwegian mass media on the whole supported membership. Why then did the Yes vote lose out? Labor's voters were split and there was a minor split as well among the party's leaders, with the anti-EU Labor party leaders establishing their own campaign organizations. Thus, the Labor party majority could not campaign as early or enthusiastically as it wanted, fearing a formal party split. The final decision on the party's EU position in 1994 was in fact left to local party organizations, and the big Norwegian Trade Union Confederation (LO) voted No in 1994, as opposed to its Yes stand in 1972.

The No side possessed four advantages. First, a No campaign was organized inside the governing Labor party both in 1972 and 1994. Second, opponents of EU membership had a strong constituency in public opinion and the grass roots. The agriculture and fisheries sectors, profoundly against membership, provided financial support and intense activism in the campaigns. Third, and very important, the No side ("Nei til EF" or "No to the EC") mobilized much earlier than the other side. Sensing the 1972 referendum on the way, the No side was active already from 1970. The 1994 referendum found the "No to the EU" side mobilized already since 1989–1990, first to discredit the EC-EFTA negotiations for a "European Economic Area," then, in 1992 following Norways' new application to join the EU, for the almost certain referendum.

The No side stressed the negative impact membership would have on Norwegian self-determination. The Yes side emphasized the positive impact on Norway's economy, security, and influence in Europe. How these arguments succeeded in convincing voters correlated with various social, economic, geographic, and political variables.

Attitudes toward EC/EU membership generally correspond with socioeconomic status. Simply put, a higher income and education are correlated with a favorable attitude toward Norway's membership. This correlation was even stronger in 1994 than in 1972, a change perhaps the result of diminished impact of the well-educated 1960s radical leftists.

Geography is another crucial variable. Regional cleavages over the EC/EU issue are remarkable both in strength and stability. In 95 percent of local governments (a total of 435), the Yes or No vote was the same in 1994 as in 1972. The general pattern has been that of center versus periphery, that is, urban regions favorable to membership versus rural regions against it. The core of the Yes voters are found in and around the capital of Oslo, the No voters are densest by far in the rural north of Norway.

The explanation is rather clear (see table 6.1), mainly the importance of primary industries—agriculture and fisheries in the rural northern regions voting 93 percent combined No in 1972, 94 percent combined No in 1994!—versus the Yes vote of urban and industrial growth areas around Oslo. It seems evident that a referendum exposes regional differences whereas national party politics, life in the Storting, buffers them, since national parties want a unified point of view on each main political issue for their electorate.

Table 6.1   Percentage of No votes in the 1994 Norwegian referendum, by region

Oslo	33
Oslofjord region	47
Eastern Norway	53
West Norway	58
Trondelag County	58
North Norway	72

Party politics were central in 1972, and in 1994 it seemed that little had changed. A big majority of the Labor party anchored the Yes vote, as said, along with the Conservatives. On the No side, in 1972 and again in 1994, were the Center party (previously called the Agrarian party), the Christian People's party, and a small Socialist Left party.

The Liberal party, Norway's second oldest, split and then reunited over the European issue. This illustrated the fact that split parties lose votes whereas No parties tend to gain votes. The winners of the 1973 and 1993 general elections, which both turned into "EC/EU elections," were all No parties.

Gender, public versus private occupation, and age are also indicators of Euro-skepticism or Euro-enthusiasm. Gender seemed to have no correlation with referendum voting in 1972, when about 51 percent of men and women voted No. But by 1994 women had increased to 57 percent No voters while the male No vote had declined to 48 percent. This might be explained by the emancipation of women increasing throughout the 1970s, which, among other things, changed their position in the labor market, a large number finding jobs in the public sector. With regard to occupation, in 1972 there was a near-even split, 46-45 percent, between private and public sector workers. In 1994 public sector employees voted No to the tune of 53 percent, while the private sector No vote declined somewhat, to 43 percent. In the agriculture and fisheries sector the No vote, as mentioned, remained adamant at 93-94 percent over the two decades. Clearer it couldn't be.

To sum up, the EC/EU issue uncovered a deep cleavage in 1972 and again in 1994 between the Norwegian people and its elites, and between the center (or the Oslo-centered south) and the periphery (or the rural north). In socioeconomic terms, the further down the social ladder, opposition to membership grows and tends to grow stronger. High education and income produce greater Yes votes for EU membership. The center/periphery gap is both geographical and social, a difference between the cosmopolitan, economically advanced area around Oslo and the rural, agriculture/fishing economy of the north.

Economic interest plays a huge role in attitudes toward joining the EU. Norwegian farmers are strongly subsidized and there were strong indications that Norwegian agriculture would get less from the EU's Common Agricultural Policy (CAP) than the subsidies received from the national budget.

Opposition by fishermen was similarly self-interested. First, they feared having to share their fish quotas with the EU fleet, well-known for its huge capacity. Second, they feared Norway losing influence on future regimes for fishery management. Nevertheless the fishermen were somewhat split themselves, with the No majority worried about the quotas and influence but a minority on the refining side espousing a Yes vote to gain free access to EU markets. The Norwegian government had to pay attention to the fishermen, whose 30 billion Kroner represent about 9 percent of Norway's total yearly exports.

But of course economic self-interest of farmers and fishermen—approximately 5 percent of the rural workforce as such—does not explain the entire No movement in rural areas, nor is the national interest of having a viable, vital farming and fishing sector a matter of the two groups alone. Throughout the postwar period Norwegian authorities have pursued a "rural friendly" policy. This was due first to strategic considerations, to securing a strong "buffer" zone in the north to deter expansion of Soviet influence, just across the border. The unusual scattered settlement pattern along the extremely long Norwegian coastline has given the fishing industry a particularly crucial place in Norwegian regional policy, since fishing is the major economic activity along the coast. To secure settlement on equal terms all over the country, a whole range of economic support schemes has been established. Since the rural and coastal areas benefited disproportionately from Oslo's regional policies, it was logical to believe that the EU's increasingly market-oriented economic culture could only disadvantage them. In addition, the rural parts of Norway would be still further from the power center in the EU than in the home country. Thus the slogan, "It's a long way to Oslo, but much longer to Brussels."

As for political reasons for saying No to the EU, the long periods when Norway was under foreign rule—first in a union with Denmark (1380–1814) and then in union with Sweden (1814–1905)—indicate why the concept of national self-determination, of being master in your own house, resonates so strongly in Norway, whereas the concept of "union" has a negative connotation. Given that the union with Sweden lasted until 1905 and the drive for Norway's independence corresponded with democratic development, opposition to EC/EU membership often has been seen as a continuation of these great advances. Rational or not, the concept of "union" has a particular Norwegian significance, meaning a vague threat to Norway's independence and freedom of choice. In this perspective, the Maastricht treaty complicated the 1994 referendum by replacing the looser EC with the more federalist EU.

The well-known Norwegian sociologist Stein Rokkan explained the center/periphery gap as much due to Norway's subordination for centuries to other Scandinavian "masters."[3] In particular, Danish and Swedish dominance in Norway were channeled through the cities; consequently, the central authority had the cities as their base and never managed to penetrate the periphery, which remained opposed to the life-style and culture of the urban areas. Some of these cultural differences have survived the homogenization that has occured during the post-World War II prosperity. Three historical countercultures, so defined by Tor Bjorklund, have persisted: the teetotal movement, the Lutheran lay movement, and the struggle for a language based on the Norwegian rural dialects ("new Norwegian"), to combat Danish influence in standard urban Norwegian.

THE INTERNATIONAL CONTEXT:
NORWAY IN A CHANGING EUROPE

Given the demise of communism and divided Europe, it should have been easier in 1994 than in 1972 to get a Yes referendum vote on joining the EU, especially the few percent needed for victory. Why was this not the case?

By 1992 the Norwegian prime minister, Mrs. Gro Harlem Brundtland, had concluded negotiations with the EU on the European Economic Area, and Sweden and Finland both had applied for EU membership. Opinion polls indicated a growing movement favorable to Norwegian membership as well. The EC in the 1980s and then the EU at the beginning of the 1990s seemed to many Norwegians to be truly pan-European organizations. By the time of the Norwegian referendum the EU had even announced its plans for eastern enlargement.

By 1994 the situation was in this respect contrary to 1972. At the earlier time the No side was able to argue that Norwegian EC membership would accentuate the two-bloc Europe. It would be bad for Europe and perhaps dangerous for Norway. However, after the European revolution of 1989–1991, parts of the No side in Norway argued that only *after* the EU's eastern extension occurs should Norway reconsider its own membership.

As opposed to 1972, in 1994 the Norwegian governing parties sought a common solution regarding all the Nordic countries. Membership for Finland, Sweden, and Norway could pave the way for Iceland as well. With Denmark inside since 1972, a strong Nordic block inside the EU might emerge. A hoped-for domino effect in holding three Nordic referenda—Finland first, then Sweden, and finally Norway—would possibly increase Yes support in Norway.

There was a notable difference however. Sweden and Finland had serious economic difficulties that EU membership could ameliorate, whereas Norway's economy was in much better shape. Nevertheless, economic benefit from EU membership was the main argument put forward by the Norwegian political and business elites in 1994, as had been the case in 1972. But whereas 63 percent of the Finns and 52 percent of the Swedes equated EU membership with economic benefits, only 28 percent of the Norwegians thought this, and 31 percent of the Norwegians told pollsters they believed the national economic situation would worsen with EU membership. As opposed to Swedish and Finnish exports, Norway's main exports are global commodities: 60 percent of net export is made up of offshore oil and natural gas, fisheries, and shipping. Thus, the Norwegian trading perspective is necessarily broader, or rather less Europe-bound, than that of EU members. In fact, because Norway is a large exporter of raw materials, Norwegian interests often contradict those of continental European partner countries.

THE SEA, OIL, AND GAS

Norway is the most sea-oriented and also the most sea-dependent country in Europe. The enormous sea areas under Norwegian jurisdiction, more or less 2,000,000 square kilometers, considered with Norway's territory, make the country approximately equivalent in size to the entire EU before the last enlargement. Norway has been described therefore as "a small nation with the economy of a giant." Or to put it differently, the country is "a strange animal in the European zoo." And it seems obvious that in a country where *80 percent* of the population lives less than ten kilometers from the sea, where the main pillars of economic wealth are found, there should be very different economic and political priorities than in a country with a land-based economy.

Norway's merchant fleet, the world's eighth largest, brings in 14 percent of total export income. EU membership would be more or less irrelevant to this sector, because shipping is global in character and is still an industry denominated in U.S. dollars. This latter factor could create particular distortions if Norway were to join the euro-zone, especially so long as the euro remains weak compared to the dollar.

Offshore oil and natural gas, however, are the main pillars of Norway's economic strength and her peculiarity among European countries. Since the early 1970s, Norway has become the largest oil-producing country in Europe and the third largest oil-exporting country in the world after Saudi Arabia and Russia, as well as the second largest supplier of natural gas to Europe. Largely because of this, the Norwegian state budget has run in surplus for the past ten to fifteen years.

Oil is transported on ships and operates in a global market, whereas natural gas, which has to be transported through pipelines, depends on a regional market. Hence, all Norwegian gas is exported to Europe. In 1998 about 20 percent of EU natural gas imports came from Norway, approximately 22 percent in Germany, and 28 percent in France and Belgium. The outlook is for increases in these percentages, to between 30 and 40 percent, respectively. The economic differences of interest between Norway and the continental countries are evident, even if modulated by other convergences.

THE IMPACT OF NEUTRALITY VERSUS NATO MEMBERSHIP

Whereas applications for EU membership by the cold war neutral countries—Sweden, Finland, and Austria (but not Switzerland)—were a break with the past, Norway's EU application was considered, at home and abroad, as a continuation of the country's committed alliance policy. It turned out, however, that whereas concerns about external security added strength to the pro membership side in the neutral countries, particularly Finland, the country most exposed to developments in Russia, in Norway concerns about security had little or no visible effect on votes in the 1994 referendum.

Norway, which had been occupied by Nazi Germany in spite of its proclaimed neutrality policy, understandably abandoned neutrality for NATO in 1949. U.S. guarantees did what neutrality could not: keep Norway safe from all threats whatsoever in its near surroundings. NATO's continuation despite the end of the cold war allowed the No side in 1994 to argue that EU membership would not offer Norway, which already had access to the EU Single Market through the EEA, anything important that it did not already have. The North Atlantic Cooperation Council (NACC) and the Partnership for Peace (PfP) innovations showed NATO was the more dynamic organization anyway, when compared with vague EU plans in the Maastricht treaty for a Common Foreign and Security Policy and a European Security and Defense Identity. Many Norwegians believe that such plans would weaken NATO and reduce American interest in European security, and all the more so if they were to succeed. Indeed, in 1994 even the Yes side could only admit that the Atlantic connection in security matters was more reliable than the European Union.

THE EU'S INTERNAL DEVELOPMENT
AND NORWEGIAN ATTITUDES

Opposition to the Maastricht treaty's plan for a more unified "Europe" had probably the most significant effect in producing the No outcome in the 1994 referendum.

The No side stigmatized Maastricht's federalist character. It defended "national self-determination" against joining in a political integration that most probably was leading toward a federal European supranational state with a serious democratic deficit. The favorable parties, it must be said, did very little to impart nuances to this vision of a supranational union with old national states gradually fading away. Quite to the contrary, the Yes side argued implicitly that this process was inevitable. Its main argument was that national self-determination was becoming an illusion in a world of interdependence and globalization. The EU was portrayed as the means to regain democratic control, necessarily beyond the level of nation-states.

The Norwegian anti-federalists had counterparts in all the European countries, of course, but most of all in the EFTA and former EFTA free-trade association countries, with Britain and Denmark being the most reluctant "Maastricht Europeans." Seen in this light, the Norwegian opposition to a federal superstate was in line with strong minorities, in some cases majorities, in several EU member states.

CONCLUSION: A THIRD REFERENDUM?

As one of Europe's small nations Norway can neither shape the institutions and structures of Europe nor escape them. Heavily dependent on global and European trade regimes and on overall political and strategic developments in Europe, Norway in strategic terms has few choices other than to adapt to realities created by others. In the year 2000 one might make a double conclusion about the debate in 1994: the opponents of EU membership tended to overestimate Norway's independent position and freedom of maneuver outside the EU, while proponents of membership probably overestimated the impact membership could have on Norway's influence in Brussels, as well as the extent of the country's isolation and marginalization outside.

Nevertheless, Norway is not internationally isolated, nor is it a true EU outsider. Norway has no vote in EU decision-making processes, yet it participates in the Single Market through the EEA agreement in force since January 1994. Norwegian manufactured goods and services therein have full access to the EU market, and a stable framework is assured for commercial cooperation with main trading partners. In 1997 Norway even joined the Schengen agreement, which created a common European external border control. This continued the old Nordic passport union after Sweden and Finland became EU members. In addition to these formal structures, Norway has, to quote former foreign affairs minister Knut Vollebaek, a "whole toolbox" of international links and memberships at its disposal. These include NATO, the UN, EFTA, the OSCE, the Council of Europe, the WEU, and several regional arrangements such as the Nordic and Nordic–Baltic Cooperation Group, the Barents Council, and the Council of the Baltic Sea States. Norway has also played a significant role as a neutral peace intermediary, for example in the Middle East conflict and in Latin America. This peace role might have suffered had Norway been an EU member.

On the other hand, the EU is engaged again in a process of transformation likely to change the size and character of the union. Especially if monetary union is well completed and current opt-outs (Britain, Sweden, and Denmark) join; if the foreign policy and military initiatives are successfully launched;

and if eastern enlargement occurs, Norway could hardly avoid a new consideration of its own membership.

But if enlargement loosens the union, the same result might ensue. A more flexible EU, where member states could choose their areas of integration, would probably be more attractive to anti-federalist Norwegians. The Danish no to the euro in autumn 2000 indicates that this development cannot be ruled out. The current foreign affairs minister and leader of the Labor party, Torbjorn Jagland, is already talking of sending a new membership application during the next parliament, 2001–2005.

Yet, even if external events once again put EU membership on Norway's agenda, domestic political currents will be once again decisive. No political party on the Yes side would raise this sensitive issue without a significant shift in public opinion in favor of membership. As foreign affairs minister Jagland puts the matter, "A third No would be totally devastating. We cannot make another application before we are certain of getting a Yes vote at a referendum." But this is not yet the case.

But is Norway dancing so much out of line after all? In 1994 when a tiny 2.2 percent of the vote kept Norway out of the EU, there was widespread Euro-skeptical opposition to the supranational aspirations of the Maastricht treaty in many member and potential member countries. Seen against the perspective of large Euro-skeptical minorities, and a few Euro-skeptical majorities, the Norwegian No in 1994 was not as unique as commonly understood both abroad and, one must add, by both sides in the domestic debate.

Thus, Norway is just one of many "strange animals in the European zoo," unique but not so peculiar after all.

NOTES

1. It should be mentioned that Greenland, which became an EC member as a consequence of Danish membership in 1973, quit the EC in 1985.

2. The European Economic Area (EEA) consists of the fifteen EU countries and three EFTA countries (Norway, Iceland, and Liechtenstein), whereas the fourth EFTA country, Switzerland, chose to stay outside. Through the EEA agreement, the EFTA countries are part of the EU's internal market.

3. Stein Rokkan, "Norway: Numerical Democracy and Corporate Pluralism," in, Political Opposition in Western Democracies, ed. Robert A. Dahl (New Haven, Conn.: Yale University Press, 1957), pp. 70–115.

SELECTED REFERENCES AND FURTHER READING IN ENGLISH

Bjorklund, Tor. "The Three Nordic 1994 Referenda Concerning Membership in the EU." In *Cooperation and Conflict*. Vol. 31(1). Thousand Oaks, Calif.: Sage, 1996.

Einhorn, Eric S., and John Logue. "Scandanavia: Still the Middle Way?" In *Europe Today: National Politics, European Integration, and European Security,* ed. Ronald Tiersky. Lanham, Md.: Rowman & Littlefied, 1999.

Gaarder, Godrun. "Norway—Outside the EU." In *Europe at the End of the 90s,* ed. Jon Bingen and W. Schütze. Oslo: Europa-programmet, 1996.

Haidar, Knut. *Norway: Center and Periphery* (2000).

Ingebritsen, Cristina. *The Nordic States and the European Union: From Economic Interdependence to Political Integration.* Ithaca, N.Y.: Cornell University Press, 1998.

Shaffer, William R. *Politics, Parties, and Parliaments: Political Change in Norway.* Columbus: Ohio State University Press, 1998.

CHAPTER 7

Back to the Future: Instability in Europe after the Cold War

John J. Mearsheimer

John J. Mearsheimer is the R. Wendell Harrison Distinguished Service Professor at the University of Chicago. He is codirector of Chicago's Program on International Security Policy. He is the author of Liddell Hart and the Weight of History *(1988) and* Conventional Deterrence *(1983). Mearsheimer is best known, however, for his vigorous reassertion of the realist perspective in international security matters, as expressed in his editorship (with Stephen Van Evera and others) of the journal* International Security *and especially in the controversial article reproduced here, "Back to the Future: Instability in Europe after the Cold War." "Back to the Future" caused a salutary political and intellectual firestorm on its publication because its argumentation contradicted rosy liberal internationalist predictions, or hopes, of an undisturbed European peace after the demise of communism and the Soviet Union. Forecasting the kinds of wars and violence that consumed the Balkans a short time later, Mearsheimer became an early, frank advocate of outright partition of Bosnia, even at the expense of shrinking it to the gain of Serbia and Croatia, to stop the killing. A few years later Mearsheimer published "The False Promise of International Institutions," (*International Security *19, no. 3[Winter 1994/95]: 5–49), reprinted several times in international affairs readers.*

The profound changes now underway in Europe have been widely viewed as harbingers of a new age of peace. With the Cold War over, it is said, the threat

From John J. Mearsheimer, "Back to the Future: Instability in Europe after the Cold War," *International Security* 15, no. 1 (Summer 1990): 5-56. © by the President and Fellows of Harvard College and the Massachusetts Institute of Technology; reprinted by permission of the publisher.

of war that has hung over Europe for more than four decades is lifting. Swords can now be beaten into ploughshares; harmony can reign among the states and peoples of Europe. Central Europe, which long groaned under the massive forces of the two military blocs, can convert its military bases into industrial parks, playgrounds, and condominiums. Scholars of security affairs can stop their dreary quarrels over military doctrine and balance assessments, and turn their attention to finding ways to prevent global warming and preserve the ozone layer. European leaders can contemplate how to spend peace dividends. So goes the common view.

This article assesses this optimistic view by exploring in detail the consequences for Europe of an end to the Cold War. Specifically, I examine the effects of a scenario under which the Cold War comes to a complete end. The Soviet Union withdraws all of its forces from Eastern Europe, leaving the states in that region fully independent. Voices are thereupon raised in the United States, Britain, and Germany, arguing that American and British military forces in Germany have lost their principal *raison d'être*, and these forces are withdrawn from the Continent. NATO and the Warsaw Pact then dissolve; they may persist on paper, but each ceases to function as an alliance.[1] As a result, the bipolar structure that has characterized Europe since the end of World War II is replaced by a multipolar structure. In essence, the Cold War we have known for almost half a century is over, and the postwar order in Europe is ended.[2]

How would such a fundamental change affect the prospects for peace in Europe?[3] Would it raise or lower the risk of war?

I argue that the prospects for major crises and war in Europe are likely to increase markedly if the Cold War ends and this scenario unfolds. The next decades in a Europe without the superpowers would probably not be as violent as the first 45 years of this century, but would probably be substantially more prone to violence than the past 45 years.

This pessimistic conclusion rests on the argument that the distribution and character of military power are the root causes of war and peace. Specifically, the absence of war in Europe since 1945 has been a consequence of three factors: the bipolar distribution of military power on the Continent; the rough military equality between the two states comprising the two poles in Europe, the United States and the Soviet Union; and the fact that each superpower was armed with a large nuclear arsenal.[4] Domestic factors also affect the likelihood of war, and have helped cause the postwar peace. Most importantly, hyper-nationalism helped cause the two world wars, and the decline of nationalism in Europe since 1945 has contributed to the peacefulness of the postwar world. However, factors of military power have been most important in shaping past events, and will remain central in the future.

The departure of the superpowers from Central Europe would transform Europe from a bipolar to a multipolar system.[5] Germany, France, Britain, and perhaps Italy would assume major power status; the Soviet Union would decline from superpower status but would remain a major European power, giving rise to a system of five major powers and a number of lesser powers. The resulting system would suffer the problems common to multipolar systems, and would therefore be more prone to instability.[6] Power inequities could also appear; if so, stability would be undermined further.

The departure of the superpowers would also remove the large nuclear arsenals they now maintain in Central Europe. This would remove the pacifying effect that these weapons have had on European politics. Four principal scenarios are possible. Under the first scenario, Europe would become nuclear-free, thus eliminating a central pillar of order in the Cold War era. Under the second scenario, the European states do not expand their arsenals to compensate for the departure of the superpowers' weapons. In a third scenario, nuclear proliferation takes place, but is mismanaged; no steps are taken to dampen the many dangers inherent in the proliferation process. All three of these scenarios would raise serious risks of war.

In the fourth and least dangerous scenario, nuclear weapons proliferate in Europe, but the process is well-managed by the current nuclear powers. They take steps to deter preventive strikes on emerging nuclear powers, to set boundaries on the proliferation process by extending security umbrellas over the neighbors of emerging nuclear powers, to help emerging nuclear powers build secure deterrent forces, and to discourage them from deploying counterforce systems that threaten their neighbors' deterrents. This outcome probably provides the best hope for maintaining peace in Europe. However, it would still be more dangerous than the world of 1945–90. Moreover, it is not likely that proliferation would be well-managed.

Three counter-arguments might be advanced against this pessimistic set of predictions of Europe's future. The first argument holds that the peace will be preserved by the effects of the liberal international economic order that has evolved since World War II. The second rests on the observation that liberal democracies very seldom fight wars against each other, and holds that the past spread of democracy in Europe has bolstered peace, and that the ongoing democratization of Eastern Europe makes war still less likely. The third argument maintains that Europeans have learned from their disastrous experiences in this century that war, whether conventional or nuclear, is so costly that it is no longer a sensible option for states.

But the theories behind these arguments are flawed, as I explain; hence their prediction of peace in a multipolar Europe is flawed as well.

Three principal policy prescriptions follow from this analysis. First, the United States should encourage a process of limited nuclear proliferation in Europe. Specifically, Europe will be more stable if Germany acquires a secure nuclear deterrent, but proliferation does not go beyond that point. Second, the United States should not withdraw fully from Europe, even if the Soviet

Union pulls its forces out of Eastern Europe. Third, the United States should take steps to forestall the re-emergence of hyper-nationalism in Europe.

METHODOLOGY: HOW SHOULD WE THINK ABOUT EUROPE'S FUTURE?

Predictions on the future risk of war and prescriptions about how best to maintain peace should rest on general theories about the causes of war and peace. This point is true for both academics and policymakers. The latter are seldom self-conscious in their uses of theory. Nevertheless, policymakers' views on the future of Europe are shaped by their implicit preference for one theory of international relations over another. Our task, then, is to decide which theories best explain the past, and will most directly apply to the future; and then to employ these theories to explore the consequences of probable scenarios.

Specifically, we should first survey the inventory of international relations theories that bear on the problem. What theories best explain the period of violence before the Cold War? What theories best explain the peace of the past 45 years? Are there other theories that explain little about pre-Cold War Europe, or Cold War Europe, but are well-suited for explaining what is likely to occur in a Europe without a Soviet and American military presence?

Next, we should ask what these theories predict about the nature of international politics in a post-Cold War multipolar Europe. Will the causes of the postwar peace persist, will the causes of the two world wars return, or will other causes arise?

We can then assess whether we should expect the next decades to be more peaceful, or at least as peaceful, as the past 45 years, or whether the future is more likely to resemble the first 45 years of the century. We can also ask what policy prescriptions these theories suggest.

The study of international relations, like the other social sciences, does not yet resemble the hard sciences. Our stock of theories is spotty and often poorly tested. The conditions required for the operation of established theories are often poorly understood. Moreover, political phenomena are highly complex; hence precise political predictions are impossible without very powerful theoretical tools, superior to those we now possess. As a result, all political forecasting is bound to include some error. Those who venture to predict, as I do here, should therefore proceed with humility, take care not to claim unwarranted confidence, and admit that later hindsight will undoubtedly reveal surprises and mistakes.

Nevertheless, social science *should* offer predictions on the occurrence of momentous and fluid events like those now unfolding in Europe. Predictions can inform policy discourse. They help even those who disagree to frame their ideas, by clarifying points of disagreement. Moreover, predictions of events soon to unfold provide the best tests of social science theories, by making clear what it was that given theories have predicted about those events. In short, the world can be used as a laboratory to decide which theories best explain international politics. In this article I employ the body of theories that I find most persuasive to peer into the future. Time will reveal whether these theories in fact have much power to explain international politics.

The next section offers an explanation for the peacefulness of the post–World War II order. The section that follows argues that the end of the Cold War is likely to lead to a less stable Europe. Next comes an examination of the theories underlying claims that a multipolar Europe is likely to be as peaceful, if not more peaceful, than Cold War Europe. The concluding section suggests policy implications that follow from my analysis.

EXPLAINING THE "LONG PEACE"

The past 45 years represent the longest period of peace in European history.[7] During these years Europe saw no major war, and only two minor conflicts (the 1956 Soviet intervention in Hungary and the 1974 Greco-Turkish war in Cyprus). Neither conflict threatened to widen to other countries. The early years of the Cold War (1945-63) were marked by a handful of major crises, although none brought Europe to the brink of war. Since 1963, however, there have been no East-West crises in Europe. It has been difficult—if not impossible—for the last two decades to find serious national security analysts who have seen a real chance that the Soviet Union would attack Western Europe.

The Cold War peace contrasts sharply with European politics during the first 45 years of this century, which saw two world wars, a handful of minor wars, and a number of crises that almost resulted in war. Some 50 million Europeans were killed in the two world wars; in contrast, probably no more than 15,000 died in the two post-1945 European conflicts.[8] Cold War Europe is far more peaceful than early twentieth-century Europe.

Both Europeans and Americans increasingly assume that peace and calm are the natural order of things in Europe and that the first 45 years of this century, not the most recent, were the aberration. This is understandable, since Europe has been free of war for so long that an ever-growing proportion of the Western public, born after World War II, has no direct experience with great-power war. However, this optimistic view is incorrect.

The European state system has been plagued with war since its inception. During much of the seventeenth and eighteenth centuries war was underway somewhere on the European Continent.[9] The nineteenth century held longer periods of peace, but also several major wars and crises. The first half of that century witnessed the protracted and bloody Napoleonic Wars; later came the Crimean War, and the Italian and German wars of unification.[10] The wars of 1914–45 continued this long historical pattern. They represented a break from the events of previous centuries only in the enormous increase in their scale of destruction.

This era of warfare came to an abrupt end with the conclusion of World War II. A wholly new and remarkably peaceful order then developed on the Continent.

The Causes of the Long Peace: Military Power and Stability

What caused the era of violence before 1945? Why has the postwar era been so much more peaceful? The wars before 1945 each had their particular and unique causes, but the distribution of power in Europe—its multipolarity and the imbalances of power that often occurred among the major states in that multipolar system—was the crucial permissive condition that allowed these particular causes to operate. The peacefulness of the postwar era arose for three principal reasons: the bipolarity of the distribution of power on the Continent, the rough equality in military power between those two polar states, and the appearance of nuclear weapons, which vastly expanded the violence of war, making deterrence far more robust.[11]

These factors are aspects of the European state system—of the character of military power and its distribution among states—and not of the states themselves. Thus the keys to war and peace lie more in the structure of the international system than in the nature of the individual states. Domestic factors—most notably hyper-nationalism—also helped cause the wars of the pre-1945 era, and the domestic structures of post-1945 European states have been more conducive to peace, but these domestic factors were less important than the character and distribution of military power between states. Moreover, hyper-nationalism was caused in large part by security competition among the European states, which compelled European elites to mobilize publics to support national defense efforts; hence even this important domestic factor was a more remote consequence of the international system.

Conflict is common among states because the international system creates powerful incentives for aggression.[12] The root cause of the problem is the anarchic nature of the international system. In anarchy there is no higher body or sovereign that protects states from one another. Hence each state living under anarchy faces the ever-present possibility that another state will use force to harm or conquer it. Offensive military action is always a threat to all states in the system.

Anarchy has two principal consequences. First, there is little room for trust among states because a state may be unable to recover if its trust is betrayed.

Second, each state must guarantee its own survival since no other actor will provide its security. All other states are potential threats, and no international institution is capable of enforcing order or punishing powerful aggressors.

States seek to survive under anarchy by maximizing their power relative to other states, in order to maintain the means for self-defense. Relative power, not absolute levels of power, matters most to states. Thus, states seek opportunities to weaken potential adversaries and improve their relative power position. They sometimes see aggression as the best way to accumulate more power at the expense of rivals.

This competitive world is peaceful when it is obvious that the costs and risks of going to war are high, and the benefits of going to war are low. Two aspects of military power are at the heart of this incentive structure: the distribution of power between states, and the nature of the military power available to them. The distribution of power between states tells us how well-positioned states are to commit aggression, and whether other states are able to check their aggression. This distribution is a function of the number of poles in the system, and their relative power. The nature of military power directly affects the costs, risks, and benefits of going to war. If the military weaponry available guarantees that warfare will be very destructive, states are more likely to be deterred by the cost of war.[13] If available weaponry favors the defense over the offense, aggressors are more likely to be deterred by the futility of aggression, and all states feel less need to commit aggression, since they enjoy greater security to begin with, and therefore feel less need to enhance their security by expansion.[14] If available weaponry tends to equalize the relative power of states, aggressors are discouraged from going to war. If military weaponry makes it easier to estimate the relative power of states, unwarranted optimism is discouraged and wars of miscalculation are less likely.

One can establish that peace in Europe during the Cold War has resulted from bipolarity, the approximate military balance between the superpowers, and the presence of large numbers of nuclear weapons on both sides in three ways: first, by showing that the general theories on which it rests are valid; second, by demonstrating that these theories can explain the conflicts of the pre-1945 era and the peace of the post-1945 era; and third, by showing that competing theories cannot account for the postwar peace.

The Virtues of Bipolarity Over Multipolarity

The two principal arrangements of power possible among states are bipolarity and multipolarity.[15] A bipolar system is more peaceful for three main reasons. First, the number of conflict dyads is fewer, leaving fewer possibilities for war. Second, deterrence is easier, because imbalances of power are fewer and more easily averted. Third, the prospects for deterrence are greater because miscalculations of relative power and of opponents' resolve are fewer and less likely.[16]

In a bipolar system two major powers dominate. The minor powers find it difficult to remain unattached to one of the major powers, because the major powers generally demand allegiance from lesser states. (This is especially true in core geographical areas, less so in peripheral areas.) Furthermore, lesser states have little opportunity to play the major powers off against each other, because when great powers are fewer in number, the system is more rigid. As a result, lesser states are hard-pressed to preserve their autonomy.

In a multipolar system, by contrast, three or more major powers dominate. Minor powers in such a system have considerable flexibility regarding alliance partners and can opt to be free floaters. The exact form of a multipolar system can vary markedly, depending on the number of major and minor powers in the system, and their geographical arrangement.

A bipolar system has only one dyad across which war might break out: only two major powers contend with one another, and the minor powers are not likely to be in a position to attack each other. A multipolar system has many potential conflict situations. Major power dyads are more numerous, each posing the potential for conflict. Conflict could also erupt across dyads involving major and minor powers. Dyads between minor powers could also lead to war. Therefore, *ceteris paribus,* war is more likely in a multipolar system than in a bipolar one.

Wars in a multipolar world involving just minor powers or only one major power are not likely to be as devastating as a conflict between two major powers. However, local wars tend to widen and escalate. Hence there is always a chance that a small war will trigger a general conflict.

Deterrence is more difficult in a multipolar world because power imbalances are commonplace, and when power is unbalanced, the strong become hard to deter.[17] Power imbalances can lead to conflict in two ways. First, two states can gang up to attack a third state. Second, a major power might simply bully a weaker power in a one-on-one encounter, using its superior strength to coerce or defeat the minor state.[18]

Balance of power dynamics can counter such power imbalances, but only if they operate efficiently.[19] No state can dominate another, either by ganging up or by bullying, if the others coalesce firmly against it, but problems of geography or coordination often hinder the formation of such coalitions.[20] These hindrances may disappear in wartime, but are prevalent in peacetime, and can cause deterrence failure, even where an efficient coalition will eventually form to defeat the aggressor on the battlefield.

First, geography sometimes prevents balancing states from putting meaningful pressure on a potential aggressor. For example, a major power may not be able to put effective military pressure on a state threatening to cause trouble, because buffer states lie in between.

In addition, balancing in a multipolar world must also surmount difficult coordination problems. Four phenomena make coordination difficult. First, alliances provide collective goods, hence allies face the formidable dilemmas of collective action. Specifically, each state may try to shift alliance burdens onto the shoulders of its putative allies. Such "buck-passing" is a common feature of alliance politics.[21] It is most common when the number of states required to form an effective blocking coalition is large. Second, a state faced with two potential adversaries might conclude that a protracted war between those adversaries would weaken both, even if one side triumphed; hence it may stay on the sidelines, hoping thereby to improve its power position relative to each of the combatants. (This strategy can fail, however, if one of the warring states quickly conquers the other and ends up more powerful, not less powerful, than before the war.) Third, some states may opt out of the balancing process because they believe that they will not be targeted by the aggressor, failing to recognize that they face danger until after the aggressor has won some initial victories. Fourth, diplomacy is an uncertain process, and thus it can take time to build a defensive coalition. A potential aggressor may conclude that it can succeed at aggression before the coalition is completed, and further may be prompted to exploit the window of opportunity that this situation presents before it closes.[22]

If these problems of geography and coordination are severe, states can lose faith in the balancing process. If so, they become more likely to bandwagon with the aggressor, since solitary resistance is futile.[23] Thus factors that weaken the balancing process can generate snowball effects that weaken the process still further.

The third major problem with multipolarity lies in its tendency to foster miscalculation of the resolve of opposing individual states, and of the strength of opposing coalitions.

War is more likely when a state underestimates the willingness of an opposing state to stand firm on issues of difference. It then may push the other state too far, expecting the other to concede, when in fact the opponent will choose to fight. Such miscalculation is more likely under multipolarity because the shape of the international order tends to remain fluid, due to the tendency of coalitions to shift. As a result, the international "rules of the road"—norms of state behavior, and agreed divisions of territorial rights and other privileges—tend to change constantly. No sooner are the rules of a given adversarial relationship worked out, than that relationship may become a friendship, a new adversarial relationship may emerge with a previous friend or neutral, and new rules must be established. Under these circumstances, one state may unwittingly push another too far, because ambiguities as to national rights and obligations leave a wider range of issues on which a state may miscalculate another's resolve. Norms of state behavior can come to be broadly understood and accepted by all states, even in multipolarity, just as basic norms of diplomatic conduct became generally accepted by the European powers during the eighteenth century. Nevertheless, a well-defined division of rights is generally more difficult when the number of states is large, and relations among them are in flux, as is the case with multipolarity.

War is also more likely when states underestimate the relative power of an opposing coalition, either because they underestimate the number of states who will oppose them, or because they exaggerate the number of allies who will fight on their own side.[24] Such errors are more likely in a system of many states, since states then must accurately predict the behavior of many states, not just one, in order to calculate the balance of power between coalitions.

A bipolar system is superior to a multipolar system on all of these dimensions. Bullying and ganging up are unknown, since only two actors compete. Hence the power asymmetries produced by bullying and ganging up are also unknown. When balancing is required, it is achieved efficiently. States can balance by either internal means—military buildup—or external means—diplomacy and alliances. Under multipolarity states tend to balance by external means; under bipolarity they are compelled to use internal means. Internal means are more fully under state control, hence are more efficient, and are more certain to produce real balance.[25] The problems that attend efforts to balance by diplomatic methods—geographic complications and coordination difficulties—are bypassed. Finally, miscalculation is less likely than in a multipolar world. States are less likely to miscalculate others' resolve, because the rules of the road with the main opponent become settled over time, leading both parties to recognize the limits beyond which they cannot push the other. States also cannot miscalculate the membership of the opposing coalition, since each side faces only one main enemy. Simplicity breeds certainty; certainty bolsters peace.

There are no empirical studies that provide conclusive evidence of the effects of bipolarity and multipolarity on the likelihood of war. This undoubtedly reflects the difficulty of the task: from its beginning until 1945, the European state system was multipolar, leaving this history barren of comparisons that would reveal the differing effects of multipolarity and bipolarity. Earlier history does afford some apparent examples of bipolar systems, including some that were warlike—Athens and Sparta, Rome and Carthage—but this history is inconclusive, because it is sketchy and incomplete and therefore does not offer enough detail to validate the comparisons. Lacking a comprehensive survey of history, we cannot progress beyond offering examples pro and con, without knowing which set of examples best represents the universe of cases. As a result the case made here stops short of empirical demonstration, and rests chiefly on deduction. However, I believe that this deductive case provides a sound basis for accepting the argument that bipolarity is more peaceful than multipolarity; the deductive logic seems compelling, and there is no obvious historical evidence that cuts against it. I show below that the ideas developed here apply to events in twentieth century Europe, both before and after 1945.

The Virtues of Equality of Power Over Inequality

Power can be more or less equally distributed among the major powers of both bipolar and multipolar systems. Both systems are more peaceful when equality is greatest among the poles. Power inequalities invite war by increasing the potential for successful aggression; hence war is minimized when inequalities are least.[26]

How should the degree of equality in the distribution of power in a system be assessed? Under bipolarity, the overall equality of the system is simply a function of the balance of power between the two poles—an equal balance creates an equal system, a skewed balance produces an unequal system. Under multipolarity the focus is on the power balance between the two leading states in the system, but the power ratios across other potential conflict dyads also matter. The net system equality is an aggregate of the degree of equality among all of the poles. However, most general wars under multipolarity have arisen from wars of hegemony that have pitted the leading state— an aspiring hegemon—against the other major powers in the system. Such wars are most probable when a leading state emerges, and can hope to defeat each of the others if it can isolate them. This pattern characterized the wars that grew from the attempts at hegemony by Charles V, Philip II, Louis XIV, Revolutionary and Napoleonic France, Wilhelmine Germany, and Nazi Germany.[27] Hence the ratio between the leader and its nearest competitor—in bipolarity or multipolarity—has more effect on the stability of the system than do other ratios, and is therefore the key ratio that describes the equality of the system. Close equality in this ratio lowers the risk of war.

The polarity of an international system and the degree of power equality of the system are related: bipolar systems tend more toward equality, because, as noted above, states are then compelled to balance by internal methods, and internal balancing is more efficient than external balancing. Specifically, the number-two state in a bipolar system can only hope to balance against the leader by mobilizing its own resources to reduce the gap between the two, since it has no potential major alliance partners. On the other hand, the second-strongest state in a multipolar system can seek security through alliances with others, and may be tempted to pass the buck to them, instead of building up its own strength. External balancing of this sort is especially attractive because it is cheap and fast. However, such behavior leaves intact the power gap between the two leading states, and thus leaves in place the dangers that such a power gap creates. Hence another source of stability under bipolarity lies in the greater tendency for its poles to be equal.

The Virtues of Nuclear Deterrence

Deterrence is most likely to hold when the costs and risks of going to war are obviously great. The more horrible the prospect of war, the less likely it is to occur. Deterrence is also most robust when conquest is most difficult. Aggressors then are more likely to be deterred by the futility of expansion, and all states feel less compelled to expand to increase their security, making them easier to deter because they are less compelled to commit aggression.

Nuclear weapons favor peace on both counts. They are weapons of mass destruction, and would produce horrendous devastation if used in any numbers. Moreover, if both sides' nuclear arsenals are secure from attack, creating a mutually assured retaliation capability (mutual assured destruction or MAD), nuclear weapons make conquest more difficult; international conflicts revert from tests of capability and will to purer tests of will, won by the side willing to run greater risks and pay greater costs. This gives defenders the advantage, because defenders usually value their freedom more than aggressors value new conquests. Thus nuclear weapons are a superb deterrent: they guarantee high costs, and are more useful for self-defense than for aggression.[28]

In addition, nuclear weapons affect the degree of equality in the system. Specifically, the situation created by MAD bolsters peace by moving power relations among states toward equality. States that possess nuclear deterrents can stand up to one another, even if their nuclear arsenals vary greatly in size, as long as both sides' nuclear arsenals are secure from attack. This situation of closer equality has the stabilizing effects noted above.

Finally, MAD also bolsters peace by clarifying the relative power of states and coalitions.[29] States can still miscalculate each other's will, but miscalculations of relative capability are less likely, since nuclear capabilities are not elastic to the specific size and characteristics of forces; once an assured destruction capability is achieved, further increments of nuclear power have little strategic importance. Hence errors in assessing these specific characteristics have little effect. Errors in predicting membership in war coalitions also have less effect, since unforeseen additions or subtractions from such coalitions will not influence war outcomes unless they produce a huge change in the nuclear balance—enough to give one side meaningful nuclear superiority.

The Dangers of Hyper-Nationalism

Nationalism is best defined as a set of political beliefs which holds that a nation—a body of individuals with characteristics that purportedly distinguish them from other individuals—should have its own state.[30] Although nationalists often believe that their nation is unique or special, this conclusion does not necessarily mean that they think they are superior to other peoples, merely that they take pride in their own nation.

However, this benevolent nationalism frequently turns into ugly hyper-nationalism—the belief that other nations or nation-states are both inferior and threatening and must therefore be dealt with harshly. In the past, hyper-nationalism among European states has arisen largely because most European states are nation-states—states comprised of one principal nation—and these nation-states exist in an anarchic world, under constant threat from other states. In such a situation people who love their own nation and state can develop an attitude of contempt and loathing toward the nations who inhabit opposing states. The problem is exacerbated by the fact that political elites often feel compelled to portray adversary nations in the most negative way so as to mobilize public support for national security policies.

Malevolent nationalism is most likely to develop under military systems that require reliance on mass armies; the state may exploit nationalist appeals to mobilize its citizenry for the sacrifices required to sustain large standing armies. On the other hand, hyper-nationalism is least likely when states can rely on small professional armies, or on complex high-technology military organizations that do not require vast manpower. For this reason nuclear weapons work to dampen nationalism, since they shift the basis of military power away from pure reliance on mass armies, and toward greater reliance on smaller high-technology organizations.

In sum, hyper-nationalism is the most important domestic cause of war, although it is still a second-order force in world politics. Furthermore, its causes lie largely in the international system.

The Causes of the Long Peace: Evidence

The historical record shows a perfect correlation between bipolarity, equality of military power, and nuclear weapons, on the one hand, and the long peace, on the other hand. When an equal bipolarity arose and nuclear weapons appeared, peace broke out. This correlation suggests that the bipolarity theory, the equality theory, and the nuclear theory of the long peace are all valid. However, correlation alone does not prove causation. Other factors still may account for the long peace. One way to rule out this possibility is to enumerate what the three theories predict about both the pre-war and post-war eras, and then to ask if these predictions came true in detail during those different periods.

Before the Cold War

The dangers of multipolarity are highlighted by events before both world wars. The existence of many dyads of potential conflict provided many possible ways to light the fuse to war in Europe. Diplomacy before World War I involved intense interactions among five major powers (Britain, France, Russia, Austria-Hungary, and Germany), and two minor powers (Serbia, and Belgium). At least six significant adversarial relationships emerged: Germany versus Britain, France, Russia, and Belgium; and Austria-Hungary versus Serbia and Russia. Before World War II five major powers (Britain, France, the Soviet Union, Germany, and Italy) and seven minor powers (Belgium, Poland, Czechoslovakia, Austria, Hungary, Romania, and Finland) interacted. These relations produced some thirteen important conflicts: Germany versus Britain, France, the Soviet Union, Czechoslovakia, Poland, and Austria; Italy versus Britain and France; the Soviet Union versus Finland and Poland; Czechoslovakia versus Poland and Hungary; and Romania versus Hungary. This multiplicity of conflicts made the outbreak of war inherently more likely. Moreover, many of the state interests at issue in each of these conflicts were interconnected, raising the risk that any single conflict that turned violent would trigger a general war, as happened in both 1914 and 1939.

Before World War II Germany was able to gang up with others against some minor states, and to bully others into joining with it. In 1939 Germany bolstered its power by ganging up with Poland and Hungary to partition Czechoslovakia, and then ganged up with the Soviet Union against Poland. In 1938 Germany bullied the Czechs into surrendering the Sudetenland, and also bullied the Austrians into complete surrender.[31] By these successes Germany expanded its power, leaving it far stronger than its immediate neighbors, and thereby making deterrence much harder.

German power could have been countered before both world wars had the other European powers balanced efficiently against Germany. If so, Germany might have been deterred, and war prevented on both occasions. However, the other powers twice failed to do so. Before 1914 the scope of this failure was less pronounced; France and Russia balanced forcefully against Germany, while only Britain failed to commit firmly against Germany before war began.[32]

Before 1939, failure to balance was far more widespread.[33] The Soviet Union failed to aid Czechoslovakia against Germany in 1938, partly for geographic reasons: they shared no common border, leaving the Soviets with no direct access to Czech territory. France failed to give effective aid to the Czechs and Poles, partly because French military doctrine was defensively oriented, but also because France had no direct access to Czech or Polish territory, and therefore could not easily deploy forces to bolster Czech and Polish defenses.

Britain and France each passed the buck by transferring the cost of deterring Germany onto the other, thereby weakening their combined effort. The Soviet Union, with the Molotov-Ribbentrop Pact, sought to turn the German armies westward, hoping that they would become bogged down in a war of attrition similar to World War I on the Western Front. Some of the minor European powers, including Belgium, the Netherlands, Denmark, and the Scandinavian states, passed the buck to the major powers by standing on the side-lines during the crises of 1938 and 1939.

Britain and the United States failed to recognize that they were threatened by Germany until late in the game—1939 for Britain, 1940 for the United States—and they therefore failed to take an early stand. When they finally recognized the danger posed by Germany and resolved to respond, they lacked appropriate military forces. Britain could not pose a significant military threat to Germany until after it built up its own military forces and coordinated its plans and doctrine with its French and Polish allies. In the meantime deterrence failed. The United States did not launch a significant military buildup until after the war broke out.

Multipolarity also created conditions that permitted serious miscalculation before both world wars, which encouraged German aggression on both occasions. Before 1914, Germany was not certain of British opposition if it reached for continental hegemony, and Germany completely failed to foresee that the United States would eventually move to contain it. In 1939, Germany hoped that France and Britain would stand aside as it conquered Poland, and again failed to foresee eventual American entry into the war. As a result Germany exaggerated its prospects for success. This undermined deterrence by encouraging German adventurism.

In sum, the events leading up to the world wars amply illustrate the risks that arise in a multipolar world. Deterrence was undermined in both cases by phenomena that are more common under a multipolar rather than a bipolar distribution of power.[34]

Deterrence was also difficult before both wars because power was distributed asymmetrically among the major European powers. Specifically, Germany was markedly stronger than any of its immediate neighbors. In 1914 Germany clearly held military superiority over all of its European rivals; only together were they able to defeat it, and then only with American help. 1939 is a more ambiguous case. The results of the war reveal that the Soviet Union had the capacity to stand up to Germany, but this was not apparent at the beginning of the war. Hitler was confident that Germany would defeat the Soviet Union, and this confidence was key to his decision to attack in 1941.

Finally, the events leading up to both world wars also illustrate the risks that arise in a world of pure conventional deterrence in which weapons of mass destruction are absent. World War I broke out partly because all of the important states believed that the costs of war would be small, and that successful offense was feasible.[35] Before World War II these beliefs were less widespread, but had the same effect.[36] The lesser powers thought war would be costly and conquest difficult, but the leaders of the strongest state—Germany—saw the prospect of cheap victory, and this belief was enough to destroy deterrence and produce war. Had nuclear weapons existed, these beliefs would have been undercut, removing a key condition that permitted both wars.

What was the role of internal German politics in causing the world wars? So far I have focused on aspects of the international system surrounding Germany. This focus reflects my view that systemic factors were more important. But German domestic political and social developments also played a significant role, contributing to the aggressive character of German foreign policy. Specifically, German society was infected with a virulent nationalism between 1870 and 1945 that laid the basis for expansionist foreign policies.[37]

However, two points should be borne in mind. First, German hyper-nationalism was in part fueled by Germany's pronounced sense of insecurity, which reflected Germany's vulnerable location at the center of Europe, with relatively open borders on both sides. These geographic facts made German security problems especially acute; this situation gave German elites a uniquely strong motive to mobilize their public for war, which they did largely by fanning nationalism. Thus even German hyper-nationalism can be ascribed in part to the nature of the pre-1945 international system.

Second, the horror of Germany's murderous conduct during World War II should be distinguished from the scope of the aggressiveness of German foreign policy.[38] Germany was indeed aggressive, but not unprecedentedly so. Other states have aspired to hegemony in Europe, and sparked wars by their efforts; Germany was merely the latest to attempt to convert dominant into hegemonic power. What was unique about Germany's conduct was its policy of mass murder toward many of the peoples of Europe. The causes of this murderous policy should not be conflated with the causes of the two world wars. The policy of murder arose chiefly from domestic sources; the wars arose mainly from aspects of the distribution and character of power in Europe.

The Cold War Record

The European state system abruptly shifted from multipolar to bipolar after 1945. Three factors were responsible: the near-complete destruction of German power, the growth of Soviet power, and the permanent American commitment to the European Continent. The weakening of the German Reich was accomplished by allied occupation and dismemberment. Silesia, Pomerania, East Prussia, and parts of West Prussia and Brandenburg were given to other countries, the Sudetenland was returned to Czechoslovakia, and Austria was restored to independence. The rest of the German Reich was divided into two countries, East and West Germany, which became enemies. This reduction of German power, coupled with the physical presence of American and Soviet military might in the heart of Europe, eliminated the threat of German aggression.[39]

Meanwhile the Soviet Union extended its power westward, becoming the dominant power on the Continent and one of the two strongest powers in the world. There is no reason to think that the Soviets would not have reached for continental hegemony, as the Spanish, French, and Germans did earlier, had they believed they could win a hegemonic war. But the Soviets, unlike their predecessors, made no attempt to gain hegemony by force, leaving Europe in peace.

Bipolarity supplies part of the reason. Bipolarity made Europe a simpler place in which only one point of friction—the East-West conflict—had to be managed to avoid war. The two blocs encompassed most of Europe, leaving few unprotected weak states for the Soviets to conquer. As a result the Soviets have had few targets to bully. They have also been unable to gang up on the few states that are unprotected, because their West-bloc adversary has been their only potential ganging-up partner.

Bipolarity also left less room for miscalculation of both resolve and capability. During the first fifteen years of the Cold War, the rules of the road for the conflict were not yet established, giving rise to several serious crises. However, over time each side gained a clear sense of how far it could push the other, and what the other would not tolerate. A set of rules came to be agreed upon: an understanding on the division of rights in Austria, Berlin, and elsewhere in Europe; a proscription on secret unilateral re-deployment of large nuclear forces to areas contiguous to the opponent; mutual toleration of reconnaissance satellites; agreement on rules of peacetime engagement between naval forces; and so forth. The absence of serious crises during 1963–90 was due in part to the growth of such agreements on the rights of both sides, and the rules of conduct. These could develop in large part because the system was bipolar in character. Bipolarity meant that the same two states remained adversaries for a long period, giving them time to learn how to manage their conflict without war. By contrast, a multipolar world of shifting coalitions would repeatedly have forced adversaries to re-learn how their opponents defined interests, reach new accords on the division of rights, and establish new rules of competitive conduct.

Bipolarity also left less room to miscalculate the relative strength of the opposing coalitions. The composition of possible war coalitions has been clear because only two blocs have existed, each led by an overwhelmingly dominant power that could discipline its members. Either side could have miscalculated its relative military strength, but bipolarity removed ambiguity about relative strength of adversarial coalitions arising from diplomatic uncertainties.

The East-West military balance in Europe has been roughly equal throughout the Cold War, which has further bolstered stability. This approximate parity strengthened deterrence by ensuring that no state was tempted to use force to exploit a power advantage. Parity resulted partly from bipolarity: because the two blocs already encompassed all the states of Europe, both sides have balanced mainly by internal rather than external means. These more efficient means have produced a more nearly equal balance.

Nuclear weapons also played a key role in preventing war in post–World War II Europe.

Western elites on both sides of the Atlantic quickly recognized that nuclear weapons were vastly destructive and that their widespread use in Europe would cause unprecedented devastation. The famous *Carte Blanche* exercises conducted in Germany in 1955 made it manifestly clear that a nuclear war in Europe would involve far greater costs than another World War II.[40] Accordingly, Western policymakers rarely suggested that nuclear war could be "won," and instead emphasized the horrors that would attend nuclear war. Moreover, they have understood that conventional war could well escalate to the nuclear level, and have in fact based NATO strategy on that reality.

Soviet leaders also recognized the horrendous results that a nuclear war would produce.[41] Some Soviet military officers have asserted that victory is possible in nuclear war, but even they have acknowledged that such a victory would be Pyrrhic. Soviet civilians have generally argued that victory is impossible. Furthermore, the Soviets long maintained that it was not possible to fight a purely conventional war in Europe, and that conventional victory would only prompt the loser to engage in nuclear escalation.[42] The Soviets later granted more possibility that a conventional war might be controlled, but still recognized that escalation is likely.[43] Under Gorbachev, Soviet military thinking has placed even greater emphasis on the need to avoid nuclear war and devoted more attention to the dangers of inadvertent nuclear war.[44]

Official rhetoric aside, policymakers on both sides have also behaved very cautiously in the presence of nuclear weapons. There is not a single case of a leader brandishing nuclear weapons during a crisis, or behaving as if nuclear war might be a viable option for solving important political problems. On the contrary, policymakers have never gone beyond nuclear threats of a very subtle sort, and have shown great caution when the possibility of nuclear confrontation has emerged.[45] This cautious conduct has lowered the risk of war.

Nuclear weapons also imposed an equality and clarity on the power relations between the superpowers. This equality and clarity represented a marked change from the earlier non-nuclear world, in which sharp power inequalities and miscalculations of relative power were common.[46]

During the Cold War, the United States and the Soviet Union have exhibited markedly less hyper-nationalism than did the European powers before 1945. After World War II, nationalism declined sharply within Europe, partly because the occupation forces took active steps to dampen it,[47] and also because the European states, no longer providing their own security, now lacked the incentive to purvey hyper-nationalism in order to bolster public support for national defense. More importantly, however, the locus of European politics shifted to the United States and the Soviet Union—two states that, each for its own reasons, had not exhibited nationalism of the virulent type found earlier in Europe. Nor has nationalism become virulent in either superpower during the Cold War. In part this reflects the greater stability of the postwar order, arising from bipolarity, military equality, and nuclear weapons; with less expectation of war, neither superpower has faced the need to mobilize its population for war. It also reflects a second effect of nuclear weapons: they have reduced the importance of mass armies for preserving sovereignty, thus diminishing the importance of maintaining a hyper-nationalized pool of manpower.

The Causes of the Long Peace: Competing Explanations

The claim that bipolarity, equality, and nuclear weapons have been largely responsible for the stability of the past 45 years is further strengthened by the absence of persuasive competing explanations. Two of the most popular theories of peace—*economic liberalism* and *peace-loving democracies*—are not relevant to the issue at hand.

Economic liberalism, which posits that a liberal economic order bolsters peace (discussed in more detail below), cannot explain the stability of post-war Europe, because there has been little economic exchange between the Soviet Union and the West over the past 45 years. Although economic flows between Eastern and Western Europe have been somewhat greater, in no sense has all of Europe been encompassed by a liberal economic order.

The peace-loving democracies theory (also discussed below) holds that democracies do not go to war against other democracies, but concedes that democracies are not especially pacific when facing authoritarian states. This theory cannot account for post–World War II stability because the Soviet Union and its allies in Eastern Europe have not been democratic over the past 45 years.

A third theory of peace, *obsolescence of war,* proposes that modern conventional war had become so deadly by the twentieth century that it was no longer possible to think of war as a sensible means to achieve national goals.[48] It took the two world wars to drive this point home, but by 1945 it was clear that large-scale conventional war had become irrational and morally unacceptable, like institutions such as slavery and dueling. Thus, even without nuclear weapons, statesmen in the Cold War would not seriously have countenanced war, which had become an anachronism. This theory, it should be emphasized, does not ascribe the absence of war to nuclear weapons, but instead points to the horrors of modern conventional war.

This argument probably provides the most persuasive alternative explanation for the stability of the Cold War, but it is not convincing on close inspection. The fact that World War II occurred casts serious doubt on this theory;

if any war could have convinced Europeans to forswear conventional war, it should have been World War I, with its vast casualties. There is no doubt that conventional war among modern states could devastate the participants. Nevertheless, this explanation misses one crucial difference between nuclear and conventional war, a difference that explains why war is still a viable option for states. Proponents of this theory assume that all conventional wars are protracted and bloody wars of attrition, like World War I on the Western front. However, it is possible to score a quick and decisive victory in a conventional war and avoid the devastation that usually attends a protracted conventional war.[49] Conventional war can be won; nuclear war cannot be, since neither side can escape devastation by the other, regardless of the outcome on the battlefield. Thus, the incentives to avoid war are far greater in a nuclear than a conventional world, making nuclear deterrence much more robust than conventional deterrence.[50]

PREDICTING THE FUTURE:
THE BALKANIZATION OF EUROPE?

What new order will emerge in Europe if the Soviets and Americans withdraw to their homelands and the Cold War order dissolves? What characteristics will it have? How dangerous will it be?

It is certain that bipolarity will disappear, and multipolarity will emerge in the new European order. The other two dimensions of the new order—the distribution of power among the major states, and the distribution of nuclear weapons among them—are not pre-determined, and several possible arrangements could develop. The probable stability of these arrangements would vary markedly. This section examines the scope of the dangers that each arrangement would present, and the likelihood that each will emerge.

The distribution and deployment patterns of nuclear weapons in the new Europe is the least certain, and probably the most important, element of the new order. Accordingly, this section proceeds by exploring the character of the four principal nuclear worlds that might develop: a denuclearized Europe, continuation of the current patterns of nuclear ownership, and nuclear proliferation either well- or ill-managed.

The best new order would incorporate the limited, managed proliferation of nuclear weapons. This would be more dangerous than the current order, but considerably safer than 1900-45. The worst order would be a non-nuclear Europe in which power inequities emerge between the principal poles of power. This order would be more dangerous than the current world, perhaps almost as dangerous as the world before 1945. Continuation of the current pattern, or mismanaged proliferation, would be worse than the world of today, but safer than the pre-1945 world.

Europe Without Nuclear Weapons

Some Europeans and Americans seek to eliminate nuclear weapons from Europe, and would replace the Cold War order with a wholly non-nuclear order. Constructing this nuclear-free Europe would require Britain, France and the Soviet Union to rid themselves of nuclear weapons. Proponents believe that a Europe without nuclear weapons would be the most peaceful possible arrangement; in fact, however, a nuclear-free Europe would be the most dangerous among possible post-Cold War orders. The pacifying effects of nuclear weapons—the security they provide, the caution they generate, the rough equality they impose, and the clarity of relative power they create—would be lost. Peace would then depend on the other dimensions of the new order—the number of poles, and the distribution of power among them. However, the new order will certainly be multipolar, and may be unequal; hence the system may be very prone to violence. The structure of power in Europe would look much like it did between the world wars, and it could well produce similar results.

The two most powerful states in post-Cold War Europe would probably be Germany and the Soviet Union. They would be physically separated by a band of small, independent states in Eastern Europe. Not much would change in Western Europe, although the states in that area would have to be concerned about a possible German threat on their eastern flank.

The potential for conflict in this system would be considerable. There would be many possible dyads across which war might break out. Power imbalances would be commonplace as a result of the opportunities this system would present for bullying and ganging up. There would be considerable opportunity for miscalculation. The problem of containing German power would emerge once again, but the configuration of power in Europe would make it difficult to form an effective counterbalancing coalition, for much the same reason that an effective counterbalancing coalition failed to form in the 1930s. Eventually the problem of containing the Soviet Union could also re-emerge. Finally, conflicts may erupt in Eastern Europe, providing the vortex that could pull others into a wider confrontation.

A reunified Germany would be surrounded by weaker states that would find it difficult to balance against German aggression. Without forces stationed in states adjacent to Germany, neither the Soviets nor the Americans would be in a good position to help them contain German power. Furthermore, those small states lying between Germany and the Soviet Union might fear the Soviets as much as the Germans, and hence may not be disposed to cooperate with the Soviets to deter German aggression. This problem in fact arose in the 1930s, and 45 years of Soviet occupation in the interim have done nothing to ease East European fears of a Soviet military presence. Thus, scenarios in which Germany uses military force against Poland, Czechoslovakia, or even Austria become possible.

The Soviet Union also might eventually threaten the new status quo. Soviet withdrawal from Eastern Europe does not mean that the Soviets will never feel compelled to return to Eastern Europe. The historical record provides abundant instances of Russian or Soviet involvement in Eastern Europe. Indeed, the Russian presence in Eastern Europe has surged and ebbed repeatedly over the past few centuries.[51] Thus, Soviet withdrawal now hardly guarantees a permanent exit.

Conflict between Eastern European states is also likely to produce instability in a multipolar Europe. There has been no war among the states in that region during the Cold War because the Soviets have tightly controlled them. This point is illustrated by the serious tensions that now exist between Hungary and Romania over Romanian treatment of the Hungarian minority in Transylvania, a region that previously belonged to Hungary and still has roughly 2 million Hungarians living within its borders. Were it not for the Soviet presence in Eastern Europe, this conflict could have brought Romania and Hungary to war by now, and it may bring them to war in the future.[52] This will not be the only danger spot within Eastern Europe if the Soviet empire crumbles.[53]

Warfare in Eastern Europe would cause great suffering to Eastern Europeans. It also might widen to include the major powers, because they would be drawn to compete for influence in that region, especially if disorder created fluid politics that offered opportunities for wider influence, or threatened defeat for friendly states. During the Cold War, both superpowers were drawn into Third World conflicts across the globe, often in distant areas of little strategic importance. Eastern Europe is directly adjacent to both the Soviet Union and Germany, and has considerable economic and strategic importance; thus trouble in Eastern Europe could offer even greater temptations to these powers than past conflicts in the Third World offered the superpowers. Furthermore, because the results of local conflicts will be largely determined by the relative success of each party in finding external allies, Eastern European states will have strong incentives to drag the major powers into their local conflicts.[54] Thus both push and pull considerations would operate to enmesh outside powers in local Eastern European wars.

Miscalculation is also likely to be a problem in a multipolar Europe. For example, the new order might well witness shifting patterns of conflict, leaving insufficient time for adversaries to develop agreed divisions of rights and agreed rules of interaction, or constantly forcing them to re-establish new agreements and rules as old antagonisms fade and new ones arise. It is not likely that circumstances would allow the development of a robust set of agreements of the sort that have stabilized the Cold War since 1963. Instead, Europe would resemble the pattern of the early Cold War, in which the absence of rules led to repeated crises. In addition, the multipolar character of the system is likely to give rise to miscalculation regarding the strength of the opposing coalitions.

It is difficult to predict the precise balance of conventional military power that would emerge between the two largest powers in post–Cold War Europe, especially since the future of Soviet power is now hard to forecast. The Soviet Union might recover its strength soon after withdrawing from Central Europe; if so, Soviet power would overmatch German power. Or centrifugal national forces may pull the Soviet Union apart, leaving no remnant state that is the equal of a united Germany.[55] What seems most likely is that Germany and the Soviet Union might emerge as powers of roughly equal strength. The first two scenarios, with their marked inequality between the two leading powers, would be especially worrisome, although there is cause for concern even if Soviet and German power are balanced.

Resurgent hyper-nationalism will probably pose less danger than the problems described above, but some nationalism is likely to resurface in the absence of the Cold War and may provide additional incentives for war. A non-nuclear Europe is likely to be especially troubled by nationalism, since security in such an order will largely be provided by mass armies, which often cannot be maintained without infusing societies with hyper-nationalism. The problem is likely to be most acute in Eastern Europe, but there is also potential for trouble in Germany. The Germans have generally done an admirable job combatting nationalism over the past 45 years, and in remembering the dark side of their past. Nevertheless, worrisome portents are now visible; of greatest concern, some prominent Germans have lately advised a return to greater nationalism in historical education.[56] Moreover, nationalism will be exacerbated by the unresolved border disputes that will be uncovered by the retreat of American and Soviet power. Especially prominent is that of the border between Germany and Poland, which some Germans would change in Germany's favor.

However, it seems very unlikely that Europe will actually be denuclearized, despite the present strength of anti-nuclear feeling in Europe. For example, it is unlikely that the French, in the absence of America's protective cover and faced with a newly unified Germany, would get rid of their nuclear weapons. Also, the Soviets surely would remain concerned about balancing the American nuclear deterrent, and will therefore retain a deterrent of their own.

The Current Ownership Pattern Continues

A more plausible order for post-Cold War Europe is one in which Britain, France and the Soviet Union keep their nuclear weapons, but no new nuclear powers emerge in Europe. This scenario sees a nuclear-free zone in Central Europe, but leaves nuclear weapons on the European flanks.

This scenario, too, also seems unlikely, since the non-nuclear states will have substantial incentives to acquire their own nuclear weapons. Germany would probably not need nuclear weapons to deter a conventional attack by its neighbors, since neither the French nor any of the Eastern European states would be capable of defeating a reunified Germany in a conventional war. The Soviet Union would be Germany's only legitimate conventional threat, but as long as the states of Eastern Europe remained independent, Soviet ground forces would be blocked from a direct attack. The Germans, however, might not be willing to rely on the Poles or the Czechs to provide a barrier and might instead see nuclear weapons as the best way to deter a Soviet conventional attack into Central Europe. The Germans might choose to go nuclear to protect themselves from blackmail by other nuclear powers. Finally, given that Germany would have greater economic strength than Britain or France, it might therefore seek nuclear weapons to raise its military status to a level commensurate with its economic status.

The minor powers of Eastern Europe would have strong incentives to acquire nuclear weapons. Without nuclear weapons, these Eastern European states would be open to nuclear blackmail from the Soviet Union and, if it acquired nuclear weapons, from Germany. No Eastern European state could match the conventional strength of Germany or the Soviet Union, which gives these minor powers a powerful incentive to acquire a nuclear deterrent, even if the major powers had none. In short, a continuation of the current pattern of ownership without proliferation seems unlikely.

How stable would this order be? The continued presence of nuclear weapons in Europe would have some pacifying effects. Nuclear weapons would induce greater caution in their owners, give the nuclear powers greater security, tend to equalize the relative power of states that possess them, and reduce the risk of miscalculation. However, these benefits would be limited if nuclear weapons did not proliferate beyond their current owners, for four main reasons.

First, the caution and the security that nuclear weapons impose would be missing from the vast center of Europe. The entire region between France and the Soviet Union, extending from the Arctic in the north to the Mediterranean in the south, and comprising some eighteen significant states, would become a large zone thereby made "safe" for conventional war. Second, asymmetrical power relations would be bound to develop, between nuclear and non-nuclear states and among non-nuclear states, raising the dangers that attend such asymmetries. Third, the risk of miscalculation would rise, reflecting the multipolar character of this system and the absence of nuclear weapons from a large portion of it. A durable agreed political order would be hard to build because political coalitions would tend to shift over time, causing miscalculations of resolve between adversaries. The relative strength of potential war coalitions would be hard to calculate because coalition strength would depend heavily on the vagaries of diplomacy. Such uncertainties about relative capabilities would be mitigated in conflicts that arose among nuclear powers:

nuclear weapons tend to equalize power even among states or coalitions of widely disparate resources, and thus to diminish the importance of additions or defections from each coalition. However, uncertainty would still be acute among the many states that would remain non-nuclear. Fourth, the conventionally-armed states of Central Europe would depend for their security on mass armies, giving them an incentive to infuse their societies with dangerous nationalism in order to maintain public support for national defense efforts.

Nuclear Proliferation, Well-Managed or Otherwise

The most likely scenario in the wake of the Cold War is further nuclear proliferation in Europe. This outcome is laden with dangers, but also might provide the best hope for maintaining stability on the Continent. Its effects depend greatly on how it is managed. Mismanaged proliferation could produce disaster, while well-managed proliferation could produce an order nearly as stable as the current order. Unfortunately, however, any proliferation is likely to be mismanaged.

Four principal dangers could arise if proliferation is not properly managed. First, the proliferation process itself could give the existing nuclear powers strong incentives to use force to prevent their non-nuclear neighbors from gaining nuclear weapons, much as Israel used force to preempt Iraq from acquiring a nuclear capability.

Second, even after proliferation was completed, a stable nuclear competition might not emerge between the new nuclear states. The lesser European powers might lack the resources needed to make their nuclear forces survivable; if the emerging nuclear forces were vulnerable, this could create first-strike incentives and attendant crisis instability. Because their economies are far smaller, they would not be able to develop arsenals as large as those of the major powers; arsenals of small absolute size might thus be vulnerable. Furthermore, their lack of territorial expanse deprives them of possible basing modes, such as mobile missile basing, that would secure their deterrents. Several are landlocked, so they could not base nuclear weapons at sea, the most secure basing mode used by the superpowers. Moreover, their close proximity to one another deprives them of warning time, and thus of basing schemes that exploit warning to achieve invulnerability, such as by the quick launch of alert bombers. Finally, the emerging nuclear powers might also lack the resources required to develop secure command and control and adequate safety procedures for weapons management, thus raising the risk of accidental launch, or of terrorist seizure and use of nuclear weapons.

Third, the elites and publics of the emerging nuclear European states might not quickly develop doctrines and attitudes that reflect a grasp of the devastating consequences and basic unwinnability of nuclear war. There will probably be voices in post-Cold War Europe arguing that limited nuclear war is feasible, and that nuclear wars can be fought and won. These claims might be taken seriously in states that have not had much direct experience with the nuclear revolution.

Fourth, widespread proliferation would increase the number of fingers on the nuclear trigger, which in turn would increase the likelihood that nuclear weapons could be fired due to accident, unauthorized use, terrorist seizure, or irrational decision-making.

If these problems are not resolved, proliferation would present grave dangers. However, the existing nuclear powers can take steps to reduce these dangers. They can help deter preventive attack on emerging nuclear states by extending security guarantees. They can provide technical assistance to help newly nuclear-armed powers to secure their deterrents. And they can help socialize emerging nuclear societies to understand the nature of the forces they are acquiring. Proliferation managed in this manner can help bolster peace.

How broadly should nuclear weapons be permitted to spread? It would be best if proliferation were extended to Germany but not beyond.[57] Germany has a large economic base, and can therefore sustain a secure nuclear force. Moreover, Germany will feel insecure without nuclear weapons; and Germany's great conventional strength gives it significant capacity to disturb Europe if it feels insecure. Other states—especially in Eastern Europe—may also want nuclear weapons, but it would be best to prevent further proliferation. The reasons are, as noted above, that these states may be unable to secure their nuclear deterrents, and the unlimited spread of nuclear weapons raises the risk of terrorist seizure or possession by states led by irrational elites. However, if the broader spread of nuclear weapons proves impossible to prevent without taking extreme steps, the existing nuclear powers should let the process happen, while doing their best to channel it in safe directions.

However, even if proliferation were well-managed, significant dangers would remain. If all the major powers in Europe possessed nuclear weapons, history suggests that they would still compete for influence among the lesser powers and be drawn into lesser-power conflicts. The superpowers, despite the security that their huge nuclear arsenals provide, have competed intensely for influence in remote, strategically unimportant areas such as South Asia, Southeast Asia, and Central America. The European powers are likely to exhibit the same competitive conduct, especially in Eastern Europe, even if they possess secure nuclear deterrents.

The possibility of ganging up would remain: several nuclear states could join against a solitary nuclear state, perhaps aggregating enough strength to overwhelm its deterrent. Nuclear states also might bully their non-nuclear neighbors. This problem is mitigated if unbounded proliferation takes place, leaving few non-nuclear states subject to bullying by the nuclear states, but such widespread proliferation raises risks of its own, as noted above.

Well-managed proliferation would reduce the danger that states might miscalculate the relative strength of coalitions, since nuclear weapons clarify the relative power of all states, and diminish the importance of unforeseen additions and defections from alliances. However, the risk remains that resolve will be miscalculated, because patterns of conflict are likely to be somewhat fluid in a multipolar Europe, thus precluding the establishment of well-defined spheres of rights and rules of conduct.

Unbounded proliferation, even if it is well-managed, will raise the risks that appear when there are many fingers on the nuclear trigger—accident, unauthorized or irrational use, or terrorist seizure.

In any case, it is not likely that proliferation will be well-managed. The nuclear powers cannot easily work to manage proliferation while at the same time resisting it; there is a natural tension between the two goals. But they have several motives to resist. The established nuclear powers will be reluctant to give the new nuclear powers technical help in building secure deterrents, because it runs against the grain of state behavior to transfer military power to others, and because of the fear that sensitive military technology could be turned against the donor state if that technology were further transferred to its adversaries. The nuclear powers will also be reluctant to undermine the legitimacy of the 1968 Nuclear Non-Proliferation Treaty by allowing any signatories to acquire nuclear weapons, since this could open the floodgates to the wider proliferation that they seek to avoid, even if they would otherwise favor very limited proliferation. For these reasons the nuclear powers are more likely to spend their energy trying to thwart the process of proliferation, rather than managing it.

Proliferation can be more easily managed if it occurs during a period of relative international calm. Proliferation that occurred during a time of crisis would be especially dangerous, since states in conflict with the emerging nuclear powers would then have a strong incentive to interrupt the process by force. However, proliferation is likely not to begin until the outbreak of crisis, because there will be significant domestic opposition to proliferation within the potential nuclear powers, as well as significant external resistance from the established nuclear powers. Hence it may require a crisis to motivate the potential nuclear powers to pay the domestic and international costs of moving to build a nuclear force. Thus, proliferation is more likely to happen under disadvantageous international conditions than in a period of calm.

Finally, there are limits to the ability of the established nuclear powers to assist small emerging nuclear powers to build secure deterrents. For example, small landlocked powers cannot be given access to sea-based deterrents or land-mobile missile systems requiring vast expanses of land; these are geographic problems that technology cannot erase. Therefore even if the existing nuclear powers move to manage the proliferation process early and wisely, that process still may raise dangers that they cannot control.

ALTERNATIVE THEORIES THAT PREDICT PEACE

Many students of European politics will reject my pessimistic analysis of post–Cold War Europe and instead argue that a multipolar Europe is likely to be at least as peaceful as the present order. Three specific scenarios for a peaceful future have been advanced. Each rests on a well-known theory of international relations. However, each of these theories is flawed and thus cannot serve as the basis for reliable predictions of a peaceful order in a multipolar Europe; hence the hopeful scenarios they support lack plausibility.

Under the first optimistic scenario, even a non-nuclear Europe would remain peaceful because Europeans recognize that even a conventional war would be horrific. Sobered by history, national leaders will take great care to avoid war. This scenario rests on the "obsolescence of war" theory.

Although modern conventional war can certainly be very costly, there are several flaws in this argument. There is no systematic evidence demonstrating that Europeans believe war is obsolete. However, even if it were widely believed in Europe that war is no longer thinkable, attitudes could change. Public opinion on national security issues is notoriously fickle and responsive to elite manipulation and world events. Moreover, only one country need decide war is thinkable to make war possible again. Finally, it is possible that a conventional war could be fought and won without suffering grave losses, and elites who saw this possibility could believe war is a viable option.

Under the second optimistic scenario, the existing European Community (EC) grows stronger with time, a development heralded by the Single European Act, designed to create a unified Western European market by 1992. A strong EC then ensures that this economic order remains open and prosperous, and the open and prosperous character of the European economy keeps the states of Western Europe cooperating with each other. In this view, the present EC structure grows stronger, but not larger. Therefore, while conflict might emerge in Eastern Europe, the threat of an aggressive Germany would be removed by enmeshing the newly unified German state deeply in the EC. The theory underpinning this scenario is "economic liberalism."

A variant of this second scenario posits that the EC will spread to include Eastern Europe and possibly the Soviet Union, bringing prosperity and peace to these regions as well.[58] Some also maintain that the EC is likely to be so successful in the decade ahead that it will develop into a state apparatus: a unified Western European super-state would emerge and Germany would be subsumed in it. At some future point, the remainder of Europe would be incorporated into that super-state. Either way, suggest the proponents of this second scenario and its variants, peace will be bolstered.

Under the third scenario, war is avoided because many European states have become democratic since the early twentieth century, and liberal democracies simply do not fight against each other. At a minimum, the presence of liberal democracies in Western Europe renders that half of Europe free from armed conflict. At a maximum, as democracy spreads to Eastern Europe and the Soviet Union, it bolsters peace among these states, and between these states and Western Europe. This scenario is based on the theory that can be called "peace-loving democracies."

Economic Liberalism

The Logic of the Theory

Economic liberalism rejects the notion that the prospects for peace are tightly linked to calculations about military power, and posits instead that stability is mainly a function of international economic considerations. It assumes that modern states are primarily motivated by the desire to achieve prosperity, and that national leaders place the material welfare of their publics above all other considerations, including security. This is especially true of liberal democracies, where policymakers are under special pressure to ensure the economic well-being of their populations.[59] Thus, the key to achieving peace is establishment of an international economic system that fosters prosperity for all states.

The taproot of stability, according to this theory, is the creation and maintenance of a liberal economic order that allows free economic exchange between states. Such an order works to dampen conflict and enhance political cooperation in three ways.[60]

First, it makes states more prosperous; this bolsters peace because prosperous states are more economically satisfied, and satisfied states are more peaceful. Many wars are waged to gain or preserve wealth, but states have less motive for such wars if they are already wealthy. Wealthy societies also stand to lose more if their societies are laid waste by war. For both reasons they avoid war.

Moreover, the prosperity spawned by economic liberalism feeds itself, by promoting international institutions that foster greater liberalism, which in turn promotes still greater prosperity. To function smoothly, a liberal economic order requires international regimes or institutions, such as the EC, the General Agreement on Tariffs and Trade (GATT), and the International Monetary Fund (IMF). These institutions perform two limited but important functions. First, they help states to verify that partners keep their cooperative commitments. Second, they provide resources to governments experiencing short-term problems arising from their exposure to international markets, and by doing so they allow states to eschew beggar-thy-neighbor policies that might otherwise undermine the existing economic order. Once in place, these institutions and regimes bolster economic cooperation, hence bolster prosperity. They also bolster themselves: once in existence they cause the expansion of their own size and influence, by proving their worth and selling themselves to states and publics. And as their power grows they become better able to promote cooperation, which promotes greater prosperity, which further bolsters their prestige and influence. In essence, a benevolent spiral-like relationship sets in between cooperation-promoting regimes and prosperity, in which each feeds the other.

Second, a liberal economic order fosters economic interdependence among states. Interdependence is defined as a situation in which two states are mutually vulnerable; each is a hostage of the other in the economic realm.[61] When interdependence is high, this theory holds, there is less temptation to cheat or behave aggressively towards other states because all states could retaliate. Interdependence allows states to compel each other to cooperate on economic matters, much as mutual assured destruction allows nuclear powers to compel each other to respect their security. All states are forced by the others to act as partners in the provision of material comfort for their home publics.

Third, some theorists argue that with ever-increasing political cooperation, international regimes will become so powerful that they will assume an independent life of their own, eventually growing into a super-state. This is a minority view; most economic liberals do not argue that regimes can become so powerful that they can coerce states to act against their own narrow interests. Instead most maintain that regimes essentially reflect the interests of the states that created and maintain them, and remain subordinate to other interests of these states. However, the "growth to super-statehood" view does represent an important strand of thought among economic liberals.

The main flaw in this theory is that the principal assumption underpinning it—that states are primarily motivated by the desire to achieve prosperity—is wrong. States are surely concerned about prosperity, and thus economic calculations are hardly trivial for them. However, states operate in both an international political environment and an international economic environment, and the former dominates the latter in cases where the two systems come into conflict. The reason is straightforward: the international political system is anarchic, which means that each state must always be concerned to ensure its own survival. Since a state can have no higher goal than survival, when push comes to shove, international political considerations will be paramount in the minds of decision-makers.

Proponents of economic liberalism largely ignore the effects of anarchy on state behavior and concentrate instead on economic considerations. When this omission is corrected, however, their arguments collapse, for two reasons.

First, competition for security makes it very difficult for states to cooperate. When security is scarce, states become more concerned about relative gains than absolute gains.[62] They ask of an exchange not, "will both of us gain?" but instead, "who will gain more?"[63] When security is scarce, they reject even cooperation that would yield an absolute economic gain, if the other state would gain more of the yield, from fear that the other might convert its gain to military strength, and then use this strength to win by coercion in later rounds.[64] Cooperation is much easier to achieve if states worry only about absolute gains, as they are more likely to do when security is not so scarce. The goal then is simply to insure that the overall economic pie is expanding and each state is getting at least some part of the resulting benefits. However, anarchy guarantees that security will often be scarce; this heightens states' concerns about relative gains, which makes cooperation difficult unless gains can be finely sliced to reflect, and thus not disturb, the current balance of power.

In contrast to this view, economic liberals generally assume that states worry little about relative gains when designing cooperative agreements, but instead are concerned mainly about absolute gains. This assumption underlies their optimism over the prospects for international cooperation. However, it is not well-based: anarchy forces states to reject agreements that result in asymmetrical payoffs that shift the balance of power against them.

Second, interdependence is as likely to lead to conflict as cooperation, because states will struggle to escape the vulnerability that interdependence creates, in order to bolster their national security. States that depend on others for critical economic supplies will fear cutoff or blackmail in time of crisis or war; they may try to extend political control to the source of supply, giving rise to conflict with the source or with its other customers. Interdependence, in other words, might very well lead to greater competition, not to cooperation.[65]

Several other considerations, independent of the consequences of anarchy, also raise doubts about the claims of economic liberals.

First, economic interactions between states often cause serious frictions, even if the overall consequences are positive. There will invariably be winners and losers within each state, and losers rarely accept defeat gracefully. In modern states, where leaders have to pay careful attention to their constituents, losers can cause considerable trouble. Even in cases where only winners are involved, there are sometimes squabbles over how the spoils are divided. In a sense, then, expanding the network of contacts among states increases the scope for international disagreements among them. They now have more to squabble about.

Second, there will be opportunities for blackmail and for brinkmanship in a highly dynamic economic system where states are dependent on each other. For example, although mutual vulnerabilities may arise among states, it is likely that the actual levels of dependence will not be equal. The less vulnerable states would probably have greater bargaining power over the more dependent states and might attempt to coerce them into making extravagant concessions. Furthermore, different political systems, not to mention individual leaders, have different capacities for engaging in tough bargaining situations.

The Historical Record

During two periods in the twentieth century, Europe witnessed a liberal economic order with high levels of interdependence. Stability should have obtained during those periods, according to economic liberalism.

The first case clearly contradicts the theory. The years between 1890 and 1914 were probably the time of greatest economic interdependence in Europe's history. Yet World War I broke out following this period.[66]

The second case covers the Cold War years. During this period there has been much interdependence among the EC states, while relations among these states have been very peaceful. This case, not surprisingly, is the centerpiece of the economic liberals' argument.

The correlation in this second case does not mean, however, that interdependence has *caused* cooperation among the Western democracies. It is more likely that the prime cause was the Cold War, and that this was the main reason that intra-EC relations have flourished.[67] The Cold War caused these results in two different but mutually reinforcing ways.

First, old-fashioned balance of power logic mandated cooperation among the Western democracies. A powerful and potentially dangerous Soviet Union forced the Western democracies to band together to meet the common threat. Britain, Germany, and France no longer worried about each other, because all faced a greater menace from the Soviets. This Soviet threat muted concerns about relative gains arising from economic cooperation among the EC states by giving each Western democracy a vested interest in seeing its alliance partners grow powerful, since each additional increment of power helped deter the Soviets. The Soviet threat also muted relative-gains fears among Western European states by giving them all a powerful incentive to avoid conflict with each other while the Soviet Union loomed to the east, ready to harvest the gains of Western quarrels. This gave each Western state greater confidence that its Western partners would not turn their gains against it, as long as these partners behaved rationally.

Second, America's hegemonic position in NATO, the military counterpart to the EC, mitigated the effects of anarchy on the Western democracies and facilitated cooperation among them.[68] As emphasized, states do not trust each other in anarchy and they have incentives to commit aggression against each other. America, however, not only provided protection against the Soviet threat, but also guaranteed that no EC state would aggress against another. For example, France did not have to fear Germany as it rearmed, because the American presence in Germany meant that the Germans were not free to attack anyone. With the United States serving as night watchman, relative-gains concerns among the Western European states were mitigated and, moreover, those states were willing to allow their economies to become tightly interdependent.

In effect, relations among EC states were spared the effects of anarchy—

fears about relative gains and an obsession with autonomy—because the United States served as the ultimate arbiter within the Alliance. If the present Soviet threat to Western Europe is removed, and American forces depart for home, relations among the EC states will be fundamentally altered. Without a common Soviet threat and without the American night watchman, Western European states will begin viewing each other with greater fear and suspicion, as they did for centuries before the onset of the Cold War. Consequently, they will worry about the imbalances in gains as well as the loss of autonomy that results from cooperation.[69] Cooperation in this new order will be more difficult than it has been in the Cold War. Conflict will be more likely.

In sum, there are good reasons for looking with skepticism upon the claim that peace can be maintained in a multipolar Europe on the basis of a more powerful EC.

Peace-Loving Democracies

The peace-loving democracies theory holds that domestic political factors, not calculations about military power or the international economic system, are the principal determinant of peace. Specifically, the argument is that the presence of liberal democracies in the international system will help to produce a stable order.[70] The claim is not that democracies go to war less often than authoritarian states. In fact, the historical record shows clearly that such is not the case.[71] Instead, the argument is that democracies do not go to war against other democracies. Thus, democracy must spread to Eastern Europe and the Soviet Union to insure peace in post–Cold War Europe.

It is not certain that democracy will take root among the states of Eastern Europe or in the Soviet Union. They lack a strong tradition of democracy; institutions that can accommodate the growth of democracy will have to be built from scratch. That task will probably prove to be difficult, especially in an unstable Europe. But whether democracy takes root in the East matters little for stability in Europe, since the theory of peace-loving democracies is unsound.

The Logic of the Theory

Two explanations are offered in support of the claim that democracies do not go to war against one another.

First, some claim that authoritarian leaders are more prone to go to war than leaders of democracies, because authoritarian leaders are not accountable to their publics, which carry the main burdens of war. In a democracy, by contrast, the citizenry that pays the price of war has greater say in the decision-making process. The people, so the argument goes, are more hesitant to start trouble because it is they who pay the blood price; hence the greater their power, the fewer wars.

The second argument rests on the claim that the citizens of liberal democracies respect popular democratic rights—those of their fellow countrymen, and those of individuals in other states. As a result they are reluctant to wage war against other democracies, because they view democratic governments as more legitimate than others, and are loath to impose a foreign regime on a democratic state by force. This would violate their own democratic principles and values. Thus an inhibition on war is introduced when two democracies face each other that is missing in other international relationships.

The first of these arguments is flawed because it is not possible to sustain the claim that the people in a democracy are especially sensitive to the costs of war and therefore less willing than authoritarian leaders to fight wars. In fact, the historical record shows that democracies are every bit as likely to fight wars as are authoritarian states.

Furthermore, mass publics, whether democratic or not, can become deeply imbued with nationalistic or religious fervor, making them prone to support aggression, regardless of costs. The widespread public support in post-revolutionary France for Napoleon's wars of aggression is just one example of this phenomenon. On the other hand, authoritarian leaders are just as likely as democratic publics to fear going to war, because war tends to unleash democratic forces that can undermine the regime.[72] War can impose high costs on authoritarian leaders as well as on their citizenries.

The second argument, which emphasizes the transnational respect for democratic rights among democracies, rests on a weaker factor that is usually overridden by other factors such as nationalism and religious fundamentalism. There is also another problem with the argument. The possibility always exists that a democracy will revert to an authoritarian state. This threat of backsliding means that one democratic state can never be sure that another democratic state will not change its stripes and turn on it sometime in the future. Liberal democracies must therefore worry about relative power among themselves, which is tantamount to saying that each has an incentive to consider aggression against the other to forestall future trouble. Lamentably, it is not possible for even liberal democracies to transcend anarchy.

The Historical Record

Problems with the deductive logic aside, the historical record seems to offer strong support for the theory of peace-loving democracies. There appears to have been no case where liberal democracies fought against each other. Although this evidence looks impressive at first glance, closer examination shows it to be indecisive. In fact, history provides no clear test of the theory. Four evidentiary problems leave the issue in doubt.

First, democracies have been few in number over the past two centuries, and thus there have not been many cases where two democracies were in a position to fight with each other. Only three prominent cases are usually cited: Britain and the United States (1832–present); Britain and France (1832–49, 1871–1940); and the Western democracies since 1945.

Second, there are other persuasive explanations for why war did not occur in those three cases, and these competing explanations must be ruled out before the peace-loving democracies theory can be accepted. While relations between the British and the Americans during the nineteenth century were hardly free of conflict,[73] their relations in the twentieth century were quite harmonious, and thus fit closely with how the theory would expect two democracies to behave towards each other. That harmony, however, can easily be explained by the presence of a common threat that forced Britain and the United States to work closely together.[74] Both faced a serious German threat in the first part of the century, and a Soviet threat later. The same basic argument applies to France and Britain. While Franco-British relations were not the best throughout most of the nineteenth century,[75] they improved significantly around the turn of the century with the rise of a common threat: Germany.[76] Finally, as noted above, the Soviet threat can explain the absence of war among the Western democracies since 1945.

Third, it bears mention that several democracies have come close to fighting one another, which suggests that the absence of war may be due simply to chance. France and Britain approached war during the Fashoda crisis of 1898. France and Weimar Germany might have come to blows over the Rhineland during the 1920s, had Germany possessed the military strength to challenge France. The United States has clashed with a number of elected governments in the Third World during the Cold War, including the Allende regime in Chile and the Arbenz regime in Guatemala.

Lastly, some would classify Wilhelmine Germany as a democracy, or at least a quasi-democracy; if so, World War I becomes a war among democracies.[77]

CONCLUSION

This article argues that bipolarity, an equal military balance, and nuclear weapons have fostered peace in Europe over the past 45 years. The Cold War confrontation produced these phenomena; thus the Cold War was principally responsible for transforming a historically violent region into a very peaceful place.

There is no doubt that the costs of the Cold War have been substantial. It inflicted oppressive political regimes on the peoples of Eastern Europe, who were denied basic human rights by their forced membership in the Soviet empire. It consumed national wealth, by giving rise to large and costly defense establishments in both East and West. It spawned bloody conflicts in the Third World; these produced modest casualties for the superpowers, but large casualties for the Third World nations. Nevertheless, the net human and economic cost of the Cold War order has been far less than the cost of the European order of 1900–45, with its vast violence and suffering.

A Cold War order without confrontation would have been preferable to the order that actually developed; then the peace that the Cold War order produced could have been enjoyed without its attendant costs. However, it was East-West enmity that gave rise to the Cold War order; there would have been no bipolarity, no equality, and no large Soviet and American nuclear forces in Europe without it. The costs of the Cold War arose from the same cause—East-West confrontation—as did its benefits. The good could not be had without the bad.

This article further argues that the demise of the Cold War order is likely to increase the chances that war and major crises will occur in Europe. Many observers now suggest that a new age of peace is dawning; in fact the opposite is true.

The implications of my analysis are straightforward, if paradoxical. The West has an interest in maintaining peace in Europe. It therefore has an interest in maintaining the Cold War order, and hence has an interest in the continuation of the Cold War confrontation; developments that threaten to end it are dangerous. The Cold War antagonism could be continued at lower levels of East-West tension than have prevailed in the past; hence the West is not injured by relaxing East-West tension, but a complete end to the Cold War would create more problems than it would solve.

The fate of the Cold War, however, is mainly in the hands of the Soviet Union. The Soviet Union is the only superpower that can seriously threaten to overrun Europe; it is the Soviet threat that provides the glue that holds NATO together. Take away that offensive threat and the United States is likely to abandon the Continent, whereupon the defensive alliance it has headed for forty years may disintegrate. This would bring to an end the bipolar order that has characterized Europe for the past 45 years.

The foregoing analysis suggests that the West paradoxically has an interest in the continued existence of a powerful Soviet Union with substantial military forces in Eastern Europe. Western interests are wholly reversed from those that Western leaders saw in the late 1940s: instead of seeking the retraction of Soviet power, as the West did then, the West now should hope that the Soviet Union retains at least some military forces in the Eastern European region.

There is little the Americans or the Western Europeans can or are likely to do to perpetuate the Cold War, for three reasons.

First, domestic political considerations preclude such an approach. Western leaders obviously cannot base national security policy on the need to maintain forces in Central Europe for the purpose simply of keeping the Soviets there. The idea of deploying large forces in order to bait the Soviets into an order-keeping competition would be dismissed as bizarre, and contrary to the general belief that ending the Cold War and removing the Soviet yoke from Eastern Europe would make the world safer and better.[78]

Second, the idea of propping up a declining rival runs counter to the basic behavior of states. States are principally concerned about their relative power position in the system; hence, they look for opportunities to take advantage of each other. If anything, they prefer to see adversaries decline, and thus will do whatever they can to speed up the process and maximize the distance of the fall. In other words, states do not ask which distribution of power best facilitates stability and then do everything possible to build or maintain such an order. Instead, they each tend to pursue the more narrow aim of maximizing their power advantage over potential adversaries. The particular international order that results is simply a byproduct of that competition, as illustrated by the origins of the Cold War order in Europe. No state intended to create it. In fact, both the United States and the Soviet Union worked hard in the early years of the Cold War to undermine each other's position in Europe, which would have ended the bipolar order on the Continent. The remarkably stable system that emerged in Europe in the late 1940s was the unintended consequence of an intense competition between the superpowers.

Third, even if the Americans and the Western Europeans wanted to help the Soviets maintain their status as a superpower, it is not apparent that they could do so. The Soviet Union is leaving Eastern Europe and cutting its military forces largely because its economy is foundering. It is not clear that the Soviets themselves know how to fix their economy, and there is little that Western governments can do to help them solve their economic problems. The West can and should avoid doing malicious mischief to the Soviet economy, but at this juncture it is difficult to see how the West can have significant positive influence.[79]

The fact that the West cannot sustain the Cold War does not mean that the United States should abandon all attempts to preserve the current order. The United States should do what it can to direct events toward averting a complete mutual superpower withdrawal from Europe. For instance, the American negotiating position at the conventional arms control talks should aim toward large mutual force reductions, but should not contemplate complete mutual withdrawal. The Soviets may opt to withdraw all their forces unilaterally anyway; there is little the United States could do to prevent this.

Policy Recommendations

If complete Soviet withdrawal from Eastern Europe proves unavoidable, the West faces the question of how to maintain peace in a multipolar Europe. Three policy prescriptions are in order.

First, the United States should encourage the limited and carefully managed proliferation of nuclear weapons in Europe. The best hope for avoiding war in post–Cold War Europe is nuclear deterrence; hence some nuclear proliferation is necessary to compensate for the withdrawal of the Soviet and American nuclear arsenals from Central Europe. Ideally, as I have argued, nuclear weapons would spread to Germany, but to no other state.

Second, Britain and the United States, as well as the Continental states, will have to balance actively and efficiently against any emerging aggressor to offset the ganging up and bullying problems that are sure to arise in post–Cold War Europe. Balancing in a multipolar system, however, is usually a problem-ridden enterprise, either because of geography or because of significant coordination problems. Nevertheless, two steps can be taken to maximize the prospects of efficient balancing.

The initial measure concerns Britain and the United States, the two prospective balancing states that, physically separated from the Continent, may thus conclude that they have little interest in what happens there. They would then be abandoning their responsibilities and, more importantly, their interests as off-shore balancers. Both states' failure to balance against Germany before the two world wars made war more likely in each case. It is essential for peace in Europe that they not repeat their past mistakes, but instead remain actively involved in maintaining the balance of power in Europe.

Specifically, both states must maintain military forces that can be deployed to the Continent to balance against states that threaten to start a war. To do this they must also socialize their publics to support a policy of continued Continental commitment. Support for such a commitment will be more difficult to mobilize than in the past, because its principal purpose would be to preserve peace, rather than to prevent an imminent hegemony, and the latter is a simpler goal to explain publicly. Moreover, it is the basic nature of states to focus on maximizing relative power, not on bolstering stability, so this prescription asks them to take on an unaccustomed task. Nevertheless, the British and American stake in peace is real, especially since there is a sure risk that a European war might involve large-scale use of nuclear weapons. It should therefore be possible for both countries to lead their publics to recognize this interest and support policies that protect it.[80]

The other measure concerns American attitudes and actions toward the Soviet Union. The Soviets may eventually return to their past expansionism and threaten to upset the status quo. If so, we are back to the Cold War; the West should respond as quickly and efficiently as it did the first time. However, if the Soviets adhere to status quo policies, Soviet power could play a key role in balancing against Germany and in maintaining order in Eastern Europe. It is important that, in those cases where the Soviets are acting in a balancing capacity, the United States recognize this, cooperate with its former adversary, and not let residual distrust from the Cold War interfere with the balancing process.

Third, a concerted effort should be made to keep hyper-nationalism at bay, especially in Eastern Europe. This powerful force has deep roots in Europe and has contributed to the outbreak of past European conflicts. Nationalism has been contained during the Cold War, but it is likely to reemerge once Soviet and American forces leave the heart of Europe.[81] It will be a force for trouble unless it is curbed. The teaching of honest national history is especially important, since the teaching of false chauvinist history is the main vehicle for spreading virulent nationalism. States that teach a dishonestly self-exculpating or self-glorifying history should be publicly criticized and sanctioned.[82]

On this count it is especially important that relations between Germany and its neighbors be handled carefully. Many Germans rightly feel that Germany has behaved very responsibly for 45 years, and has made an honest effort to remember and make amends for an ugly period of its past. Therefore, Germans quickly tire of lectures from foreigners demanding that they apologize once again for crimes committed before most of the current German population was born. On the other hand, peoples who have suffered at the hands of the Germans cannot forget their enormous suffering, and inevitably ask for repeated assurance that the past will not be repeated. This dialogue has the potential to spiral into mutual recriminations that could spark a renewed sense of persecution among Germans, and with it, a rebirth of German-nationalism. It is therefore incumbent on all parties in this discourse to proceed with understanding and respect for one another's feelings and experience. Specifically, others should not ask today's Germans to apologize for crimes they did not commit, but Germans must understand that others' ceaseless demands for reassurance have a legitimate basis in history, and should view these demands with patience and understanding.

None of these tasks will be easy to accomplish. In fact, I expect that the bulk of my prescriptions will not be followed; most run contrary to powerful strains of domestic American and European opinion, and to the basic nature of state behavior. Moreover, even if they are followed, this will not guarantee the peace in Europe. If the Cold War is truly behind us, the stability of the past 45 years is not likely to be seen again in the coming decades.

NOTES

This article emerged from a paper written for a February 1990 conference at Ditchley Park, England, on the future of Europe, organized by James Callaghan, Gerald Ford, Valéry Giscard d'Estaing, and Helmut Schmidt. An abridged version of this article appears in the *Atlantic,* August 1990. I am grateful to Robert Art, Stacy Bergstrom, Richard Betts, Anne-Marie Burley, Dale Copeland, Michael Desch, Markus Fischer, Henk Goemans, Joseph Grieco, Ted Hopf, Craig Koerner, Andrew Kydd, Alicia Levine, James Nolt, Roger Petersen, Barry Posen, Denny Roy, Jack Snyder, Ashley Tellis, Marc Trachtenberg, Stephen Van Evera, Andrew Wallace, and Stephen Walt for their most helpful comments.

1. There is considerable support within NATO's higher circles, including the Bush administration, for maintaining NATO beyond the Cold War. NATO leaders have not clearly articulated the concrete goals that NATO would serve in a post-Cold War Europe, but they appear to conceive the future NATO as a means for ensuring German security, thereby removing possible German motives for aggressive policies; and as a means to protect other NATO states against German aggression. However, the Germans, who now provide the largest portion of the Alliance's standing forces, are likely to resist such a role for NATO. A security structure of this sort assumes that Germany cannot be trusted and that NATO must be maintained to keep it in line. A united Germany is not likely to accept for very long a structure that rests on this premise. Germans accepted NATO throughout the Cold War because it secured Germany against the Soviet threat that developed in the wake of World War II. Without that specific threat, which now appears to be diminishing rapidly, Germany is likely to reject the continued maintenance of NATO as we know it.

2. I am not arguing that a complete end to the Cold War is inevitable; also quite likely is an intermediate outcome, under which the status quo is substantially modified, but the main outlines of the current order remain in place. Specifically, the Soviet Union may withdraw much of its force from Eastern Europe, but leave significant forces behind. If so, NATO force levels would probably shrink markedly, but NATO may continue to maintain significant forces in Germany. Britain and the United States would withdraw some but not all of their troops from the Continent. If this outcome develops, the basic bipolar military competition that has defined the map of Europe throughout the Cold War will continue. I leave this scenario unexamined, and instead explore what follows from a complete end to the Cold War in Europe because this latter scenario is the less examined of the two, and because the consequences, and therefore the desirability, of completely ending the Cold War would still remain an issue if the intermediate outcome occurred.

3. The impact of such a change on human rights in Eastern Europe will not be considered directly in this article. Eastern Europeans have suffered great hardship as a result of the Soviet occupation. The Soviets have imposed oppressive political regimes on the region, denying Eastern Europeans basic freedoms. Soviet withdrawal from Eastern Europe will probably change that situation for the better, although the change is likely to be more of a mixed blessing than most realize. First, it is not clear that communism will be promptly replaced in all Eastern European countries with political systems that place a high premium on protecting minority rights and civil liberties. Second, the longstanding blood feuds among the nationalities in Eastern Europe are likely to re-emerge in a multipolar Europe, regardless of the existing political order. If wars break out in Eastern Europe, human rights are sure to suffer.

4. It is commonplace to characterize the polarity—bipolar or multipolar—of the international system at large, not a specific region. The focus in this article, however, is not on the global distribution of power, but on the distribution of power in Europe. Polarity arguments can be used to assess the prospects for stability in a particular region, provided the global and regional balances are distinguished from one another and the analysis is focused on the structure of power in the relevant region.

5. To qualify as a pole in a global or regional system, a state must have a reasonable prospect of defending itself against the leading state in the system by its own efforts.

The United States and the Soviet Union have enjoyed clear military superiority over other European states, and all non-European states, throughout the Cold War, hence they have formed the two poles of both the global and European systems. What is happening to change this is that both the Soviet Union and the United States are moving forces out of Central Europe, which makes it more difficult for them to project power on the Continent and thus weakens their influence there; and reducing the size of those forces, leaving them less military power to project. Because of its proximity to Europe, the Soviet Union will remain a pole in the European system as long as it retains substantial military forces on its own territory. The United States can remain a pole in Europe only if it retains the capacity to project significant military power into Central Europe.

6. Stability is simply defined as the absence of wars and major crises.

7. The term "long peace" was coined by John Lewis Gaddis, "The Long Peace: Elements of Stability in the Postwar International System," *International Security*, Vol. 10, No. 4 (Spring 1986), pp. 99–142.

8. There were approximately 10,000 battle deaths in the Russo-Hungarian War of October–November 1956, and some 1500–5000 battle deaths in the July-August 1974 war in Cyprus. See Ruth Leger Sivard, *World Military and Social Expenditures 1989* (Washington, D.C.: World Priorities, 1989), p. 22; and Melvin Small and J. David Singer, *Resort to Arms: International and Civil Wars, 1816-1980* (Beverly Hills, Calif.: Sage, 1982), pp. 93–94.

9. For inventories of past wars, see Jack S. Levy, *War In the Modern Great Power System, 1495-1975* (Lexington: University Press of Kentucky, 1983); and Small and Singer, *Resort to Arms.*

10. Europe saw no major war from 1815-1853 and from 1871-1914, two periods almost as long as the 45 years of the Cold War. There is a crucial distinction, however, between the Cold War and these earlier periods. Relations among the great powers deteriorated markedly in the closing years of the two earlier periods, leading in each case to a major war. On the other hand, the Cold War order has become increasingly stable with the passage of time and there is now no serious threat of war between NATO and the Warsaw Pact. Europe would surely remain at peace for the foreseeable future if the Cold War were to continue, a point that highlights the exceptional stability of the present European order.

11. The relative importance of these three factors cannot be stated precisely, but all three had substantial importance.

12. The two classic works on this subject are Hans J. Morgenthau, *Politics Among Nations: The Struggle for Power and Peace*, 5th ed. (New York, Knopf, 1973); and Kenneth N. Waltz, *Theory of International Politics* (Reading, Mass.: Addison-Wesley, 1979).

13. The prospects for deterrence can also be affected by crisis stability calculations. See John J. Mearsheimer, "A Strategic Misstep: The Maritime Strategy and Deterrence in Europe," *International Security*, Vol. 11, No. 2 (Fall 1986), pp. 6-8.

14. See Robert Jervis, "Cooperation Under the Security Dilemma," *World Politics*, Vol. 30, No. 2 (January 1978), pp. 167-214; and Stephen Van Evera, "Causes of War" (unpub. PhD dissertation, University of California at Berkeley, 1984), chap. 3. As noted below, I believe that the distinction between offensive and defensive weapons and, more generally, the concept of an offense-defense balance, is relevant at the nuclear

level. However, I do not believe those ideas are relevant at the conventional level. See John J. Mearsheimer, *Conventional Deterrence* (Ithaca: Cornell University Press, 1983), pp. 25-27.

15. Hegemony represents a third possible distribution. Under a hegemony there is only one major power in the system. The rest are minor powers that cannot challenge the major power, but must act in accordance with the dictates of the major power. Every state would like to gain hegemony, because hegemony confers abundant security: no challenger poses a serious threat. Hegemony is rarely achieved, however, because power tends to be somewhat evenly distributed among states, because threatened states have strong incentives to join together to thwart an aspiring hegemon, and because the costs of expansion usually outrun the benefits before domination is achieved, causing extension to become overextension. Hegemony has never characterized the European state system at any point since it arose in the seventeenth century, and there is no prospect for hegemony in the foreseeable future; hence hegemony is not relevant to assessing the prospects for peace in Europe.

16. The key works on bipolarity and multipolarity include Thomas J. Christensen and Jack Snyder, "Chain Gangs and Passed Bucks: Predicting Alliance Patterns in Multipolarity," *International Organization,* Vol. 44, No. 2 (Spring 1990), pp. 137-168; Karl W. Deutsch and J. David Singer, "Multipolar Power Systems and International Stability," *World Politics,* Vol. 16, No. 3 (April 1964), pp. 390-406; Richard N. Rosecrance, "Bipolarity, Multipolarity, and the Future," *Journal of Conflict Resolution,* Vol. 10, No. 3 (September 1966), pp. 314-327; Kenneth N. Waltz, "The Stability of a Bipolar World," *Daedalus,* Vol. 93, No. 3 (Summer 1964), pp. 881-909; and Waltz, *Theory of International Politics,* chap. 8. My conclusions about bipolarity are similar to Waltz's, although there are important differences in our explanations, as will be seen below.

17. Although a balance of power is more likely to produce deterrence than an imbalance of power, a balance of power between states does not guarantee that deterrence will obtain. States sometimes find innovative military strategies that allow them to win on the battlefield, even without marked advantage in the balance of raw military capabilities. Furthermore, the broader political forces that move a state towards war sometimes force leaders to pursue very risky military strategies, impelling states to challenge opponents of equal or even superior strength. See Mearsheimer, *Conventional Deterrence,* especially chap. 2.

18. This discussion of polarity assumes that the military strength of the major powers is roughly equal. The consequences of power asymmetries among great powers is discussed below.

19. See Stephen M. Walt, *The Origins of Alliances* (Ithaca: Cornell University Press, 1987); and Waltz, *Theory of International Politics,* pp. 123-128.

20. One exception bears mention: ganging up is still possible under multipolarity in the restricted case where there are only three powers in the system, and thus no allies available for the victim state.

21. See Mancur Olson and Richard Zeckhauser, "An Economic Theory of Alliances," *Review of Economics and Statistics,* Vol. 48, No. 3 (August 1966), pp. 266-279; and Barry R. Posen, *The Sources of Military Doctrine: France, Britain, and Germany between the World Wars* (Ithaca: Cornell University Press, 1984).

22. Domestic political considerations can also sometimes impede balancing be-

havior. For example, Britain and France were reluctant to ally with the Soviet Union in the 1930s because of their deep-seated antipathy to communism.

23. See Walt, *Origins of Alliances*, pp. 28-32, 173-178.

24. This point is the central theme of Waltz, "The Stability of a Bipolar World." Also see Geoffrey Blainey, *The Causes of War* (New York: Free Press, 1973), chap. 3.

25. Noting the greater efficiency of internal over external balancing is Waltz, *Theory of International Politics*, pp. 163, 168.

26. This discussion does not encompass the situation where power asymmetries are so great that one state emerges as a hegemon. See note 15.

27. This point is the central theme of Ludwig Dehio, *The Precarious Balance: Four Centuries of the European Power Struggle*, trans. Charles Fullman (New York: Knopf, 1962). Also see Randolph M. Siverson and Michael R. Tennefoss, "Power, Alliance, and the Escalation of International Conflict, 1815-1965," *American Political Science Review*, Vol. 78, No. 4 (December 1984), pp. 1057-1069. The two lengthy periods of peace in the nineteenth century (see note 10 above) were mainly caused by the equal distribution of power among the major European states. Specifically, there was no aspiring hegemon in Europe for most of these two periods. France, the most powerful state in Europe at the beginning of the nineteenth century, soon declined to a position of rough equality with its chief competitors, while Germany only emerged as a potential hegemon in the early twentieth century.

28. Works developing the argument that nuclear weapons are essentially defensive in nature are Shai Feldman, *Israeli Nuclear Deterrence: A Strategy for the 1980s* (New York: Columbia University Press, 1982), pp. 45-49; Stephen Van Evera, "Why Europe Matters, Why the Third World Doesn't: American Grand Strategy after the Cold War," *Journal of Strategic Studies*, Vol. 13, No. 2 (June 1990); and Van Evera, "Causes of War," chap. 13.

29. See Feldman, *Israeli Nuclear Deterrence*, pp. 50-52; and Van Evera, "Causes of War," pp. 697-699.

30. This definition is drawn from Ernest Gellner, *Nations and Nationalism* (Ithaca: Cornell University Press, 1983), which is an excellent study of the origins of nationalism. Nevertheless, Gellner pays little attention to how nationalism turns into a malevolent force that contributes to instability in the international system.

31. Austria is not a pure case of bullying; there was also considerable pro-German support in Austria during the late 1930s.

32. Britain's failure to commit itself explicitly to a Continental war before the July Crisis was probably a mistake of great proportions. There is evidence that the German chancellor, Bethmann-Hollweg, tried to stop the slide towards war once it became apparent that Britain would fight with France and Russia against Germany, turning a Continental war into a world war. See Imanuel Geiss, ed., *July 1914: The Outbreak of the First World War* (New York: Norton, 1967), chap. 7. Had the Germans clearly understood British intentions before the crisis, they might have displayed much greater caution in the early stages of the crisis, when it was still possible to avoid war.

33. See Williamson Murray, *The Change in the European Balance of Power, 1938-1939: The Path to Ruin* (Princeton: Princeton University Press, 1984); Posen, *Sources of Military Doctrine*; and Arnold Wolfers, *Britain and France between Two Wars: Conflicting Strategies of Peace from Versailles to World War II* (New York:

Norton, 1968); and Barry R. Posen, "Competing Images of the Soviet Union," *World Politics,* Vol. 39, No. 4 (July 1987), pp. 579-597.

34. The problems associated with multipolarity were also common in Europe before 1900. Consider, for example, that inefficient balancing resulted in the collapse of the first four coalitions arrayed against Napoleonic France. See Steven T. Ross, *European Diplomatic History, 1789-1815: France Against Europe* (Garden City, N.Y.: Doubleday, 1969).

35. Stephen Van Evera, "The Cult of the Offensive and the Origins of the First World War," *International Security,* Vol. 9, No. 1 (Summer 1984), pp. 58-107. Also see Jack Snyder, *The Ideology of the Offensive: Military Decision-Making and the Disasters of 1914* (Ithaca: Cornell University Press, 1984).

36. Mearsheimer, *Conventional Deterrence,* chaps. 3-4.

37. See Ludwig Dehio, *Germany and World Politics in the Twentieth Century,* trans. Dieter Pevsner (New York: Norton, 1967); Fritz Fischer, *War of Illusions: German Policies from 1911 to 1914,* trans. Marian Jackson (New York: Norton, 1975); Paul M. Kennedy, *The Rise of the Anglo-German Antagonism, 1860-1914* (London: Allen and Unwin, 1980), chap. 18; Hans Kohn, *The Mind of Germany: The Education of a Nation* (New York: Harper Torchbook, 1965), chaps. 7-12; and Louis L. Snyder, *German Nationalism: The Tragedy of a People* (Harrisburg, Pa.: Telegraph Press, 1952).

38. There is a voluminous literature on the German killing machine in World War II. Among the best overviews of the subject are Ian Kershaw, *The Nazi Dictatorship: Problems and Perspectives of Interpretation,* 2nd ed. (London: Arnold, 1989), chaps. 5, 8, 9; Henry L. Mason, "Imponderables of the Holocaust," *World Politics,* Vol. 34, No. 1 (October 1981), pp. 90-113; and Mason, "Implementing the Final Solution: The Ordinary Regulating of the Extraordinary," *World Politics,* Vol. 40, No. 4 (July 1988), pp. 542-569.

39. See Anton W. DePorte, *Europe between the Superpowers: The Enduring Balance,* 2nd ed. (New Haven: Yale University Press, 1986).

40. See Hans Speier *German Rearmament and Atomic War: The Views of German Military and Political Leaders* (Evanston, Ill.: Row, Peterson, 1957), chap. 10.

41. See Robert L. Arnett, "Soviet Attitudes Towards Nuclear War: Do They Really Think They Can Win?" *Journal of Strategic Studies,* Vol. 2, No. 2 (September 1979), pp. 172-191; and David Holloway, *The Soviet Union and the Arms Race* (New Haven: Yale University Press, 1983).

42. Thus Nikita Khrushchev explained, "Now that the big countries have thermonuclear weapons at their disposal, they are sure to resort to those weapons if they begin to lose a war fought with conventional means. If it ever comes down to a question of whether or not to face defeat, there is sure to be someone who will be in favor of pushing the button, and the missiles will begin to fly." Nikita Khrushchev, *Khrushchev Remembers: The Last Testament,* trans. and ed. by Strobe Talbott (New York: Bantam, 1976), pp. 603-604.

43. See James M. McConnell, "Shifts in Soviet Views on the Proper Focus of Military Development," *World Politics,* Vol. 37, No. 3 (April 1985), pp. 317-343.

44. See Stephen M. Meyer, "The Sources and Prospects of Gorbachev's New Political Thinking on Security," *International Security,* Vol. 13, No. 2 (Fall 1988), pp. 134-138.

45. See Hannes Adomeit, *Soviet Risk-taking and Crisis Behavior: A Theoretical and Empirical Analysis* (London: Allen and Unwin, 1982); Richard K. Betts, *Nuclear*

Blackmail and Nuclear Balance (Washington, D.C.: Brookings, 1987); and McGeorge Bundy, *Danger and Survival: Choices about the Bomb in the First Fifty Years* (New York: Random House, 1988). Also see Joseph S. Nye, Jr., "Nuclear Learning and U.S.-Soviet Security Regimes," *International Organization,* Vol. 41, No. 3 (Summer 1987), pp. 371-402.

46. Some experts acknowledge that nuclear weapons had deterrent value in the early decades of the Cold War, but maintain that they had lost their deterrent value by the mid-1960s when the Soviets finally acquired the capability to retaliate massively against the American homeland. I reject this argument and have outlined my views in John J. Mearsheimer, "Nuclear Weapons and Deterrence in Europe," *International Security,* Vol. 9, No. 3 (Winter 1984/85), pp. 19-46.

47. See Paul M. Kennedy, "The Decline of Nationalistic History in the West, 1900-1970," *Journal of Contemporary History,* Vol. 8, No. 1 (January 1973), pp. 77-100; and E.H. Dance, *History the Betrayer* (London: Hutchinson, 1960).

48. This theory is most clearly articulated by John E. Mueller, *Retreat from Doomsday: The Obsolescence of Major War* (New York: Basic Books, 1989). See also Carl Kaysen, "Is War Obsolete? A Review Essay," *International Security,* Vol. 14, No. 4 (Spring 1990), pp. 42-64.

49. See Mearsheimer, *Conventional Deterrence,* chaps. 1-2.

50. German decision-making in the early years of World War II underscores this point. See Mearsheimer, *Conventional Deterrence,* chap. 4. The Germans were well aware from their experience in World War I that conventional war among major powers could have devastating consequences. Nevertheless, they decided three times to launch major land offensives: Poland (1939); France (1940); and the Soviet Union (1941). In each case, the Germans believed that they could win a quick and decisive victory and avoid a costly protracted war like World War I. Their calculations proved correct against Poland and France. They were wrong about the Soviets, who thwarted their blitzkrieg and eventually played the central role in bringing down the Third Reich. The Germans surely would have been deterred from attacking the Soviet Union if they had foreseen the consequences. However, the key point is that they saw some possibility of winning an easy and relatively cheap victory against the Red Army. That option is not available in a nuclear war.

51. See, inter alia: Ivo J. Lederer, ed., *Russian Foreign Policy: Essays in Historical Perspective* (New Haven: Yale University Press, 1962); Andrei Lobanov-Rostovsky, *Russia and Europe, 1825-1878* (Ann Arbor, Mich.: George Wahr Publishing, 1954); and Marc Raeff, *Imperial Russia, 1682-1825: The Coming of Age of Modern Russia* (New York: Knopf, 1971), chap. 2.

52. To get a sense of the antipathy between Hungary and Romania over this issue, see *Witnesses to Cultural Genocide: First-Hand Reports on Romania's Minority Policies Today* (New York: American Transylvanian Federation and the Committee for Human Rights in Romania, 1979). The March 1990 clashes between ethnic Hungarians and Romanians in Tirgu Mures (Romanian Transylvania) indicate the potential for savage violence that is inherent in these ethnic conflicts.

53. See Zbigniew Brzezinski, "Post-Communist Nationalism," *Foreign Affairs,* Vol. 68, No. 5 (Winter 1989/1990), pp. 1-13; and Mark Kramer, "Beyond the Brezhnev Doctrine: A New Era in Soviet-East European Relations?" *International Security,* Vol. 14, No. 3 (Winter 1989/90), pp. 51-54.

54. The new prime minister of Hungary, Jozsef Antall, has already spoken of the need for a "European solution" to the problem of Romania's treatment of Hungarians in Transylvania. Celestine Bohlen, "Victor in Hungary Sees '45 as the Best of Times," *New York Times,* April 10, 1990, p. A8.

55. This article focuses on how changes in the strength of Soviet power and retraction of the Soviet empire would affect the prospects for stability in Europe. However, the dissolution of the Soviet Union, a scenario not explored here in any detail, would raise dangers that would be different from and in addition to those discussed here.

56. Aspects of this story are recounted in Richard J. Evans, *In Hitler's Shadow: West German Historians and the Attempt to Escape from the Nazi Past* (New York: Pantheon, 1989). A study of past German efforts to mischaracterize history is Holger H. Herwig, "Clio Deceived: Patriotic Self-Censorship in Germany After the Great War," *International Security,* Vol. 12, No. 2 (Fall 1987), pp. 5–44.

57. See David Garnham, "Extending Deterrence with German Nuclear Weapons," *International Security,* Vol. 10, No. 1 (Summer 1985), pp. 96–110.

58. Jack Snyder, "Averting Anarchy in the New Europe," *International Security,* Vol. 14, No. 4 (Spring 1990), pp. 5–41.

59. This point about liberal democracies highlights the fact that economic liberalism and the theory of peace-loving democracies are often linked in the writings of international relations scholars. The basis of the linkage is what each theory has to say about peoples' motives. The claim that individuals mainly desire material prosperity, central to economic liberalism, meshes nicely with the belief that the citizenry are a powerful force against war, which, as discussed below, is central to the theory of peace-loving democracies.

60. The three explanations discussed here rest on three of the most prominent theories advanced in the international political economy (IPE) literature. These three are usually treated as distinct theories and are given various labels. However they share important common elements. Hence, for purposes of parsimony, I treat them as three strands of one general theory: economic liberalism. A caveat is in order. The IPE literature often fails to state its theories in a clear fashion, making them difficult to evaluate. Thus, I have construed these theories from sometimes opaque writings that might be open to contrary interpretations. My description of economic liberalism is drawn from the following works, which are among the best of the IPE genre: Richard N. Cooper, "Economic Interdependence and Foreign Policies in the Seventies," *World Politics,* Vol. 24, No. 2 (January 1972), pp. 158–181; Ernst B. Haas, "Technology, Pluralism, and the New Europe," in Joseph S. Nye, Jr., ed., *International Regionalism* (Boston: Little, Brown, 1968), pp. 149–176; Robert O. Keohane and Joseph S. Nye, Jr., *Power and Interdependence: World Politics in Transition* (Boston: Little, Brown, 1977); Robert O. Keohane, *After Hegemony: Cooperation and Discord in the World Political Economy* (Princeton: Princeton University Press, 1984); David Mitrany, *A Working Peace System* (Chicago: Quadrangle Press, 1966); Edward L. Morse, "The Transformation of Foreign Policies: Modernization, Interdependence, and Externalization," *World Politics,* Vol. 22, No. 3 (April 1970), pp. 371–392; and Richard N. Rosecrance, *The Rise of the Trading State: Commerce and Conquest in the Modern World* (New York: Basic Books, 1986).

61. See Kenneth N. Waltz, "The Myth of National Interdependence," in Charles P.

Kindelberger, ed., *The International Corporation* (Cambridge: MIT Press, 1970), pp. 205–223.

62. See Joseph M. Grieco, "Anarchy and the Limits of Cooperation: A Realist Critique of the Newest Liberal Institutionalism," *International Organization*, Vol. 42, No. 3 (Summer 1988), pp. 485–507; and Grieco, *Cooperation among Nations: Europe, America and Non-Tariff Barriers to Trade* (Ithaca: Cornell University Press, 1990).

63. Waltz, *Theory of International Politics*, p. 105.

64. It is important to emphasize that because military power is in good part a function of economic might, the consequences of economic dealings among states sometimes have important security implications.

65. There are numerous examples in the historical record of vulnerable states pursuing aggressive military policies for the purpose of achieving autarky. For example, this pattern of behavior was reflected in both Japan's and Germany's actions during the interwar period. On Japan, see Michael A. Barnhart, *Japan Prepares for Total War: The Search for Economic Security, 1919–1941* (Ithaca: Cornell University Press, 1987); and James B. Crowley, *Japan's Quest for Autonomy* (Princeton: Princeton University Press, 1966). On Germany, see William Carr, *Arms, Autarky and Aggression: A Study in German Foreign Policy, 1933–39* (New York: Norton, 1973). It is also worth noting that during the Arab oil embargo of the early 1970s, when it became apparent that the United States was vulnerable to OPEC pressure, there was much talk in America about using military force to seize Arab oil fields. See, for example, Robert W. Tucker, "Oil: The Issue of American Intervention," *Commentary*, January 1975, pp. 21–31; Miles Ignotus [said to be a pseudonym for Edward Luttwak], "Seizing Arab Oil," *Harpers*, March 1975, pp. 45–62; and U.S. Congress, House Committee on International Relations, *Report on Oil Fields as Military Objectives: A Feasibility Study*, prepared by John M. Collins and Clyde R. Mark, 94th Cong., 1st sess. (Washington, D.C.: U.S. Government Printing Office [U.S. GPO], August 21, 1975).

66. See Richard N. Rosecrance, et al., "Whither Interdependence?" *International Organization*, Vol. 31, No. 3 (Summer 1977), pp. 432–434.

67. This theme is reflected in Barry Buzan, "Economic Structure and International Security: The Limits of the Liberal Case," *International Organization*, Vol. 38, No. 4 (Autumn 1984), pp. 597–624; Robert Gilpin, *U.S. Power and the Multinational Corporation: The Political Economy of Foreign Direct Investment* (New York: Basic Books, 1975); and Robert A. Pollard, *Economic Security and the Origins of the Cold War, 1945–1950* (New York: Columbia University Press, 1985).

68. See Josef Joffe, "Europe's American Pacifier," *Foreign Policy*, No. 54 (Spring 1984), pp. 64–82.

69. Consider, for example, a situation where the European Community is successfully extended to include Eastern Europe and the Soviet Union, and that over time all states achieve greater prosperity. The Germans, however, do significantly better than all other states. Hence their relative power position, which is already quite strong, begins to improve markedly. It is likely that the French and the Soviets, just to name two states, would be deeply concerned by this situation.

70. This theory has been recently articulated by Michael Doyle in three articles: "Liberalism and World Politics," *American Political Science Review*, Vol. 80, No. 4 (December 1986), pp. 1151–1169; "Kant, Liberal Legacies, and Foreign Affairs," *Philosophy and Public Affairs*, Vol. 12, No. 3 (Summer 1983), pp. 205–235; and "Kant,

Liberal Legacies, and Foreign Affairs, Part 2," *Philosophy and Public Affairs,* Vol. 12, No. 4 (Fall 1983), pp. 323-353. Doyle draws heavily on Immanuel Kant's classic writings on the subject. This theory also provides the central argument in Francis Fukuyama's widely publicized essay on "The End of History?" in *The National Interest,* No. 16 (Summer 1989), pp. 3-18. For an excellent critique of the theory, see Samuel P. Huntington, "No Exit: The Errors of Endism," *The National Interest,* No. 17 (Fall 1989), pp. 3-11.

71. There is a good empirical literature on the relationship between democracy and war. See, for example, Steve Chan, "Mirror, Mirror on the Wall . . . Are the Freer Countries More Pacific?" *Journal of Conflict Resolution,* Vol. 28, No. 4 (December 1984), pp. 617-648; Erich Weede, "Democracy and War Involvement," in ibid., pp. 649-664; Bruce M. Russett and R. Joseph Monsen, "Bureaucracy and Polyarchy As Predictors of Performance," *Comparative Political Studies,* Vol. 8, No. 1 (April 1975), pp. 5-31; and Melvin Small and J. David Singer, "The War-Proneness of Democratic Regimes, 1816-1965," *The Jerusalem Journal of International Relations,* Vol. 1, No. 4 (Summer 1976), pp. 50-69.

72. See, for example, Stanislav Andreski, "On the Peaceful Disposition of Military Dictatorships," *Journal of Strategic Studies,* Vol. 3, No. 3 (December 1980), pp. 3-10.

73. For a discussion of the hostile relations that existed between the United States and Britain during the nineteenth century, see H. C. Allen, *Great Britain and the United States: A History of Anglo-American Relations, 1783-1952* (London: Odhams, 1954).

74. For a discussion of this rapprochement, see Stephen R. Rock, *Why Peace Breaks Out: Great Power Rapprochement in Historical Perspective* (Chapel Hill: University of North Carolina Press, 1989), chap. 2.

75. For a good discussion of Franco-British relations during the nineteenth century, see P. J. V. Rolo, *Entente Cordiale: The Origins and Negotiation of the Anglo-French Agreements of 8 April 1904* (New York: St. Martins, 1969), pp. 16-109.

76. Stephen Rock, who has examined the rapprochement between Britain and France, argues that the principal motivating force behind their improved relations derived from geopolitical considerations, not shared political beliefs. See Rock, *Why Peace Breaks Out,* chap. 4.

77. Doyle recognizes this problem and thus has a lengthy footnote that attempts to deal with it. See "Kant, Liberal Legacies, and Foreign Affairs [Part One]," pp. 216-217, n. 8. He argues that "Germany was a liberal state under republican law for domestic issues," but that the "emperor's active role in foreign affairs . . . made imperial Germany a state divorced from the control of its citizenry in foreign affairs." However, an examination of the decision-making process leading to World War I reveals that the emperor (Wilhelm II) was not a prime mover in foreign affairs and that he was no more bellicose than other members of the German elite, including the leading civilian official, Chancellor Bethmann-Hollweg.

78. This point is illustrated by the 1976 controversy over the so-called "Sonnenfeldt Doctrine." Helmut Sonnenfeldt, an adviser to Secretary of State Henry Kissinger, was reported to have said in late 1975 that the United States should support Soviet domination of Eastern Europe. It was clear from the ensuing debate that whether or not Sonnenfeldt in fact made such a claim, no administration could publicly adopt that position. See U.S. Congress, House Committee on International Relations, *Hearings on*

United States National Security Policy Vis-à-Vis Eastern Europe (The "Sonnenfeldt Doctrine"), 94th Cong., 2nd sess. (Washington, D.C.: U.S. GPO, April 12, 1976).

79. For an optimistic assessment of how the West can enhance Gorbachev's prospects of succeeding, see Jack Snyder, "International Leverage on Soviet Domestic Change," *World Politics,* Vol. 42, No. 1 (October 1989), pp. 1–30.

80. Advancing this argument is Van Evera, "Why Europe Matters, Why the Third World Doesn't."

81. On the evolution of nationalistic history-teaching in Europe see Kennedy, "The Decline of Nationalistic History," and Dance, *History the Betrayer.*

82. My thinking on this matter has been influenced by conversations with Stephen Van Evera.

CHAPTER 8

The Case against "Europe"

Noel Malcolm

Noel Malcolm is a political columnist for London's The Daily Telegraph. *His most recent books are* Kosovo: A Short History *(1999) and* Bosnia: A Short History *(1996), published by New York University Press. He is also author of* The Origins of English Nonsense *(1999) and editor of "The Correspondence, 1622-1659," in* The Clarendon Edition of the Works of Thomas Hobbes.

A FLAWED IDEAL

The case against "Europe" is not the same as a case against Europe. Quite the contrary. "Europe" is a project, a concept, a cause: the final goal that the European Community (EC) has been moving toward ever since its hesitant beginnings in the 1950s. It involves the creation of a united European state with its own constitution, government, parliament, currency, foreign policy, and army. Some of the machinery for this is already in place, and enough of the blueprints are in circulation for there to be little doubt about the overall design. Those who are in favor of Europe—that is, those who favor increasing the freedom and prosperity of all who live on the European continent—should view the creation of this hugely artificial political entity with a mixture of alarm and dismay.

The synthetic project of "Europe" has almost completely taken over the natural meaning of the word. In most European countries today, people talk simply about being "pro-Europe" or "anti-Europe"; anyone who questions more political integration can be dismissed as motivated by mere xenophobic hostility toward the rest of the continent. Other elements of the "Euro-

Reprinted by permission of *Foreign Affairs* (March/April 1995). Copyright 1995 by the Council on Foreign Relations, Inc.

pean" political language reinforce this attitude. During the 1991–93 debate over the Maastricht treaty, for example, there was an almost hypnotic emphasis on clichés about transport. We were warned that we must not miss the boat or the bus, that we would be left standing on the platform when the European train went out, or that insufficient enthusiasm would cause us to suffer a bumpy ride in the rear wagon. All these images assumed a fixed itinerary and a preordained destination. Either you were for that destination, or you were against "Europe." The possibility that people might argue in favor of rival positive goals for Europe was thus eliminated from the consciousness of European politicians.

The concept of "Europe" is accompanied, in other words, by a doctrine of historical inevitability. This can take several different forms: a utopian belief in inevitable progress, a quasi-Marxist faith in the iron laws of history (again involving the withering away of the nation-state), or a kind of cartographic mysticism that intuits that certain large areas on the map are crying out to emerge as single geopolitical units. These beliefs have received some hard knocks from twentieth-century history. Inevitability is, indeed, a word most often heard on the lips of those who have to turn the world upside down to achieve the changes they desire.

ON LITTLE CAT FEET

The origins of the "European" political project can be traced back to a number of politicians, writers, and visionaries of the interwar period: people such as the half-Austrian, half-Japanese theorist Richard Coudenhove-Kalergi, former Italian Foreign Minister Carlo Sforza, and Jean Monnet, a French brandy salesman turned international bureaucrat. When their idea of a rationalized and unified Europe was first floated in the 1920s and 1930s, it sounded quite similar in spirit to the contemporaneous campaign to make Esperanto the world language. Who, at that stage, could confidently have declared that one of these schemes had the force of historical inevitability behind it and the other did not? Both had theoretical benefits to offer, although they were almost certainly outweighed by the practical difficulties of attaining them. It is not hard, surely, to imagine an alternative history of Europe after World War II in which the EC never came into existence and in which, therefore, the project of a united Europe would occupy a footnote almost as tiny as that devoted to the work of the International Esperanto League. Things seem inevitable only because people made them happen.

The impetus behind the "European" idea came from a handful of politicians in France and Germany who decided that a supranational enterprise might solve the problem of Franco-German rivalry, which they saw as the root cause of three great European wars since 1870. For this purpose alone, an arrangement involving just those two countries might have sufficed. But other factors coincidentally were at work, in particular the Cold War, which made the strengthening of Western Europe as a political bloc desirable, and the barely concealed resentment of French President Charles de Gaulle toward "les Anglo-Saxons," which made him look more favorably on the EC as an Anglo-Saxon-free area that could be politically dominated by France.

Even with these large-scale factors at work, however, it is doubtful whether the "European" project would have got off the ground without the ingenuity of a few individuals, notably Monnet and former French Foreign Minister Robert Schuman. The method they invented was what political theorists now call "functionalism." By meshing together the economies of participating countries bit by bit, they believed a point would eventually be reached where political unification would seem a natural expression of the way in which those countries were already interacting. As Schuman put it in 1950, "Europe will not be built all at once, or as a single whole: it will be built by concrete achievements which first create de facto solidarity."

And so the method has proceeded, from coal and steel (European Coal and Steel Community Treaty), through agriculture and commerce (Treaty of Rome), environmental regulation and research and development (Single European Act), to transport policy, training, immigration policy, and a whole battery of measures designed to bring about full economic and monetary union (the Maastricht treaty). Step by step with these developments has been the march toward political unification, with the growth of a European Court, the development of the European Parliament from a talking-shop of national appointees into a directly elected assembly with real legislative powers, the extension of majority voting at the Council of Ministers, and even the announcement, in the Maastricht treaty, of something called European citizenship, the rights and duties of which have yet to be defined. Almost every one of these political changes was justified at the time on practical grounds: just a slight adjustment to make things easier, or more effective, or to reflect new realities. The economic changes and the transfers of new areas of competence to EC institutions are likewise usually presented as mere practical adjustments. At the same time, many continental European politicians (such as German Chancellor Helmut Kohl and French President François Mitterrand) talk openly of the ultimate grand political goal: the creation of a federal European state.

There is a strange disjunction between these two types of "European" discourse, the practical and the ideal. But this is just a sign of functionalism successfully at work. The argument for "Europe" switches to and fro, from claims about practical benefits to expressions of political idealism and back again. If one disagrees with advocates of "Europe" about the practical advantages, they say, "Well, you may be right about this or that disadvantage, but surely it's a price worth paying for such a wonderful political ideal." And if one casts doubt on the political desirability of the ideal, they reply, "Never mind about that, just think of the economic advantages." The truth is that both arguments for "Europe" are fundamentally flawed.

DUNCE CAP

The economic project embodied in the European Economic Community (EEC) was a true reflection of its origins in a piece of Franco-German bargaining. German industry was given the opportunity to flood other member states with its exports, thanks to a set of rules designed to eliminate artificial barriers to competition and trade within the "common market." France, on the other hand, was given an elaborate system of protection for its agriculture, the so-called Common Agricultural Policy.

The general aims of the CAP, as set out in Article 39 of the Treaty of Rome, included stable markets and "a fair standard of living for the agricultural community." On that slender basis, France established one of the most complex and expensive systems of agricultural protectionism in human history. It is based on high external tariffs, high export subsidies, and internal price support by means of intervention buying (the most costly system of price support yet invented, since it involves collecting and storing tens of millions of tons of excess produce). By the time this system was fully established in 1967, EEC farm prices had been driven up to 175 percent of world prices for beef, 185 percent for wheat, 400 percent for butter, and 440 percent for sugar. The annual cost of the CAP is now $45 billion and rising; more than ten percent of this is believed to be paid to a myriad of scams. Thanks to this policy, a European family of four now pays more than $1,600 a year in additional food costs—a hidden tax greater than the poll tax that brought rioters out onto the streets of London.

Even the most hardened advocates of "Europe" are always a little embarrassed by the CAP. The massive corruption that flows from it—phantom exports picking up export subsidies, smuggled imports relabeled as EC products, nonexistent Italian olive groves receiving huge subsidies, and so on—is embarrassing enough, but it is the system itself that requires defense. Ten or twenty years ago, one used to hear its proponents arguing that at least there would be stocks of food available if Western Europe came under siege. That argument seemed thin then and sounds positively fatuous today. If pressed, they will insist that the CAP is gradually being reformed, pointing out that the beef mountains and wine lakes are getting smaller. These reforms, however, are achieved only by spending more money in such schemes as the infamous set-aside payments given to farmers as a reward for not growing anything. More commonly, though, the defenders of "Europe" will say that the CAP is just an unfortunate detail, that they are aware of its problems, and that one really should not use it to blacken "Europe's" name.

But the CAP is not just a detail. It is, by a huge margin, the largest single item of EC spending, taking up roughly 60 percent of the budget every year. It dominates the EC'S external trade policy, distorting the world market and seriously undermining the ability of poorer countries elsewhere to export their own agricultural produce. It almost broke the Uruguay round of the General Agreement on Tariffs and Trade (GATT), thanks to the French government's irrational obsession with agricultural protectionism—irrational, that is, because agriculture accounts for only four percent of French GDP, and much of the other 96 percent would have benefited from lower world tariffs.

No account of the economic functioning of "Europe" can fail to begin with the CAP, and no study that examines it can fail to conclude that it is a colossal waste of money. Even the European Commission, which administers the scheme, has admitted that "farmers do not seem to have benefited from the increasing support which they have received." Enthusiasts for "Europe" often wax lyrical about European achievements such as the German highway system or the French railways—things that were built by national governments. Almost the only major achievement of the EC—the only thing it has constructed and operated itself—is the CAP. It is not an encouraging precedent.

LEVELING THE PLAYING FIELD

The CAP sets the tone for other areas of the EC's trading policy. Although it would be unfair to describe the EC as behaving like a "Fortress Europe" (so far), it is nevertheless true that "Europe" has evolved an elaborate system of tariffs and discriminatory trading agreements to protect its sensitive industries. Agriculture has the highest tariffs; ranging below it are such products as steel, textiles, clothing, and footwear (as Poland, Hungary, and the Czech Republic have discovered to their dismay—food, steel, textiles, clothing, and footwear being their own most important products). The EC has been at the forefront in developing so-called voluntary export restraints with countries such as Japan. In addition, "Europe" has shown extraordinary ingenuity in adapting the GATT's "antidumping" measures to block the flow of innumerable imports: electronic typewriters, hydraulic excavators, dot-matrix printers, audiocassettes, and halogen lights from Japan; compact disc players from Japan and Korea; small-screen color televisions from Korea, China, and Hong Kong, and so on.

A recent study of EC trade policy by L. A. Winters uses the phrase "managed liberalization" to describe the EC's foot-dragging progress toward freer trade. "Managed liberalization," notes Winters, "is a substitute for genuine liberalization, but a poor one, because it typically attenuates competition in precisely those sectors which are most in need of improved efficiency." Nor is this surprising, since the trade policy emerges from a system of political bargaining in which the governments of EC member states compete to protect their favorite industries. Massive state subsidies to flagship enterprises (French car manufacturers, Spanish steel mills, Belgian and Greek national airlines) are common practice. In addition, the officials at the European Commission in Brussels are strongly influenced by the French *dirigiste* tradition, which sees it as the role of the state to select and nurture special "champion" industries. This was the driving force behind the new powers granted to the EC in 1986 to "strengthen the scientific and technological basis of European industry." In practice, this means spending millions of taxpayers' dollars developing French microchips that will never compete with East Asian ones on the open market.

Inside the tariff wall, a kind of free trade area has indeed been created. Many obstacles to trade have been removed (though important barriers remain in the realm of services, as British insurance firms are still discovering when they try to break into the German market), and industry as a whole has benefited from this process of internal liberalization. However, the long-term effects may be more harmful than beneficial. In their attempt to create a level playing field for competition on equal terms within the EC, the administrators of "Europe" have leveled up, not down. They have tried to raise both the standards and the costs of industry throughout the community to the high levels practiced in Europe's foremost industrial country, Germany. When this process is complete, industrialists inside the EC may indeed sell goods to one another on equal terms, but their goods will all be uncompetitive on the world market.

This leveling up occurs in two areas. The first is the harmonization of standards. Brussels has issued a mass of regulations laying down the most minute specifications for industrial products and processes; the dominant influence on these has been the German Institute for Norms, which has the strictest standards in Europe. Harmonization is meant to simplify matters for producers, who now have only one standard within the EC instead of various national ones. But in many cases, as the task of matching product to standard becomes relatively simpler, it is also made absolutely more expensive. In addition, the EC has powers relating to environmental protection and health and safety at work, which are increasingly used to impose German-style costs on industries and services. The costs fall especially heavily on small enterprises, which have to pay disproportionately for monitoring equipment, inspection, and certification. This distorts the market in favor of large corporations, penalizing the small enterprises that are the seed corn of any growing economy.

The second way in which the playing field is leveled up to German standards is in the social costs of labor. German employers pay heavily for the privilege of giving people jobs: there are generous pension schemes to pay for health insurance, long holidays, maternity and paternity leave, and other forms of social insurance. As a consequence, labor costs are $25 per hour in the former West Germany (the highest in the world), as opposed to $17 in Japan, $16 in the United States, and $12 in the United Kingdom. German work practices mean that a machine in a German factory operates an average of only 53 hours a week, as opposed to 69 hours in France and 76 in Britain. And the average worker in Germany spends only 1,506 hours each year actually at work, as opposed to 1,635 hours in Britain, 1,847 in the United States, and 2,165 in Japan.

Over the last five years, the European Commission has proposed a whole range of measures to increase the rights of workers and limit their working hours. When measures in this so-called social action program could not gain the required unanimous support from member states (notably Britain), they were dressed up as health and safety matters, for which only a majority vote is required. Further costs on employers were imposed by a "social protocol" added to the Maastricht treaty. Although Britain was able to gain a special exemption from this agreement, it is likely that many of the new measures adopted under the protocol eventually will filter back to Britain through other parts of the "European" administrative machine.

Some of these measures are inspired, no doubt, by concern for the plight of the poorest workers in the community's southern member states. But the general aim of the policy is clearly to protect the high-labor-cost economies (above all, Germany) from competitors employing cheaper labor. In the short or medium term, this policy will damage the economies of the poorer countries, which will have artificially high labor costs imposed on them. In the long term, it will harm Germany, too, by reducing its incentive to adapt to worldwide competition. "Europe," whose share of world trade and relative rate of economic growth are already in decline, will enter the next century stumbling under the weight of its own costs like a woolly mammoth sinking into a melting tundra.

The final expression of this leveling-up syndrome is the plan for monetary union. As outlined in the Maastricht treaty, the idea is to create a Euro-deutsche mark, operated by a body closely modeled on the Bundesbank and situated in Frankfurt. Earlier moves in this direction were not encouraging: the European Exchange Rate Mechanism, which linked the currencies of member states to the deutsche mark, fell apart spectacularly in October 1992. In the process, the British government spent nearly $6 billion in a doomed attempt to prop up the pound, and Germany is thought to have spent roughly $14 billion in an equally futile effort to support the Italian lira. The artificially high interest rates that countries such as Britain had imposed to maintain their currency's parity with the deutsche mark severely intensified the 1989–93 recession; the human costs of the unnecessary indebtedness, bankruptcies, and unemployment cannot be calculated.

The Exchange Rate Mechanism was, as Professor Sir Alan Walters, an adviser to former British Prime Minister Margaret Thatcher, famously put it, "half-baked." Currencies were neither fully fixed nor freely floating but pegged to so-called fixed rates that could be changed. This provided the world markets, at times of pressure on any particular currency, with an irresistible one-way bet. That problem, of course, will not arise once the currencies of "Europe" are merged into a single Euro-mark—though the activities of the world currency markets in the days just before the conversion terms are announced will be a wonder to behold.

Once the Euro-mark is in place, a different set of problems will arise. Whatever the "economic convergence programs" dutifully embarked on by the governments of member states, this single currency will be covering a number of national economies with widely varying characteristics. Hitherto, changes in the values of their national currencies have been one of the essential ways in which the relative strengths and weaknesses of those countries were both expressed and adjusted. With that mechanism gone, other forms of expression will operate, such as the collapse of industries or the mass migration of labor.

The European Commission understands this problem and has a ready solution: massive transfers of money to the weaker economies of "Europe." The machinery to administer this huge program of subsidies is already in place, in the form of regional funds, "structural" funds, and "cohesion payments." All that is lacking so far is the actual money, for which purpose the outgoing president of the European Commission, Jacques Delors, recently proposed increasing the European budget by more than $150 billion over the next five years.

A model for the future of an economically unified Europe can be found in modern Italy, which united the prosperous, advanced provinces of the north with the Third World poverty of the south. After more than a century of political and economic union, huge disparities still remain between the two halves of Italy—despite (or indeed partly because of) all the subsidies that are poured into the south via institutions such as the Cassa del Mezzogiorno, the independent society established by the Italian government to help develop the south. As southern Italians have had the opportunity to discover, an economy based on subsidies unites the inefficiencies of state planning with almost limitless opportunities for graft and corruption. It is a sad irony that today, just as the leaders of "Europe" are preparing for unification, the politicians of Italy are seriously considering dismantling their country into two or three separate states.

DECAFFEINATED POLITICS

So much for the economic benefits of European unity. At this point the advocates of "Europe" usually shift to their other line of defense. This is not just a money-grubbing enterprise, they say, to be totted up in terms of profit and loss: "Europe" is a political ideal, a spiritual adventure, a new experiment in brotherhood and cooperation. Has it not made war in Europe unthinkable? Is it not the natural next step for mankind, at a time when the old idea of national sovereignty is evidently obsolete? Does it not show the way to the abolition of old-fashioned national feeling, with all its hostilities, prejudices, and resentments?

The answer to all these questions, unfortunately, is no. The argument that the EC is responsible for the lack of war in post-1945 Europe is hard to substantiate. A far more obvious reason is the Cold War, which obliged Western Europe to adopt a common defensive posture and a system of deterrence so effective that war between Western and Eastern Europe never happened. The fact that a group of West European countries were able to cooperate in the EC was more a symptom of the lack of belligerent tensions in postwar Western Europe than a cause. Liberal democracies had been established in most West European countries after 1945; even if the EEC had not existed, it is hard to imagine a scenario in which Germany would have wanted to invade France, or France drop nuclear bombs on Germany. Even if one concedes for the sake of argument that the EEC did ensure peace for the last generation or two, this cannot be used as a reason for closer integration, since the EEC had this supposed effect at a time when it was not a unified supranational entity but a group of cooperating nation-states.

The idea of "Europe" is founded, however, on the belief that the nation-state is obsolete. This is an article of faith against which rational arguments cannot prevail. It is no use pointing out that the most successful countries in the modern world—Japan, the United States, and indeed Germany itself—are nation-states. It matters little if one says that some of the most dynamic economies today belong to small states—South Korea, Taiwan, Singapore—that feel no need to submerge themselves in large multinational entities. And it is regarded as bad taste to point out that the multinational federations most recently in the news were the U.S.S.R. and the Federal Republic of Yugoslavia. They are merely the latest in a long list of multinational states that have collapsed in modern times, from the Austro-Hungarian Empire to the various postcolonial federations set up by the British in central Africa, east Africa, and the West Indies. Nigeria, for example, kept Biafra only by warfare and starvation; India needs armed force to retain Nagaland and Kashmir. "But Europe will not be like that," say the federalists. "We have traditions of mutual tolerance and civilized behavior." Yes, we have some such traditions; they are the traditions that have evolved within fairly stable nation-states. Whether they last indefinitely under the new conditions of multinational politics remains to be seen.

What will political life be like in the sort of European federation currently proposed in Brussels and Bonn? Some of the powers of national governments will be transferred upward to the European level, while others will move down to a "Europe of the regions" (Catalonia, Bavaria, Wales, etc.). The official vision of political life at the uppermost level is essentially that of Jean Monnet, the original inventor of the community: a technocrat's ideal, a world in which large-scale solutions are devised to large-scale problems by far-sighted expert administrators. (The most common argument for abolishing nation-states is that problems nowadays are just too big for individual states to handle. In fact, there have always been issues that cross international borders, from postal services to drug enforcement to global trade. It cannot be the size of the problem that dictates that it must be dealt with by supranational authority rather than international cooperation, but some other reason that the advocates of European federation have yet to explain.)

This technocratic vision is of a decaffeinated political world, from which real politics has been carefully extracted. Things will surely turn out differently. Real politics will still operate at the European level. The one form it will not take, however, is that of federation-wide democratic politics. For that, we would need "Europe"-wide parties, operating across the whole federation in the way that the Republican and Democratic parties operate across the United States.

There are already some ghostly transnational groupings in the European Parliament: the Socialist Group, the European People's Party (the Christian Democrats), and so on. But these are just alliances formed at Strasbourg by members of the European Parliament elected on the tickets of their own national parties. No one can really envisage ordinary voters in, say, Denmark being inspired by the leader of their preferred Euro-party, who might make his or her speeches in Portuguese. The basic facts of linguistic, cultural, and geographic difference make it impossible to imagine federation-wide mass politics ever becoming the dominant form of political life in Europe. Instead, the pursuit of national interests by national politicians will continue at the highest "European" levels. Yet it will do so in a way subtly different from the way in which local representatives within a national political system press for the interests of their localities. Although a member of parliament for Yorkshire may push hard on Yorkshire's behalf, on all major issues the member votes according to what he or she thinks is in Britain's interest; the MP belongs to a national party that addresses those issues with national policies.

The art of "European" politics, on the other hand, will be to do nothing more than dress up national interests as if they were Europe-wide ones. With any particular nation paying only a small proportion of the European budget, each set of national politicians will seek to maximize those European spending projects that benefit their own country. The modus operandi of European politics, therefore (already visible in the Council of Ministers today), will be logrolling and back-scratching: you support my pet proposal, even though you think it is a bad one, and in return I shall back yours. This is a recipe not only for nonstop increases in spending, but also for radical incoherence in policymaking. And with politics at the highest level operating as a scramble for funds, it is hard to see how politicians at the lower level of Europe's "regions" can fail to replicate it: they will have fewer real governmental powers but more populist opportunities to woo their voters with spending.

This type of political life is accompanied by two grave dangers. In any system where democratic accountability is attenuated and the powers of politicians to make deals behind closed doors is strengthened, the likely consequence is a growth in political corruption. Corrupt practices are already common in the political life of several European countries: their exposure has led recently to the prosecution, flight into exile, or suicide of former prime ministers in Italy, Greece, and France. A federal Europe, far from correcting these vices, will offer them a wider field of action.

A more serious danger, however, lies in store for the political life of a federal "Europe": the revival of the politics of nationalist hostility and resentment. Aggressive nationalism is typically a syndrome of the dispossessed, of those who feel power has been taken from them. Foreigners are often the most convenient focus of such resentment, whatever the true causes of the powerlessness may be. But in a system where power really has been taken from national governments and transferred to European bodies in which, by definition, the majority vote will always lie in the hands of foreigners, such nationalist thinking will acquire an undeniable logic. Of course, if "Europe" moves ever onward and upward in an unprecedented increase in prosperity for all its citizens, the grounds for resentment may be slight; that is not, however, a scenario that anyone can take for granted.

In this respect, the whole "European" project furnishes a classic example of the fallacious belief that the way to remove hostility between groups, peoples, or states is to build new structures over their heads. Too often that method yields exactly the opposite result. The most commonly repeated version of this argument is that Germany needs to be "tied in" or "tied down" by a structure of European integration to prevent it from wandering off dangerously into the empty spaces of Mitteleuropa. If Germany really has different interests from the rest of "Europe," the way to deal with it, surely, is not to force it into an institutional straitjacket (which can only build up German resentment in the long run), but to devise ways of pursuing those interests that are compatible with the interests of its allies and partners. So far, Germany's involvement in "Europe" looks rather like the action of a jovial uncle at a children's party who, to show goodwill, allows his hands to be tied behind his back. It is not a posture that he will want to stay in for long, and his mood may change when he becomes aware of innumerable little fingers rifling through his pockets.

FIRST AS FARCE . . .

The final question is whether "Europe" has a valuable role to play on the world stage. The "Europe" we have at present is a product of the Cold War era. Now that the whole situation in Eastern Europe has changed, one might expect the engineers of the EC to go back to the geopolitical drawing board. Instead, they are pressing ahead with the same old set of plans at a faster pace. Some enthusiasts for "Europe," such as former EC Commissioner Ralf Dahrendorf or British Foreign Minister Douglas Hurd, have even claimed that the internal development of the EC in the 1980s played a decisive part in bringing about the fall of communism in the east. One rather doubts many East European dissidents ever said: "Have you heard about the new Brussels Directive on Permitted Levels of Lawnmower Noise? This means we really must bring down the communist regime!" The Hurd/Dahrendorf thesis bears a curious resemblance to the recent Michael Jackson music video entitled "Redeeming Eastern Europe," in which the pop star defeats the Red Army singlehandedly while adoring children chant messages of goodwill in (coincidentally) Esperanto.

Since the removal of the Iron Curtain, the new democracies of Eastern Europe have found their ostensible savior strangely reluctant to help it in the one way that matters—namely, by buying their goods. They all want to join "Europe," of course, for two simple reasons: because it is a rich man's club in which fellow members possess huge funds for investment, and because they want to be part of some kind of security grouping. The first requirement could be met by any economic club of nations, of the sort that the EC was for its first couple of decades; it does not call for European political integration. Indeed, any such development would be a strange reward for those East European countries that have only just freed themselves from the embrace of another multinational empire.

The question of European security raises a similar point. The long-term effect of the end of the Cold War will be a gradual reduction in the American defense commitment to Europe. This prospect even causes some pleasure in those parts of Europe—above all, France and Germany—where anti-Americanism has long flourished. Clearly, the Europeans will have to take more care of their own defense. But the question is whether this requires political integration, a Euro-army, a Euro-foreign policy, and a Euro-government. For more than 50 years, NATO has managed to defend Western Europe without any such political integration, and NATO is clearly the most successful international organization in modern history.

"Of course," comes the reply, "NATO was able to function as a loose intergovernmental body because its members were facing a clear common threat. The threats and challenges will be more various now, so intergovernmental agreement will be harder to obtain." But that is precisely why such matters should not be funneled into a "European" government operating by majority vote. "Europe" is indeed a collection of countries with different national interests and foreign commitments. On each separate security issue, individual states may have concerns of their own that are not shared by their fellow members (Britain over the Falklands, France over North Africa, Germany and

Italy over Yugoslavia, and so on). To try to form a single "European" policy on such issues, whether by unanimity, consensus, or majority voting, is to guarantee at best ineffective compromise and at worst total self-paralysis.

This simple truth has been demonstrated twice in the last four years—the first time as farce, the second as tragedy. The farce was "Europe's" reaction to Iraq's 1990 invasion of Kuwait, when Germany agonized over sending a few trainer jets to Turkey, France sent an aircraft carrier to the Persian Gulf bearing helicopters instead of planes, and Belgium refused to sell ammunition to the British army. The tragedy is Yugoslavia. "This is the hour of Europe!" cried the egregious Jacques Poos, foreign minister of Luxembourg, when Yugoslavian President Slobodan Milošević's army first opened fire in Slovenia and Croatia in the summer of 1991. "We do not interfere in American affairs; we trust that America will not interfere in European affairs," said Jacques Delors, voicing the only consistent and distinctive theme of "European" foreign policy: graceless anti-Americanism. The desire to produce a foreign policy by consensus was just strong enough to ensure that those countries who did understand what was happening in Yugoslavia (above all, Germany) were kept in check by those who did not (above all, Britain). As a result, the recognition of Croatia and Slovenia was delayed by six months, and when it finally came it did so unaccompanied by any measures to protect Milošević's other prospective victims from attack.

The mentality behind the drive for a "European" foreign policy displays a childlike logic. "Think how strong and effective our foreign policies will be if we add them all together!" it says. Similarly, one might say: think what a beautiful color we can make if we mix all the colors of the paint box! The result, inevitably, is a muddy shade of brown.

CHAPTER 9

Jean-Marie Le Pen, the French National Front, and "Europe"

Jean-Marie Le Pen was born in 1928 and entered far-right politics early on. He founded the French National Front Party (FN) in 1972, but as a young man he had marked himself already two decades earlier as a nationalist extremist in the Algèrie française *cause of keeping Algeria French. He was a soldier during France's brutal Algerian war in the late 1950s and early 1960s, and has been accused of having participated in torture. He has been elected to the French Parliament and was elected to the European Parliament in 1984, with the goal of combating federalist tendencies. He has also been a presidential candidate several times. In 1988 he won 16 percent on the first ballot of France's two ballot system, in which, it is said, on the first ballot people "vote their heart" before they "vote their wallet" on the second ballot. Worryingly, more or less one-third of the French people regularly tell opinion pollsters that they agree with some of the National Front's ideas.*

Le Pen and other European leaders like him reject being called "far right" or "extreme right." They want to be called the "national right," meaning a patriotic party and cause. Naturally there is much acrimony on this point. The National Front has long been associated with the goal of harsh repatriation of illegal immigrants, "France for the French," and support for capital punishment (which was abolished by the first François Mitterrand government in 1981). Altogether Le Pen and the National Front generally have been considered a racist and xenophobic element in French politics. Their largest political scores were achieved in the mid-1980s. The top party leadership—Le Pen and Bruno Megret—have since split and the National Front is weakened today.

The first of two interviews with Jean-Marie Le Pen reproduced here is from Le Figaro *of December 1, 1991, as the Maastricht treaty was in final negotiation. In it he explains his intense opposition to a federal Europe. In inflammatory language, he calls the Maastricht blueprint a Europe of the "federastes," a "suicidal policy" for the French. He advocates a confederal Europe based on nation-state sovereignty. In the second interview, from*

191

the National Front's own complaisant newspaper, National Hebdo *(Decem-ber 12, 1991), Le Pen asserts that the Maastricht treaty will mean "the death of [European] nations."*

INTERVIEW BY *LE FIGARO*: DECEMBER 1, 1991

Le Figaro: Are you favorable to signing the [Maastricht] treaty of political union?

Le Pen: No, absolutely against it. We have been fighting for years in the European Parliament—mainly by ourselves I have to add—against the rise of European federal-ism and against the construction of a "super-state" that would rapidly empty the nations of their substance. The Centrist-Socialist Europe that MM. Dumas, Mitterrand, Delors, plus their accomplices in the [French Parliamentary Conservative] opposition, want to create would mean the death of French independence and the disappearance of its historical individuality. . . .

Le Figaro: To be clear, you hoped for the Maastricht summit to fail?

Le Pen: Yes, I say it frankly, I hoped that Maastricht would fail. Because I believe that the federal Europe that is being foisted on us, that has the immense defect of being run by an anonymous and irresponsible bureaucracy—generally socialist to boot—that Europe might have been a good idea at the end of the nineteenth century. It might have prevented the two world wars. But as we head into the third millennium I believe it to be totally contrary to trends expressed in public opinion, in Western as well as Eastern Europe. A lot of the French have kept silent because they have allowed them-selves to be convinced that being part of Europe in 1993 would mean an economic rebound and new growth. I think that, unfortunately, the year 1992 will not see the arrival of Santa Claus but rather of a hard taskmaster! All the European agreements have been achieved on the back of French interests. . . .

Le Figaro: Will the National Front lead the fight against a federal Europe?

Le Pen: You can be sure of it! The Brussels socialist technocrats want a federal Europe, that is a super-state. Jacques Delors [president of the EU Commission] doesn't hide it. He says that 80 percent of the laws that will regulate French life will be decided in Brussels. But this process is not democratic, and the majority of the French don't want this European super-state. Those who would impose it will thus, in my opinion, commit a genuine treason against the French nation, and all the means we dispose of will be used against it.

The FN quite naturally leads the patriotic fight against the creation of this Europe that would destroy France! Because we are being led, without any democratic poll of the peoples, toward a monster that we [in the FN] call the "Europe of the federasts," a super-structure that is directly contrary to the main currents in public opinion today.

In the European Economic Community, we are already fighting the ever stronger hold of Brussels on our economy, above all the idea of equalization, of massification, which you find for example in the matter of equalizing value added tax. There was no reason to equalize value added taxes.

Translated from "Contre l'Europe des 'federastes' " (*Le Figaro,* December 11, 1991) and printed by permission of the publisher.

Le Figaro: Are you equally against any form of economic union?

Le Pen: We agree with the idea of creating a common currency as a unit of account, with the ecu [precursor of the euro] coexisting with national currencies. But we are completely against the idea that a common currency should lead to the abolition of national currencies, which would mean that we would lose our national budgetary independence.

I believe that economic union has not had only advantages for our country, far from it. In my opinion it has resulted in the destruction of French agriculture and the promotion of competing agricultures, when originally we joined the Common Market with the view that our agriculture would be some sort of a protected domain.

I observe in addition that the Rome treaty was violated, because it foresaw a European preference that has not been respected. It foresaw as well an equalization of incomes between industry and agriculture. But all of that has been a tremendous failure.

Le Figaro: What form of European cooperation do you propose?

Le Pen: In the European Parliament I am fighting for the idea of "l'Europe des patries" [a Europe of nation-states], a confederation that would have a clear goal: seeking political, economic, and even military cooperation of the European states among themselves. This cooperation in confederal form would be structured with respect for the identity of the peoples, of the institutions of the different states, and of national independence.

I don't exclude that there could be a specific form of cooperation between the European nations. To the contrary. I even believe that we must give to the European peoples of the east the hope of joining the European confederation of tomorrow, a confederation that is in no way the "common house" talked about by [Soviet leader Mikhail] Gorbachev, but rather a confederation that would put together all those countries that are historically and geographically European.

Le Figaro: Do you believe that the Schengen agreement [eliminating internal boundaries between states] should be denounced?

Le Pen: We have put the cart before the horse! First it would have been necessary to decide what the boundaries of Europe are. The problem is that they don't exist. We are bringing down the borders between Germany, Benelux, and France, and, as a consequence, with the other countries that are our neighbors. This is a suicidal policy at a time when our country and our continent are faced with increasingly pressing immigration.

Today we should not be abolishing our frontiers but rather reinforcing them. Some people say, "The FN wants to create a fortress." But there are situations in which it is useful to close oneself into a fortress: It is when the enemy wants to submerge you and attack you.

And a border may be open or closed, or even half-opened. I think it is utopian, and even suicidal, to place one's confidence in the generalized free circulation of goods, capital, and people, because if until now national structures have proven themselves indispensable, it is because they are congruent with the interest of nations. . . .

INTERVIEW BY THE *NATIONAL-HEBDO* NEWSPAPER: DECEMBER 12, 1991

National Hebdo: M. Le Pen, the French media . . . reported with gusto the hostile reception you received in London. What really happened?

Le Pen: There were the usual two hundred socialist/communist demonstrators. Nothing out of the ordinary. . . . The attacks of a part of the British press didn't seem to me to represent a widespread feeling.

National Hebdo: . . . A recent poll indicated that 75 percent of the French didn't know what was going to happen at Maastricht. What do you think of this?

Le Pen: It's not surprising, given the clever dissimulation in the way the matter was presented to the French people. It was necessary to hide from them the fact that after fifteen centuries of existence [the French nation] was going to enter the night of inexistence because of Maastricht. The death of nations is being plotted at Maastricht. And this is being done by the will of a handful of politicians. . . . This is all the more serious and criminal in that what will be decided at Maastricht isn't even in the competence of the [French] National Assembly. For this kind of giving up of sovereignty a reform of the constitution is necessary. . . .

The [just-concluded London Congress of the] European Organization of Rightist Movements has formally condemned this entire federalist enterprise and the attempts by the technocratic commission at Brussels to destroy national sovereignty. It is furthermore demanding the abolition of the commission and its replacement by a secretariat, a simple organ of administration. [The official convention document] speaks out against policies whose goal is to replace "a dying communism by a senile socialism."

National Hebdo: Great Britain continues to oppose including the term "federalism" in [European] agreements. Where do you think this could lead?

Le Pen: The Eurocrats naturally will try to get around this obstacle by creating an exception: the concept of federalism will hold for everyone but Great Britain. This of course would be contrary to all the rules and logic. . . .

Translated from the French (*Le National-Hebdo*, December 12, 1991) and printed by permission of the publisher.

CHAPTER 10

Europe: Escaping the Trap

Jean-Pierre Chevènement

Jean-Pierre Chevènement is a maverick French left-wing politician, a combination of classic French statist republican and Euro-skeptic. Long a French Socialist (PS) party member, deputy, and government official, he finally quit the Socialists in 1993 in the wake of the Maastricht Treaty success and close victory in a French referendum in September 1992. As a government minister Chevènement had resigned in 1983 as minister of industry to protest President François Mitterrand's pro-Europe decisions in the "Union of the Left" government's monetary crisis, again in 1986 over agricultural policy, and in 1991, as Socialist defense minister, to protest France's participation, still under President François Mitterrand, in the Gulf War.

Remaining nevertheless close to the Socialist party, he in 1993 founded a separate "left republican" splinter movement, the "Mouvement des Citoyens" (MDC or Citizens' Movement). He was then interior minister from 1997 in the Socialist Lionel Jospin's government, until a fourth resignation in August 2000 over a controversial bill to give the Corsican Regional Assembly limited legislative autonomy. The Mouvement des Citoyens, hovering at 3–5 percent of the vote, nevertheless runs with the mother Socialist party on joint European Parliament electoral lists.

Chevènement's uniqueness is to combine left- and right-wing positions. He is socialist, left-wing, and "republican," yet also nationalist, a normally conservative appellation. His upholds the French centralizing, statist tradition, standing guard over threats to national sovereignty from federalist European integration projects. Like Charles Pasqua on the right, Chevènement espouses not mere national sovereignty as such but the historical distinctiveness of French institutions—centralization, the crucial role historically of the state in defining French society and identity, and the "indi-

visibility of the republic," meaning that the republic must be a single constitutional space with no special laws or status for regional or other subnational considerations.

Chevènement's leftism, by contrast, is based on a vague doctrine of the role of the citoyen, a glorified and anachronistic version of the citizen in French revolutionary mythology. As a gauge of leftist authenticity, Chevènement still advocates formal alliance and even "historic reunification" of the French Socialists with the French Communist party (PCF), to get the best from, and to correct the defects of, social democracy and Stalinism. The MDC's "republican leftism" is in fact a third and fourth republic label, reflected in its poor showing at the polls.

In July-August 2000 Chevènement's "republican" rejection of damaging the "indivisibility of the republic" came to the fore over a Jospin government bill to offer the Corsican Regional Assembly limited legislative autonomy for the island. Chevènement resigned as interior minister saying that he could not in good conscience present to the French National Assembly the government's bill. Jospin's intention was to do something to mitigate the perennial separatist violence and demands for autonomy in Corisca, hoping that limited autonomy would rally Corsican moderates to oppose the separatists and stand up against the violence. Chevènement replied that Paris should rather fight what was in fact an alliance of separatists and organized crime, a growing presence on Corsica as Mafia groups shifted operations northward from Sicily.

More than a difference of opinion about Corsican strategy, Chevènement's belief is that Jospin's plan put in danger "the unity of France," that it was "a threat to the very definition of France . . . Next we might imagine seeing a Basque or a Breton parliament. The law must be the same for all." This is the French republican tradition going back to the time of Bonaparte, who, although himself born in Corsica, did the most to smother regional identities and create the centralized modern French state. French republican nationalists fear that the Jospin plan will legitimize the idea of different kinds of French citizens, fostering the new idea of a multicultural nation in which the traditional assimilationist concept of French nationality would give way.

In sum, Jean-Pierre Chevènement's Euro-skepticism, like Charles Pasqua's, is hostile both to European federalism and to French decentralization. And both contain a large worry about attaching France to German standards in European integration. In 1993, when the article here included appeared, this meant continuing criticism of the Maastricht treaty, which unexpectedly had won only 51 percent in the referendum of September 20, 1992. Chevènement's book, France-Germany: Let's Speak Frankly *(Paris: Plon, 1993), argued that French attachment to the German model of hard money (the so-called* pensée unique *or orthodox view) would result in per-*

manent high French unemployment and low growth. This lack of economic growth would leave France defenseless against American and global economic and cultural domination. Chevènement wanted a political monetary policy controlled by the government. Through formal or informal devaluations, exchange rates could be used to increase exports and stimulate industrial strength, thus creating a stronger economic base for national independence. This was contrary to President Mitterrand's controversial decision of March 1983 to keep the franc inside the European Monetary System to preserve the goal of full monetary union that was concreted in the 1991 Maastricht Treaty.

In June-July 2000 Chevènement's long-standing worry about German power and the danger for France in linking up to German policies caused a political storm when he responded to German foreign minister Joschka Fischer's unexpected (and unexpectedly well-received) call for new steps toward a genuinely federal Europe. Chevènement said that a German wish for a federalist Europe was a sublimated expression of old German dreams of empire because Germany would surely predominate.

Reality avenges itself on governments that ignore the facts. [Conservative Prime Minister Edouard] Balladur, a prisoner of the logic of Maastricht, has just learned this lesson. He flattered himself thinking he inspired confidence with his fine face, forgetting that a country that today has 3.2 million unemployed and is set to have 3.5 million in 1994 cannot pride itself on having a "healthy" economy.

The markets, which are more political than the experts, include unemployment among the "fundamentals" of an economy. They know that the French economy cannot be left in disrepair for years while waiting for Germany to finish its reunification. This is why the policy of independent interest rate cuts begun this spring by M. Balladur has been a fiasco. And by denationalizing the Bank of France, [Economics and Finance Minister] Alphandéry said he was "sending a strong signal" to the international financial markets. The response was clear: The implosion of the European monetary system, August 2, 1993, has tolled the bell for the single European currency project. It is now necessary to rethink the European structure with new premises.

Alas, our government leaders are stubbornly holding on to a policy of hypocrisies. M. Balladur says that "the policy direction will be maintained." He refuses to admit that the franc has effectively been devalued, instead saying that it has "depreciated." At his request Chancellor Kohl has just declared that the calendar for economic and monetary union will be kept, "insofar as

Translated from "Europe: sortir du piège" (*Le Monde*, September 3, 1993) and printed by permission of the publisher.

the conditions for doing so are fulfilled." But we know they will not be. As a good prince, he agrees to "rediscuss" the GATT pre-accord on agriculture, but says he will not "renegotiate" it with the United States. M. Balladur's government seems to be satisfied with these "verbal phrases." It cannot however ignore that French policy is entirely in the hands of German choices, in the GATT negotiation as in the matter of interest rates. France is caught in a trap.

THE BITTER FRUIT OF MAASTRICHT

Forgetting about the "social priority" dear to [his Gaullist colleagues] MM. Séguin and Pasqua, M. Balladur's government is reduced to seeking escape paths by deregulating the right to work or in social protection, or in muddy debates on the "constitutionalization" of the Schengen agreements [eliminating internal borders in the EU]. He refuses the alternative policy, which, through a devalued currency and structural actions to jump start the economy, would mean rethinking "Europe" around a genuine European growth policy extended to the continent as a whole.

M. Balladur is thus harvesting the bitter fruit of Maastricht. He is the bankruptcy receiver of the economic policies pursued for years, by the right as well as the establishment left [i.e., the Socialist and Communist governing parties]. The Maastricht treaty misread the immense event that was communism's collapse. From this arose the grave diplomatic errors regarding former Yugoslavia. The project for economic and monetary union, which is the heart of the [Maastrict] treaty, is totally unrealistic. It foresaw neither the German economic crisis nor the cost of German reunification, nor the priority the Germans are giving to it—quite understandably—in relation to other considerations.

The collective error of our so-called elites, both conservative and left wing, has ancient roots. Obsessed by the need to fight inflation, they are ignoring the need for economic growth that demography imposes on France. Because of a hard money policy, our elites have sacrificed industry to finance. Even more, our ruling classes have not been willing to see that German industry, because of structural reasons, could resist an objectively overvalued currency much better than ours.

But these ancient errors are multiplied today by a suicidal political illusion. The right and left favorable to Maastricht both imagine that they can prevent Germany, through the single currency project, from transforming its economic influence into political influence. They live on the myth of a federal Europe, now ruined by communism's collapse and the necessities of an unavoidable enlargement of the European structure, which is in itself desirable.

The president of the Republic [François Mitterrand] recently declared, "There will be no durable monetary convergence without more economic [and business cycle] convergence." M. Balladur speaks the same language. Both are wrong and are leading the country astray. The Maastricht criteria [for joining the single currency zone] will not be met for a long time. The single currency with twelve [of the fifteen] member states [i.e., minus those who say they don't want to join] won't be possible for decades.

For too long France has put her economic growth on a low flame, wearing herself out in this exercise of reaching the fixed criteria for membership. [French] leaders have put the issue of Franco-German relations the wrong way. Germany is master of the calendar. She can pose her conditions and get what she wants, for example in [former] Yugoslavia [diplomatic recognition for Slovenia and Croatia], in the GATT, in the matter of interest rates, regarding the location [in London rather than Paris] of the future Bank for European Reconstruction and Development. And [Germany will again do so] tomorrow in renegotiation of the Maastricht treaty and the [decision-making] reform of European institutions. France should recogize that even in the highly improbable case of a European Central Bank limited to the countries of the "Carolingian core," its influence within would be zero . . . because of the text of the treaty and because of the new equation of forces in Europe.

The right and the established left misunderstand the dissymmetry now existing between France and Germany, which is less in demography than in economics and geopolitics. German industry is twice as weighty as ours. The same is true for savings rates. The deutschemark is the second [European] reserve currency in the world (more than 20 percent of central bank reserves as against 3 percent in francs). Germany, finally, is [geopolitically] at the heart of Europe. No one can reproach them for this, but Mitteleuropa is recreating itself naturally in Germany's orbit. The dangerous problem is not Germany's strength but France's weakness.

Germany has a project; France does not. Germany is playing a world-level game. France plays at the regional level (and besides "Europe" France has no project of its own). France thus depends on Germany much more than the latter depends on her. Making of economic and monetary union a new "blue line in the Vosges" [rapprochement], France has damagingly attached herself to Germany. It is time to get out of this trap.

In the interest of a Franco-German cooperative relation necessary to Europe, French policy must break with the old asphixiating dogmas and find a freedom of action once again. To answer to the [French] national interest rightly understood, this means giving priority to [French] social reunification! France must also learn to play a world game. France has assets: her people, her culture and language, the quality of her education, her landscape, her institutions, her geopolitical stability, her research and technological capabilities, her tradition of a global outlook, her receptiveness to the [developing world].

It is time, finally, for France to show imagination in rethinking Europe.

Though it might displease the prophets of "postnational" ideas, Europe—the genuine, grand Europe—has no need for France to dissolve herself, exactly the contrary. Europe needs a France strong and conscious of herself.

TO REINVENT FRANCE

In a liberal Europe in which the democratic legitimacy of states will continue to be undermined by so-called postnational ideology painted over in supranational colors, the German nation will survive because of the very definition it has of itself and its specific weight. But not the French nation. [France] is in fact a political and cultural reality, not an ethnic one. [The French nation] exists only through the republican state.

In France as in the rest of Europe the social question today dominates all others. It requires a political response and the active participation of citizens. Because democracy cannot be separated from national sovereignty, the social question implies the national question. It is therefore necessary to reinvent France as a project of citizenship in order to change policies and meet the challenges of our time, which are (1) lowering unemployment, (2) integrating the excluded, (3) stabilizing central and eastern Europe plus the southern rim of the Mediterranean, which all equally need a dynamic Europe, (4) inventing a new model of development to meet the technological and commercial competition of the new industrializing states, and, finally, (5) to provide a balance to American power. For all this France is necessary to Europe. Instead of just blindly following liberal and monetarist ideas, France must once again find her confidence in the values of citizenship, of secularism, and of public service. France must play a role of stimulus and balance in Europe.

Is there a hope that our "elites" will overcome their obstinacy for choosing unearned income rather than work, finance rather than industry, cultivating capital rather than the human resources of the country? The [governing neo-Gaullist RPR conservatives], by avoiding the social question, cannot pose the [real] French problem. The party that calls itself socialist, that is incapable of putting correctly the national question, takes refuge once again in irresponsible social chattering.

THE MEANING OF GENERAL DE GAULLE

The truth is that France today is a democracy without an opposition. Where could resistance come from? Not from the right. That would require not only General de Gaulle's vocabulary but above all a social base. The right-wing candidates for the presidential election [coming in 1995] are prisoners not only of Maastricht but also of an electorate in which those who live from capital carry more weight than those who are productive. Resistance cannot come from the working world, from those who work, invent, create. The difficulty today is in the gap that exists between that social base and the established left.

To get out of the trap and escape from this theater of shadows—which is a mixture of demagogic talk ("social Europe") and impotence put into concepts ("there is no serious alternative policy")—one must obviously get past the split at Tours [in 1920, when the French Communist party split off from the existing Socialist party]. There is no solution in reforming only the Socialist party or the Communist party. It is necessary to lift up the entire left with France around *l'idée républicaine* [the French idea of the republic and republican sentiments]. We must resolve the social question and the national question simultaneously. We must show what we can do in France to resist a "social Munich" and [the American-inspired] "New World Order."

This is the struggle that the Citizens' Movement wants to lead, first of all to start a change in mentalities. We must change the lay of the land on the left to make possible a wider set of changes necessary to drag the country out of decline. We will go to the voters in the European parliamentary elections of June 1994. We won't hide the difficulties; the storm winds are already on the horizon. Given the great existing emptiness of hope, the people must have a real alternative in order to get out of the trap in which they are enclosed by the consensus of the right and the established left. If we don't do it, who will do it in our place?

CHAPTER 11

Which France for Which Europe?

Charles Pasqua

Charles Pasqua is a gruff, hard-talking French politician, a heritor of Charles de Gaulle. A former interior minister in conservative governments, he is one of France's most compelling neo-Gaullists in defining politics and the centrality of the French state in conceiving and protecting national interests. Faced with frightening terrorist attacks in Paris in the 1986–88 government of Jacques Chirac, Pasqua's declaration that his police force would turn the tables and "terrorize the terrorists" aptly captured his provocative, voluntarist idea of political leadership.

Charles Pasqua is one of the minority of neo-Gaullists who has defied President Jacques Chirac, rejecting his Rally for the Republic's acceptance of European integration. (The neo-Gaullist RPR was founded in 1976 by Chirac as successor to the previous Gaullist UNR and UDR parties.) For Pasqua as for other European politicians, negotiating and voting the Maastricht treaty was a turning point in the history of European integration, especially the plan for monetary union, a European central bank, and the euro. The euro and the ECB, they rightly saw, were milestones toward European Union federalism.

Charles Pasqua thus rejected Jacques Chirac's controversial call for neo-Gaullists to vote in favor of François Mitterrand's Maastricht referendum of September 20, 1992, a Yes vote "without enthusiasm but without second thoughts," said Chirac. Pasqua, in the same vein, later also opposed the 1997 Amsterdam treaty and the French constitutional amendments necessary for its application.

In 1999, he, along with Philippe de Villiers, deserted the RPR and ran a separate Euro-skeptical list in the European parliamentary elections. Unexpectedly, the Pasqua-de Villiers list won more votes, about 16 percent, than the RPR itself. The two Euro-skeptics thereupon founded a national-sovereignty-oriented "Rally for France" (RPF), one of several "sovereignist" groupings in current French political jargon. But already by summer 2000 Pasqua and the emotional de Villiers had fallen out, leaving the RPF's leadership in disarray, its future in doubt.

Pasqua is a more thoughtful politician than his reputation for abruptness would indicate. One of his substantive objections to federalist integration is to say that breaking up national sovereignty, even to "pool" it rather than to hand it over to a federalist Brussels bureaucracy, causes special damage to France's political character. Historically, the national state in France, from the monarchy forward, has been crucial, much more influential and even necessary than in other countries, in molding French society and providing economic and political dynamism. In a unique way, France needs statism, according to Pasqua. Therefore, to amputate the national state's sovereignty and its multifarious roles in creating civil society will, at least in France, dilute national identity and weaken the country's traditional economic and political strengths. France will thus become prey to stronger neighbors more adapted to the structures of the European Union being built. Pasqua, like other French leaders (e.g., Jean-Pierre Chevènement), of course is thinking of Germany. That such thoughts appear on both the right and the left in France illustrates how the German neighbor was, and still is, an obsession in the French political class.

Pasqua's Euro-skeptic ideas are genuinely substantive, as compared with either the demagogic Euro-phobia of extreme rightist Jean-Marie Le Pen or with leftist Jean-Pierre Chevènement's nostalgia for a national-republican synthesis focused on the mythic citoyen of French revolutionary lore. His defense of French sovereignty against European federalism is without question the most pertinent and contemporary of the several French "sovereignist" doctrines in circulation today. From 1958 through 1974, under de Gaulle and Georges Pompidou, this rejection of European federalism was, it is well to remember, literally the doctrine of French government, as it was in the 1980s in British policy under Margaret Thatcher.

That said, Charles Pasqua's Euro-rejectionism seems to assume permanent French economic weakness vis-à-vis Germany, and a lack of confidence in general that French business is capable of competing successfully in a liberalized, Europeanized, globalized economy. Hidden here may also be a Corsican's nostalgia for leaving things the way they have long been, which Pasqua's critics see as a reactionary mind-set. Pasqua's Corsican origin, given the island's violent independist movement and mafia-like public life, may also contribute to his fierce attachment to the French republic's territorial integrity. The following article is taken from the Revue des deux mondes, *April 1997.*

No wish seems to me more justified than to see the Europeans united. A united Europe, which General de Gaulle called "the dream of wise men and the ambition of the strong," is without doubt the natural and welcome continuation of our national history, as it is for each of the old nations that, after having fought among themselves and after having spread out across the world, now realize, because it is obvious, that their individual destinies depend above all on their capacity to join together. Two world wars, which were in essence two European wars, have imposed on us the vital obligation to achieve European unity.

No project is more important than that of building a stable and accepted political order on our continent. We are far from it, although the threats to peace seem to have disappeared along with the Soviet Union, and we have pushed the perils "outside the walls" of our clever castle. We thus conceived of the war in Bosnia, occuring at our gates, as a foreign war. We were wrong. It was a European war, the first since 1945.

I am of those who regretted that, when the Berlin Wall fell and then the Soviet empire collapsed, we didn't seize the historic occasion given to us to reconcile Europe with its geography, to erase Yalta and to trace the outline of that "cathedral" that General de Gaulle sketched [in his speech] at Warsaw in 1969, the union of all of Europe [i.e., including the eastern countries]. François Mitterrand [in 1989-90] spoke fleetingly of that sort of "confederation," only to forget it immediately. However, as futurist as that idea was and still seems, I believe it is the right political approach for Europe's future, once we focus on the ends—peace first of all—rather than getting lost in debates over the means.

THE DASH TO CREATE THE "EURO" RESEMBLES A GAME OF MUSICAL CHAIRS

Instead of this we were given Maastricht, that is, a choice for accelerated integration of western Europe. In 1992 the issue that above any other caused me to oppose the Maastricht treaty was that it seemed to me to be a huge historic and geopolitical error. This withdrawal of the European Community inside its own shell, whatever the economic or financial reasons, seemed to me then and still does today a vast underestimation of the potential of the European continent. Of course, the worst is never certain; but neither is it totally to be excluded. Thus, I think that we did not, at that moment, take the measure of the stake that we had before us. And we have since forgotten it, encouraged to do so by economic considerations.

However this may be, the choice was made. The euro has thus become the symbol of Europe. A mechanism, if not a dynamic, was thus put into gear. At least officially, nothing else is supposed to stand in the way of launching the single currency into orbit according to the calendar and criteria set down five

Translated from "Quelle France pour Quelle Europe" (*Revue des Deux Mondes,* April 1997) and printed by permission of the publisher.

years ago [in 1992]. I admit to perplexity, but also to a certain admiration, listening to so many certitudes [about the euro] repeated with such constancy, all the more so in that serious doubt, even if not shown, exists quite clearly even among those most tenaciously committed to creating the single currency.

This doubt is quite obviously created by three questions, which are complementary or rather consecutive. None has been given an answer, or can be, before the fateful date. The race for the euro thus somewhat resembles a round of musical chairs in which we don't know beforehand either the number of chairs or the real desire of the participants to sit down or not when the time comes.

First Question:

Looking at the convergence criteria, I am not a forecaster, but it seems to me, if I believe what I read, that none of the big European countries will in a strict sense meet the criteria that were precisely set out for automatic admission into the euro group. The [difficult] economic situation, which the criteria themselves will aggravate, having defeated this method, it will therefore be necessary to choose subjectively rather than objectively, that is to say, simply, to make political choices. And when it is a matter of politics among nations rather than accounting, we don't necessarily stick to the criteria. And at that point it is much more difficult to camouflage interests, calculations, even hidden designs. To take a comparison: It is easier to create a Franco-German brigade or a Eurocorps than to agree on the places where it will intervene. It is much easier to agree about techniques or means than it is to align policies.

Quite clearly this problem will affect the [European] currency, once dry numbers alone prove insufficient to select among the candidates. The question is going to be whether the countries of the south of Europe, and first of all Italy, which is not only a founding member of the Common Market but much more than that a source of European civilization, can be excluded by France and by Germany (they will in fact decide) from the euro train, when it cannot be known when or whether a second train will leave. The problem is intensified because the euro's very functioning risks creating a rapid divergence of interests of EU euro-zone countries as opposed to those remaining outside.

It is hard to see how France, whose geopolitical interest here is blinding, can accept being only the "Finistère" [the end part of Brittany] in a Europe totally recentered on the ancient Lotharingia [the northwestern part of the empire Charlemage left divided among his sons; here, meaning a Germanic-centered EU], instead of being the anchoring pier in a European space of the Italian, Hispanic, and, why not, British worlds. To do so would be ipso facto to renounce our Mediterranean calling, that is to say a large part of our political influence as such.

Second Question, Which Arises from the First:

How to arrange the [temporary] cohabitation, in a "single" market, of currencies that will not be one, even if it is evident that the euro will be the dominant currency among them? What should be done if these currencies—the pound, the lira, the peseta—are devalued or are de facto devalued by the markets?

We already saw, in the light of the competitive devaluations of 1992, what damage was done to our industries. I know very well that the idea is to create a kind of new European monetary system (EMS), linking these currencies to the euro within defined margins. What should be done, however, if their situation leads them, by their own decision or by the decision of the markets, to leave the system again? One can't very well deprive these countries simultaneously of the advantages, real or supposed, of the single currency, and also of all national means of development, if necessary to save their economies. As of today there is no answer to this question, which by the way is no longer even asked, because it would lead directly back to the first question.

Third Question, Underlying the Two Previous Ones:

It is a matter of the nature itself of the kind of Europe whose construction is foreseen because of, and through the process of, monetary integration. For me it is the most important, inasmuch as I believe the current outbidding between France and Germany is leading us directly either toward a failure or toward the irremediable abandonment of all sovereignty for France.

Everything is happening, it seems, as if each of the two countries were trying to project, so to speak, onto the European level the way in which it manages its national currency. Against the "stability pact" imposed by Germany—new criteria that, according to the nice expression of M. Theo Weigel [German finance minister], shield a currency from "political arbitrariness"—France tries to reply by proposing a "council for stability," a hoped-for political counterweight to the proposed European central bank, which is to run on the statutes, missions, and the philosophy of the Bundesbank. It is hard to see, whatever camouflage is set up to hide differences, how two such opposed visions of things could find a point of compromise.

However, the stability pact sought by Germany under Bundesbank pressure is neither in the spirit of the Maastricht treaty nor in the interest of the European economies. Neither is it necessary to the good functioning of a single currency, given that the European central bank is already given independence [from political influence] and assigned the objective of monetary stability. What is being done is neither more nor less than putting European economies and states on a leash, a control furthermore augmented with sanctions. I don't know if the European currency will be more solid for this, but I do know that in the best of cases Europe will not be the greater for it.

IS IT TOO LATE FOR ANOTHER ROAD THAN INTEGRATION?

The proof of the pudding is in the eating, the English say. Such seems also to be the nature and destiny of the European currency. But, like a pudding, everyone has his own recipe and swears by it. I would like there to be a little less dogmatism about the issue and more flexibility, that all the European countries be included and not just a few, that there be political dialogue and not sovereign technocracy, and economic growth in addition. In such a case I believe the European currency would be really European, at the service of the European economies and not, as looks to be the case, a simple consolidation of the affiliation of France to the deutschemark zone. But let us not jump to a conclusion regarding a negotiation whose color we will see on the occasion of the next European summit, in June 1997 at Amsterdam.

That said, we can still observe today that if German ideas should prevail, as comprehensible as they are given German history, psychology, and the determinant weight of the mark in the future European currency, that is to say, if France, through the euro and the stability pact had to give up all sovereignty and all monetary freedom of action—thus budgetary, thus fiscal, thus, in the end, economic and social freedom of maneuver—it would be appropriate to bring the issue before the French people, sole possessor of this sovereignty and therefore sole authorized to give it up, in a referendum. Is it thus really too late to choose another road than that of integration, when we see clearly, along with even those who want it, that integration is intrinsically incompatible with any form of sovereignty, thus with a democracy recognizable as such by the European peoples themselves? Is it really too late to launch a Europe founded on the basis of the nations that compose it rather than to pursue the technocratic chimera of an integrated European nation? At every step of the European construction, those who express the least doubt as to the aptness of the means employed are immediately suspected of wanting to question the whole enterprise. Having already had to put up with this heavy accusation, I will try to discuss the large alternative policies that in my view could give to Europe the human face from which it seems evermore to distance itself. Emmanuel Berl is correct in suspecting "these technocrats who are trying to make Europe without the Europeans themselves, dreaming of building in secret, in silence, structures such that the old peoples of western Europe will wake one day united without having noticed that they were being so molded. For how long?" In my view there is no better definition of totalitarianism than to want to make people happy against their will.

The truth is that the game is not yet up, that renegotiation of the Maastricht treaty would be legitimate, and, if we want it, a true change of direction. In reality the treaty mixed together, with a political pragmatism that allowed ratification by all the countries, the three conceptions of Europe that from the beginning put the large nations in opposition among themselves. These are a Europe of free trade; a Europe of cooperation; and a federal Europe. Obviously we have, *grosso modo*, the British, French, and German conceptions. In ratifying the treaty, the European nations—and as regards France, French citizens—did not explicitly choose any one of these three alternatives. They simply gave up to their governments the authority to choose for them and without their knowledge.

A EUROPEAN EUROPE OR AMERICAN TUTELAGE?

Naturally the treaty concealed, inside the process leading to the single currency, all the linkages that led inevitably toward the third alternative. The big goal of the [coming Amsterdam] intergovernmental conference will thus be to make the law agree with the facts. And there once again it seems to me that France is evolving from its own conceptions toward those of its neighbor [Germany], notably in terms of the treaty "pillar" concerning internal security and justice affairs, where we are shifting from the intergovernmental pattern contained in the treaty toward the [EU] communitarization wanted by the Germans. And there again it is necessary to judge by the facts the results of the forthcoming intergovernmental conference, looking at the whole architecture that will be proposed, at the institutional "compromise" that will be found, if it is still possible to find one at this stage of the game. Each of us will then have to make a new judgment.

The single currency and the stability pact; institutions; and finally the matter of defense. Here in this fundamental, determining matter I get to the heart of my argument, which is the idea that Europe intends to have of itself, it being understood that it is in relation to [how defense is conceived] that France can or cannot inscribe its national future. Are we talking about a "European Europe," or putting ourselves once again under American tutelage?

I want national independence. I understand, even if I don't share all their conclusions, those who believe that, given what the world has become, only Europe is potentially capable of embodying this independence even if we have to create this independence from scratch, better adapted to a new epoch. But I don't understand how it can be that the argument made about the single currency, necessary to stand up against the dollar, is exactly the inverse of that we hear made about defense, where we are told it is on the contrary necessary to negotiate a few pieces of [American] hegemony [in NATO].

One can't want something and its contrary at the same time, in this case a sovereign currency and a strategic, thus political dependency. It isn't necessary to be a great thinker to see that, this being the case, the independence and thus the value of a European currency would in fact depend on the good will and the interests of the tutelary power. And at present the good will that [the United States] shows for the process of European monetary integration is the counterpart of the strategic advantage that it expects from the now generalized acceptance in Europe of the preeminence of NATO in the matter of European defense.

Thus, on the one hand, who could seriously contest the fact that Europe alone is potentially a counterbalance to the American superpower? But on the other hand, who could equally seriously argue that Europe is launched in the direction of genuinely giving herself the means to do so? The former *porte-parole* [spokesman] for François Mitterrand, Jean Musitelli, wrote a few days ago: "It is about as realist to want to build a European defense inside NATO as to put the European central bank at Fort Knox." No Gaullist could have put the point better.

The reality, which everyone is beginning to see behind the smoke and mirrors of official declarations of intent as the different pieces of the European puzzle get put into place, is that *the European model which is appearing before our eyes is a whole—monetarist, federal, Atlanticist—and it is impossible to accept one part of it without being forced to accept the others, nor to reject one part without renouncing the others.* The coherence of the scheme that we are "proposed"—the term is a euphemism—now is clear in all of its scope.

This is why, if the European question until now was tied up with the German question, from now on it is the French question. And no one should think that in saying this I am imputing any bad motives to German leaders or, a fortiori, to French leaders. But the fact is that it is the entire history, the entire organization, and, above all, the psychology of the two nations that are going to collide, now that they are on the way to passing concretely from cooperation to a sort of unification.

The Germans think sincerely that their federal structure is the best one for unifying the European peoples, just as it has unified the German people. The French know that their identity was given to them by a unitary state and that it alone knew how to make the best of their diversity in joining them together in a great common ambition with a goal of universality. It is exactly that ambition, which General de Gaulle gave back to them, that is in the balance today, Germany for its part having sacrificed that which made its own pride, which is to say its currency.

Thus, the choices that remain in this European matter cannot be taken, and even less ratified, in the secrecy of top-level trading or in the half-light of diplomatic discussions or the opacity of administrative measures. Whatever the opinions of each on the choices at hand, we should all be in agreement that the debate be public, that is to say political. To avoid open discussion would perhaps be a short-term advantage, but I am convinced that such agility would contain the seeds of all the dangers for the European enterprise as a whole.

A NEW STRATEGY FOR FRANCE

However determinant for France will be the answers to the questions just posed, Europe is not the only solution to the numerous challenges we face today. I often say, "No one will do for France what France doesn't do for itself." And I know well that for twenty years Europe, whatever its intrinsic virtues, has had for successive governments the advantage of allowing them to shirk their responsibilities by wrapping their actions in exterior constraints, a policy that M. Jacques Delors [former French finance minister, former president of the EU commission, one of the principal authors of the Maastricht treaty] summarized in a motto, "For France through Europe."

I think that what we now call globalization is rendering this strategy rather obsolete, in that it moves so much more quickly than our patient construction [of Europe]. We have only to observe how our [European social democratic] social model is the object of a vigorous debate in which any specifically European dimension has more or less disappeared. "Flexibility" [of labor markets] or pension funds are the answers—whatever one may think of them in general—to the acceleration of the various forms of exchange and to a uniformization of modes of thought in which the boundaries of place, time, and action are now the world as a whole.

Globalization is stopped neither by borders nor by costly institutions. Globalization is the true challenge at this end of century because of its force of attraction, increasing every day, in finance—in the [finance] markets—in communications—the Internet for example—and in the immediate placing into competition of all products and services, thus soon of all individuals! Still attached to its old strategy, neither France nor Europe has taken the full measure of this situation.

Nevertheless it is on the scale of this new world economy that we must now imagine a new strategy for France, which must not let itself be locked into the European project alone, even if the latter remains the main arena in which her future is decided.

Our country possesses her own particular trump cards because of her history, her culture, and, above all, the political originality that France represents in the eyes of the world. This originality, which General de Gaulle redressed, cannot be transferred or combined without dissolving it. We have recently seen in Bosnia, in the Middle East, and in Africa, that France's voice can carry when that of Europe stammers.

All through its history our country, renewing its character when necessary, has succeeded in preserving this exceptional character of a sovereign nation to which the world pays attention. Today, as General de Gaulle had foreseen, the end of ideologies opens a vast field of action for France. Who cannot see that in a world dominated now by a fascination with increasingly more numerous, easy, and rapid forms of interaction, the individual risks soon appearing as the least important element of development? Who cannot see, thus, that the fading away of [France's particularity] would be disastrous for the world as a whole?

This point would be certainly more probing if our country had undertaken itself to redefine the major outlines necessary for a reform of its economic, social, and political life, instead of seeming to allow, like it or not, the imposition from outside of models that are not part of its republican character.

As for me, I tried [as a government official], by rehabilitating and I believe by adapting regional planning to the new realities of European construction and decentralization, to aid our country in having something to offer in the European and international competition, something founded on France's global assets, its special qualities, and its various geographies, instead of exacerbating the competition among them. I hoped to reestablish an equality of opportunity among the country's regions and among its citizens, so that access to markets, to knowledge, to jobs, to the entrepreneurial spirit, would allow each part of French territory to be used to advantage, because I am convinced that territorial cohesion, just as social cohesion, is in the end a decisive advantage for the local growth of economies and jobs, even if there is a cost in the short run.

It is in this same spirit that we must now reweave, thread by thread, the fabric of our national community, not by making identical copies of old patterns, but by interpreting from them the only unifying frame with which all the French can identify and recognize themselves. I am talking about the Republic, this political project that is simultaneously in permanent creation and universal, and which, whatever European model it finally chooses, is the only one capable of giving to France and to the French that interior force that, alone, is a winning attitude.

Europe, yes. But not under just any conditions. Let Europe be European, and let sovereignty—which means the right to say no—be preserved! As for France, let it find within itself the capacity to deal with a world that will increasingly see as evermore irrelevant its borders, but above all its ideals! There one can see a vast field for political action.

CHAPTER 12

EU Ostracism of Austria

EU Review

In February 2000, the fourteen other European Union governments imposed sanctions on Austria because its conservative party (VPÖ or "blacks") had accepted the far-right "national" Freedom party (FPÖ) headed by the controversial Jörg Haider into a government coalition.

The Social Democratic party, SPÖ or "reds," had come in first in elections in late 1999 with 33 percent. However, the SPÖ was unable to form a large-enough coalition with the Greens, on their left, to create a governmental majority. The conservative party broke a taboo by agreeing, in this situation, to accept the Freedom party as its coalition partner. This provoked EU sanctions, as other governments had made it clear to the ÖVP leader, Wolfgang Schüssel, that it would not be "business as usual" if Mr. Haider's party were made respectable and legitimate in this way. The new chancellor got Haider to sign a three-page document committing his party to work for an Austria in which "xenophobia, anti-Semitism, and racism have no place." And none of Haider's pet policies—a ban on immigration, a flat-tax fiscal system, $400 monthly checks for new mothers to encourage larger families, and a crackdown on crime and child molesting—were taken up.

Haider himself was given no national office. Indeed, he resigned as official Freedom party leader to mollify international outcry at the FPÖ's governmental role in Austria, although he remained the leading influence in a party that was, at the national level, still basically a one-man show. His official role is still limited to governor of Carinthia Province.

France, in the "cohabitation" enthusiasm of the president, Jacques Chirac, and the prime minister, Lionel Jospin, became the point country in the ostracism by the European Union of the new Austrian government. "Sanctions" imposed combined minimization of all bilateral contacts with Austrian officials, reduction of EU contacts to necessary official business, and humiliation in formal ceremonies, where leaders from other countries went to great lengths to avoid, for example, being in the same photograph with Austrian officials.

In explanation of how Haider's party had ended up in the national government, Austrians themselves blamed the long-standing, encrusted "grand coalition" of the Socialist party and the Popular party, which had long prevented liberalizing economic and social reform in order not to disturb their vested electoral-political interests. This grand coalition of conservatives and social democrats shared out, as permanent patronage, positions in government, public enterprises, public television, etc.

The Freedom party, against the grand coalition, was able to monopolize opposition to this red-black regime, albeit with the minor exception of the Greens. The sudden rise in FPO votes (from 5 percent in 1986 to 27 percent in the October 1999 election) and the Popular party's acceptance of a "small coalition" with Haider's Freedom party was, according to this view, not a vote for xenophobia, populism, and anti-Semitism, but a vote for modernization and unblocking a rigidified society. Reinvigorating the Austrian economy along EU lines required ousting the hidebound Socialists.

Whether or not the Austrians themselves were voting for Haider's ideology, other governments, especially France's, with a large extreme-right electoral force, feared the setting of a precedent, and even more the potential contagion of legitimizing extreme right-wing parties in government. Thus arose French leadership in imposing sanctions.

Already by July 2000, however, other EU governments, especially the smaller states, were concluding the sanctions had been an overreaction that had its own dangers. They began to seek a face-saving way to end ostracism of the Austrians.

The positive report submitted in September 2000 of a three-man blue-ribbon commission named by the EU to investigate the new Austrian government's human rights record provided the occasion. The report found that the Austrian government was respecting "common European values," and that respect for human rights there was "not inferior to that of other EU member states" and even better than in a few others. On September 12 the sanctions were lifted. The EU had escaped an increasingly embarrassing situation, though it vowed to maintain "especial vigilance" regarding the Freedom party, which the report had harshly termed "a right-wing populist party with radical elements" whose leaders and members continue to use xenophobic language and racist sentiments in electoral campaigns.

An exuberant Jörg Haider retaliated against the French, calling President Jacques Chirac "a pocket-sized Napoleon who has just met his Waterloo." The conservative party chancellor, Wolfgang Schüssel, who had naturally vehemently denounced his ostracism, claimed "a great success for Austria resulting from our patience and firmness." Ending the ostracism also headed off a possible referendum on Austria's relations with the EU, which the government had threatened if sanctions were not lifted, not to mention the threat of a Viennese veto in the looming December 2000 Nice conference to agree on treaty changes necessary to enlargement. Finally, the inglorious end to EU disciplining of a small member country was applauded especially in Denmark, where a referendum would be held September 28 on whether to join the single currency zone and adopt the euro. The Danes, in the occurence, said no anyway.

Indeed, all or nearly all of the small European Union countries—governments and public opinion—had shown themselves worried about the Austrian case. Whatever its particular merits, the imposition of sanctions against the Vienna government showed that a small EU country might face discipline by the larger states whereas this would be highly unlikely vis-à-vis a large country such as Italy, where a far right-wing government coalition is also possible.

At the same time, the Freedom party is having its own problems. Its electoral success has already in a few months' time declined sharply in local and regional elections following its entry into the government. This indicates that its populist protest electoral appeal is waning. Nor is the Freedom party suited well to government. It had to replace three of its six ministers in the first months in office, and a fourth, the justice minister, currently faces investigations by his own office into his actions as a lawyer for Haider and the FPO. Even Jörg Haider's own popularity has slumped, whereas Chancellor Schüssel has gained stature in Austrian opinion for his behavior vis-à-vis EU sanctions.

The attitudes, policies, and rhetoric of Haider and the Freedom party toward European integration resemble other far-right European parties, such as the French National Front. Far-right attitudes toward "Europe" are vague and hysterical versions—demagogic, xenophobic, and anti-immigrant—of Gaullist and Thatcherite "Europe des patries" conceptions of European integration anchored in a certain idea of national identity, of the nation-state as the basis of democracy, and the maximum preservation of national sovereignty. Beyond that, it goes without saying, the latter have little to do with the former.

AUSTRIA PRESS PACK

Quotes from Jörg Haider

The Associated Press Thursday, Feb. 3, 2000; 2:06 p.m. EST
Quotes from Jörg Haider, leader of the far-right Freedom Party in Austria:

"Our soldiers were not criminals, at most they were victims."—October 1990, to an annual meeting of World War II war veterans, which included former Waffen SS members.

"In the Third Reich they had an orderly employment policy."—June 1991, in the Carinthia state legislature.

In February 1995, Haider referred to "the punishment camps of National Socialism" and said later that day he meant to say "concentration camps."

"There are still decent people of good character who also stick to their convictions, despite the greatest opposition and have remained true to their convictions until today."—September 1995, in an address to World War II war veterans, including former Waffen SS members.

"The Waffen SS was a part of the Wehrmacht and hence it deserves all the honor and respect of the army in public life."—December 1995, in a television interview.

"In the past, some remarks have been attributed to me in connection with Nazism which were certainly insensitive or open to misunderstanding. I am personally sorry for this, firstly because I believe I hurt the feelings of people who were themselves victims of Nazism or whose relatives were, and secondly because the statements were not in line with the personal values of tolerance and humanity which are the basis of my political work."—November 1999, after his party did well in the elections.

"Austria accepts her responsibility arising out of the tragic history of the 20th century and the horrendous crimes of the National Socialist regime. Our country is facing up to the light and dark sides of its past and to the deeds of all Austrians, good and evil, as its responsibility.". . . In a statement signed by Haider and a coalition partner. President Thomas Klestil demanded the declaration before he would approve their coalition government.

Supplement to the *EU Review*, No. 861, February 11, 2000. Issued by the Directorate General for Foreign Relations.

Statement from the Portuguese Presidency of the EU on Behalf of XIV Member States

Today, Monday 31 January, the Portuguese Prime Minister informed both the President and the Chancellor of Austria and the Portuguese Minister of Foreign Affairs notified his Austrian counterpart of the following joint reaction agreed by the Heads of State and Government of XIV Member States of the EU in case it is formed in Austria a Government integrating the FPÖ.

- Governments of XIV Member States will not promote or accept any bilateral official contacts at political level with an Austrian Government integrating the FPÖ;
- There will be no support in favor of Austrian candidates seeking positions in international organizations;
- Austrian Ambassadors in EU capitals will only be received at a technical level.

The Portuguese Prime Minister and the Minister of Foreign Affairs had already informed the Austrians authorities that there would be no business as usual in the bilateral relations with a Government integrating the FPÖ.

Lisbon, 31 January 2000[1]

Prime Minister's Office Press Release on the constitution of the new Austrian Cabinet

The Portuguese Government deeply regrets that FPÖ has been included in the newly formed Austrian Cabinet.

As a consequence, Portugal will henceforth enforce the three decisions made by the 14 Member States of the EU, announced on 31 January.

The Portuguese Presidency of the EU Council will do its best, within its competence, to uphold the values and principles of humanism and democratic tolerance underlying the European project. FPÖ and its leader have repeatedly questioned said values and principles.

Lisbon, 3 February 2000[2]

Commission statement on Austria

The Commission notes the agreed joint view expressed by 14 Member States of the Union on January 31st and shares the concerns which underlie that decision.

The Commission will continue to fulfill its duty as guardian of the provisions and values set down in the Treaties, which provide that the Union is founded on the principles of liberty, democracy, respect of human rights and fundamental freedoms and the rule of law, as set out notably in Articles 6 and 7 of the Treaty on European Union.

At this stage the working of the European institutions is not affected. In this context the Commission, in close contact with the Governments of the Member States, will follow the situation carefully, maintaining its working relations with the Austrian authorities.[3]

Personal statement by Commissioner Fischler on the new government in Austria

I am well aware of the immense responsibility resting on me, as both a convinced European and an Austrian citizen, as a result of the inclusion of the Austrian Freedom Party in Austria's new national government. I share the concern expressed by the Commission in its statement. The Commission has a duty as guardian of the EU Treaties and is determined to exercise that role to the full, remaining watchful and quick to reprimand the slightest breach of EU law. However, it is not the Commission's place to isolate a member country. On the contrary, our duty is to prevent any country cutting itself adrift from the rest of Europe. This is why the Commission must and will maintain its working relationship with Austria.

One part of my responsibility is and always has been to convey the present international concern to my countrymen and to explain that the European Union is not turning against Austria as a country or a people. The Union has made clear that its basic values—tolerance, solidarity, respect for human rights—have to be automatic for every Member State. No Austrians who are attached to their country will want to disagree with me on this.

But another part of my responsibility, as I see it, is to help defend Austria's well-deserved reputation abroad. Austria is not a stronghold of fascism, of intolerance, but a functioning democracy. My fellow-countrymen, as the sovereign people of an independent state, naturally have every right to make up their own democratic mind. That is what has taken place, whether one likes the results or not. What would not be acceptable is any policy running counter to the essential and fundamental values of the European Union.

I personally expressed myself clearly in December towards the head of the Freedom Party when I said that nationalism, anti-foreign feeling and intolerance have no place in our common Europe. I still stand to what I said then and would not take back a single word. My own membership of the Austrian People's Party, whose values are the same as those of all Christian-Democrat parties in Europe, is a reflection of this. It goes without saying that I would be the first to reconsider my membership in the Austrian People's Party, if these principles would not be upheld. I have read the introduction of the programme put out by the new coalition government very thoroughly and have found no passage in it which would clash with these high requirements. It contains a definite "no" to discrimination, as well as to xenophobia and intolerance. It also contains a clear commitment to eastward enlargement, to European integration in general and to shared responsibility among Austrians for the darkest chapter of our history, the holocaust. This is an important step towards gaining international acceptance which I welcome. I can only hope that this is an unambiguous signal that the Freedom Party has broken with its past. But words alone are not enough. This Austrian Government, as no other, will be judged by its deeds.[4]

Austria—Haider's views condemned

Thursday 3 February—In adopting this resolution by 406 votes to 53, with 60 abstentions, Parliament condemned the "insulting xenophobic and racist statements" made by the leader of the Austrian Freedom Party, Jörg HAIDER. The resolution also expresses the belief that the admission of the Freedom Party into a coalition government legitimises the extreme right in Europe and considers that such sentiments can play no part in the evolution of Austria-EU relations. It stresses that any Austrian government must respect the spirit and the letter of the fundamental principles of the Treaty. It welcomes the "timely political intent of the Portuguese Presidency in as far as it reiterates member states' common concern to defend common European values." It calls on the Commission and Council to monitor developments regarding racism both in Austria and throughout Europe and to be prepared to suspend any state's rights in the event of a serious breach of the Treaty principles of freedom, democracy and respect for human rights. An amendment calls on Council and Commission to give their full support to activities in Austria organised to counter racist views.[5]

Article 6 (ex Article F)

1. The Union is founded on the principles of liberty, democracy, respect for human rights and fundamental freedoms, and the rule of law, principles which are common to the Member States.
2. The Union shall respect fundamental rights, as guaranteed by the European Convention for the Protection of Human Rights and Fundamental Freedoms signed in Rome on 4 November 1950 and as they result from the constitutional traditions common to the Member States, as general principles of Community law.
3. The Union shall respect the national identities of its Member States.

4. The Union shall provide itself with the means necessary to attain its objectives and carry through its policies. Treaty on European Union 13.

Article 7 (ex Article F.1)

1. The Council, meeting in the composition of the Heads of State or Government and acting by unanimity on a proposal by one third of the Member States or by the Commission and after obtaining the assent of the European Parliament, may determine the existence of a serious and persistent breach by a Member State of principles mentioned in Article 6(1), after inviting the government of the Member State in question to submit its observations.
2. Where such a determination has been made, the Council, acting by a qualified majority, may decide to suspend certain of the rights deriving from the application of this Treaty to the Member State in question, including the voting rights of the representative of the government of that Member State in the Council. In doing so, the Council shall take into account the possible consequences of such a suspension on the rights and obligations of natural and legal persons. The obligations of the Member State in question under this Treaty shall in any case continue to be binding on that State.
3. The Council, acting by a qualified majority, may decide subsequently to vary or revoke measures taken under paragraph 2 in response to changes in the situation which led to their being imposed.
4. For the purposes of this Article, the Council shall act without taking into account the vote of the representative of the government of the Member State in question. Abstentions by members present in person or represented shall not prevent the adoption of decisions referred to in paragraph 1. A qualified majority shall be defined as the same proportion of the weighted votes of the members of the Council concerned as laid down in Article 205(2) of the Treaty establishing the European Community. This paragraph shall also apply in the event of voting rights being suspended pursuant to paragraph 2.
5. For the purposes of this Article, the European Parliament shall act by a two-thirds majority of the votes cast, representing a majority of its members.[6]

Article 309 (ex Article 236)

1. Where a decision has been taken to suspend the voting rights of the representative of the government of a Member State in accordance with

Article 7(2) of the Treaty on Europe Union, these voting rights shall also
be suspended with regard to this Treaty.

2. Moreover, where the existence of a serious and persistent breach by a
   Member State of principles mentioned in Article 6(1) of the Treaty on
   European Union has been determined in accordance with Article 7(1)
   of that Treaty, the Council, acting by a qualified majority, may decide to
   suspend certain of the rights deriving from the application of this Treaty
   to the Member State in question. In doing so, the Council shall take into
   account the possible consequences of such a suspension on the rights
   and obligations of natural and legal persons. The obligations of the Member State in question under this Treaty shall in any case continue to be
   binding on that State.

3. The Council, acting by a qualified majority, may decide subsequently to
   vary or revoke measures taken in accordance with paragraph 2 in
   response to changes in the situation which led to their being imposed.

When taking decisions referred to in paragraphs 2 and 3, the Council shall
act without taking into account the votes of the representative of the government of the Member State in question. By way of derogation from Article 205(2)
a qualified majority shall be defined as the same proportion of the weighted
votes of the members of the Council concerned as laid down in Article 205(2).

This paragraph shall also apply in the event of voting rights being suspended in accordance with paragraph 1. In such cases, a decision requiring
unanimity shall be taken without the vote of the representative of the government of the Member State in question.[7]

Declaration: Responsibility for Austria—A Future in the Heart of Europe

The Federal Government reaffirms its unswerving adherence to the spiritual and moral values which are the common heritage of the peoples of
Europe and the true source of individual freedom, political liberty and the
rule of law, principles which form the basis of all genuine democracy.

The Federal Government stands for respect, tolerance and understanding
for all human beings irrespective of their origin, religion, or *weltanschauung*.
It condemns and actively combats any form of discrimination, intolerance and
demagoguery in all areas. It strives for a society imbued with the spirit of
humanism and tolerance towards the members of all social groups.

The Federal Government works for an Austria in which xenophobia, anti-
Semitism and racism have no place. It will take vigorous steps to counter
every way of thinking which seeks to denigrate human beings, will actively
combat the dissemination of such ideas and is committed to full respect for

the rights and fundamental freedoms of people of any nationality—irrespective of the reason for their stay in Austria. It acknowledges its special responsibility as regards the respectful treatment of ethnic and religious minorities.

The Federal Government supports the Charter of European Political Parties for a Non-Racist Society and commits itself to work for the exemplary realisation of its fundamental principles in Austria.

The Federal Government is committed to the protection and promotion of human rights as well as to their unconditional implementation at national and international levels. This also makes an important contribution to the prevention of wars and domestic conflicts which result in violations of the rights of people, who may find themselves displaced or even forced to leave their home country.

The Federal Government is committed to the principles of pluralistic democracy and the rule of law common to all members of the European Union, which are also anchored in the Austrian constitution and form the precondition for membership in the Council of Europe. The rights and freedoms enshrined in the European Convention on Human Rights, which are constitutionally guaranteed in Austria, are a clear expression of this commitment.

The Federal Government is committed to the European peace project. Cooperation between the coalition parties is based on a commitment to Austria's membership in the European Union. The Federal Government is bound by those principles of liberty, democracy, respect for human rights and fundamental freedoms, and the rule of law, which under Article 6 of the Treaty of the European Union are common to all member states of the European Union. Austria's future, too, lies in the deepening of integration and the enlargement of the Union. Austria's history and geopolitical situation represent a special responsibility to further the process of integration and to anchor the European idea even more firmly in everyday life. The Transatlantic Partnership will have a special significance in order to assure peace and stability during the 21st century.

The European Union as a community of values corresponds to a definite concept for the future development of European integration. This includes, in particular, work on the Charter of Fundamental Rights of the European Union. Austria supports further work towards combating all forms of discrimination according to Article 13 of the EU Treaty.

A living culture of democracy and the rule of law demands a relationship between state and citizens that creates new areas of freedom and responsibility for the individual. In a modern efficient state there are functions which can best be carried out by the individual or by non-state actors.

The Federal Government is, however, committed with all emphasis to the maintenance in solidarity of the state welfare services for every citizen who needs state help and support. This applies especially to those people who are unable to take advantage of the opportunities induced by modernisation which are increasingly dominating our lives.

The principle of solidarity also means that consideration must be shown towards the needs and expectations of future generations in order to ensure fair chances for all members of society and their plans for the future.

The Federal Government desires to strengthen Austria's position as a performance and competition oriented economic location. That is the basis for securing existing employment, creating new jobs and ensuring prosperity in our country. Austria's accession to the European Union and an assured participation in the European Monetary Union were and remain important preconditions for the future of the economy and employment in Austria.

Austria's social partnership has proved itself as an important instrument for the location of industry and jobs in Austria, and has contributed thereby to the maintenance of social peace. The Federal Government is committed to comprehensive cooperation with the social partners, but at the same time recommends the necessary readiness to reform the social partnership, for example in respect of the social security structures including the election of representatives of the insured, and strengthening the service character of the social partnership institutions.

The Federal Government is aware that the Austrian people must energetically continue to build on their great achievements of the past and develop Austria's strengths still further.

Austria accepts her responsibility arising out of the tragic history of the 20th century and the horrendous crimes of the National Socialist regime. Our country is facing up to the light and dark sides of its past and to the deeds of all Austrians, good and evil, as its responsibility. Nationalism, dictatorship and intolerance brought war, xenophobia, bondage, racism and mass murder. The singularity of the crimes of the Holocaust which are without precedent in history are an exhortation to permanent alertness against all forms of dictatorship and totalitarianism.

The European Union's project for a broad, democratic and prosperous Europe, to which the Federal Government is unconditionally committed, is the best guarantee against a repetition of this darkest chapter of Austrian history.

The Federal Government is committed to a self-critical scrutiny of the National Socialist past. It will ensure unreserved clarification, exposure of the structures of injustice, and the transmission of this knowledge to coming generations as a warning for the future. As regards the question of forced labour under the National Socialist regime, the Federal Government will endeavour to arrive at objective solutions in the light of the intermediate report by the Austrian commission of historians, while having regard to the primary responsibility of the companies concerned.

The government parties are committed to a new form of government and cooperation. They desire to solve problems, deal with challenges and make consistent use of opportunities, because they are committed to Austria's future in Europe. Austria, as a stable reliable country, will make her contribution in partnership for a peaceful and secure life together in Europe and the world.

Vienna, 3rd February 2000

(Dr. Wolfgang Schüssel) (Dr. Jörg Haider)[8]

The White House
Office of the Vice President
For Immediate Release February 2, 2000
Statement by the Vice President on Austrian Government

I am concerned about developments in Vienna that apparently will allow into the Austrian Government the FRP, whose leader has made statements interpreted in Austria and abroad as expressing sympathy for the Nazis and minimizing the tragedy of the Holocaust.

Austria has a democratically-elected government; that is true, and we must be respectful of Austria's constitutional processes. It is also true the world has suffered horribly in the past century at the hands of leaders who have used the tools of democracy to undermine the spirit and purpose of democracy. There are reasons for us to remain watchful.

The United States will continue to follow the situation closely and remain in touch with our EU allies, as we look for the Austrian government to uphold its commitments to openness, expansion of democracy, support of free markets, and tolerance for others.[9]

NOTES

1. January 31, 2000 statement by the Portuguese EU presidency for the "14" countries [excepting Austria](www.portugal.ue-2000.pt/uk/frame.htm).

2. Press release from the Portuguese Prime Minister's office, dated 3 February, "On the Constitution of the new Austrian Cabinet" (www.portugal.ue-2000.pt/uk/frame. htm).

3. IP/00/93 Brussels, 1st February 2000.

4. IP/00/112 Brussels, 4 February 2000.

5. A summary of Parliament's Resolution of February 3 *(Also to be found in the EU-REVIEW No. 860, pt III:1.)*

6. Articles 6 and 7 of the Treaty on European Union.

7. Article 309 of the Treaty Creating the European Community.

8. February 2000 Preamble Declaration by the Austrian Federal Government, "Responsibility According to Austria A Future in the Heart of Europe."

9. February 2, 2000 statement by the U.S. Vice President (www.washingtonpost.com/wp-srv/aponline/20000203/aponline140642001.htm).

CHAPTER 13

The Haider Phenomenon

Interview by Melanie Sully

Melanie Sully is an American professor of politics who has written several works on Austrian politics and also recently published The New Politics of Tony Blair *(2000). This 1997 interview she did with Jörg Haider is striking for its personal insights into his family background and personal itinerary.*

VIENNA, FEBRUARY, 1997

Q. You come from Bad Goisern, Upper Austria. How did you see Vienna as a child?

A. Vienna really played no role at all. We were in the northern part of the Salzkammergut. The provincial capital of Linz was for us nearer. No one really thought of Vienna at all. Everyone was very concerned with their own region.

Q. When did you first visit Vienna?

A. It wasn't until I was 18 and of course I was very impressed with the splendid buildings and so on. It was another world.

Q. You decided then to study in Vienna instead of Linz.

A. No, instead of Salzburg. To begin with I wanted to study in Salzburg. I had rooms reserved and everything and then suddenly I made a spontaneous decision not to go. I wanted to study German and history in Salzburg and then I opted for law in Vienna. I thought well, you can do more with that. First of all I did military service for a year and then I went to Vienna in 1969 and in 1972 I started as an academic under Professor Winkler which really taught me a lot.

Q. When did you decide to go into politics?

A. It was in 1976 although before I had been leader of the Ring of Free Youth for Austria and then I gave that up since I was in disagreement with the policies of the

From Melanie A. Sully, *The Haider Phenomenon* (Eastern European Monographs, no. 484), 210–19; reprinted by permission of the publisher.

federal party at that time. I withdrew from politics for a time until 1976 when my Carinthian friends took me by storm and said "we're beginning anew and we're going to reform the party and you should join us." I was attracted by this and said to Professor Winkler "what do you think?" and he said "it's a good opportunity. You can always come back to me; your academic career will still be open but it's good to get some practical experience and see how things really work. Give it a try—it's a challenge."

Q. I believe you originally wanted to be an actor?

A. As a school kid I really did dream of this. We had a stage and a school theatre in Bad Ischl which put on some very successful performances. We did Nestroy and Gerhard Hauptmann and Raimund. I had some lead roles in plays such as "einen Jux will er sich machen" and "Lumpazivagabundus."

Q. Were your parents against an acting career?

A. Well I wasn't really that serious about it—it was a schoolboy wish like wanting to be a train driver.

Q. I think you may use some acting in politics?

A. Of course the experience certainly wasn't wasted!

Q. What was your school like—was it very strict?

A. Firstly it was a private school which wasn't very common for Austria, but a private school where you could do public exams—but you had to pay 260 Schillings a month which was a lot then especially as my father didn't earn much and my mother wasn't employed. My sister was also studying. My parents even took out credit in order to finance our studies. It was a strict school, yes—but it didn't do any harm.

The school was 9 kilometres away from where I lived, in the "Kaiser town" of Bad Ischl. It was really good—we used to go by train and very often in the winter when there was a lot of snow, it was late so we missed some classes. Generally though I liked studying especially Latin. Some subjects not so much like maths for example that annoyed me for a while.

The director of the school was a conservative ÖVP man, I think he was of Jewish descent and one of his closest colleagues was a pan-German nationalist. A funny sort of mixture.

Q. Your parents were former Nazis . . .

A. Well, they were like hundreds of thousands of others, members of low rank with small functions in the party. My father was responsible in Upper Austria for organising the Reich apprentices' competitions for young people and my mother was in the League of German Maidens. After the war they were classified as small Nazis, whilst the really big ones sought their careers with the ÖVP and the SPÖ. They became the mayors and ministers and politicians for the province whilst the little people were penalised including my parents. They were banned from normal jobs and had to do work in hospitals or homes for the elderly cleaning up and doing menial tasks. My father was forced to work in the cemetery as a gravedigger. This didn't last very long though.

Q. This was the American zone of occupation?

A. Yes although I always had very positive impressions of the Americans. The first things we got were huge cans with delicious yellow cheese, milk and lots of other goodies.

Q. And your grandparents?

A. My granddad on my father's side was an innkeeper in Mondsee—I think he also had a butcher's shop. On my mother's side, the mother came from South Tyrol and the father was a gynaecologist who studied in London and worked there. He was a real Anglophile. He travelled a lot as a medical doctor, a real cosmopolitan or "globe-trotter" as we would say today.

Q. And as a student you were a member of the student duelling societies?

A. Even in Bad Ischl. There were two—one was the catholic and the other was if you like "Freiheitlich" and this one I joined. The director's son who went to school with me went to the catholic society. We had a good friendship both personally and between our groups and competed with each other to see who could get the most members. It was fun.

Q. Was this also a Protestant area?

A. Partly, the "inner" Salzkammergut if you like was a retreat for Protestants during the Counter-Reformation. Especially in and around Bad Goisern there is a strong Protestant community and nearby, on a mountain you can reach in about two hours by foot, there's a so-called church, an enormous cave where the Protestants celebrated a service to commemorate this as a sanctuary. It's really interesting—you have to go through a dark passage for about 20 minutes in this cave right in the middle of a mountain and suddenly there opens up in front of you a huge vault just like a church and this is where the Protestants held their service. Salzkammergut is the heart of Alpine territory which many know from "Sound of Music" with its wonderful lakes and the famous salt works or the Hallstatt Lake at the foot of a glacier. One of the most beautiful mountains is the Dachstein which has inspired many songs like "Hoch vom Dachstein an, wo der Aar noch haust." . . . and then there's the famous Erzherzog Johann Yodel. Erzherzog Johann was a native of these parts and for me is a symbolic figure and a model since he was a revolutionary against Vienna, against the Kaiser house although he was a son of this imperial family and was then in 1848 the first president of the Frankfurt national assembly which was concerned with the first constitution and an attempt to set up basic rights and freedoms. He was a real reformer. He then came back to Styria and fell in love with a well-to-do lady. He then put through many social reforms and was amazingly innovative and creative and also was a great mountain climber. My political model.

I can't think of so many contemporary models—I was once impressed by Helmut Schmidt, the former Social Democratic chancellor of Germany.

Q. And Kreisky?

A. He was one of the last ones who really tried to reform this country and open it up. I talked with him just before he died. The account of the meeting is always disputed by the Social Democrats who are obviously annoyed that it took place at all especially as most of them never knew it happened. The then ambassador Gredler who knew Kreisky well and who was "Freiheitlich" requested a meeting. What sticks in my mind from what he said was that in the future there will no longer be a two party system but there will be a trend to a three party system, three roughly the same strength with the Social Democrats just in front but one must ensure, and this is what he expected of me, a dialogue between all is kept up because we in the FPÖ are an important element in Austria's democracy and therefore it was important to maintain discussions with all sides. And I think our struggle against political isolation is connected with this—we say it has nothing at all to do with Kreisky's legacy when the Social Democrats try to isolate us since that is exactly what he didn't want.

Q. You have experienced many victories but also setbacks. Was there ever a time when you thought you would rather pack it in?

A. There are always situations when you might say, "Do I really have to do this?" That was the case for example in 1986 at the party conference when there were some savage debates and after 7 hours I said to myself, "Do you really need to be insulted in this way?" But my friends encouraged me and said stick it out, it'll be all right. It was always like that and I have the advantage of having really good friends who have stuck with me through thick and thin and of course the solid backing of my family has been important else I would probably not have carried on with it.

Q. Would you do it again if you had the chance?

A. It's difficult to say since I've experienced it this way. But many personal chances in life are lost since there is an enormous concentration on specific goals. On the other hand I'm not sure if I would really be satisfied with a so-called normal life when you go home at four o'clock or whatever or as a university professor and you do your lectures and exams and that's it. It's not me. I need the challenges.

Q. Was one of these "downs" after the 1995 election?

A. Yes, for me personally it was since I really couldn't understand how dishonesty could be so rewarded in politics—that really disturbed me that this blatant lack of truth which was dished out to people in the socialist propaganda led to a great election victory but you see poetic justice comes a year later which wouldn't have come in this form if they hadn't lied to the people. There's always some good which comes out of bad.

Q. In your speech at Krumpendorf you referred to the "Hafenstraßen" delegation in Hamburg—what happened there?

A. I had been invited to a meeting of the Bund Freier Bürger with Mr. Brunner and a lot of people showed up at this square in Hamburg and the "Hafenstraße" that's where a lawless bunch have occupied a particular area of the docks and not even the police dare go in—it's a kind of "wild west." There are really radical elements, above all left extremists and they turned up and tried to start off fights and so on amongst the crowd. They then chucked everything possible at us on the speakers' platform—stones, bricks and I don't know what—it was really nice. Anyway we carried on with the meeting and the police tried to give us some protection and took into custody some of them who had dangerous weapons—one just in front of me drew out a long knife. They were completely vicious characters. And then this guy in Krumpendorf who came from Hamburg apologised and said how embarrassing it had all been and really the people in Hamburg are quite friendly.

Q. Then you spoke of someone who should have come the year before but couldn't land . . . .

A. That was Fasslabend, the Minister of Defence, who was down to be the speaker in 1994 but he got cold feet for political reasons and cried off but the official reason was that it was so foggy the plane wouldn't be able to land although in actual fact it was a lovely bright and sunny day so it wouldn't really have been a problem. Anyhow he showed up the year after.

Q. What did you mean when you referred to the "decent" people—the former Waffen SS?

A. I was talking about the older generation and then I mentioned the Freedomites who represent a kind of elite in this democracy since we will bring about change and without us this rigid system in Austria won't be broken. There were journalists from *Stern* and *Profil* there—no one got excited about the speech until months later they started to criminalise it.

Q. In a subsequent interview you referred to the memorial to the Soviet army still standing in Vienna . . . .

A. What I was trying to point out was the contradiction we have in Austria when on the one hand people try to do away with war memorials dedicated to those who fell in the war from all political sides and religious denominations whilst on the other side we still have a Soviet war memorial in Vienna. This should be demolished in the post cold war era just as those people in countries once under communist oppression have got rid of Lenin and Stalin memorials.

Q. You have three large flags here in your office—one naturally enough the Austrian flag and then also the Star Spangled Banner . . . .

A. And the third is the flag of the state of California which has a bear on it and reminds me of my home in "Bear Valley" Carinthia. I've always liked the Stars and Stripes. I'm a big fan of pretty flags and I think the US flag is really great.

Q. If you were in America would you be a Republican or Democrat?

A. More of a Republican I suppose but it's difficult to say. In economics I'd be more on the liberal side and for the market economy and for deregulation. In social and family policy etc., I'd be more on the conservative side.

Q. You studied at Harvard University last Summer. . . .

A. Yes, privatisation policy. It was wonderful to be there and have some peace to think. It's a wonderful country—so uncomplicated in comparison with us and yet it's unconventional. Then I liked the way they study there and the staff student relationships are a real partnership and the professors usually come from the real world not like here where you often get professors who hold the same lectures for thirty years or more. It's what I imagined it should be like at university where professors have practical and up-to-date experience. There were experts who had been engaged in consultancy in privatisation in Eastern Europe and who had made reports for the World Economic Forum; real economic gurus. It's a different system from Austria of course but there students who get on and become famous put something back into their universities financially.

Q. Were you ever in Chicago? What was behind these posters "Vienna must not become Chicago?"

A. I've been there but the placards had more to do with this historical image since the city used to be synonymous with organised crime and there are many politicians in Europe from different parties who use such slogans. But the city itself in the centre is a modern, fascinating city.

Q. America is a multi-cultural society, something which you reject for Austria. . . .

A. I don't think you can stop it but you should not make an ideology out of "multi-culturalism." People understandably defend their own homeland and we should be able to do this in Europe and Austria. The Palestinians fight for their right to a homeland and the Kurds, so it's difficult to understand why in the heart of Europe through a wrong immigration policy the peoples are being substituted by others from outside. Also the speed and the volume of immigration is important and makes it difficult to absorb.

Q. You visited the Wiesenthal Centre in America—where did you see your portrait?

A. Right at the beginning of the exhibition which depicts the suffering of the Jews in the Holocaust. First of all there's a section on the violation of human rights in the whole world such as what the Americans did to the Indians and the execution of civil rights fighters and at the end of this there's a huge wall with lots of photos which serves as a warning that many politicians still plan to eliminate human rights in the world of today. There's Idi Amin and Saddam Hussein and then there's me. Then I asked the guide, "Who's that guy?" and he said "Oh, that's a dangerous right wing politician from Austria!"

And then you go on further through a door and it's cool and dark and that shows the suffering of the Jews in the Holocaust. It's really well done but it's the overall impression—first of all outside with these photos and then you go straight into a section dealing with the extermination of peoples.

I also went to the Holocaust Museum in Washington but at least I'm not shown there. It's quite effective with a history of the family of Daniel. It's the story of little Daniel who with his family grows up in the ghetto in Eastern Europe and you feel his experiences as he goes through life. You see how he started in peace at school and see his little school bag in his room and so on and then they go to the ghetto and the entire family is split up. It makes quite an impression.

Q. Have you visited the exhibition in Austria on the German army?

A. No, certainly not since I don't think I need to be told anything by former Soviet and East German communist historians. It's a falsification of history they've been carrying on as is clear since the Berlin Wall fell and we have access to the archives.

I went to the Mauthausen concentration camp site once on a private visit but it's got nothing constructive to say in comparison with the Washington Holocaust Museum.

Q. If we switch to the future from the past, are you a follower of astrology?

A. No, but I get all possible kinds of horoscopes sent. As an Aquarian I'm in good company with Reagan, Kreisky and Paul Newman. I think some things fit like the general characteristics. For example they love freedom and you can never pin down an Aquarian.

Q. With Klima you have the chance of a co-operation with the Social Democrats.

A. I see this just as normalisation, the beginnings of normal parliamentary practice. Klima can't suddenly throw Vranitzky's legacy out of the window. I think the SPÖ is working on a coalition with the Greens and Liberals. If that doesn't work they might consider something with us. When power is at stake the Socialists can be very flexible. You can feel this change in the provinces and the ÖVP will have to think about things since it has been really stupid the way it has looked on. It was always frightened to co-operate with us now they see the Socialists might do it. You have to understand we have had many negative experiences with the People's Party, as for example in Carinthia when it broke a pact with us and then supported a Socialist as provincial governor instead. Provincial governor of Carinthia would still interest me since I think the province is in a terrible state and needs important reforms.

Q. How do you see things developing at the European level?

A. I can't see how with over 19 million unemployed there will be a secure peace in the future in Europe. This has been completely ignored. Some countries may become successful but then they will say we're not prepared to finance the others.

We are for a Europe of the nations where the nation state has still an important role to play since the nation states are the only corrective against the power of the multinational concerns. The nation states can develop to a large degree an autonomous economic policy for people in small and medium-sized firms.

Q. Is Austria a nation or a fatherland?

A. Austria is a state nation and the fatherland is a broader concept consisting of different ethnic groups such as the classic minorities such as the Croats, Hungarians, Slovenes and Czechs and then the majority of Austrians who belong historically and linguistically to the German Volk and cultural community.

Q. Your party is now very successful as a party of the workers. . . .

A. Actually a party of the working people, i.e., of those who are not employed in the protected sectors of the economy. Small tradesmen, farmers, workers, salaried employees—all are in our voting alliance. These people should no longer have to bear the brunt of cut-backs and with the opening up of these protected privileged sectors we have a big opportunity to help those who now vote for us. We could then have more chances for greater competition, more privatisation in electricity, radio and television, and the whole state sector.

Q. How can you avoid the temptation of building up your own power network in place of the Reds and the Blacks?

A. When I was governor in Carinthia I could see it will work if you want. You have to have jobs allocated on an objective basis. This was good for Carinthia and it wasn't important whether someone was a socialist or a member of the ÖVP or a party member at all, but the decision to appoint someone must be made on the basis of merit and qualifications. People want to be rid of this political pressure and they want an end to political abuse when it comes to getting accommodation or credit at the bank, and jobs etc. We want to see real competition between the public and private sectors instead of a monopoly of politicised housing cooperatives which hand out apartments. This whole party book system must be a thing of the past. If someone wants to join us or have an Info card because they want to know more about our aims or support us—OK. But if they think it's a ticket for their personal enrichment they're wrong.

CHAPTER 14

Diary of a Trip to Vienna: Jörg Haider's Austria

Jacques Le Rider

Jacques Le Rider is a French historian and journalist, author of Journaux intimes Viennois *(Private Vienna Diaries)* (Presses Universitaires de France, 2000), *and winner of the Humboldt Foundation prize for research in spring 2000. His "diary of a trip to Vienna" in April 2000 is a vivid, on-the-ground account of the effects of the "sanctions" imposed by the fourteen other European Union governments on Austria in February 2000, because of the Christian conservative party's (VPÖ, or "blacks") government coalition in February 2000 with the extreme-right "national" Freedom party (FPÖ) headed by the controversial Jörg Haider.*

Monday, April 3

On the way to dinner after our arrival, the car radio news includes the archbishop of Vienna, Mgr. Schönborn, who expresses indignation over the fact that because of a government problem the Austrian people as a whole have been put into a quarantine. Saturday afternoon in Paris while packing my bags, I had heard part of Christine Lecerf's program on Austrian intellectuals and artists commenting on the political crisis. . . . One of the "experts" questioned emphasized that anti-Semitism and Holocaust revisionism, which are part of Haider's ideology, remained limited to what is not said, and that [Haider], the governor of Carinthian province, only allows them to appear in his controlled verbal asides. Jörg Haider watches himself, and those who say that, between the lines and words, his entire discourse insidiously mocks the "work of memory" have few objective instances to enter into evidence. . . .

In the evening an old friend welcoming me to Austria suddenly launched into a political analysis. We badly needed a change, she explained, from this Socialist party (SPÖ) which sabotaged the action of the Popular party (ÖVP). A change was necessary. The economic sectors in particular needed it. The small (alternative) coalition of the Popular party and Haider's Freedom party (FPÖ) has unblocked everything.

Tuesday, April 4

Die Presse newspaper: On the first page is a 1998 photo showing [French president] Jacques Chirac in the company of Serbian war criminal Krajisnik who has just been arrested. To the left of this "accusatory" photo: Denmark asks for a lifting of European Union sanctions [against Austria] by summer. Under the photo: The EU sanctions have not affected Austria's foreign trade. *Der Standard* newspaper, much more sober and objective, reports the vigorous ÖVP and FPÖ campaign in favor of a "national union" of all parties against the sanctions. Neither the Socialists nor the Green party accept.

Die Presse reports that Haider, invited to Trieste [Italy] by the mayor, M. Illy, . . . had wanted to visit the former fascist and Nazi concentration camp in the nearby area. The Jewish community protested and Illy quickly retracted his official invitation. The visit will be a private one. . . .

9 p.m.

This evening we had dinner again at the Heuriger, located in a rustic, popular spot as one's leaves Bad Vöslau. The owner's son came over to converse with us. He's employed at the transportation ministry and is thus under the authority now of a Freedom party minister. Does he have a problem with this? No. It's the media that created out of whole cloth the so-called FPÖ problem. Austria is neither more nor less racist than before. The sanctions, he explained to us, are unjustified because they hit the Austrian population as a whole. The entire population? When I ask him to be specific he talks of the tourism sector. I remarked to him that these bilateral and EU "sanctions" only concern governments and that individual decisions by tourists are not dictated by governments. During the ensuing conversation this son of a wine grower-innkeeper gets agitated: He denounces "Socialist corruption." For him, the Socialist party is the cause of the whole problem. To get rid of the Socialist

Translated from *Commentaire*, no. 90 (Summer 2000): 311–20, and reprinted by permission of the publisher.

scourge, the Austrians voted for the Freedom party. But the FPO is not the problem in itself. The issue is the individual case of Jörg Haider. . . .

The excellent weekly *Falter* . . . has published a piece . . . on the theme of "sanctions," the subject that obsesses all the editorial staffs and all conversations in the country: "Here one is interpreting the sanctions as a terrible mistake by the European Union, unjust for Austria. . . . But we feel ourselves important; every occasion to find once again a bit of grandeur is to be seized. The sanctions signify a paradoxical recognition of our little country's importance." [The author] Thurnher emphasizes the contradiction that weakens the sanctions policy: Since 1986, since the FPÖ was taken in hand by Haider, the party and its leader had never been "sanctioned," despite sitting in numerous elected bodies in Austria and in Europe. But Thurnher adds that the sanctions do have the merit of translating a new awareness: Populism is incompatible with democracy. . . . Used to a "social partnership" government and to a "grand coalition" [of the Socialist and Popular parties] that attenuated all conflicts like a soft comforter, Austria has suddenly been taken back to confrontations of an intensity not seen since the 1920s and 1930s. The use of the word "resistance," whose usage the old generation of wartime resistants so severely reproaches today's young opponents [of Haider] for using, is a sign of this return to violence, for the moment ideological, symbolic, and verbal.

On Portuguese television Haider now says that it is not Austria but the European Union that must change. Yet, surprisingly, a large majority of Austrians remains in favor of Europe according to opinion polls. I fear that Europe is as vague an idea in public opinion here as was [cold war] neutrality, which had been brandished as a fundamental element of Austrian identity without realizing that since German reunification and the emancipation of the former eastern Europe, now become central Europe, this neutrality hardly had any more meaning.

THE SANCTIONS: A NATIONAL OBSESSION

The newspaper *Die Presse* foams with rage against the sanctions. It consoles itself by highlighting a study from some Irish political science institute concluding that the sanctions against Austria are illegal.

In the late afternoon I meet with a leader, G.K., of the "underground" movement of "resistance" to the new blue-black [Popular party-Freedom party] political culture. . . . [He] is ferocious toward the SPO party and harps on the theme of Socialist recycling in their ranks of former Nazis after 1945. . . . The historic error of Popular party chancellor Wolfgang Schüssel was to take the FPÖ inside the institutions of the Austrian State, it having been until then a protest party confined to its provincial bastions, thus giving it the experience and stature of a government party. In sum [Schüssel] has normalized the political abnormality. . . .

April 6

Die Presse rejoices at the news that the [German conservative] CDU party is trying to find a way to end the sanctions without disavowing the European Union. For some time readers of the *Frankfurther Allgemeine* and *Die Welt* know where these newspapers stand: The German right supports [Austrian chancellor] Schüssel and doesn't accept that there is a "Haider problem."

Friday, April 7

Der Standard publishes an entire page on the theme, "What do the French [who lead the battle for sanctions] have against us?"

Yesterday the [Austrian] foreign affairs minister, outraged at having been snubbed at the very official inauguration of the European Racism Watch institute, declared . . . that it is the European Union that must change its position, not Austria.

This afternoon I go to visit a Germanist of the University of Vienna, the world's best known specialist in "Austrian" literature since 1945. Very much against the "black-blue" coalition, on his coat he has the badge—a bow tie covered by a red bar, like the cigarette covered with a red bar to indicate nonsmoking places—which is an allusion to the ever-present bow tie of [chancellor] Wolfgang Schüssel. He talks of his hope soon to see a Socialist-Green majority to succeed the current "small coalition." He fears people getting accustomed to the "new regime." He mentions Haider's recent speech meant to be a homage to the Slovenians complete with phrases in Slovenian. This populist is a protean politician ready to wear a caftan and to stand at the entrance to a synagogue to disprove those who think he is anti-Semitic.

Saturday, April 8

We have dinner this evening . . . with very old friends. . . . They are convinced partisans of the Schüssel government. R.K. is indignant that Austria is being charged with racism when his country is one of those that produces the fewest number of crimes and other racist incidents, and when Austria has accepted so many refugees coming from the countries of former Yugoslavia. P.K., also up in arms, is furious that the European Union puts on gloves to receive [Vladimir] Putin and receives [Moamar] Ghadafi, at the same time multiplying harassments against Austria.

For him everything is explained by the bankruptcy of the Socialist party's reign. The only way to contain the rise of the FPÖ was to assign it governmental responsibilities. He is disgusted by French newspaper presentations of the Austrian situation. I reply that the countries that are being severe with Austria worry about the extension of extreme-right populism into all of Europe and that Austria holds a sad record (27 percent for Haider's FPÖ in the last elections). What fascinates foreign observers is the fact that a personality like Haider, who would be considered in Germany as a marginal troublemaker and perhaps even charged legally with Holocaust revisionism, in Austria takes on the dimensions of a very popular statesman. P.K., a bit shaken but not convinced, replies that Haider has been around for fifteen years at least, and that it isn't serious for the European Union to present the situation as a political thunderclap.

SAVAGED MEMORIES

Sunday, April 9

Today, an excursion with the L. to the wine country up to the border with Moravia. At Wagram we visited the small Napoleon museum. Then, in the open-air museum of peasant arts and traditions, there was a memorial stand dedicated to the "south Moravian deported," meaning those Sudeten [Czech] Germans chased out after 1945 who found refuge in Austria. One more painful Austrian memory. Those people never "forgave" the Czechs and don't want to be forgotten.

J.L. is very moderate in his political views. He remarks only that the "sanctions" came much too late to serve a useful purpose. Europe would have had to take up the problem at its beginning, from the time of [Austrian] negotiations prior to membership.

As a consequence of the "sanctions," the Austrians are becoming "sovereigntists." . . . In the *Kurier* [newspaper], I read that France and Portugal are now "boycotted" by Austrian tourists. . . . The *Kurier* says that Jörg Haider is officially renouncing his idea of seeking the chancellorship. The paper judges this to be a direct consequence of the sanctions. "One of the most popular political leaders of the Second [Austrian] Republic" will have thus been constrained to take the consequences of his status of pariah within the international political class. . . .

Austria has lost at this moment all influence on the international policy of the EU. To the contrary, it is obvious that the European partners will try to neutralize Austria, above all on the question of enlargment since no doubt it is possible on this point: The Freedom party is vigorously opposed to admitting countries such as Hungary, the Czech Republic, or Slovenia into the European Union, for the same reasons that once lead France to slow down Spain's membership: fears of competition, for example in agriculture and artisan trades, fear of economic immigration, etc. . . .

Monday, April 10

Antipathy here toward France [for its strong denunciation and leadership on sanctions] is so widespread in Vienna that our friend T.S., an Alsatian restaurant owner, says he has lost 30 percent of his clientele in relation to last year's first quarter.

I meet with Peter Engelmann, the top publisher in Vienna . . . who says that defending democracy with nondemocratic discourse and behavior is wrong. . . . And it's a genuine, serious problem to judge the Haider party government ministers not on their acts but by a preference for condemnations of principle. On the other hand, those people want precisely to be judged as perfect democrats. We get back once again to the distinction between democratic procedures and democratic values. If the FPÖ has uncontestably not violated democratic procedures since [its accession to government] last February, is it also so certain that it has respected democratic values?

THIS PAST WHICH NEVER IS OVER . . .

Tuesday, April 11

[The writer] Thurnher devotes an enlightening chapter to Haider and to his party's rise since 1986. In 1991 there was the infamous speech to the Carinthian Regional Parliament that praised the "Third Reich's judicious labor market policy," over which Haider was forced to resign from the office of governor. In his anger he said that "blue acid" . . . should be thrown over all that "vermin" (the Blausäure, or blue acid, was the slang word for the Zyklon B gas used in the gas chambers in the death camps). In the 1989 elections his party had 29 percent. In the following elections in 1994 it reached 33.3 percent. In 1995 there was the speech before the Kameradschaft IV [veterans organization] of the Waffen SS. You are "good people," Haider shouted. In 1999 came the FPÖ's electoral victory and Haider became governor again. He observed, "For the first time since 1945, the FPÖ has won a majority in a region." Since 1945—what a slip of the tongue! The FPÖ has existed in its present form only since 1956. . . .

[Haider] is the son of a militant Nazi of the first hour, from the time when the Nazi Party was illegal in Austria. His father participated in the 1934 putsch; later he became chief of the Hitler Youth of the Gau Upper Danube region in Upper Austria. In 1986, the year he became FPÖ president, Jörg Haider inherited a huge property that had been "Aryanized" in 1939 (stolen from an Italian Jewish woman). . . .

In the afternoon I see Peter Engelmann again. . . . For him the sanctions represent a fading of the European idea, a kind of violence done to Austria, a small country, when no one ever thought of acting in the same manner against the Italy of Berlusconi and Fini. We think that behind the French-Austria tensions lies a profound Franco-German difference of view. France only wants to hear the voices of Chancellor [Gerhard] Schröder and Foreign Affairs Minister Joschka Fischer, thus avoiding the facts: These leaders are very isolated domestically on the Austrian question and the majority of Germans don't understand at all the agitation within the French political class. . . . On the question of sanctions, [the historian E.B.] moderately but firmly informs me that the reaction of the EU and certain countries such as France deeply affronts Austrian legalism; the latter are still wondering what treaty or rule allows [for such sanctions].

Wednesday, April 12

The *Kurier* newspaper: The CDU party convention has voted a motion of solidarity with Wolfgang Schüssel's Austria against the sanctions. The Austrian ambassador, excluded from the meeting to present French proposals for its turn at the presidency of the EU, threatens France with reprisals that could affect the French presidency. Schüssel . . . raises the tone, talking of "judicial actions" by his government against the bad behavior of the French authorities. . . .

The only argument that would allow Chancellor Schüssel to renew a dialog with his European partners would be to say: "The problem dominating Austria's political life for a decade has been the rise of Jörg Haider's populist party. The socialists (and the conservatives in forming a coalition with it) have failed in the strategy of exclusion of Haider and his party. On the contrary we have seen the rise of the populist FPÖ and the weakening of the government parties. Since February 2000 I have taken the risk of exploring a new option, which consists of fighting against the FPÖ with the weapon of making it assume government responsibilities. Don't complicate my life by maintaining the sanctions and thus giving new protest themes to Haider." . . . The charismatic FPÖ leader has understood very well already that comanagement of the government, with its parade of unpopular measures, could durably weaken the party. . . .

Haider's reckless declarations at Brussels ("Europe is acting like a colonial power toward Austria") are echoed in a frighteningly nationalist editorial by Karl-Peter Schwarz in *Die Presse*: "It is more and more clear that the 'values' cultivated by *this* European community of values consist in emphasizing preconceptions, slander, and contempt for democratic procedures. . . . To continue to implore the European Union would be humiliating. Austria should adopt a wait-and-see policy, reducing its European contacts to current business. We too have national interests to defend."

WILL ITALY BE SANCTIONED?

Saturday, April 15, Paris

"Russia disapproves the EU sanctions and supports Austria." The foreign affairs minister, Ferrero-Waldner, visiting Moscow and Chechenya, supposedly was told this.

Sunday, April 16

In my mail I find a letter from Kurt Jungwirth . . . furiously critical of the sanctions and asking if in the future the EU "will vet all the parties of all the member countries before all elections." . . .

Monday, April 17

In *Le Monde* of April 16–17 I learn that the Italian regional elections could be the occasion for Berlusconi and his grouping of the extreme right parties to return to a leading position. If this unfortunate possibility were to happen, would Europe apply "sanctions" to Italy? And if it didn't, Austria would have an easy time complaining about being a "small country" completely mistreated by the "big powers." . . .

Tuesday, April 18

A huge dossier is published on the plundering of French Jews during the Vichy period and German occupation. . . . Would such an accounting be possible in Austria . . . ? Jörg Haider is one of the largest landowners in Carinthia, owing his considerable fortune to the handover of "Aryanized" property. But that apparently doesn't bother anyone. If the legitimacy of this sort of patrimony were questioned, how many happy Austrian property owners would be threatened! . . .

The declarations of Joschka Fischer regarding the question, "How to raise the sanctions against Austria when in Germany you, with Chancellor Schröder, are completely alone [in supporting them]?" Fischer's reply: "The constitution makes it our duty to defend German interests. These were not to allow Haider to divide the European Union on the conception it has of itself. I completely understand the [strong anti-Haider] reaction of the French. If the EU partners had not reacted together . . . we would have found ourselves in a different predicament: Austria would have been faced with an even harder reaction from Israel, the U.S., or other countries. By considering that it was a 'family affair,' we rendered a service to Austria. I hope that Chancellor Schüssel succeeds in keeping Haider inside the democratic camp. . . . In any case we won't make the mistake of allowing Haider to become a German problem."

CHAPTER 15

The Euro: The Engine That Couldn't

Josef Joffe

Josef Joffe is the editor of Die Zeit *(Hamburg) and was previously manag-ing editor of the* Süddeutsche Zeitung *(Munich). He is author of* The Lim-ited Partnership: Europe, the United States, and the Burdens of Alliance *(1987), and, among many articles, has contributed chapters recently to Ronald Tiersky's* Europe Today: National Politics, European Integration, and European Security *(1999) and Robert A. Pastor's* A Century's Journey: How the Great Powers Shape the World *(1999). The following short piece is from* The New York Review of Books, *December 4, 1997.*

1.

"European Monetary Union—The Movie" would have to begin with the fol-lowing scene. The place is the library of the Elysée Palace, the time is about March 1990. Only three people are present: François Mitterrand, the French president; Helmut Kohl, the chancellor of soon-to-be reunited Germany; finally, since neither speaks the language of the other, a faceless interpreter sworn to silence.

Mitterrand is in a melancholy mood. During the last few months, ever since the collapse of the Berlin Wall in November 1989, he has tried every con-ceivable diplomatic strategem to stop, or at least brake, the quickening pace of German reunification. But to no avail. Glumly, he stares into the fireplace, as his friend Helmut talks. "Look, François, this time it won't be like Versailles in 1871, when Paris was encircled by German armies, when the new Reich was proclaimed on the ruins of French pride. We have Franco-German friendship, we have the European Union, our forces are completely integrated in NATO; indeed, we don't even have our own general staff any more."

The mention of NATO, America's foot in Europe's door, hardly cheers Mitterand. So Kohl goes on. "My dear friend, this is 1990—not 1914 and not 1939. These days, my countrymen are polishing their BMWs, not their jackboots. Come on, François, what do you say?"

Mitterrand continues to stare into the fire for a minute that seems to stretch on forever. Finally, he bursts out, *"Bon, Helmut, c'est ce qu'on va faire.* You get all of Deutschland, if I get half of the Deutschemark."

2.

The point of this imaginary scene is that the euro, Europe's soon-to-be common money, is a political currency. It was born out of the abrupt transformation of world politics: Moscow's capitulation in the cold war, which suddenly revealed the true power relationships on the Continent. In a few months, Germany would be "whole and free" again, as George Bush had put it. Once united, the country would also shed the ancient dependencies that had tied two thirds of it, the Federal Republic, to France.

But Helmut Kohl is not Wilhelm II. Like Bismarck, he understood the precarious position of Germany about to become the most powerful country in Europe again—at least if power is measured by the size of Germany's population and GDP, and by its central strategic position. Like Konrad Adenauer and Willy Brandt, Kohl knew that Germany was too weak to act alone, but too strong for the rest of Europe to leave it alone. The lesson of the past hundred years for him was clear. When Germany, its power untrammeled, struck out on its own, the result was ever greater disaster. When it was safely locked into European institutions—when its power was tamed by cooperative arrangements with other countries—Germany flourished beyond anyone's expectations.

Now the division of the country imposed by the cold war was about to end, and Kohl wanted to reassure France and all of Europe. The Deutschemark, the strongest currency on the Continent, was the very symbol of German primacy. What better way to soften its edge than by *more* integration? By way of the euro, one might say, Gulliver proposed to tie *himself* down. The sentiment and the logic of self-containment were as commendable as Kohl's intentions were historically honorable.

But Gulliver would not actually immobilize himself—that was the elegant part of the deal. In essence, the euro would be the Deutschemark writ large. It would be administered by a European central bank patterned after the

German Bundesbank which, in turn, was largely modeled after the American Federal Reserve. This super-Bundesbank would be totally independent of political control; with its mighty autonomy, it would impose strict financial discipline on countries like France or Italy, whose central banks usually acted as handmaidens to their profligate political masters in Paris and Rome. So Germany would not so much sacrifice its precious currency as it would extend its sway beyond the informal Deutschemark zone that already encompasses Austria, Denmark, and the Benelux countries.

To the French, invaded three times by Germany in the space of a lifetime, the euro nonetheless offered fair compensation. The losers of the Franco-Prussian War of 1871, the French had emerged from World War I and II only as nominal victors. In each case, they saw their strategies for postwar containment of Germany come to nothing. By 1922, at the time of the Rapallo Treaty, with Soviet Russia in economic difficulty and the Anglo Saxon powers turning in on themselves, Weimar Germany had actually improved on the strategic position of the Wilhelmine Reich. By 1955, West Germany, freshly installed in NATO, was free of occupation forces and had become a junior partner of the United States. And now, in 1990, the last constraints would melt away. On October 3, reunification day, the Federal Republic would expand by one half while regaining complete sovereignty. Kohl's offer to give up the Deutschemark was a godsend for Mitterand. And so, on they went to Maastricht—with good instincts, but bad economics and politics.

3.

In Maastricht, a small town in the Netherlands, the twelve members of the European Union (now fifteen) gathered in early 1992 to pledge something history had never recorded before. They would sign away several of the largest sovereign powers at the command of the modern nation-state. These are the power to mint money and the power to regulate its quantity as well as its price both at home (the interest rate) and abroad (the exchange rate).

The Maastricht Treaty contains two critical dates. At the beginning of 1999, those countries whose economies meet the standards set at Maastricht—the fabled "criteria"—will yield their monetary sovereignty to a European Central Bank, which is to manage both the money supply and interest rates of all the European countries taking part, with national currencies irrevocably chained to one another. For the next three years, the euro and the various national currencies will exist side by side. But on January 1, 2002, marks, guilders, francs, etc. will vanish. There will only be euros and cents.

Such a brief summary of the Maastricht Treaty hardly suggests the enormity of the task ahead. Before national currencies can become *e pluribus unum* they must be brought into line. To conceive of what that will involve, we can visualize several locomotives, each running under its own power, strung together to make up a single train. Each engine must steam ahead at the same speed in the same direction at the same time. All currencies must behave as one, with no fluctuations among them and hence with virtually identical interest and inflation rates—as if there were only one lead locomotive that pulls all the others with their engines switched off. If there is no strict coordination, the locomotives will run into one another and go off the rails, or the couplings linking them will break. In the real world, the required degree of coordination is called "political union" or "federation"—something like the United States.

Had Messrs. Kohl and Miterrand made this logic explicit, the euro would have died right after it was conceived. Frenchmen and Germans don't want to be like the citizens of Michigan and New York; nor do Italians, Spaniards, or Britons. They like Europe, but they like even better their national homelands, which have been around for one or two millennia. They don't speak each other's languages; they do not share each other's memories.

So the would-be members of the euro club are not like railroad cars just coasting along or waiting passively in the Brussels switching yard. Each has its own "engineer"—its government whose politicians face reelection. Each has its own "engine"—its macroeconomic policy that determines spending and taxing, debt and interest. Each follows its own "timetable"—i.e., it is situated at different points in the business cycle.[1] And none can ignore its own history and the basic national assumptions and habits that define the unwritten social contract by which the state gives to, and takes from, its citizens. By comparison with France's, only a small part of the British economy is state-based or state-controlled; Germany's falls somewhere in between.

Compare this to the United States: Michigan and New York don't conduct macroeconomic policy; their money, like that of every other state, is managed nationally by the Federal Reserve. Lansing and Albany have limited powers to tax and spend, but the country's fiscal policy is decided in Washington, by the US Congress and by the executive branch. France, Germany, and other members of the European Union are not and will not be like any of the fifty American states. They are sovereign entities, with national parliaments and executives, and the large countries like Britain, Spain, and Italy have proportionally far more effect on the European economy than the economy of California does on the economy of the US.

How can they be kept on the same track? This is where the famous "criteria" of the Maastricht regime come in—the gates to the inner sanctum of monetary union. In essence, the criteria demand of each would-be member that it stop behaving like a sovereign state. In order to qualify for euro membership, their annual budget deficits must not exceed 3 percent of GDP. Accumulated public debt must stay within 60 percent of GDP. Long-term interest rates must be lower than 10 percent, and the inflation rate must be lower than 3 percent.

In short, though each state, like a locomotive, still obeys its own driver, engine, and timetable, it has to act as if it were Michigan or New York. It has to forget virtually everything that turned fiefdoms, duchies, and city-states into modern nation-states between the fourteenth and the nineteenth century: first the king's, and later the parliament's, supremacy over public finance.

At this point, only Luxembourg qualifies on all counts, if the criteria are applied rigorously. By next May, the European Union must decide who else makes the cut on the basis of the 1997 figures. "Eurostat," the statistical research branch of the European Commission in Brussels, has just announced that, except for Greece, all the members of the European Union are likely to squeeze by.[2] How will they do so? By creative bookkeeping, if not outright cheating.

4.

Take Germany, once the fiscal disciplinarian of Europe. Without some imaginative maneuvers, its annual budget deficit would be closer to 4 than 3 percent of GDP at the end of the year; and its total debt, rising of course, has passed the 60 percent limit. How, then, will Germany fulfill the criteria? Deutsche Telekom, the state-owned telephone service, is being sold off on the stock market. So is Lufthansa. The receipts will look good on the nation's books by the end of the year. Also Theo Waigel, the finance minister, has conveniently discovered that the gold held by the Bundesbank—the German version of the Federal Reserve—has been badly undervalued for many years. Revalue it to reflect the market price for gold, shunt the paper profits into the federal till, and the deficit shrinks some more.

The Italians, whose country, next to Greece, has the largest deficits, are desperate to be founding members of the euro club, and so they are prettying up the books *all'italiana,* while trying to impose austerity measures on the economy. This led to a bit of political commedia dell'arte in October. Assaulted by the Communists on grounds of excessive social cruelty, the Prodi government fell—only to be resurrected forty-eight hours later. This does not bode well for a sustained budget-cutting policy past the magic date in May, when the EU must decide on admission to the euro club.

First prize for creative accounting must go to the French, though. There is no way that the defiant Socialist government of Lionel Jospin, which took power from the Chirac coalition earlier this year with promises of 350,000 public jobs, can bring about a budget deficit as low as 3 percent of GDP. But the French have told the Germans they have found a brilliant solution. They will simply withhold tax refunds for a while, thus "proving" that France, when the 1997 figures are tallied, is marching straight toward the 3 percent deficit target.

Why the obsession with meeting criteria which are more or less arbitrary anyway? Theoretically, the European governments and central bankers could have set the deficit-to-GDP standard at 5 rather than 3 percent, and the public debt-to-GDP ration at 80 or 100 rather than 60 percent. But the exact limits are not the critical issue. The real point, to recall the railroad metaphor, is simultaneity, with everybody moving at the same speed in the same direction.

Unless they do, the couplings break. This is exactly what happened in 1992 when George Soros, betting on the Deutschemark, sold billions of pounds sterling on the international market, forcing Britain to devalue the pound and leave the European Exchange Rate Mechanism (ERM). This was the system set up in 1979 to preserve rough parity among European currencies—a forerunner of the euro. Italy followed and devalued, too. So did Spain, Portugal, and Sweden. This episode may now seem past history, but its lesson is still valid. Nations may pledge the kind of fiscal and monetary probity that keeps exchange rates in lockstep. But then governments look at their unemployment rates and think of their coming elections. They then choose economic policies—a bit of easy money there, a few more public works there—that strain, and then break, international monetary agreements.

The history of the ERM nicely illustrates the skeptic's worries about the euro. It worked as long as the dictatorship of virtue was regularly relieved by an occasional brush with sin. Until 1987, there were many realignments of the different currencies, on the average once every eighteen months. Everybody could stay on the wagon precisely because he could take an occasional swig from the bottle. But after 1987, currencies became fixed, to be defended at all costs and against all comers. Hence, the pressures derived from incompatible economic policies began to build up, exploding five years later with Britain's withdrawal in 1992. Thereafter, realism was given its due: exchange rates, previously within a range of 4.5 percent, were allowed a leeway of 30 percent, which is another word for "floating currency."

Today, life on the wagon has become a bit easier, above all because inflation and interest rates have been dropping throughout Europe, even among famously improvident states like Italy. Advocates of the euro have been citing this cheerful news as proof that Maastricht is working. Alas, this may be like that famous correlation that links the decline of the stork population to the receding birth rate, both of which happen to be the case in postwar Europe. The fact is that inflation has been falling throughout the entire Western world since the early 1990s. If Maastricht had acted as such an effective taskmaster, why did inflation also ebb in the US and in Britain, countries that were not clamoring to get into the euro club?

5.

By next May, most of the European countries, prodded by France and Germany, will most likely certify themselves ready for the euro. They will look at the dressed-up numbers, wink and nod; in the case of countries where even the most creative accountant could not hide the gaps between rule and reality, the others may agree to be charitable and say that since they are trying so hard they can join anyway.

What then? Traditionally, states have used the exchange rate as a major cushion against external shocks, and they have manipulated the money supply, the interest rate, taxes, and spending for the sake of stability and growth at home. But in 1999, the exchange rate, as an instrument of national policy, will have gone the way of the halberd. Monetary policy will be set by the European Central Bank. And fiscal policy, including taxes and spending, though legally still in the hands of states, will be severely constrained by the demands of the "stability pact" that the Germans have insisted other members of the European Union must sign. Essentially, the pact says that the Maastricht criteria must rule forever. Or as some French politicians suspect, it will be the Bundesbank-writ-large that will rule, plus a softer version of the US balanced-budget amendment. (This is why the French above all have been pushing for an Economic Council that would set macroeconomic policy for the euro zone and thus counteract or dilute the stringent monetary policies of the European Central Bank.)

The resulting loss of autonomy is an economist's nightmare. Individual governments in the euro zone will no longer be able to do what they have done since the invention of the printing press. They will no longer be able to increase the money supply to drive down interest rates and stimulate investment. They will no longer be able to devalue their currency so their exports will grow. If they are obedient to the stability pact, they will have a very limited ability to increase aggregate demand through deficit spending. With national monetary policy determined supranationally, and fiscal policy heavily limited, a national economy is left with three, and only three, ways out of trouble. And each of them spells more trouble.

To take a simplified example, let us assume that there is stubborn and growing unemployment in the northeast of France, a traditional industrial region. There are only three solutions to the problem. One: wages fall, attracting new investment and generating new employment. But wages do not fall in Europe, and least of all in France. National or industrywide collective bargaining agreements inhibit payment of different wage rates in different regions. In the United States, the Carolinas or Alabama, with wages lower than California's or Connecticut's, may lure capital investment from inside and outside the country. European capital in search of profits migrates to the Czech Republic, if not China.

The second solution is geographical mobility. If capital does not come to the workers, they go where the jobs are. In the early 1970s, Sunday papers from Houston and Dallas sold well in depressed Detroit, where the Big Three auto makers were being done in by foreign competition. Unemployed auto workers would scan the want ads and then pack up their families to move to Texas towns that were then booming. Some of the workers by now have moved back to Michigan, which is again in strong economic shape.

By comparison, Europeans do not move. Theoretically, Lille's unemployed could migrate to high-growth regions like southern England or Munich. But unlike relatively poor Turks or Serbs, they don't. First of all, a lavish welfare state, plus large benefits for shrinking industries (steel or agriculture), allow people to stay in places from which the jobs have departed. Second, if they *did* want to move, they would face intimidating cultural barriers, above all a new language, unlike Detroit workers in Texas. Third, although Germans have used Turks for menial labor, much as the French have used North Africans, Europeans are less and less willing to accept "cheap foreign labor" that can do more skilled work. Construction workers' unions in high-wage Germany have been fighting hard against Polish migrants. They would not welcome migrates from Lille either.

Which leaves the third, and most troublesome solution: transfer payments on a Europe-wide scale. In the absence of wage and labor flexibility, this has been for decades the favorite European economic strategy for dealing with unproductive regions. The rich Italian North subsidizes the *mezzogiorno,* the agrarian South. Prosperous Bavaria pays large subsidies to Bremen, a Social Democrat–ruled city-state on the North Sea, which has been keeping ship-yards alive against all economic reason. Indeed, Western Germany has annually been plowing the equivalent of the entire Marshall Plan—which gave aid to fifteen countries for three years—into Eastern Germany, a region of 15 million people, since reunification.

Bavaria pays grudgingly for Bremen, but it pays. Lombardy supports the Italian South, but resentfully so; indeed, the secessionist Lega Nord has been demanding partition for years. Now imagine that Germany and Italy have to shell out billions to help their less fortunate brethren in Euro-Land. What is, and will be, lacking is the kind of common identity that justifies expenditures, often rather grudging ones, on behalf of poor regions or groups. "Europe" is a construct, not a country. Though it has a flag (fifteen golden stars on deep blue), it does not evoke the kind of loyalty the Stars and Stripes evokes among Americans. The European Union is not—and will not be for a long time—a community of identity and obligation. And money, as a German saying cautions, is where friendship stops.

6.

The larger point is that Europe, by plunging into monetary union, is putting last things first. It is erecting a vast structure without having prepared the indispensable foundation, a common state. One might think that so sweeping a sacrifice of sovereignty would require a "general will," expressed in an institution that transcends the feeble European Parliament in Strasbourg and the rudimentary apparatus of governance in Brussels. Power in the EU is still lodged in the Council of Ministers representing the fifteen member states, not Europe. History confirms such a somber assessment. Bismarck had to force twenty-five little Germanies to accept the Reich before the new state could move on to a national market and currency. It took the United States from 1788 to 1913, from the approval of the Constitution to the founding of the Federal Reserve Board, before it established a central bank and true monetary union (with a murderous civil war in between).

Political union must precede monetary union—that is what historical experience keeps stressing. Nor is monetary union a kind of furtive shortcut to political union, as Europe's federalists might presume. Money, in fact, does not bind what pulls apart. The first thing secessionist states do is to print their own tender—as the American Confederacy did in 1861, as Slovakia did in 1993. Money, as every unhappy family knows, is a prime cause of discord and divorce.

Still, the euro will spawn powerful benefits. Big business, even in Britain, loves it because it will do away with costly hedging operations to insure against currency fluctuations. It will make the mechanics of international payments easier and sweep away the exchange-rate risks of long-term investments. Europe's exporters also surmise that the euro will be "softer" than, say, the mark, franc, or pound, and thus give them a competitive edge over exports that must be paid for in dollars and yen. Europe's large banks and insurance companies can hardly wait for the euro. They see a vast market awaiting them in which every bond, stock, and insurance policy will be denominated in a single currency. That will bulldoze barriers of habit and tradition and deliver a continent-sized playing field for the best and biggest financial institutions in Europe. Corporate capitalism salivates over the euro, and for good reason.

But the citizens of France and Germany do not do so, if we are to believe the opinion polls—at least the polls not conducted by the European Commission, which likes to produce good news for its masters. In those countries whose economies have the most valid chance of meeting the criteria next May, opposition to the euro or desire for a delay unites up to two thirds of the populace. And fondness for the euro tends to grow with the distance from the Maastricht criteria, most dramatically in Italy.

Kohl, Chirac, and their colleagues are thus plunging head-on into a current of popular distaste against the euro. They have been able to brave the resistance to the plan because only very few politicians, whether on the center left or center right, have dared to seek votes by turning against it. To oppose the euro is to oppose Europe—the equivalent of motherhood. On the Continent, at least, nobody of stature and ambition wants to be seen in the company of the main opposition to Maastricht—whether the neo-right, like Germany's Republikaners, or the paleo-left, like the French Communists. That has deadened the debate, leaving behind a mood of sullen passivity fed by hopes for postponement.

7.

A lengthy trial run of, say, three or five years of strict observance of the rules of economic convergence would be a wiser course than adopting the euro now. For it might or might not prove what the euro enthusiasts merely assume: that nations, though they remain nations, will act as if they were not. To repeat the cruel textbook truth, they must remain in tandem not just in the period before the deadline, but forever more. *They must stop acting like sovereign states* in matters monetary and economic.

By next May, when the cut is to be made, the euro-aspirants will have proven only one thing: that they are capable of making a desperate dash for the 3 percent deficit line. But in order to cut the deficit, they have sold off public assets instead of reducing government expenditures. These are one-time solutions that do not change the underlying dynamics of fiscal policy. And since the states act as their own referees, they have been able to fudge the numbers quite nicely.

True, inflation has dropped throughout Europe, and medium-term interest rates are converging. But there is less progress than meets the eye. Inflation rates, as was noted before, are down in the entire West, reflecting a mildly deflationary world economy rather than the fiscal virtue of the euro candidates. Italians today dwell proudly on the fact that the yield spread between Italian and German government bonds, about six percentage points just two years ago, has come down to less than two. But Italy's plummeting rates do not prove that the Italians have really changed their ways, and that goes, *mutatis mutandis,* for the others, too. Money traders have simply concluded that, for political reasons, France and Germany will have to take in Italy, a founding member of the old European Economic Community, no matter what. They are happily buying lire bonds (which drives down Italian rates) because they no longer need to fear yesterday's devaluation risks. And why not? In 1999, these bonds can simply be converted into euros or Deutschmarks at predictably fixed rates.

In short, the EU countries have not proven that they can sustain convergence over the long run. Long-term discipline was precisely the test set up more than five years ago. But Europe cannot be said to have met it. Hence the wisdom of postponing the plunge for three or five years. During such a period, the candidates could confound the skeptics by actually doing what they should have been doing since 1992. They would live up to the logic of monetary union by scrupulously sticking to parallel macroeconomic and monetary policies as opposed to merely selling off the family silver and cooking the books.

By definition, inflation and interest rates would then remain in lockstep, and so would exchange rates. This would be de facto monetary union, though with national currencies still in circulation. At the end of the "trial marriage," real monetary union would be a mere formality, or, to return to the train metaphor, visible proof that everybody had maintained the same speed and direction not just in the run-up but over the long haul.

In so submitting to a general will, each of the European nation-states would prove that it is indeed ready for self-transcendence. But the European nation-state is still vigorously alive—that is the problem. Nor do Kohl and Chirac even contemplate yielding their power to a European president lodged in Brussels. And their citizens, who do not really understand the enormous loss of sovereignty the euro entails, still want to be ruled from Paris and Berlin, and not from Brussels. But who is going to read through the 250 pages of the Maastricht Treaty, which flummox even trained lawyers?

Never in the history of democracy have so few debated so little about so momentous a transformation in the lives of men and nations. And so the train will probably leave the station on time, on January 1, 1999, but with screeching wheels and shaky couplings. If it goes off the rails, as economics and politics suggest it will, the consequences may contaminate much of what Europe has achieved during the past forty years.

NOTES

1. A recent report by the British treasury made this point in warning of the dangers posed by the euro to the British economy. As the *London Observer* reported on October 19:

> The Treasury review underlines that the British economy is seriously out of line with continental economies, with Britain's recovery years more advanced. Treasury officials have warned that cutting British interest rates to continental rates— appropriate for countries where economic conditions are more depressed— could detonate a runaway boom, with inflationary pressures that could not be responded to by devaluation.

In view of such advice, we can understand the government's position that any decision on the euro must be delayed until after the next election.

2. Eurostat is not a totally independent body. Attached to the European Commission, it assembles and evaluates economic and budgetary data given to it by each national government. For a sober analysis of Eurostat's operations and the bookkeeping tricks of EU governments, see Andreas Oldag, "Schlüssel zur Währungsunion liegt bei Eurostat" (The Key to Monetary Union Rests with Eurostat) and "EU-Mitgliedstaaten entwickeln immer neue Ideen, um ihre Haushaltsdaten zu schönen" (EU Member States Come Up with Ever New Ideas on How to Prettify Their Budget Data), *Süddeutsche Zeitung,* October 25–26, 1997, p. 2.

CHAPTER 16

Democratic Values
and the Currency

Michael Portillo

Michael Portillo was Secretary of State for Defense in the John Major Conservative party government from 1995 to 1997. He is presently a member of the Conservative shadow cabinet in opposition. In 1983 he was Special Adviser to the Chancellor of the Exchequer, Nigel Lawson. His February 1998 lecture "Democratic Values and the Currency" has been widely remarked as one of the most memorable and eloquent statements of Euroskepticism regarding the single European currency.

1. INTRODUCTION

I am honoured to be able to deliver a lecture to the IEA, and I thank John Blundell for the invitation to do so. The triumvirate of Antony Fisher, Arthur Seldon and Ralph Harris has provided a remarkable demonstration of the power and influence of ideas. They patiently expounded a remarkable combination of common sense and academic excellence; never afraid to yell out from the crowd, when, as was usually the case, the ruling emperor of conventional wisdom was actually wearing no clothes. Their thinking deeply affected the last Conservative government, many other governments around the world, and new Labour. I cannot think of a better forum in which to deliver what follows.

My object is to discuss the single currency, but not as it is often talked of in Britain, as though it were merely an economic device which can be mea-

Reprinted with permission from the IEA publication *Democratic Values and Currency* (0-255 36412-1, occasional paper no. 103), 9-31.

sured in terms of costs and benefits. I wish to examine it in the terms used by our partners, who see it as a project in re-shaping the way our Continent is governed, to create a political union that can free Europe from the fear of conflict between the nations.

2. THE COST AND CAUSES OF WAR

In the last two centuries the peoples of Europe have paid a terrible price in wars. In the First World War, 15 million were killed, mainly soldiers. In the Second World War, the toll was at least 41 million, of whom most were civilians. Those terrible events have naturally and rightly led highly distinguished statesmen to dedicate their lives to creating conditions in which war would not occur again. There is no higher or more important objective for politicians in Europe than to work for policies that may better guarantee the security of our Continent and avoid a repetition of the dreadful slaughter of our modern history.

We can distinguish two causes at the root of past conflicts in Europe. The first is Franco-German rivalry. Prussia and Austria invaded France in 1793 and 1813. France occupied Prussian and Austrian territory between 1805 and 1813. Prussia dealt the French army a swift defeat in 1870, and went on to besiege the French capital causing many Parisians to die of starvation. Germany invaded France in the opening stages of both world wars. Understandably therefore, much effort since the last war has been devoted to creating political institutions, and other links, to bind the former adversaries together.

A second cause of past conflict was the so-called Eastern Question in its various forms. There was the clash between the empires of Christendom and Islam, both ideological and territorial. The assassination in Sarajevo of an Austrian archduke, and Austria's revenge for it on Serbia, provided the spark for the outbreak of the Great War. But Germany's suspicion and fear of Russia, another part of the Eastern Question, were a more fundamental cause of that war. The mutual aggression between totalitarian régimes in Germany and Russia supplied the bitterest and most costly conflict of the Second World War.

Comparatively little effort has been devoted to bringing Russia fully into the family of Western nations, or to building bridges between Christendom and Islam in Europe, and I shall return to that later. First, let us look at how efforts to resolve the conflict between France and Germany have been taken forward.

3. THE IDEAL OF A UNITED EUROPE

The ideal of creating a United Europe, even a United States, grew up as part of the humanist-pacifist tradition even before the wars of the 20th century, but until the end of the second war was largely confined to academics and dreamers. Thereafter, it was taken up by statesmen like Altiero Spinelli and Jean Monnet.

The two men embodied two distinct approaches to European unity, and the distinction is important even today. Spinelli was a federalist, believing that local, regional, national and European authorities should complement each other. Monnet did not describe himself as a federalist but as a functionalist, believing that functions one by one, and therefore sovereignty, should be transferred from the national to the European level.

In the official European Community literature of the 1990s it is argued that 'Today the two approaches have been merged.'[1] Perhaps so. The Maastricht Treaty appears to owe much to a functionalist approach with its proposals that Europe should acquire its own defence and foreign policies and its own currency. But federalists will be happy with that, since the result is none the less federation, that is, the creation of a new political entity. It has the critical characteristic of a federation, in that the federation's laws are binding on the member-states.

Those who support the creation of a federation sometimes argue that federalism is generally misunderstood in Britain, and tell us that in continental Europe it is about de-centralisation, and that federal constitutions in a number of European states emphasise the devolution of powers to states or regions. But the federalism that is being unfolded at European level is not like that. It does not emphasise the devolution of powers to member-states. The process of integration now being pursued from one inter-governmental conference to the next, is highly centralising and owes much to the Monnet-functionalist approach.

British Policy on European Security

While Spinelli, Monnet and others were advancing European unity by whatever means they could, which in their day meant mostly devising institutions governing economic and trading relations in Europe, Britain held aloof from that process, but committed itself directly to European security.

There is a myth that Britain has never cared about Europe. That is an extraordinary claim. The British Empire lost nearly a million combatants in the First World War, despite beginning the war with what the Kaiser called a 'contemptibly small army.' In the Second World War, hundreds of thousands of British people died at home, or fighting in and around Europe for the freedom of Europe.

Following that war, at a time when the nature of the Soviet Empire was becoming clear, the British foreign secretary, Ernest Bevin, committed Britain to a Western Union, an alliance of European and non-European states dedicated to providing their peoples with security. In 1954, attempts to create a European Defence Community were scuppered by France at the Paris Conference. But the British foreign secretary, Anthony Eden, made an historic commitment on behalf of this country to maintain land and air forces in Europe for the following 40 years, thus providing a clear and unmistakable guarantee of Britain's willingness to fulfil its obligations if the security of our allies were ever violated. It was a remarkable undertaking for an island nation to make, especially given our traditional strategy of maintaining a small army and avoiding Continental military commitments.

Different Models for Europe

We need to understand the history in order to understand how strong is the impetus to European integration. The momentum derives from an understandable fear of war. That is what lies behind Chancellor Kohl's famous remark that European integration is 'a question of war and peace.'[2] We all subscribe wholeheartedly to the objective of achieving peace and security. More importantly, British foreign policy over five decades has been committed to that objective, and Britain's actions have followed its words.

Everyone can appreciate the terrible suffering experienced by Europe and share in the objective of never allowing it to happen again. Furthermore, Europe is right to sweep away barriers to trade, investment and mobility across the boundaries of the nation states of our Continent. But there are many different means by which those objectives can be achieved. The functionalist, that is to say, centralising model now being applied by the Commission, and by most of our partner countries, is not the only paradigm that could be used. Nor is it the case that those who oppose the present course are anti-European, still less chauvinist or xenophobic.

General de Gaulle was famously in favour of a 'Europe des patries,' and opposed the tendency of the European Commission to acquire new powers for itself. He employed rough tactics to establish the principle that nation states should not be over-ruled by majorities on matters of vital national interest. How could it be that someone who valued Europe, who had fought for its freedom and knew as much as any about war, still nurtured a belief in the nation state?

The answer to that question requires us to consider a little more deeply what are the causes of conflict. It seems that those who want to create a United States of Europe believe that nationalism has been the principle cause. They think that if you can replace the nation states, and make the nations of Europe dependent on each other in a new European state, you will have dealt with the problem of nationalism and therefore abolished the main cause of war.

But it is not enough to assert that European wars have been caused by rampant nationalism. Two other things have also been necessary: despotism and a sense of grievance. Take any of the wars of the last two centuries, and it will be seen that the aggressors were despots: French revolutionaries, kaisers, emperors, Hitler and Stalin. They capitalised ruthlessly on some supposed injustice done to their nation, some piece of territory that had to be restored to the mother- or fatherland, some minority that yearned to be set free from its foreign repressor.

4. THE SPREAD OF DEMOCRACY—AND OF SECURITY

The great victory in Europe at the end of the Second World War was the restoration of democracy in Germany and Italy, and the liberation of those countries that had been conquered by the axis powers. Subsequently Spain, Portugal and Greece rejoined the family of democratic nations. My father fought for democracy in Spain and was a refugee from tyranny for 20 years. To see democracy restored there brought my family great joy. Following the fall of the Iron Curtain, most of Eastern Europe and even Russia have become young democracies, to the joy of millions who had suffered there. Democracy is precious to everyone, but its value is most appreciated by those who know what it is to be without it.

The European Union, along with NATO and other European institutions, has played an important part in the extension of democracy through Europe. Their member-states have provided a shining example of both freedom and material success, and Western institutions have supplied the template of democratic values to be reproduced by the new democracies if they are to aspire to join them as new members. Europe is more secure from conflict within the Continent now than ever before, because there have never been so many democracies as now, and it is inconceivable that democracies would go to war with one another.

Viewed like that, democracy acquires a special value. It is not merely, as Churchill said, the worst system except for all the rest, it is *the* form of government that best assures peace. If we do not have security, we cannot hope to achieve anything decent in life, because we have seen repeatedly in Europe that without it we risk descending into absolute barbarity. Democracy provides the best guarantee of security. Without democracy, for all its alleged deficiencies, the abyss would yawn before us.

European integration is not the means to achieve the security of our Continent. It is the wrong route. Integration is being designed in a way that sharply reduces democratic control. If we shoe-horn the nations of Europe into an artificial union, we will not abolish nationalism, indeed we risk stirring it up. The danger is that we make people feel that their national interests will be overlooked, and that they cannot assert them through the ballot. That risks exactly what the architects of the new Europe say they wish to avoid: destabilising Europe, creating tensions and releasing resentments that damage the present good relations between European nations.

What Is Democracy?

Let us consider what democracy is and how it works. The origins of the word are illuminating: *demos* meaning the people or commons of an ancient Greek state and hence the populace, and *cracy* meaning rule or power. The earliest Greek democracy depended on a very small populace, those of a city, those that could be expected to gather together in one place. Their *commonality* was evident. In the modern world it is more difficult to be precise about what constitutes a *people.* It is obviously a matter of great controversy and can be subject to change. Most nation states have a common language, but not all. Many nation states have a principal nationality or ethnic group, but not all. Most nation states are geographically homogeneous, but not all. The United States of America would not score very high on any of those criteria, and yet it is undoubtedly a nation state. Its people are explicitly bound together by a clearly articulated sense of national purpose and by a set of shared values, by a vision of themselves and by a notion of their place in the world. All of that provides them with the things in common that make them a people. Much of the same could be said of most of the nation states of Europe, though admittedly some to a greater and others to a lesser extent.

For democracy to work, people have to have more than just a vote. They need to feel a part of the institutions to which they elect representatives. They need to feel properly represented in those bodies. They need to believe that their vote can change things.

Scottish Frustration

That can give rise to problems within nation states. It seems that a majority of Scottish people do not now feel confident on those points with regard to the parliament at Westminster. Evidently they do not feel properly represented there, sensing that Scotland has particular interests that may tend to be overlooked in London, experiencing frustration when at general elections the United Kingdom produces a different sort of government from that which Scotland alone would have selected. Whether that leads in due course to a break-up of the United Kingdom remains to be seen, and that is not within the scope of this paper. The point is that recent events in Scotland give us an indication of a mood, also to be found well beyond Scotland, about representative government. Such government must be seen to be sensitive and responsive to the way in which people perceive themselves and the sense of commonality which they feel.

The Scottish example is interesting because there is no ethnic or linguistic difference between the Scots and the English. England, Scotland and Wales are, taken together, geographically homogeneous and distinct. We three nations share many common values and sense of national identity, and yet the Scots are unhappy about certain things done in their name and decided at Westminster. People in democracies have to feel that the critical decisions that affect their daily lives are taken in a forum within which they see themselves as properly represented. The Basques, Catalonians, Bretons, Bavarians and other groups in Europe feel that too.

The important conclusion for the purposes of this lecture is that we will be storing up the causes of future resentment and unrest if policy which affects people's lives and livelihoods is made by bodies which are thought to be too distant, or made by people who are not democratically accountable at all. The sort of political decisions about which people rightly feel very strongly are those that affect the level of interest rates, taxes and unemployment.

5. THE SINGLE CURRENCY

That brings us to the single currency. Most of the remainder of this lecture is concerned with the political consequences of introducing a single currency. The economic arguments against the scheme were made brilliantly in the speech that William Hague gave to the CBI, and I concur completely. I have a few comments on the economic consequences, but I cannot improve on what he said.

The proposal to institute a single currency in Europe involves a bigger step towards centralised decision-making than any that has been taken before. It seems difficult for many people in Britain to grasp that the motivation is political, not economic. As Dr. Helmut Hesse, a member of the directorate of the Bundesbank, has said, monetary union is to be seen 'as the last step in a process of integration that began only a few years after the Second World War in order to bring peace and prosperity to Europe.'[3] And Dr. Hesse sees it in those clear terms even though as a banker you might expect him rather to highlight the economic significance of the change.

The responsibility for monetary policy will pass from the governments of the member-states, or from their central banks, to the European Union central bank. Member-states will be compelled also to transfer their foreign reserves from their national central banks to the European central bank. They will be required to limit their borrowing to maintain convergence. The effect of the first is to make it extremely difficult for any member-state to run a deficit, and the effect of the second is to provide for sanctions against it should it none the less succeed in doing so. It does not take much imagination to realise that a constraint on the level of borrowing in practice translates into a severe curtailment of the freedom to decide either the level of public spending or the rate of taxation.

Transfer of Monetary and Financial Policy Inevitable

The Chancellor of the Exchequer, Gordon Brown, has claimed that there is 'no question of giving up our ability to make decisions on tax and spending.' I do not know whether that owes more to naiveté or to dishonesty. I have respect for the Chairman of the Bundesbank, Hans Tietmeyer, who hides nothing when he says:

> a European currency will lead to member-states transferring their sovereignty over financial and wage policy, as well as in monetary affairs. It is an illusion to think that states can hold on to their autonomy over taxation policy.[4]

The consequences have been accurately represented by Chancellor Kohl, when he said plainly: 'We want the political unification of Europe. If there is no monetary union, then there cannot be political union, and vice-versa.'[5] Indeed, there is no currency in the world that is not controlled by a nation state, and no country of significant size that does not control its own currency.

In contrast to Chancellor Kohl, other advocates of the single currency often play down the significance of its implications. For example, they argue that there is not much difference between giving responsibility for the level of interest rates to a national central bank or passing it to a European institution. There is a huge difference. A national central bank should be responsible to the national parliament or to the government. Its role and scope are embedded within a democratic constitution. It should be set clear objectives and be held accountable for its performance. Failures can be punished by dismissal of the governor or board. The European central bank will not be responsible to any democratic body, and the single currency itself is claimed to be irreversible.

Decisions about interest rates in effect become decisions about rates of inflation and unemployment—the most sensitive of all policy matters. If people feel that in elections they are unable to give their view of economic management through their vote, or change the people who have made the policy, they will rightly feel that their democracy no longer counts for much. What will be the point of voting for political parties if they are powerless to change policy? Electors will feel resentful and cheated.

When people feel like that, they become vulnerable to extremist influences, something which we should all wish to avoid at all costs. Where democracy is working, intolerance and political extremism do not attract widespread support amongst the population. Nasty minorities remain merely that, because the majority retains its confidence in the democratic system. The population believes that grievances can be remedied, or at least that those responsible for things that they do not like can be despatched at the polls. Once large numbers of people cease to have faith in the system, extremism can take hold, including extremist nationalism.

The Scope for Autonomy

Enthusiasts for the single currency also contend that arguments against transferring control of the currency are based on an out-of-date view of national sovereignty, since these days the scope for independent action by each country is severely constrained by economic events elsewhere. Of course we are affected by events outside our control, but considerable scope for independent action remains. The Bundesbank evidently feels that it has considerable autonomy despite the impact of global forces. In Britain's case, the point is most easily demonstrated by contrasting our experience inside the ERM (which made it impossible for us to reduce our interest rates below 10 per cent, and indeed on the last day of membership we proposed to raise them to 15 per cent) with our experience subsequently, when we were able to cut interest rates to about 5 per cent. There are degrees of freedom, and the fact that we are not totally independent of outside influences is no argument for throwing away the considerable amount of scope for action we still possess. More importantly, our *right* to make choices for ourselves should not be given up on such spurious grounds.

Following the ignominy of Britain's exit from the ERM, the British people were free to vote against the Conservatives who had taken them into it, causing the loss of many homes, businesses and jobs. If we were members of a single currency and the key decisions were taken by the European central bank, voters would no longer be able to vote out the people who made harmful economic decisions. What is more, at least in the case of the ERM it was possible, however painfully, for Britain to leave and thus to reverse policy. There is, we are told, no exit from the single currency.

6. WHY DEMOCRACY WILL NOT WORK
AT THE EUROPEAN LEVEL

Some who know these arguments will object that democratic accountability for the European central bank's decisions could and should be established at European level through the European parliament. The point demonstrates the success that Monnet and his successors have had over the years. In the period following the war it was impossible to find many followers for the visionary notion of a United States of Europe. But the pioneers of European integration patiently made what progress they could with smaller-scale projects in the economic field, leading in due course to the idea of a single currency. The single currency, however, requires the centralisation of decision-making on issues that are so very important, that even those who oppose the whole idea may cry out for the creation of centralised democratic institutions to provide some element of people's control.

The creation of the European state has been approached in reverse order to the creation of almost any other. Normally, a new state establishes its institutions of government *first*, and goes on to create its policies and its currency. In this case, the common European policies and the currency are being created first, with the intention that that should lead to demands, in the names of logic and of democracy, for the formation of the institutions of centralised European government.

The European parliament is not presently perceived by the British people, perhaps not by any other population either, as a representative body invested with much democratic trust and authority. That is not merely because it is in its infancy. Democracy requires not only the *cracy* but also the *demos*, not only the state but also the people. You can create the apparatus of a state at European level, with a common frontier, a single immigration policy, a common foreign and defence policy, and a single currency. All the attributes of the nation state, all its *functions*, can be transferred to the European level along the Monnet-functionalist model. But what we do not have and what we cannot conjure up is a *demos*—that is, a single European people.

Diversity of European Peoples

If the Scots are now doubting that a democracy spanning from John o' Groats to Land's End is capable of making every part of the country feel properly represented, then certainly no parliament spanning from Dublin to Athens, and being charged with the critical decisions affecting our lives and livelihoods, is capable of satisfying the democratic requirements and aspirations of each of our populations.

The peoples of Europe are too different from one another, their histories, cultures and values are too diverse, for them to be brought together into one state. We can work together and co-operate for mutual benefit, but Europeans do not have a common identity, or view of their role in world affairs. They do not constitute a nation, and since they do not we should not try to create a European nation state. We should not try to do at European level things that nation states should do. Nation states should take the most sensitive policy decisions, because they require democratic control, and democracy can work only within a nation state where people share values, history and cultural tradition.

Looking Back Instead of Forward

One of the boldest efforts of propaganda by the enthusiasts for European integration, is the attempt to portray themselves as modern and forward-looking. They are the opposite. They are mainly motivated by a fear that the past may repeat itself, that is, that Franco-German rivalry or rampant German nationalism may re-awaken. They propose a centralisation of power that runs flatly in the opposite direction to the march of history. We can see around us that the old empires or unions of states have collapsed in failure. The Soviet Union and Yugoslavia both failed in their attempts, even using coercion, to sustain a centralised system of governmental control over a wide area, covering many diverse peoples and nations.

The European integrationists are out-of-date in another way too. They see a European political union as a necessary response to global competition, believing that we must react to the challenge posed by the industrial and trading giants, like the USA and Japan, by creating a giant Europe. Chancellor Kohl has claimed that 'the nation-state . . . cannot solve the great problems of the twenty-first century' and that Europe has to 'assert itself.'[6] Dr. Helmut Hesse has said that 'a multiplicity of small states is not suitable for the world economy today.'[7]

Global competition is indeed between industrial giants, but they are companies, not nation states. There may well be an argument for industrial mergers in Europe, for example between defence contractors in France, Germany and Britain. But that is a completely separate agenda from political integration. Paradoxically, some of the people who are spurring us on towards political union are also those who still believe in national protectionism, and therefore refuse to implement policies that would bring about European industrial rationalisation.

Big (Global) Competition, Bigger State?

Some of those who think that the right response to global competition is to create a bigger state, also believe in a bigger state in the other sense, meaning a bigger role for the state, through more interference and regulation. That frame of mind has produced the social chapter, and is a strong influence within New Labour. Such people believe that global competition will whittle away worker protection and social standards in the developed world, and that we must create a large European corral in which they can be defended against the pressures from outside.

New Labour, however, also spends a part of its time arguing against that, advocating the spread of flexible labour markets instead. In that second view they are right. Flexibility, along with rising educational standards, will enable us to compete *and* to improve our social standards. Excessive interference by governments, whether at national or European level, is clumsy and unresponsive, and has already played a large part in creating unemployment levels in Europe that are well above those of the USA.

We are being led towards a Europe which displays many of the characteristics of Britain 20 years ago. It is populated with over-manned and protected nationalised industries. In many places private sector managers are in thrall to trade unions. Business is tied down by government bureaucracy and interventionism. Public spending is appallingly high. There persists the belief that Europe can go its own sweet way, unaffected by the assault from international competition, provided that the fortress walls are built high enough. Twenty million unemployed Europeans give mute testimony to the failure of those policies. To present any of that as forward-looking is indeed a triumph for the spin doctors.

7. WILL THE SINGLE CURRENCY BE AN ECONOMIC SUCCESS FOR BRITAIN?

There are those, no doubt, who would argue that even if it is true that the single currency requires the centralisation of important policy-making, and even if you cannot re-create at European level the sort of representative democracy to which we have become accustomed in our nation states, we are likely to get better decisions from a European central bank than we have had from governments in the past, and that will make people happier.

That is hard to believe. Unaccountable bureaucracy does not produce better decisions than democracy. The corruption and inefficiency in the Common Agricultural Policy sufficiently tells us that. Furthermore, there is no evidence that a single currency will lead to better policies, greater stability or greater economic success for its members. It is pure conjecture. The single currency will be traded in world markets against other currencies. Whether it is more stable than the national currencies it replaces will depend on how good are the policies of those who control it.

There has been no stability between the currencies of the USA and Japan, the world's largest and second largest economies. Currency stability is an illusion, and in Asia there is now on display many a scalp of men who declared that their currencies would hold their values.

Case for Joining Weaker

The case for Britain joining a single currency has lost whatever appeal it might have had when first presented a few years back. Five or 10 years ago it was plausible to argue that Britain was forever dogged by inflation, and doomed continually to resort to devaluation in order to maintain competitiveness. Unemployment in the UK was stubbornly high. By contrast, Germany appeared to have discovered the secret of non-inflationary growth, and was able to compete successfully in the world on the basis of quality, despite the strength of its currency. How much better, the argument went, for Britain to give up control over its own economy in order to reap the benefits of the German economic miracle.

Things look rather different now. Britain has gained control of inflation by its own efforts. Britain has lower unemployment than most of its European neighbors, and that is just one of many indicators that it is competing successfully. The current concern is not with devaluation, but with the strength of the pound.

Mr. Blair has said that he wishes to decide whether to enter a single currency solely according to an assessment of whether it is in Britain's economic interest to do so. As will be clear from what I have said already, I think that misses the point of what is really involved in the decision. But anyway, the economic case appears very weak. It has been argued that the single currency is the logical completion of the single market. It is not. The greatest trading partners in the world, Canada and the USA, do not have a common currency and have no plans to establish one. At present, none of the countries with which Britain trades has the same currency as we do, and yet our trade with them goes on rising. I can see that there would be a small saving on transaction costs for companies trading with Europe if we all had the same currency, but it would be marginal. Against that, British industry has to ask itself whether it really wishes to enter the next recession with the currency locked at its present level, and with the British government powerless to vary interest rates.

"Grave Danger"

The grave danger for Europe, economically speaking, is to introduce a single currency where no single labour market exists. A single currency means that, in future, variations in economic performance between one region and another cannot result, as they do today, in a downward adjustment of the currency in the less successful areas, and interest rates must reflect policy established at the centre, not local conditions. The full impact of recession will therefore fall on unemployment.

In the USA, a vast area covered by a single currency, people who lose their jobs in a depressed area can move to another state in search of a job, however inconvenient it may be. But people cannot move at will within our Continent to find new work. They face barriers related to language, qualifications, local culture and plain prejudice. Some of those can be reduced with the passage of time, but most will prove intractable. Indeed, with the so-called Posted Workers Directive, approved under the Social Chapter, European Union labour ministers seem determined to reduce labour mobility across borders.

There is another danger. Britain presently receives a notably high proportion of the inward investment attracted into Europe. Those investors clearly see value in Britain's membership of the EU and free access to its markets. But they also see it as an advantage that the British economy is more flexible and deregulated than some others in Europe. In other words, Britain derives an advantage from not embracing all European economic policy. Investors know that wherever they invest there is an exchange rate risk. But British economic policy over the last 18 years has offered them stability and reassurance.

But if we join the Euro, economic policy in Britain will be determined principally by events in the geographical centre of the European Union. There may well be a mismatch between conditions in Britain and Germany. Interest rates could be inappropriate to British economic circumstances, as they were when we were in the ERM. That represents a bad risk for investors. It may then make more sense for them to invest where local economic conditions and interest rates are most closely related, that is, in Germany. Imagine the impact upon British public opinion if unemployment is high, and inward investors are drifting away, the government is powerless to vary interest rates, and the electorate is unable to change anything by electing a new one.

8. THE REAL QUESTIONS OF SECURITY

I began this lecture by recognising the importance of European security. All other objectives are secondary. The principal guarantor of peace in Europe has been NATO. It has provided a wholly credible deterrent against attack. With American troops positioned in Europe, any potential adversary was wise to believe that America really would go to war to preserve the territory of its European allies. America's awesome military capability was evident.

Incidentally, the establishment of NATO did not infringe the sovereignty of its members. Its Treaty is explicitly an agreement of sovereign states who undertake under Article 5 to regard the violation of the territory of another member-state as though it were a violation of their own and to respond with such action *as they deem necessary*. NATO has no federalist destiny. In the near half-century since it was founded, unlike the EU, it has passed no laws that bind its member-states, and no court has extended its influence. In no way has it increased its powers since 1948. The democratic accountability of governments has not been affected.

NATO is now responding to the new situation created since the end of the

Cold War, recognising that the greatest contribution it can make to security is to strengthen the new democracies of Europe. Membership of either NATO or the EU or of both can help underpin those democracies. The EU should follow NATO's example. It should be trying to lower the barriers for entry by the countries of Eastern Europe, rather than creating an inner core which requires qualifications that they cannot hope to attain. Negotiating admission for new members looks like being a protracted, and maybe cantankerous, business.

The EU's Remaining Security Tasks

The EU must also address itself to the remaining security issues in our Continent. We need to do all we can to make Russia feel welcome in the family of Western democracies. Membership of either NATO or the EU is impractical, not least because Russia is a vast Asian as well as European power. But again, the EU ought to be demolishing fences rather than continuing to develop its fortress.

In the case of Turkey, the EU seems to be almost careless in its relations. The EU has made it clear to Turkey that although it applied for membership years ago, there is no early prospect of admission. Meanwhile countries that have only recently become democratic and pro-Western are politely ushered to positions higher up the queue. Few things could be more important for our security than that Turkey should remain democratic and well-disposed towards the West. Turkey is being kept at bay, partly because some European leaders apparently see the EU as a subset of Christendom; and partly because with its manifest social problems, Turkey's inclusion certainly would create substantial problems of integration. We have had to put heavy reliance on Turkey as a NATO ally during our conflicts with Iraq. It is difficult for the Turkish government to sell to its people the merits of being a good member of NATO, and it is difficult for us to persuade Turkey to be reasonable over the Cyprus problem, if it is offered so little by the EU.

Here is an instance where the EU has a clear choice between on the one hand maintaining its preoccupation with achieving 'ever closer European union,' and on the other hand using its enlargement to enhance the security of its members. It appears to have made the wrong choice. It fails to think strategically.

9. CONCLUSION

This case serves to illustrate a broader truth. Those who are most influencing the progress of Europe have become dreadfully confused. They believe that

European integration is the only guarantee of future security, and they are pursuing the objective with a single-mindedness that borders on fanaticism.

They are wrong. It is democracy that provides our greatest hope of future peace and prosperity. We should use our Atlantic and European institutions in every way we can to spread democracy and nurture it where it takes root.

The European Union is entirely made up of member-states that are democracies. But the European Union itself is not democratic. Neither the Commission, nor the Council of Ministers, nor the European central bank is democratically accountable, and neither can they be made so because Europe is not a nation. It follows that the more we transfer decision-making away from the democratic member-states to the undemocratic European Union, the less shall we enjoy democratic accountability.

Moving away from democratic control is retrograde in itself, but it is also highly dangerous, because disillusion and grievance provide a breeding ground for nationalism and extremism. In the interests of security, of tolerance and harmony between nations, in the interests of preserving the most valued gain of the post-war period which is democracy, we should turn away from the headlong rush towards European political integration, in which the single currency is a decisive step.

POSTSCRIPT
ASKING FOR TROUBLE: THE SINGLE CURRENCY WILL LEAD TO REGIONAL CONFLICT, NOT ECONOMIC EFFICIENCY

Martin Feldstein

[Professor Feldstein's article was first published in *Time Magazine* in the "Viewpoint" column on 19 January 1998. Professor Feldstein is Professor of Economics at Harvard University and former Chairman of the US Council of Economic Advisers.]

The European nations hurtling toward economic and monetary union are heading for trouble. EMU is likely to bring higher unemployment and higher inflation. Pursuit of a common policy will cause conflicts among participating governments that will intensify as the monetary union evolves, into a more wide-ranging political union responsible for foreign, military and domestic policies.

Joblessness will rise because interest and exchange rates will no longer automatically counter cyclical unemployment. Today, for example, if a recession in Latin America causes Spanish exports to decline, the peseta weakens and Spanish interest rates fall. That causes Spain's other exports to rise and domestic interest-sensitive spending to increase. The net effect is a smaller rise in unemployment. But once the peseta is replaced by the euro, Spain cannot be helped by a currency adjustment or by a fall in interest rates (since these must be uniform throughout the Monetary Union). EMU membership would also deny Spain the option of easing monetary policy to stimulate growth and employment. And, because of the misnamed stability pact, the Spanish government will not be able to cut taxes or raise spending to offset a fall in demand.

Some Europeans reject such pessimism, citing the example of the US, which avoids persistent high regional unemployment despite its single currency and single central bank. Unfortunately, three basic differences between the US and Europe mean that America's success with a single currency is not relevant to Europe.

First, Americans are very mobile—moving from unemployment regions to places where there are jobs. In Europe, linguistic barriers prevent similar mobility. Second, US wages are much more flexible. Wages fall in regions where demand declines, offsetting increases in production employment and, finally, when income declines, individual and business taxes paid to the federal government decline sharply, implying a strong net transfer to that region. For these reasons, unemployment rates are far less sensitive to US regional demand fluctuations than they would be in a single-currency Europe.

Europe's current double-digit unemployment rates are not cyclical but are caused by bad structural policies—misguided regulations, high minimum wages, and generous unemployment benefits. A few countries have made progress by changing these counterproductive rules. Their experience shows what can be done and provides competitive pressures to force reform elsewhere. But the increased centralisation of policy that accompanies EMU will make it harder for individual countries to experiment with reforms. The European Commission's recent pronouncement that it will force countries to respect maximum working hours is an indication of things to come.

Inflation in Europe has fallen sharply during the past decade as individual central banks emulated Germany's fiercely anti-inflationary Bundesbank. Although other countries do not share German's fervid opposition to inflation, they have been forced to follow Germany's lead to avoid devaluing their currencies. This monetary discipline will end when EMU gives every country an equal vote at the European Central Bank. Without Germany's leadership, European inflation will be higher in the next decades than it has been in recent years.

These adverse effects on unemployment and inflation far outweigh the commercial benefits that will flow from EMU. The elimination of tariffs and other barriers by the 1992 Single Market agreement was far more important for stimulating trade and investment.

Despite these shortcomings, EMU looks likely to begin on schedule because economic issues are secondary to political aspirations. For Germany and France EMU offers the possibility of dominating European policy-making. Countries like Italy and Spain will join to show that they are economically and politically worthy of membership and the smaller countries are joining to have a seat at the table where European policies are determined. The Maastricht Treaty that created the EMU calls for a European political union with broad domestic and international responsibilities. Moreover, since no significant country exists—or has ever exited—without its own currency, the shift to a single currency for the EMU members is a giant step toward such a European state.

Ever since the end of World War II a single European government has been advocated as a way of keeping the peace. But a European political union is more likely to be a source of conflict than a foundation for European harmony. There will be quarrels over monetary policy, over taxation and over the shaping of common foreign policies. There will be disputes between Germany and France about their relative power and influence. There will be conflicts that flow from the frustrations of other EU countries—including Britain if it decides to enter—when they find that they are marginalised in the decision process. A European political union with 300 million people and the ability to project military force around the world could be the source of broader international instability in the decades ahead.

NOTES

1. P. Fontaine, *Europe in Ten Points,* European Communities, 1995.
2. Helmut Kohl, speech to University of Louvain, 5 February 1996.
3. Helmut Hesse, speech to the Stadtsparkasse, Osnabrück, 31 October 1995.
4. Quoted by Will Podmone in *The European Journal,* November 1997.
5. Helmut Kohl, speech to the Council of Europe, 28 September 1995.
6. Helmut Kohl, speech to the University of Louvain, 5 February 1996.
7. Helmut Hesse, speech to the Stadtsparkasse, Osnabrück, 31 October 1995.

CHAPTER 17

The Degeneration of EMU

Niall Ferguson and Laurence J. Kotlikoff

Niall Ferguson is Fellow and Tutor in Modern History at Jesus College, Oxford. He is the author of The Pity of War *(1999) and recently also published the second volume of* The House of Rothschild *(1999). Laurence J. Kotlikoff is Professor of Economics at Boston University and Research Associate at the National Bureau of Economic Research. Both were Houblon-Norman Fellows at the Bank of England in 1998–99. Their "generational accounting" suggests, they argue, that EMU could degenerate within the next decade, given a lack of political will to enact necessary government spending cuts and tax increases.*

HERE TODAY, GONE TOMORROW

From conception through gestation and birth, and now in its early infancy, the euro has consistently proved the skeptics wrong. Some Cassandras thought that Brussels-bashing nationalists would reject the single currency in referendums. Others doubted that Italy and other fiscally troubled applicants would fulfill the Maastricht Treaty's strict limits on budget deficits and national debt. Still others predicted that the fierce 1998 dispute over the presidency of the European Central Bank might abort the entire enterprise.

Yet economic and monetary union (EMU) has proceeded more or less according to plan. The French referendum's "petit oui" in 1992 may have required a little gentle massaging; the Maastricht fiscal criteria may have been honored partly in the breach; and of course the currency has, over the past year, depreciated markedly against the dollar. But the fixed exchange rates

Reprinted by permission of *Foreign Affairs* (March/April 2000). Copyright 2000 by the Council on Foreign Relations, Inc.

within the eurozone have held firm, despite warnings about speculative attacks during the transition. And with its depreciation spurring economic growth, the euro is likely to recover somewhat against the dollar this year.

Nevertheless, the skeptics may have the last laugh. For whether a euro equals a dollar tomorrow or the next day does not really matter. What matters is whether the entire monetary union will hold together in the years ahead. The euro's medium-term future will prove much shakier when Europe is hit by the fiscal crises looming for the majority of the eurozone's member countries.

THE NEW MATH

The notion that such fiscal problems exist is not new. Nor is the proposition that they could jeopardize monetary cohesion. But fresh evidence, drawn from a recent, comprehensive calculation of "generational accounts," shows the full extent of the fiscal crisis facing the eurozone.

Generational accounting provides answers to the following three questions: How large a fiscal burden does current policy impose on future generations? Is current fiscal policy sustainable without major additional sacrifices on the part of current or future generations? What policies are required to achieve generational balance—i.e., to ensure that future generations will pay to the government the same share of their lifetime incomes in net taxes (taxes paid minus transfer payments received) as do today's generations?

This new method of accounting was developed not to augment the conventional measure of fiscal imbalance—the official government debt—but to replace it. For neither the size of the government debt nor its change over time (the budget deficit) are well-defined economic concepts. Rather, they reflect the arbitrary choice of fiscal vocabulary, specifically in labeling government receipts and payments.

Three things follow from this. First, the debt and deficit criteria laid out in the Maastricht Treaty bear no intrinsic relation to fiscal prudence. Second, one can satisfy the Maastricht criteria simply by using the appropriate accounting terminology—something that observers of Italian entry into EMU may already have guessed. Third, the sustainability of EMU fiscal policies must be measured more objectively.

The bottom line is that generational imbalances across the eurozone gravely threaten the single currency's medium-term viability. The choice for nearly all EMU members is between tax hikes on a scale unprecedented in peacetime or drastic government spending cuts. Given the political weakness of most national governments, it is hard to see either choice being made. But the only other conceivable possibility—a sharp and unanticipated rise in inflation, which "solved" some fiscal crises in the past—also seems improbable, at least within EMU's constraints.

ADD IT UP

Generational accounts represent the sum of all future net taxes (taxes paid minus transfer payments received) that citizens born in any given year will pay over their lifetimes, given current policy. The sum of the generational accounts of all living generations indicates what those now alive will pay toward the government's bills. The government's bills, in turn, are equal to the sum (in today's prices) of all of the government's future purchases of goods and services plus its official net debt—its financial liabilities minus its financial assets, including public-sector enterprises. Bills not paid by current generations must be paid by future generations. This reflects the zero-sum nature of the government's intertemporal budget constraint: no matter what level of current deficit or debt a government reports, somebody, someday, will have to pay in net taxes what the government spends. Borrowing now to pay for government spending means paying more taxes later.

Generational imbalance results when the generational accounts of current newborns fall short of the growth-adjusted accounts of future newborns. The two accounts are directly comparable because they incorporate net taxes over entire lifetimes, allowing for population and economic growth at current official projections. If future generations face higher generational accounts than do current newborns, current policy is not only generationally unbalanced, it is also unsustainable. The government cannot continue to collect the same net taxes (adjusted for growth) from future generations as it would collect, under current policy, from current newborns without violating the intertemporal budget constraint.

This calculation imposes the entire fiscal adjustment needed to satisfy the government's budget constraint on those born in the future. It also delivers a clear message about the policy changes that governments need to achieve generational balance without foisting all the adjustment on to future generations—either through government spending cuts or tax increases, or a combination thereof. One can then calculate the precise size of the tax hike or spending cut necessary to make the growth-adjusted generational accounts of future generations equal those of newborns.

A critical feature of generational accounting is that the size of the future fiscal burden does not depend on how the government describes its receipts and payments. The same, unfortunately, is not true of the reported size of the government's official debt. Suppose that the Italian government chose to label the roughly 300 trillion lire in social security contributions in 2000 as "loans" instead of "taxes." Also suppose that instead of calling the future benefits it promises to pay current workers in exchange for these contributions "transfer payments," it called them "return of principal plus interest" on these loans minus an "old-age tax." This alternative wording would leave the Italian government reporting a deficit larger by 300 trillion lire, putting the overall deficit far higher than the Maastricht threshold of three percent of GDP. A year from now, the government's total debt would therefore be larger—but so would the generational accounts of currently living generations, since their future "old-age tax" would now be included in their accounts. Since both would be larger by the same amount, the burden on future generations would not change. The economic position of each generation would also be unaffected by this alternative set of labels; each worker would hand the government the same amount of money this year and receive from the government the same amount of money in the future. The only difference would be the words that the government used to describe these flows.

The fact that a government uses a given vocabulary to describe what it is doing does not make those words sacrosanct. Since each set of words results in a different measure of the deficit, which is correct? In economic theory, there is no correct measure. The concept of a deficit has everything to do with semantics and nothing to do with economics. Generational accounting not only dispenses with this arbitrary terminology; it is also forward-looking and comprehensive.

So what does it mean for Europe? Table 17.1 gives results for 14 countries: Austria, Belgium, Finland, France, Germany, Ireland, Italy, the Netherlands, Portugal, and Spain (10 of the 11 members of EMU) as well as Denmark, Swe-

Table 17.1 Comparing the Numbers: How to Achieve Generational Balance

Country	Percentage cut in government purchases	Percentage cut in government transfers	Percentage increase in all taxes	Percentage increase in income tax
Austria	76.4	20.5	18.4	55.6
Belgium	12.4	4.6	3.1	10.0
Finland	67.6	21.2	19.4	50.8
France	22.2	9.8	6.9	64.0
Germany	25.9	14.1	9.5	29.5
Ireland	−4.3	−4.4	−2.1	−4.8
Italy	49.1	13.3	10.5	28.2
Netherlands	28.7	22.3	8.9	15.6
Portugal	9.8	7.5	4.2	13.3
Spain	62.2	17.0	14.5	44.9
Denmark	29.0	4.5	4.0	6.7
Sweden	50.5	18.9	15.6	41.9
United Kingdom	9.7	9.5	2.7	9.5
Norway	9.9	8.1	6.3	9.7

Sources: Alan J. Auerbach, Laurence J. Kotlikoff, and Willi Leibfritz, eds., *Generational Accounting Around the World* (1999); Bernd Raffelhüschen, "Aging, Fiscal Policy, and Social Insurances: A European Perspective," mimeo., University of Freiburg, Germany, and University of Bergen, Norway, 1998.

den, and the United Kingdom (EU members outside the eurozone) and Norway (which belongs to neither). It shows 4 mutually exclusive ways these countries could achieve generational balance: cutting government purchases, cutting government transfer payments, raising all taxes, or raising income taxes (corporate as well as personal). The figures in the table indicate the immediate and permanent percentage adjustment needed, with the magnitudes of these adjustments indirectly measuring a country's generational imbalance. Education is treated as a transfer payment rather than a government purchase, and calculations are for all levels of government—local, regional, state, and central.

According to the table, 9 of the 14 countries need to cut all government spending on goods and services by more than 20 percent if they want to rely solely on such cuts to achieve generational balance. This group includes the three most important EMU members: Germany, France, and Italy. Austria, Finland, and Spain need to cut their noneducation purchases by more than half, as does Sweden; indeed, for Austria and Finland, the cut in spending needed is more than two-thirds.

Not all European countries suffer from generational imbalances. In Ireland, future generations face a smaller fiscal burden than do current ones, thereby allowing for growth. But Ireland is unique: it is the only country considered here whose government could spend more over time without unduly burdening coming generations. Four countries have only moderate generational imbalances in terms of spending adjustment: Belgium, Portugal, Norway, and the United Kingdom. But the last two of these are outside the eurozone.

Generational accounting produces a very different ranking of fiscal vulnerability from the conventional measures used in both the Maastricht Treaty and the 1997 Stability and Growth Pact, which judge fiscal stability by a nation's debt and deficit as ratios of GDP. The first column of the table shows that the EMU countries with the biggest fiscal problems are Austria, Finland, and Spain. But on the basis of Maastricht debt-GDP ratios, the three worst cases are Belgium, Italy, and the Netherlands.

Europe's generational imbalances are far from unique. For the sake of comparison, take the United States. Despite rosy projections of running "surpluses" well into the future, America in fact would have to cut government spending at all levels by 14 percent (or federal spending by 43 percent) to achieve generational balance. The figures for Japan and Brazil are 30 and 26 percent, respectively. Canada and New Zealand, by contrast, are in almost perfect generational balance. And before it recently introduced a pay-as-you-go social security system, Thailand could boast a figure of–48 percent, implying enormous latitude for government spending.

Fiscal policy and demographics explain these differences. For example, the United Kingdom has kept most transfer payments fixed over time in real (that is, inflation-adjusted) terms, thanks to a decision in the 1980s to break the link between state pensions and earnings inflation. Germany is still dealing with the colossal costs of reunification, while Ireland has a more youthful population than the European average.

One alternative to cutting government purchases is to cut transfer payments—e.g., by raising the age of retirement, as is being discussed now in the United States. Here the cuts required are somewhat smaller but nevertheless daunting for the majority of EMU members: over a fifth for Austria, Finland, and Holland; more than ten percent for Germany, Italy, and Spain. Again, only Ireland does not need an immediate cut to achieve generational balance.

These dramatic cuts would be very unpopular—as would tax increases, the third possible policy option. If Germany relied exclusively on across-the-board tax hikes, tax rates at all levels of government (federal, regional, and local) and of all types (value added, payroll, corporate income, personal income, excise, sales, property, estate, and gift) would rise overnight by more than 9 percent. In Austria and Finland, taxes would have to rise more than 18 percent, and in Spain more than 14 percent. If countries relied solely on income tax hikes, then Austria, Finland, and France would have to raise their income tax rates by over 50 percent. The requisite income-tax hikes in Germany and Italy would be just under 30 percent, compared with 10 percent for Britain and 21 percent for the United States. In contrast, Ireland could cut its income tax rates by about 5 percent before it needed to worry about overburdening future generations.

This problem will not go away. On the contrary, the longer countries wait to act, the bigger the adjustments will need to be. Britain, for example, could achieve generational balance with an immediate income-tax hike of just under 10 percent. But if it waits 5 years, that number will rise to 11 percent. After a 15-year delay, it will be 15 percent, and after 25 years, more than 20 percent.

HEY, BIG SPENDERS

These shocking figures mean that the majority of EMU countries have severe generational imbalances, even if their reported deficits do lie under the Maastricht limit of three percent of annual GDP. Yet none of the four scenarios above is likely to be realized by any government other than that of Ireland, given the immense political opposition to such retrenchment. The tax hikes or spending cuts would be, in most cases, unprecedented in peacetime. But whereas the losers would be today's taxpayers, the winners would be future generations.

Not one of the key European governments has the political strength to effect such fiscal reform. In Germany, Gerhard Schröder's SPD-Green coalition is still struggling to restrain the growth of state pensions and social spending. In France, the left-wing coalition led by Lionel Jospin is even less likely to grasp fiscal nettles now that its talented finance minister, Dominique Strauss-Kahn, has resigned to fight fraud charges. In Italy, Massimo D'Alema's left-of-center coalition limps on in a newly repackaged government, crippled by the chronic divisions of the Italian party system. Total Italian tax revenues have already risen from 39 to 44 percent of GDP since 1990; it is hard to imagine any government surviving if it asked for more.

A significant increase in economic growth could ease the fiscal positions of many European states. But this is unlikely to happen in the core European countries, given their relatively rigid labor markets. True, growth in the 11 EMU countries is generally forecast to be 3 percent in 2000. But with 10-year bond yields around 5.7 percent and inflation below 1.4 percent, real interest rates are very high by historical standards, compounding debt problems and stifling economic recovery.

What course can Europe take in the face of such tight fiscal restraints? Tinkering with the budget limits in the Maastricht Treaty and the Stability and Growth Pact may be possible for some countries, though not necessarily for those states whose generational accounts are most out of kilter. And the possibilities for creative accounting using traditional measures of debts and deficits have not yet been fully exhausted. Because the Maastricht criteria are based on measures of debt that are economically arbitrary, there is every reason to expect enforcement to be lax. Indeed, it already has been. As the German Bundesbank and others have pointed out, as many as 8 of the 11 EMU members had debts above the maximum 60 percent threshold (of debt as a percentage of annual GDP) when they qualified for entry in 1998.

A further possibility is that the countries with the most severe generational imbalances may exert pressure on the ECB to loosen monetary policy. For most of the twentieth century, after all, printing money was often the line of least resistance for governments having fiscal difficulties.

As is well known, issuing money operates as a fiscal tool in three ways. First, it permits a government to swap a depreciated currency for actual goods and services. The private sector pays for this transfer to the government (or seigniorage) while inflation eats away at the money's real value. Second, raising prices by cranking up the printing presses reduces the real value of unadjusted government wage payments, transfer payments, and official debt repayments. Third, rising inflation permits a government to push taxpayers into higher marginal tax brackets if the tax system's degree of progressivity is not inflation-indexed. Historically, this is how many states have coped with severe fiscal imbalances: the defeated powers after World War I, for example, or Russia and Ukraine after the collapse of the Soviet economy.

Here lies the crucial point for Europe's single currency. Those countries under the most severe fiscal pressure will obviously wish to print money sooner and faster than those better situated. Yet the Maastricht Treaty effectively rules out printing money; Article 104 of the treaty (now Article 101 of the treaty establishing the European Community) and Article 21 of the Statute of the European System of Central Banks enshrine a strict "no bail-out" rule. Member states that hope to inflate away their debts will simply be turned away.

Much more likely is a series of collisions between national governments struggling to bring their finances under control and the ECB, which is constitutionally bound to maintain price stability as its primary objective and appears unconcerned by sluggish growth in large parts of the eurozone. The ECB is also likely to ignore the unpleasant monetary arithmetic implied by the budget problems of the members states and instead retort with some unpleasant fiscal arithmetic of its own by keeping its monetary policy strictly anti-inflationary.

If all countries were in the same predicament, they might resolve this conflict politically. But because there is such variation in the eurozone's generational imbalances, and indeed in their rates of growth and inflation, some countries will get into difficulties sooner than others. The political conflicts are easy enough to imagine. If European governments find it hard to agree about the edibility of British beef, it is not easy to imagine them acting in unison over generational imbalances in public finance. Even the recent proposal to introduce an EU-wide withholding tax on the interest from private savings foundered in the face of U.K. opposition. As was depressingly apparent at their Helsinki summit in December 1999, European leaders would rather dream the old Gaullist dream of military independence from America than face hard fiscal facts. If they do not set their generational accounts in order, there will be no European defense budgets in the future, much less a European army.

DREAMS DEFERRED

History shows that monetary unions can be undone by fiscal imbalances. The difficulty lies in deciding which previous monetary unions most closely resemble EMU, since none does exactly. Some economic historians have sought to draw comparisons with the pre-1914 gold standard. But others see EMU as more like a national monetary union because there is a common central bank and no prescribed right to secede.

In truth, neither of these parallels is very illuminating. The gold standard was an informal system, without a single central bank, that states could always exist—like the European Exchange Rate Mechanism before the euro. On the other hand, comparing EMU with the United States, Italy, or Germany is unconvincing. In each case, political union came before monetary union.

Nor is it helpful to compare currency unions between giants and dwarves (such as that among France, Andorra, and Monaco). Rather, the best analogies are with monetary unions among multiple states with only loose confederal ties and negligible fiscal centralization.

The Austro-Hungarian monetary union after 1867 is a useful example. The historian Marc Flandreau has pointed out that post-1867 Austria-Hungary combined the free circulation of goods and capital and a unified central bank on one hand with fiscal autonomy for each constituent state and its multiple nationalities on the other. (Unlike in the EU, however, there was a common army and foreign policy.) Both Austria and Hungary regularly ran quite large deficits until 1914, but these were absorbed with little difficulty by bond markets. Yet the dramatic increase in expenditure and borrowing in World War I caused inflation to accelerate and led ultimately to the breakup of the monetary union in 1917-18.

Another illuminating precedent is the Latin Monetary Union (1865-1927) between France, Belgium, Switzerland, Italy (including the Vatican), and later Greece. True, there was no Latin Central Bank, but the LMU did have a conscious political motivation, as the economist Luca Einaudi has argued. (A driving force was Félix Parieu of France, who dreamt of an eventual "European Union" with a "European Commission" and a "European Parliament.") But the costs to the other members of Italian fiscal laxity were high. The papal government financed its deficits by churning out silver coinage to reap high seigniorage profits. In short, it debased the coinage and allowed private agents to export it to the rest of the union—a flagrant breach of the rules. At the same time, the Italian government introduced largely unconvertible paper currency to finance its growing deficits, breaking the spirit if not the letter of the convention. The war of 1870 removed the political rationale of French continental hegemony; the only reason the LMU survived after 1878 was to avoid the cost of dissolution. Like the Scandinavian Monetary Union founded in 1873 by Sweden and Denmark, the LMU was belatedly pronounced dead in the 1920s.

History therefore suggests that asymmetric fiscal problems—often generated by war—quickly cause monetary unions between fiscally independent states to dissolve. The fiscal problems caused by bloated social security and pension systems could have a similar centrifugal effect on EMU, with welfare substituting for war as the fatal solvent.

EXIT STRATEGIES

The problem is not simply that European states will continue to run deficits as conventionally measured. Past experience (for example, the German monetary union of Bismarck's day) suggests that monetary unions can coexist with federal fiscal systems where member states issue substantial volumes of bonds. Diverging levels of borrowing in the eurozone today may result in differing bond yields down the road—and the existence of yield spreads is not incompatible with monetary union. Markets cannot be forbidden to attach different default risks to different member states within a monetary union, just as companies issuing euro-denominated corporate bonds offer investors varying returns. Furthermore, high levels of state borrowing do not necessarily lead to inflation. Much depends on the international bond market's demand for high-grade sovereign debt; with more and more people living for two decades or more after retirement, that demand is likely to grow.

But generational imbalance does not simply imply that European states will run deficits. This method already assumes that they will. Rather, it points to an inevitable need to raise taxes, reduce expenditures, or print money to meet a rising burden of debt interest. But what happens when states like Austria, Finland, or Spain reach a political impasse on fiscal reform? Bond markets can absorb only so much debt before demand starts to wane. Legally, withdrawal from EMU is impossible. But history shows there is always an exit. If a country's only viable option is to print money and inflate away some of its liabilities, and if the European Central Bank abides by its "no bail-out" rule, then secession will almost certainly be considered. The question is what the costs would be.

First, higher interest rates would result in the short term, and much would depend on their impact on the government's debt-service bill. In this context, the different term structures of the various national debts are important; a country with a lot of short-term debt would gain much less from inflation. Once again, there are wide disparities among eurozone members. More than half of Spain's domestic debt is short-term, compared with 0.4 percent of Austria's.

Second, the exchange rate of seceding currency would almost certainly weaken. This could help boost the economy by making exports cheaper. But legal tangles would also arise as creditors and debtors (foreign and domestic) fought over whether the presecession debts should be valued in euros or in the national currency. This could severely destabilize the seceding country's financial system, as well as those of other countries. Again, the implications would be greater for countries with more debt held abroad.

The political will to implement spending cuts and tax increases may be strengthened by these considerations. Still, history offers few examples of successful adjustments on the scale necessary in certain European countries today. What it does offer are several examples of monetary unions disintegrating when fiscal strains became incompatible with the unpleasant arithmetic of a single currency. In this respect, conventional measures of fiscal balance like debt and deficit ratios to GDP understate the magnitude of the eurozone's problems. Generational accounting suggests that EMU could degenerate—not overnight, but within the next decade.

CHAPTER 18

Europe: The Grand Illusion

Tony R. Judt

Tony Judt is of British origin and is a French and Central European specialist. He has taught for several years at New York University, where he is founding director of the Remarque Institute for European Studies. He has been a prolific, incisive essayist and book critic for The New York Review of Books. *His books include* The Burden of Responsibility: Blum, Camus, Aron, and the French Twentieth Century *(1998);* Past Imperfect: French Intellectuals, 1944–1956 *(1994);* Marxism and the French Left: Studies on Labour and Politics in France, 1830–1981 *(1989); and the book announced by the present article* (New York Review of Books, *July 11, 1996), called* A Grand Illusion? An Essay on Europe *(1996).*

1.

The European community was founded nearly forty years ago, with the stated object of promoting the "ever-closer" union of its members. It is a remarkable accomplishment, albeit not quite so remarkable as its advocates suggest. There are few who oppose its objectives in principle, and the practical benefits it affords its members, such as unrestricted trade, are obvious. That, after all, is why nearly everyone wants to join it. It is now engaging in negotiations among its member-states to construct a single European currency and mechanisms for common decision-taking and collective action, while simultaneously holding out to the countries of former Communist Europe the promise of membership in years to come.

The likelihood that the European Union can fulfil its own promises of ever-

---

closer union while remaining open to new members on the same terms is slim indeed. In the first place the unique historical circumstances of the years between 1945 and 1989 cannot be reproduced. Indeed the disruptive effect of the events of 1989 has been at least as great in the West as in the East. The essence of the Franco-German condominium around which postwar Western Europe was built lay in a mutually convenient arrangement: the Germans would have the economic means and the French would retain the political initiative. In the early postwar years, of course, the Germans had not yet acquired their present wealth and French predominance was real. But from the mid-Fifties this was no longer true; thereafter France's hegemony in West European affairs rested upon a nuclear weapon that the country could not use, an army that it could not deploy within the continent itself, and an international political standing derived largely from the self-interested magnanimity of the three victorious Powers at the end of the war.

This curious interlude is now at an end. One economic fact may illustrate the point. In 1990 a chart of French economic influence shows it to be limited to the "Europe of Nine"—that is to say, the original six (Germany, France, Italy, and the Benelux countries)—plus Britain, Eire, and Denmark. With these countries, France was a major importer and exporter of goods and services. But Germany, in contrast, already encompassed within its range of economic influence not only the present "Europe of Fifteen" but also most of the rest of the continent to the south and east. The significance of this is clear. France has become a regional power, confined to Europe's western edge. Germany, even before unification, was once again the great power of Europe.

The impact of 1989 has also posed new difficulties for the Germans. For just as weakness and declining international power arouse difficult memories for France, so in Germany does an apparent excess of powers. German politicians from Adenauer to Helmut Kohl have made a point of playing down German strength, deferring to French political initiatives and emphasizing their own wish for nothing more than a stable Germany in a prosperous Europe; they have thus fallen victim to their own rhetoric, bequeathing to post-1989 Europe a muscle-bound state with no sense of national purpose.

As a consequence, Germany's national agenda today is a little too full. In addition to the economic and political problem of absorbing the eastern *Länder,* Germans must deal with the paradox of pre-unification *Ostpolitik*: that many German politicians, especially on the left, were well pleased with things the way they were and would have been quite content to see the Wall remain a little longer. Germans have also to reckon with embarrassments about their own capacities—now that they can and manifestly do lead Europe, where should they take it? And of what Europe are they the natural leaders—the West-leaning "Europe" forged by the French, or that traditional Europe of German interests, where Germany sits not on the eastern edge but squarely in the middle?

A Germany at the heart of Europe carries echoes and reminders that many people, Germans perhaps most of all, have sought since 1949 to set aside. But the image of a Germany resolutely turned away from troubling Eastern memories, clinging fervently to its postwar Western allies, as though they alone stood between the nation and its demons, is not very convincing.

Europe's basic economic circumstances have also changed. For a generation following the announcement of the European Coal and Steel Community in 1950, Western Europe experienced an unprecedented combination of high growth and near-full employment. From this was born the belief, reflected in a series of optimistic economic forecasts from the OECD, that the cycle of crises that had marked the European economy for the previous half-century had been broken for good. The great oil crisis of 1974 should have put an end to such illusions. In 1950 Western Europe depended upon oil for only 8.5 percent of its energy needs; most of the rest was still provided by coal, Europe's indigenous and cheap fossil fuel. By 1970 oil accounted for 60 percent of European energy consumption. The quadruple increase in oil prices thus put an end to a quarter of a century of cheap energy, sharply and definitively raising the cost of manufacture, transport, and daily living. In the Federal Republic of Germany GNP actually fell by 0.5 percent in 1974 and again, by 1.6 percent, in 1975, unprecedented blips in the postwar *Wirtschaftswunder* that were confirmed in 1981 and 1982, when the West German economy declined again, by 0.2 percent and 1 percent respectively. In Italy GNP fell (by 3.7 percent) in 1976, for the first time since the end of the war. Neither the German nor any other Western European economy has ever been the same again.

The effect of this on the European Community (later Union) itself was severe. An important feature of the community had been its capacity to serve with equal success the varied needs of its member countries, needs deriving from interwar experiences and memories that differed quite markedly. The Belgians (like the British) feared unemployment more than anything else; the French sought above all to avoid the Malthusian stagnation of earlier decades; Germans lived in terror of an unstable, inflated currency. After 1974 the stalled economy of Europe threatened them all with increasing unemployment, slow growth, and sharply rising prices. There has thus been an unanticipated return to earlier woes. Far from being able to offer the advantages of its economic miracle to an ever expanding community of beneficiaries, "Europe" can no longer even be sure of being able to provide them to itself. The events of 1989 brought this problem into the open, but the source of the Union's inability to address it can be found fifteen years earlier.

The memory of unemployment between the wars varies from country to country. It was never a great scourge in France, averaging just 3.3 percent per annum throughout the 1930s. But in Britain, where 7.5 percent of the labor force was already unemployed during the 1920s, the annual average of 11.5 percent in the Thirties was something that politicians and economists of every stripe swore should never happen again. In Belgium and Germany, where the unemployment rate was nearly 9 percent, similar sentiments prevailed. It was thus one of the glories of the postwar West European economy that it maintained close to full employment through much of the 1950s and 1960s. In the 1960s the annual average unemployment rate in Western Europe was just 1.6 percent. In the following decade it rose to an annual average of 4.2 percent. By the late 1980s it had doubled again, with annual average rates of unemployment in the EC at 9.2 percent; by 1993 the figure stood at 11 percent.

Within these depressing figures one could see patterns that were more truly disturbing. In 1993 registered unemployment among men and women under twenty-five exceeded 20 percent in six EU countries (Spain, Eire, France, Italy, Belgium, and Greece). The long-term unemployed accounted for more than one third the total of those without work in those six nations as well as the UK, the Netherlands, and the former West Germany. The redistributive impact of the inflation of the 1980s worsens the effect of these figures, widening the gap between people in work and the unemployed. What is more, upturns in the economy no longer have the effect, as they did during the boom years after 1950, of absorbing surplus labor and pulling up the worse-off. Who now remembers the fantasies of the 1960s, when it was blithely believed that production problems had been solved, and all that remained was to redistribute the benefits?

The combination of rapid urban growth and subsequent economic stagnation has brought to Western Europe not only a renewed threat of economic insecurity, something unknown to most Europeans since the late 1940s, but also greater social disruption and physical risk than at any time since the early Industrial Revolution. In Western Europe today one can now see desolate satellite towns, rotting suburbs, and hopeless city ghettos. Even the great capital cities—London, Paris, Rome—are neither as clean, as safe, nor as hopeful as they were just thirty years ago. They and dozens of provincial cities from Lyon to Lübeck are developing an urban underclass. If this has not had more explosive social and political consequences, the credit lies with the systems of social welfare with which Western Europeans furnished themselves after 1945.

The crisis of the welfare state is thus the third reason why the European Union cannot expect to project its achievements and promise into the indefinite future. The Western European population is aging. Ever since the mid-Sixties the general trend has been for fewer children per family, to the point that in some countries, notably Italy and Spain, the population is not even maintaining itself. In Spain the birth rate per thousand in 1993 was just 1.1, a historic low. Europeans must now support a large and growing population of older people on the backs of fewer and fewer younger people, many of whom are not employed. A generous system of social services designed for flourishing economies where a large number of employed young people supported the social needs of a relatively small population of the old and sick is now under serious pressure.

In Northern and Western Europe the population aged sixty-five and over has grown by between 12 percent and 17 percent (depending on the country) since the mid-1960s. Moreover, even those under sixty-five can no longer be counted automatically on the "productive" side of the national equation: in West Germany the percentage of men aged sixty to sixty-four who were in paid employment fell from 72 to 44 in the two decades after 1960; in the Netherlands the figures were 81 and 58 respectively. At the moment the underemployed elderly are merely an expensive burden. But once the baby boomers begin to retire (around 2010), the presence of a huge, frustrated, bored, unproductive, and ultimately unhealthy population of old people could become a major social crisis.

It is clear to most European politicians that the costs of maintaining the welfare state in its postwar form cannot be carried indefinitely. The difficulty lies in knowing whom to displease first—the shrinking number of contributors or the growing number of involuntary beneficiaries. Both parties can vote. So far a combination of habit and good intentions has favored retaining as many social benefits as possible. But during the past few years another factor in the "welfare" debate has threatened to distort national political judgment out of all proportion to its size. This is the so-called "immigrant question."

As a result of immigration from former colonies and from its Mediterranean fringe, attracted by job prospects in an economy sucking in labor to fuel its rapid growth, Western Europe by the early 1960s had an excess of immigrants over emigrants for the first time this century. By 1973, the high point of the "foreign presence" in Western Europe, the EEC nations together with Austria, Switzerland, Norway, and Sweden had some 7.5 million foreign workers, of whom nearly five million were in France and Germany, comprising about 10 percent of the labor force in both countries. Despite a sharp fall-off in numbers since then, because governments have restricted immigration for both economic and political reasons, the "immigrant" presence has remained significant. According to data from 1990, about 6.1 percent of the German population, 6.4 percent of the French population, 4.3 percent of the Dutch and 3.3 percent of the British population are foreigners. These figures do not include naturalized immigrants, or locally born children of foreigners, though in some countries—notably Germany—these continue to be counted as foreigners and lack full citizens' rights.

In recent years these immigrants and their children have become the target of resentment and fear on the part of the "native" population, sentiments fanned and exploited by extremist and mainstream politicians alike. Just how far this process has now gone may be seen in France. In may 1989, 28 percent of Jacques Chirac's Gaullist supporters pronounced themselves "globally in agreement" with the ideas about immigrants expressed in the program of Jean-Marie Le Pen's National Front. In 1991 the figure was 50 percent. And if the Communist and Socialist voters were less sympathetic, that was only because a significant number of them had already switched their allegiance to Le Pen: in the presidential elections of 1995, he won 30 percent of the votes of the employed working class, the socialist candidate Lionel Jospin obtaining just 21 percent.

Thus by the end of the 1980s a large minority of mainstream voters in France saw nothing disreputable about expressing agreement with policies that twenty years before would have been regarded as unacceptably close to fascism (among the proposals in Le Pen's November 1991 list of "Fifty measures to be taken on immigration" was one to withdraw previously granted naturalizations, an act of retroactive injustice last practiced in France under the government of Philippe Petain). In Austria Jörg Haider's far-right Freedom Party got 22 percent of the vote in the December 1995 national elections. In Germany, too, increasing restrictions on "guest workers" and other would-be immigrants have been imposed "in their own interest."

The politics of immigration will not soon subside, because cross-continental and intercontinental migrations are once again a feature of European society, and local fears and prejudices will ensure that they continue to be seen as disruptive and politically exploitable. Prejudice in earlier decades against Polish or Italian or Portuguese immigrants was eventually muted as their children, distinguished by neither religion nor language nor color, blended into the social landscape. These advantages of cultural and physical invisibility are not available to their successors from Turkey, Africa, India, or the Antilles. There is very little tradition in Europe of effective assimilation—or, alternatively, "multiculturalism"—when it comes to truly foreign communities. Immigrants and their children will join the ranks of the "losers" in the competition for Western Europe's reduced resources.

Hitherto, the "losers' in Europe's postwar history have been sustained by complicated, expensive systems of regional aid that the European Union put in place within and between countries. These amount to a form of institutionalized relief—constantly correcting for market deformations that have concentrated wealth and opportunity in the rich northwestern core without doing much to alter the causes of the disparity. Southern Europe, the peripheries (Eire, Portugal, Greece), the economic underclass, and the "immigrants" thus constitute a community of the disadvantaged for whom the EU is the only source of relief on the one hand—for without succor from Brussels much of Western Europe, from depressed mining communities to unprofitable peasant villages, would be in even worse trouble than it is—and envy and resentment on the other. For where there are losers there are also winners.

To see "Europe" at work for the winners one has only to spend a few days in the triangle made up by the towns of Saarbrücken (Germany), Metz (France), and Luxembourg. Here prosperous citizens of three countries travel freely across all-but-vanished frontiers. People, employment, commodities, and entertainment move easily back and forth among languages and states, seemingly unconscious of the historic tensions and enmities that marked this very region in the quite recent past. Local children continue to grow up in France, Germany, or Luxembourg, and learn their histories according to national instructional rites, but what they learn no longer corresponds very well with what they see. All in all, that is to the good. The natural logic of the union of the Saarland with Lorraine has been achieved, not under the auspices of the German high command or of a French army of occupation, but following the benign designs of the European Commission.

C'est magnifique, mais ce n'est pas l'Europe. Or, to be fair, it is indeed "Europe," but from a very distinctive angle. For of what does *this* Europe consist, geographically speaking? What are its capitals, and where are its institutions? The Commission and its civil service sit in Brussels. The Parliament and its committees meet in Strasbourg and Luxembourg. The European Court is in The Hague. Crucial decisions regarding further unification are taken at Maastricht, while an agreement to pool frontier regulations and police aliens was signed in the Luxembourg town of Schengen. All six towns, within easy reach of one another, lie athwart the line running from the North Sea to the Alps that formed the centerpiece and primary communications route of the ninth-century Carolingian monarchy. Here, one might say, lies the heart (and, some would add, the soul) of today's European Union. But the instinctive, atavistic (and politically calculated) location of these modern capitals of "Europe" should serve as a cautionary reminder that what is true about today's Europe may not be very new, and what is proclaimed as new perhaps not wholly true.

There is another curious feature of Europe today. Its winners, those people and places which have done well in the Union and associate their prosperity with an emphatically European identity, are best described by reference not to nation-states but to regions. The great success stories of contemporary Europe are Baden-Württemberg, in southwestern Germany; the Rhône-Alpes region of France; Lombardy; and Catalonia. Three of these "super-regions" (none of which contains the national capital of its country) are grouped around Switzerland, as though wishing they could somehow clamber out of the constraints of their association with poorer regions of Italy, Germany, and France and become, by proximity and affinity, prosperous little Alpine republics themselves. Their disproportionate prosperity and economic power is striking. The Rhône-Alpes region, together with Greater Paris, accounts for about a third of French gross domestic product. Catalonia, in

1993, was responsible for 19 percent of Spain's GDP, 23 percent of Spanish exports, and one quarter of all foreign investment; its per capita income was some 20 percent higher than the average for Spain as a whole.

The wealthy regions of Western Europe have discovered a strong interest in associating with one another, directly or through the institutions of Europe. And in the nature of things, it is an interest that puts them ever more at odds with the older nation-state of which they are still constituent parts. This is not a new source of disagreement. In Italy the resentment of northerners at sharing the country with a "parasitic" south is a theme as old as the state itself. Flemish national separatism in Belgium, which flourished under the Nazis and for that very reason was somewhat quiescent after the war, has benefited in recent years from the economic decline of industrial Wallonia; we Flemings, the argument now runs, claim not just linguistic equality and separate administration but our own (non-Belgian) identity—and state.

The common claim of separatists, in Spain, Italy, and Belgium, but also in Slovenia and the Czech lands before the "velvet divorce," is this: "we"—the hard-working, tax-paying, better-educated, linguistically and/or culturally distinct northerners—are "European"; while "they"—the rural, backward, lazy, subsidized (Mediterranean) "south"—are less so. The logical imperative of a "European" identity that distinguishes itself from undesirable neighbors with whom it shares a state is to seek an alternative center of authority, choosing "Brussels" over Rome or Madrid. The appeal of "European Union" under these circumstances is that of cosmopolitan modern development against old-fashioned, restrictive, and "artificial" national constraints.

This in turn may account for the special attraction of "Europe" to the younger intelligentsia in these lands. The Soviet Union once appealed to many Western intellectuals as a promising combination of philosophical ambition and administrative power, and "Europe" has some of the same allure. For its admirers, the "Union" is the latest heir to the enlightened despotism of the eighteenth century. For what is "Brussels," after all, if not a renewed attempt to achieve the ideal of efficient, universal administration, shorn of particularism and driven by reason and the rule of law, which the reforming monarchs—Catherine the Great, Frederick the Great, Maria Theresa, and Joseph II—strove to install in their ramshackle lands? It is the very rationality of the European Union ideal that commends it to an educated professional class which, in east and west alike, sees in "Brussels" an escape from hidebound practices and provincial backwardness—much as eighteenth-century lawyers, traders, and writers appealed to modernizing royals over the heads of reactionary parliaments and Diets.

But there is a price to be paid for all this. If "Europe" stands for the winners, who shall speak for the losers—the "south," the poor, the linguistically, educationally, or culturally disadvantaged, underprivileged, or despised Europeans who don't live in golden triangles along vanished frontiers? The risk is that what remains to *these* Europeans is "the nation," or, more precisely, nationalism; not the national separatism of Catalans or the regional self-advancement of Lombards but the preservation of the nineteenth-century state as a bulwark against change. For this reason, and because an ever-closer bonding of the nations of Europe is in practice unlikely, it is perhaps imprudent to insist upon it. In arguing for a more modest assessment of Europrospects I don't wish to suggest that there is something *inherently* superior about national institutions over supra-national ones. But we should recognize the reality of nations and states, and note the risk that, when neglected, they become an electoral resource of nationalists.

2.

Should the European Union take in the countries of Eastern Europe? In the former East Germany an optimistic belief that economic prosperity would bring the divided country together and wash away unhappy memories—an attempt, in short, to reproduce the "economic miracle" of the Federal Republic and its attendant benefits—has foundered not so much on the presence of those memories as upon the absence of any economic transformation comparable to that which West Germany enjoyed in the early Fifties. The same difficulty would apply to any attempt to absorb into the Union the lands to its east.

In economic terms alone such an expansion would make for onerous and unpopular burdens. In the 1992 EU budget, only four countries were net contributors: Germany, Great Britain, France, and the Netherlands (in descending order of per capita contribution). The beneficiaries, in the same order per capita, were Luxembourg, Eire, Greece, Belgium, Portugal, Denmark, Spain, and Italy. True, the subsequent newcomers—Sweden, Finland, and Austria—are all potential contributors, but their economies are small and their share will not amount to much. Conversely *all* conceivable future members of the Union (Switzerland apart) fall unambiguously into the category of beneficiaries. It has been estimated (in a 1994 study by the Bertelsmann Foundation) that the four "Visegrad Group" countries—Poland, the Czech Republic, Slovakia, and Hungary—alone would cost the European Union DM20 billion per year in direct payments. Clearly, it would cost the Union a lot of money—more than it can presently afford—to bring in such future members *on the same terms as present ones.*

For reasons I have suggested, the European Union cannot realistically promise even its existing members a future as secure and as prosperous as its past. Subterfuges like "inner core," "fast track," "variable geometry," or "Partnership for Peace" are all devices to postpone or avoid the impossible choice of either saying no to newcomers or else expanding the Union on equal terms. For the foreseeable future it would be an expensive act of charity, economically speaking, for the EU to absorb the countries to its east on any acceptable terms. But would it not, perhaps, be in Western Europe's self-interest to make the sacrifice notwithstanding (always supposing it can afford to do so)?

Let us set aside the issue of cultural affinity—whether, that is, Western Europe is lacking a vital part of itself if it is in any way separated from Central or Eastern Europe. The perceived self-interest of Western Europe today lies in securing itself against demographic and economic threats to its east and south. As for threats of a more conventional sort, it is an unspoken assumption of all European defense planners that Russia remains the only significant military threat to the rest of Europe. That the major states of Western and Central Europe have the same interest they have always had in maintaining "buffer states" to separate them from Russia is clear. But whether these perform their geo-strategic role better in or out of a formal Union remains an open question.

In any case, West European debate is now focused upon the workings of the European Union itself. Should collective European undertakings be decided by unanimous agreement (as now) or by majority voting? And in the latter case, how should majorities be construed, and how binding are their decisions to be? Helmut Kohl, the late François Mitterrand, and their political advisers favored the introduction of a system of majority voting to eliminate the risk of deadlock that would arise from any attempt to meet the needs and demands of so many member-states. The British, supported by some of the smaller member states, favor retention of the veto (the same veto wielded by Charles de Gaulle to keep the British out in January 1963!) precisely to prevent decisions being taken against their interests—and indeed, to prevent the taking of too many decisions of any sort at all. It is not by chance that these conflicts have come to the fore. In the "Europe of Fifteen" it is going to be near-impossible to find strong majorities, much less unanimity, for decisions requiring hard choices.

This will be especially true in defense and foreign policy matters in which Europe has hitherto been inactive. The option of military quiescence is no longer open to Europe; the US cannot be counted on to involve itself in European affairs whenever its services are required. The European Union has utterly failed to bring its members together for any common policy or action in military or foreign affairs. And what has proven difficult for fifteen members would be out of the question for a larger number still. Where the European Union and its forebears once resembled the UN—taking unanimous decisions on areas of common interest and agreeing to disagree, or just not make a decision, on difficult or divisive topics—it will now begin to look like the League of Nations, with members simply opting out of decisions from which they dissent. The moral and political damage that can be done when a single member forces unanimous indecision upon the whole—*vide* the Greek refusal to recognize Macedonia, or Italy's insistence that Slovenia be excluded from consideration for EU membership until longstanding but trivial legal disputes between the two countries had been addressed—would be nothing compared to a refusal by Britain or France, for example, to accept the foreign policy of a majority composed of Germany and her smaller supporters.

What, then, of Western Europe's general interest in stability, in guaranteeing countries like Hungary or Slovakia against their own internal demons? This is in fact the strongest argument Central Europeans can offer in support of their candidacy for admission to the EU—protect us against ourselves, against the domestic consequences of a failed "post-Communist transition"—and it is particularly persuasive for their neighbors immediately to the west, notably Germany. But it is a purely prudential argument, which is why the EU has tried to meet it with the offer of partial membership, interim affiliation, and so on, and it raises a hypothetical future problem at a time when the West is preoccupied with real and immediate difficulties. Even if concerns about Eastern European stability succeed in prizing open the European door, these will only do so at the cost of a significant dilution of the meaning and practices of union. And the protective arm of "Europe" will surely not extend beyond the old Habsburg center (the Czech Republic, Hungary, Slovakia, Slovenia, and Poland), making of it a sort of depressed Euro-suburb beyond which "Byzantine" Europe (from Latvia to Bulgaria) will be left to fend for itself, too close to Russia and Russian interests for it to be prudent for the West to make an aggressive show of absorption and engagement.

Meanwhile, Europe will be dominated by Germany. Since 1990, a united Germany has been seeking partners for its strategy of expansion into Central Europe. If it can act in concert with fellow-members of a European "fast track," Bonn will not seem quite so obviously to be striding out ahead. Thus investments in Eastern Europe made by German firms using Austrian subsidiaries or "fronts," for example, raise fewer local hackles than those coming directly from the Federal Republic. Just as West German foreign policy before 1989 might be characterized as a triple balancing act, neither favoring nor displeasing the US, Moscow, or Paris, so post-unification German policy is seeking to follow the logic of Germany's power, and its historical place in Central and Eastern Europe, without frightening its West European allies or arousing Germans' own fears of revived national ambition.

The difficulty, as some German writers have noted, is that Germany cannot help destabilizing Europe, its own best intentions notwithstanding. The Europe that Adenauer and his contemporaries helped to make, and that in turn allowed the Federal Republic to forge its post-Hitler identity, is now in question, the postwar settlement having come to a close. The more dramatic historical analogies are misleading—a de facto alliance of Germany with Austria inside the EU is not the *Anschluss* of 1938, and a revival of German expansionism, much less militarism, is not likely, at least for the foreseeable future. But it remains true, as it has since 1871, that a powerful Germany in the middle of Europe, with interests of its own, is an unsettling presence for its neighbors.

Yet a Europe dominated by Germany, in striking contrast to the past, may be characterized above all by its unwillingness to intervene actively in international affairs. Whether this will always be so is another matter—the legacy of Nazism cannot continue to weigh upon the German public conscience indefinitely, and there must come a point when German politicians and their electors will be less inhibited about behaving like any other power: sending soldiers abroad, using force or the threat of force to achieve national goals, and so forth. But in the meantime the chief difficulty posed to its members by a German-dominated Europe is a sort of inertia, forcing the European community to restrict its collective international interventions to uncontentious issues of an environmental or humanitarian nature.

This is the first lesson of the Yugoslav tragedy, illustrating as it does the weakness of European initiatives, the compulsion to avoid engagement, and the absence of any agreed collective strategic interest beyond maintaining the status quo. The war in Yugoslavia since 1991 is also a timely reminder that Germans are not the only people for whom German hegemony in Europe is unwelcome. One of the strongest points in Serbian propaganda, first against Slovenian and Croatian independence and then against external "interference" in Bosnia, has been its claim that Germany and Austria are seeking to restore a "German-Catholic" *Mitteleuropa* and that the whole enterprise of dismantling Yugoslavia is a sort of Teutono-Habsburg plot. Fear of giving hostages to this argument prevented Europe's most powerful state from intervening actively in the war until four years had passed, and even then the decision to send a small German military contingent—confined to strictly noncombat duties—was only taken against much opposition from intellectual and political circles in Germany.

This is not to say that the behavior of France or Great Britain has been exemplary. But the French and the British have been constrained to do *something*, however inadequate and even perfidious—hence the dispatch of a small "Rapid Reaction Force" to Sarajevo in 1995, after it became embarrassingly clear just how ineffectual the UN presence there had become.[1] But just because this force was a Franco-British one, and not operating under any sort of "European" aegis, it confirmed another lesson taught by events in the Balkans, that the "European" edifice is fundamentally hollow, selfishly obsessed with fiscal rectitude and commercial advantage. Just as there is no effective international community, so there is, for these purposes, no European one either. There are merely powers, great and not so great; and for the moment at least, a German-led Europe is not among them.

How France and Britain will use the limited international initiative this gives them will depend on what lesson, if any, their governments choose to learn from the humiliations of their Bosnian adventure. But forty years after the Anglo-French disgrace at Suez they are about to rediscover the charms, and burdens, of relative diplomatic autonomy. The United States is no longer looking over their shoulder, and "Europe" is no longer a credible bolt hole. The years 1945–1989 are coming to seem more and more like a parenthesis. As we move further away from World War II the reasons why it was so important to build something different will seem less pressing. That is why we must remind ourselves not just that real gains have been made, but that the European community which helped to make them was a means, not an end.

For if we look to European Union as a catchall solution, chanting "Europe" like a mantra, and waving the banner of "Europe" in the face of recalcitrant "nationalist" heretics, we may wake up one day to find that far from solving the problems of our continent, the myth of "Europe" has become an impediment to recognizing them. We shall discover that it has become little more than the politically correct way to paper over local difficulties, as though the mere invocation of the promise of a united Europe could substitute for solving problems and crises in the present. To be sure, there is a certain self-fulfilling advantage in speaking of Europe as though it already existed in some stronger, collective sense. But there are some things it cannot do, some problems it does not address. "Europe" is more than a geographical notion but less than an answer.

NOTE

1. It did not go unremarked in Bosnia, however, that the main objective of this force was to protect other foreign troops (French and British especially) operating under UN authority.

CHAPTER 19

"Europe" and the "Anglosphere"

Robert Conquest

The following letter to the New York Review of Books *is from British historian Robert Conquest, one of the doyens of Russian and Soviet studies, author of* The Great Terror: Stalin's Purge of the Thirties *(1968). The text, a reply to Michael Ignatieff's review of Conquest's recent* Reflections on a Ravaged Century *(2000), questions not just the progress so far of European integration but also the desirability of a united Europe trying to stand alone, the idea of a "European Europe." Conquest believes Europe must position itself not independently but together with the United States as part of "the West," which is a "group of law-and-liberty countries." Professor Conquest is not uncritical of America, but he is even more critical of Britain's tendencies to rejoin "Europe," because he doubts that the European Union's political will and common interests are sufficient to make a go of independence. Britain should instead choose what he calls the "Anglosphere," an English-speaking political union (United States, Britain, Canada, Australia, New Zealand, etc.) whose common political culture, values, and institutions would permit some sort of formal arrangement to act internationally in concept.*

To the Editors:

I don't want to carp at Michael Ignatieff's generous review of my *Reflections on a Ravaged Century* (NYR, March 23). Nor can he be faulted for giving his (hostile) view of a controversial subject—the possible development

---

of a closer association between the law-and liberty countries of, mainly, what has been called the Anglosphere. He notes the fallings-off and faults to be found in the US and the UK; so do I, over two chapters. But he does not cover the far worse failings of his European choice.

He rightly shows that I am skeptical of the European political tradition. But I, and many others, are much more so of the EU actuality. We see it as divisive of the West, and indeed divisive of "European" civilization itself; as implicitly, and often explicitly, anti-American; as already, and with the promise of worse to come, an (immensely corrupt) bureaucratic and regulationist nightmare; as contrary to the law-and-liberty tradition; and, fatally, as missing any real sense of how the feeling of citizenship arises—something that cannot be elicited by appeals to compulsions on behalf of a supranational entity.

As to British feelings about the US and "Europe," a recent poll published in *The Economist* on what ally would you trust in a crisis showed the British answer to be nearly 60 percent for the US, and 16 percent for "Europe."

Robert Conquest
Stanford, California

CHAPTER 20

Conclusion: Expansive, Fractious, but Not Yet Fearsome

Ronald Tiersky

The high-risk Treaty on European Union negotiated at Maastricht in December 1991 showed the Frenchman François Mitterrand and the German Helmut Kohl seeing the future in historical perspective and making a large bet on integration. Maastricht was anything but mere tactics and pursuit of national interest alone. To launch "Europe" decisively toward monetary union and political union was, right or wrong, a work of European statesmanship at the level of the European revolution of 1989–1991.

It was possible to believe, contrary to the Maastricht strategy, that political union must precede monetary union. It was reasonable to oppose, as did Britain and a few smaller states, the federalist inclination of the "ever closer union" goal inscribed in the treaty. But it was not plausible to accuse the makers of Maastricht of lacking audacity, of having remained inert faced with the opportunity presented by communism's collapse in the east.

Kohl and Mitterrand acted out of a deep worry as well as a desire to seize an opportunity. Carpe diem, they, who both personally had been so long engaged in European integration, realized that building "Europe" would impassion future generations less than it did the pacified west European populations that suddenly and unexpectedly experienced, in only half a decade, the Soviet Union's emotionally electrifying transformation, the end to "Yalta" Europe, cold war and east European communist regimes, the fall of the Berlin Wall, and German unification.

For Euro-skeptics, on the other hand, the Maastricht Treaty on European Union launched the next great phase in the clash of national interests and strategies, and domestic partisan political battles, over where European integration should be taken. As is clear from the selections in this reader, in the 1990s monetary union was the focus. At the turn of the century, the main issue has become the EU's eastern enlargement and the political-institutional reforms that will determine its significance. Will the result of enlargement be more or less "Europe"?

At the beginning of 2001, monetary union, after a shaky start, goes not as badly as Euro-skeptics predicted.

The acceptance without major incident of the euro as an accounting unit by euro-zone citizens in January 1999 indicates that the arrival of actual coins and bills in January 2002 has a good chance of being a fait accompli. Euro-enthusiasts, if all goes as planned, will see in this a confirmation of their strategy, whereas Euro-skeptics will see this two-stage arrival as another example of integration "by stealth."

It is also without debate that member state requirements to meet the "convergence criteria" for euro-zone acceptance did discipline national budgets to a remarkable degree during the 1990s. Final results for membership had to be fudged statistically in a few countries (e.g., in Italy and perhaps even in the newly unified Germany). Yet, the effect overall among candidate countries was a European constraint to oblige what could not, for domestic political reasons, have been done nationally. And the euro's creation from one day to the next did abruptly end speculation in financial markets between one euro-zone currency and another, by the "simple" and elegant procedure of abolishing national currencies. What was supposed to work in theory did work in reality, an astonishing enough occurence in government to warrant special emphasis.

The euro's advent was a remarkable victory for political will over the uncertainties of optimum currency union theory and, above all, over political pessimism. But doubts and problems endure. The European currency's sharp 30 percent decline in 1999–2000 against the dollar was significantly more than expected. But against a slowdown in the U.S. economy at the end of 2000 the euro began to rebound. Gaffes by the European Central Bank's president and other difficulties in testing out the ECB's procedures and personnel created other kinds of doubts. Nevertheless, the euro and the federal EU monetary system are now accepted parts of the international economy.

"For the first time in history," the Nobel economist Robert Mundell observes, "an important group of independent countries has agreed to irrevocably pool their monetary sovereignties to create a currency that will have a wordwide market." This potential, if it proves out, will provide the European Union a financial basis for transforming itself "from a place on the map into a power," as French policy puts the goal. Finance and economy are not the only aspects of a world power in a multipower world, but they are two important aspects. It may well turn out, as Zbigniew Brzezinski says, that an integrated but not unified Europe will remain basically a financial-economic power, thus only a limited kind of rival to American power and influence. And even then, as several of the texts in this book point out, the euro and the monetary union framework as a whole will need to pass a severe test, a serious recession, before their ability to cohere the various euro-zone national economies can be taken as achieved.

Euro-skepticism in any case is moving on, as it must, to the agenda created by Maastricht's treaty on political union and debated at the Nice summit of December 2000: reform of the EU's political institutions to prepare the EU's eastern enlargement, moving from fifteen EU member states to perhaps twenty-seven.

Of the Nice summit one can say that, as usual, Euro-skeptic and Euro-enthusiast points of view both have their arguments. The meeting of the European Council turned into a horse-trading session that lasted far into the night of an extended conclave. Majority voting was extended to twenty-nine new areas, but not as far as the Euro-enthusiasts wanted, notably in tax and social security policy, where a British insistence on veto prevailed. A shift in power will occur toward the big countries (meaning Germany, France, Britain, Italy, Spain, and also, when it is admitted to membership, Poland); at the same time, even though big countries will get more votes in the Council of Ministers, smaller countries will still be advantaged in votes given demography. Among the big countries, increasingly termed a "directorate," Germany has gained power. France was able to prevent Germany from getting more votes in the council, but its weight will increase because blocking minorities will be based on population: Germany and any other two countries will be able to form a blocking minority.

Indeed the Franco-German partnership at the core of European integration for four decades has become diluted by history—a change of leadership generations from the postwar to the German baby boomers—and by the brute facts of Germany's stronger economy—a third larger than France's—and by the former's twenty million greater population. As opposed to the Mitterrand-Kohl traditions of a joint letter before a summit indicating French-German common positions and a breakfast together before the summit's first day of deliberations, French President Jacques Chirac and German Chancellor Schröder seemed what they were, not European statesmen but representatives of two countries pursuing national interests. Chirac refused Schröder's demand for more German votes in the council, arguing that Franco-German voting parity was mandated "by history." The Germans, for their part, are less and less sensitive to even indirect invocations of the German past as reason for today's Germany to dampen its national interests. The *Frankfurter Allgemeine Zeitung* editorialized, "Have 50 years of hand-shaking over the graves of Verdun not been able to banish the old suspicions after all?"

Tony Blair's Britain, for its part, made clear it would have a big voice along with France in the proposed European Security and Defense Identity (ESDI), but that it would repulse French proposals, half-hearted in any case, to place ESDI in an independent position outside NATO. The smaller EU countries nearly all rebelled, arguing they were unacceptably pressured by the bigger countries.

The EU Commission, in the person of its president, Romano Prodi, was remarkably and openly critical of member states' refusal to cede more veto power in favor of qualified majority voting. At the same time, the commission was marginalized in the negotiations and the reform of its composition was put on a slow track as a sop to the small countries, who each have one commissioner.

Instead of reducing the percentage of council votes needed to form a "qualified majority," the bargaining at Nice resulted actually in raising the required threshhold from 72 to 74.6 percent. If the Nice treaty will make enlargement somewhat less difficult in certain ways, upping the "qualified majority" requirement risks making decision making more difficult.

Enlargement itself seems accepted in principle by member states, even those who will be disadvantaged most. It is the number of new members, the schedule of enlargement, and, above all, the shape of the future European Union that is most at issue.

There are two models of what the European Union will look like and how it will function as a result of enlargement to almost double size in the coming period beginning around 2004. The first is a layered "two-speed" EU, meaning an exterior confederation structure encompassing a fast-track core of countries practicing "enhanced cooperation." Significantly, the Nice treaty allows for any group of eight countries that wish to do so to integrate in a given area more deeply than the rest of the EU. Whether the Franco-German "core of the core" will be refreshed or destroyed by enhanced cooperation is a keen issue. Germany, as a result of enlargement, will find itself in a much altered position now at the geographical hub of the EU. Indeed, for the first time in its history Germany will have "Western" neighbors (postcommunist Poland, the Czech Republic, Hungary) on its eastern frontier. Paris, faced with this new EU look, will naturally worry about a loss of its traditional leading role.

The second model for the European Union, the British desire along with Denmark and other Scandanavian countries, is predicated on turning enlargement into a lever for an altogether looser, overall more confederative and intergovernmental pattern of integration. The EU would resemble a kind of patchwork union, with various groups of countries cooperating in various ways, with less and less pressure to try to match some uniform membership pattern. This kind of union, Euro-skeptic in its principle, Gaullist and Thatcherite in its lineage, would find comfort in the public opinion, still against "Europe," of these "exterior" countries. In addition, a patchwork EU would make for a less controversial American presence on the Old Continent. This is something the Atlanticist countries want, not to mention those candidate countries in the east who remember how vulnerable they were in the past when the European balance of power broke down. An American guarantee of future members' security would be relatively inexpensive and, more important, welcome.

It is far from certain that "Europe" will become a power in its own right, by which I mean a coherent geo economic, geo strategic, and diplomatic force that the United States and other potential leading powers in a multipolar world will have to reckon with. To be sure, the goal of creating a multipolar world to balance the United States unites the foreign policy aspirations of Europe, Russia, China, Japan, and yet other countries. But in the world as it is, America remains a complete superpower with no equal, or even potential equal, in a foreseeable future.

Nevertheless, pure Euro-skepticism and/or Euro-pessimism have an increasingly difficult argument to make, if the point is that the combined intergovernmental/confederal/federal variable-speed model of European integration cannot or will not work. The best Euro-skeptic argument is that a "European Europe" with a federalist core, allied with the United States but not under its wing, is the *wrong* goal, not that it is impossible. And the best argument of the Euro-enthusiasts is not that a European Europe is already happening, but that it is not impossible.

Euro-philes must be disappointed that a European Europe "whole and free" has not more distinctly emerged in the decade since the collapse of the the Soviet Union and communism. The future does last a long time, but fifty years from World War II and Yalta, and ten years after the U.S.S.R.'s shadow disappeared, these too can seem a long time. Moreover the pace of deepened integration within the EU has slowed as the union gets ready for its great eastern enlargement, and Euro-skeptics can be excused for believing that the increasing assertion, and defense, of national interests at the top of EU negotiations is a sign that the demise of the nation-state, national sovereignty, and national identification as the focus of popular perception has been overstated.

Intractable problems and political choices will hound European integration's next steps. A new phase of Euro-sclerosis or Euro-paralysis is entirely possible, especially if international economic conditions limit the EU's capacity, especially with new members, to make everyone happy to some extent. Another constitutional conference in 2004, following on the Nice summit, has already been approved at the suggestion of Germany. There will be a large menu on which to dine, although it may not be an entirely happy meal.

A last word for students: To organize the matter of the subject, tags such as Euro-skepticism, Euro-optimism, Euro-pessimism, Euro-phobia, and Euro-enthusiasm are serviceable, so long as we remember that labels are a beginning, not the end of discussion. Such concepts identify, if only imperfectly, the goals, strategies, and passions of Europe's political elites and, even less so, Europe's citizens. For those of us whose concern is first of all to understand and explain rather than to advocate, what I would call a Euro-realism is the appropriate frame of mind.

Index

About the Editor

Ronald Tiersky is Eastman Professor of Politics at Amherst College. He is the author of *François Mitterrand: The Last French President* and the editor of *Europe Today: National Politics, European Integration, and European Security.*